Typical City

By

David J. Mooney

Typical City

By

David J. Mooney

For James Keeling

Acknowledgements

My thanks go to Helen and Dave Mooney for helping me finance this project and for not complaining too much when I was always using their computers; to Paul Atherton for critiquing large parts of this book; to Daniel Rushton and Andrew Gartside for reading my blogs; to Martin Crawford for giving me a reason to write most of this; to Gary James for his advice, help and experience; to Ric Turner for encouraging me to write match reports; to Chris Prince and Dan Burns for their opinions and influence in forming mine; to Mathias Vanbuylen for keeping me going through all the bad times down the years; to Sharon Latham and Manchester City Football Club for the cover image; to Kev Robinson for have the patience to read all of this and correct my mistakes; and to Alan Bates for ideas and discussions over a cup of dreadful tea in a greasy spoon cafe.

Contents

July 2008

EB/Streymur 0-2 Manchester City
UEFA Cup Qualifying Round One, First Leg
Thursday 17 July, 2008 - 19:00 KO

City: Hart, Onuoha, Dunne (c), Richards, Ball, Ireland, Hamann (Gelson 74), Johnson, Petrov, Vassell, Jo (Evans 74)
Unused: Schmeichel, Corluka, Elano, Benjani, Castillo
Goals: Petrov (9), Hamann (28)
Man of the Match: Martin Petrov

City began the 2008-09 season with the first leg of the UEFA Cup First Qualifying Round, away to EB/Streymur of the Faroe Islands. City fans had pulled out all the stops to get to the game, including a group who began Wednesday trapped in the Shetland Islands due to rough seas (but, with a quick news appeal and a private plane journey, they arrived on time). It wasn't perhaps a classic performance that they witnessed, as the game had an air of a pre-season friendly, but City were effective and did the job they came to do.

There was an early scare when a mix up in City's half allowed Streymur to get the first shot of the game, but it was a weak effort from distance and turned out to be their only attempt on goal in the half.

City began to take the initiative and started to control possession and, with just under 10 minutes gone, a bit of neat football around the edge of the home side's box allowed Darius Vassell to pass the ball square and Petrov to drive the opener into the net, after a Michael Johnson stepover.

The former England international Vassell should have extended the lead a few minutes later, as the Streymur defence failed to execute the offside trap and the City man found himself through on goal. His left-footed drive, however, was well saved by Torgard.

Just before the half-hour, a Petrov corner was cleared only as far as Dietmar Hamann, who let fly with the outside of his right foot. It was his first goal for the club and one worth waiting for, too.

City's record signing, the Brazilian debutant Jo, showed some deft touches and was unlucky not to get himself a goal from a defensive error. A lovely interception from Johnson fell to the newboy's feet, but he fired over after cutting inside.

Manchester City 2-0 EB/Streymur
UEFA Cup Qualifying Round One, Second Leg
Thursday 31 July, 2008 - 20:00 KO

City: Hart, Corluka, Dunne (c), Richards, Ball, Johnson, Gelson (Hamann 61), Petrov (Etuhu 70), Elano, Vassell, Sturridge (Evans 70)

Unused: Schmeichel, Onuoha, Bianchi, Ireland
Goals: Petrov (48), Vassell (90)
Man of the Match: Darius Vassell

An unexpected European campaign and an unfortunately scheduled Bon Jovi concert saw City make a relatively short trip to Barnsley's Oakwell for their first home competitive game of the season.

Inside three minutes, Vassell slid in to connect with a Corluka low, driven cross, but managed to divert the ball into the Streymur keeper's face. Then, minutes later, youngster Sturridge had a shot charged down.

This passage of play set the precedent for the match, as City created more and more chances, but managed to miss them too. The Streymur goalkeeper Torgard was in fine form to tip a Sturridge turn and shot over the bar, after the youngster unleashed a fierce effort from just outside the area.

Minutes later, Streymur had their first and, as it turned out, only attack of the game. Anghel cut inside Corluka and sidestepped past Richards, before drilling his shot low into the side netting.

As the half went on, Torgard made goods saves from Elano and Sturridge, while a left-footed Johnson drive was deflected over for a corner, with the fans appealing for handball and the replays suggesting it might have been a penalty.

Dunne and Corluka got in on the act, both missing excellent chances from corners, with the Croat smashing his free header into the crossbar from six yards. Just before the interval, Petrov thought he had opened the scoring, but his controlled volley sliced through the box and smashed into Torgard's left-hand post. From the rebound, City flicked the ball up to Sturridge's head, but the England U19's attempt was cleared off the line by Olsen.

Petrov finally broke the deadlock three minutes into the second half, after a move that saw nearly everybody in City's side touch the ball. Vassell wriggled through the Streymur defence and his cross was missed by Torgard, leaving Petrov to slam the ball into the unguarded net.

With 90 minutes on the clock, a long punt up the field was flicked on by Evans and picked up by Vassell. His blistering pace was too much for the Streymur defence, and the Englishman rounded the goalkeeper and slotted the ball home from a tight angle.

July 2008 Breakdown

Games (all competitions):
Won: 2   **Drawn:** 0   **Lost:** 0

Goals (all competitions):
For: 4   **Against:** 0

Progress:
Premier League: -
League Cup: -
FA Cup: -
UEFA Cup: Into Qualifying Round Two

August 2008

Manchester City 0-1 FC Midtjylland
UEFA Cup Qualifying Round Two, First Leg
Thursday 14 August, 2008 - 19:45 KO

City: Hart, Corluka, Dunne (c), Richards, Ben-Haim, Elano (Etuhu 69), Gelson, Johnson, Petrov, Sturridge, Caicedo (Bojinov 64)
Unused: Schmeichel, Ball, Onuoha, Ireland, Hamann
Goals: -
Booked: Corluka, Ben-Haim
Man of the Match: Micah Richards

The away side began the stronger, as City struggled to find their feet in the opening stages, preferring to knock the ball (badly) across the back four and struggling to get the attacking players into the game. On 15 minutes, Dunne found himself in space in the middle of City's half and took the opportunity to stretch his legs. But he waited too long and his forward pass was blocked, falling kindly for Thygesen. Thygesen found Olsen and the Midtjylland man flashed his shot into the bottom corner, with Hart a spectator.

The goal didn't particularly wake City up, but they did begin to look a bit more comfortable on the ball. Minutes later, after some neat interplay between Petrov and Elano, the Bulgarian found himself one-on-one with the keeper, who came quickly to his feet. His shot was chipped wide.

City were just inches from going in at half time all square, as the youngster Sturridge's left-foot curler hit the underside of the crossbar, but bounced out.

Petrov went close, curling a free kick onto the crossbar from just outside the area, with the keeper rooted to the spot. It could have been worse for City midway through the second half, as a flicked header from a Midtjylland corner flashed past Hart, but Petrov was ready to clear the ball off the line. Florescu forced Hart into an excellent save, with Corluka there to complete the clearance.

City looked like they could have played all night and not scored.

Aston Villa 4-2 Manchester City
FA Premier League
Sunday 17 August, 2008 - 15:00 KO

City: Hart, Corluka, Richards (c), Ben-Haim, Garrido, Elano, Etuhu, Gelson (Ireland 81), Johnson, Petrov, Evans (Sturridge 81)
Unused: Schmeichel, Ball, Onuoha, Hamann, Caicedo
Goals: Elano (pen 64), Corluka (89)
Booked: Ben-Haim
Man of the Match: Micah Richards

City began the game the more threatening, with a Petrov corner flighted towards the edge of the area, where the unmarked Elano was ready to hit a volley. As he went to strike it, referee Phil Dowd collided with him, knocking him down and the chance went.

After the break, City's good work was undone, as Gelson gave the ball away and Young found the unmarked Carew. He rose above the defence and nodded home from inside the six-yard box.

Just after the hour, Johnson broke forward and, following a mix-up between the two Villa centre-backs, found himself through on goal. But before the youngster could pull the trigger, he was hauled over and the referee pointed to the spot. Elano stepped up and coolly slotted the ball into the bottom corner.

Then followed 10 minutes of madness: First, a Villa corner was nodded back across the box by Davies, and the ball was poked past the helpless Hart by Agbonlahor. The striker doubled his tally just six minutes later, when Barry found the Villa youngster unmarked, and headed into the net.

Agbonlahor completed his hat-trick a minute later, as City pushed forward from kick-off and failed to deal with a ball over the top. The pacey forward raced into City's box and smashed it past Hart, who must have been shell shocked.

In stoppage time, a City corner found its way to the feet of Corluka, who took a touch and slid the ball into the back of the net. City were piling on the pressure again, but it was too little too late.

Manchester City 3-0 West Ham United
FA Premier League
Sunday 17 August, 2008 - 15:00 KO

City: Hart, Corluka, Richards (c) (Hamann 54), Ben-Haim, Ball, Ireland, Kompany, Johnson, Petrov (Etuhu 77), Elano (Evans 77), Sturridge
Unused: Schmeichel, Garrido, Caicedo, Gelson
Goals: Sturridge (65), Elano (70, 76)
Booked: -
Man of the Match: Vincent Kompany

City created chance after chance from the off and had a good shout for a penalty, when debutant Kompany appeared to have his ankles nipped. The away side could only clear to Ireland, and his shot was headed off the line by Davenport, who then deflected Ben-Haim's follow up onto the bar.

Petrov thought he had opened the scoring with a sublime, 30-yard free kick, but it hit the post and flashed back into play, with Green left stranded.

On 38 minutes, West Ham's task became harder, as a needless second yellow card for Noble's tackle on Johnson produced a red from the referee. Noble had earlier been booked for a deliberate handball.

A mix-up between Richards and Ben-Haim at the start of the second half saw the two players clash heads, with the Englishman coming off the worst.

City continued to dominate the game and took the lead on 65 minutes. A Petrov cross wasn't dealt with properly by Upson, leaving Sturridge to leather the ball into the roof of the net from 10 yards.

Five minutes after, City doubled their advantage. Corluka lifted a delightful pass over the top for Ireland, who took a touch, drew the goalkeeper and squared it to Elano, who found the bottom corner. The same three players linked up down the right six minutes later, to get Elano's second and City's third, in an almost identical move.

FC Midtjylland 0-1 Manchester City (2-4 pens)
UEFA Cup Qualifying Round Two, Second Leg
Thursday 28 August, 2008 - 15:25 KO

City: Hart, Corluka, Dunne (c), Ben-Haim (Hamann 57), Ball, Richards, Ireland, Johnson, Petrov, Elano (Sturridge 57), Jo (Evans 78)
Unused: Schmeichel, Gelson, Garrido, Caicedo
Goals: Califf (og 89)
Booked: Elano, Richards
Man of the Match: Joe Hart

The first chance of the game fell to City as Ireland had a go from a corner early on, but the ball flew high and wide. Hart then came to City's rescue, saving low to his post.

Just after 20 minutes, Elano tested the home side's keeper with a low drive, but Heinze was able to hold his shot. A few minutes later, Midtjylland breached the City defence and a last-gasp tackle from Ball saved red faces from the away side. City were struggling to get going.

The visitors began to dictate possession in the second half, but chances were still few and far between. Just after the hour mark, Hart made a crucial save with his chest as Thygsen broke away from Dunne and Richards, meeting the City keeper right on the edge of the area.

But with a minute of normal time to go, Ball picked up possession in the inside left channel and swung in a cross towards Evans. His flick header looked to be going nowhere, before it took a wicked deflection off the defender Califf and beat the goalkeeper.

The best chances of extra time came one after the other, as Johnson found himself one-on-one with Heinze, but the midfielder placed his shot down the middle and it was an easy save for the keeper.

City thought they had got their second goal when Sturridge latched on to an Ireland pass before rounding the keeper and finishing off the near post, but he had already been flagged offside.

It was now all City, full of belief after their equaliser, and Sturridge had another chance to win the game, but his rising, left-footed drive smashed into the crossbar and fell clear. And with that, the game went to penalties.

Ched Evans **scored**:	0-**1**
Winston Reid **scored**:	**1**-1
Martin Petrov **scored**:	1-**2**
Christopher Poulsen **scored**:	**2**-2
Michael Johnson *missed*:	2-2
Jonas Borring *missed*:	2-2
Dietmar Hamann **scored**:	2-**3**
Danny Califf *missed*:	2-3
Vedran Corluka **scored**:	2-**4**

Sunderland 0-3 Manchester City
FA Premier League
Sunday 31 August, 2008 - 15:00 KO

City: Hart, Corluka, Richards (Ben-Haim 45), Dunne (c), Ball, Hamann, Kompany, Johnson (Gelson 80), Ireland, Wright-Phillips (Elano 85), Jo
Unused: Schmeichel, Garrido, Sturridge, Evans
Goals: Ireland (44), Wright-Phillips (50, 58)
Booked: Richards, Kompany
Man of the Match: Shaun Wright-Phillips

It was the home side who started the brighter, with Bardsley hitting Hart's left hand post on seven minutes and then, two minutes later, Cisse whipped a cross across the area, missing everyone.

A mix-up between Dunne and Hart on 42 minutes could have led to a chance, as Dunne skied it while the City keeper attempted to catch. But Hart kept his eye on the ball and was able to punch clear.

City stepped up their passing game and got their reward for good play just before half time. Hamann found Johnson on the right wing, and his low cross was cleared only to Ireland, who slotted home from eight yards.

Soon, the visitors extended their lead, when a Dietmar Hamann free kick was deflected to Jo on the left corner of the box and the Brazilian threaded the ball to Wright-Phillips, who found the net.

Eight minutes later, Wright-Phillips latched onto a chipped pass from Ball, speeding between two defenders and flicking the ball over the onrushing Gordon. It was three for City, two for Wright-Phillips and, before the hour, the game was over.

THE DAY CITY KILLED FOOTBALL

So, Manchester City get a billionaire owner and now they're ruining football. It's definitely true. It has to be. Everyone has told me so. Oh, no, hang on...

Let me start at the beginning. Round about transfer deadline day, a billionaire Arabian company bought into Manchester City and took control from Thaksin Shinawatra. There followed a day of furious bidding on various international players, Robinho signed for the club and then everyone was explaining why it was, in fact, City that destroyed football and nobody else.

Well, just hold your horses, will you? Calm down and take an objective look at the entire situation and soon you will see how that is such a ludicrous claim that it's unreal. Manchester City have not destroyed football – football is still as strong as ever and, even if it were on its last legs because of money, to place the blame solely at City's door is nothing short of ignorance.

Let's start with Chelsea. A few seasons back, the lovely London club were bought by Roman Abramovich and they then set about buying as much talent from around the world as they could. Silly money was splashed in close seasons and suddenly a team that wasn't regularly finishing in the top four was a league winner two years running.

Did they ruin football? Of course not. Not if you asked much of the media, even. It was, apparently, refreshing to see that there were more than two horses that were going to be in the Premier League title race. I don't remember there being the same criticism City are getting when Chelsea were buying players to win things.

Going back a bit further – Manchester United. I guarantee that their fans will refute this completely, but I don't think it can be denied that they were immensely lucky to have the youth squad they did when Beckham, Scholes et al arrived ready for first team action. They won the league at just the right time, and are now reaping the rewards of earning millions and millions of pounds for it.

The second a club outside of the top four breaks the English transfer record, we're told that it's getting silly. Isn't smashing that record in 1995 (£7m for Andy Cole), then again in 2001 (£28.1m for Juan Sebastian Veron) and 2002 (£29.1m for Rio Ferdinand) just as silly? Apparently not.

Incidentally, since that youth team that produced a lot of first team stars, I don't recall United's youth policy churning out youngsters that were capable of playing in their first team on a regular basis. Current City manager, Mark Hughes doesn't appear to have any problems throwing in the youngsters if they're ready for first team football; the future's certainly bright for the youth policy.

How did Blackburn win the Premier League? It was their wonderful youth policy that threw up masses of talent to lift the club up to the top of the league, wasn't it? Or was it Jack Walker's chequebook that did the damage?

I'm starting to see something of a pattern here...

If money really is the death of football, then football died many moons before Manchester City were taken over. I guess it's just convenient to blame them, since they've been starved of success recently.

August 2008 Breakdown

Games (all competitions):
Won: 3 **Drawn:** 0 **Lost:** 2

Goals (all competitions):
For: 9 **Against:** 5

Progress:
Premier League: 3rd
League Cup: -
FA Cup: -
UEFA Cup: Into Round One

Premier League Table

		P	W	D	L	F	A	GD	Pts
1	Chelsea	3	2	1	0	6	1	+5	7
2	Liverpool	3	2	1	0	3	1	+2	7
3	**Manchester City**	**3**	**2**	**0**	**1**	**8**	**4**	**+4**	**6**
4	Arsenal	3	2	0	1	4	1	+3	6
5	West Ham United	3	2	0	1	6	5	+1	6

September 2008

Manchester City 1-3 Chelsea

FA Premier League

Saturday 13 September, 2008 - 17:30 KO

City: Hart, Zabaleta, Richards, Dunne (c), Ball (Sturridge 84), Hamann (Gelson 61), Kompany, Ireland, Wright-Phillips, Robinho, Jo
Unused: Schmeichel, Ben-Haim, Evans, Garrido, Elano
Goals: Robinho (13)
Booked: -
Man of the Match: Shaun Wright-Phillips

The first action saw Jo hauled down on the edge of the area by Carvalho, giving Robinho the chance to make a dream start to his City career. His shot took a slight deflection off the top of the wall and Cech got nowhere near it as it flew into the net.

The joy was short-lived, though, as Chelsea equalised four minutes later. A corner kick took a fortunate bounce in the area and fell to Joe Cole, who knocked it back to Carvalho and the defender lashed it in.

Lampard went close when his free kick missed everyone and landed in Hart's hands, while Malouda headed a Joe Cole cross against the crossbar, as he found himself unmarked in the six-yard box.

There was controversy after the break, as Belgian Vincent Kompany appeared to be fouled in the Chelsea half, but the referee waved play on. The visitors broke quickly, and Lampard found himself with time in the box to slot home with his left foot, leaving the home fans furious.

Just after the hour, Wright-Phillips broke into the Chelsea half and squared it for Ireland in the box, but the Irishman couldn't finish. After taking a touch to steady himself, his shot was blocked by a last-ditch Carvalho challenge.

From a free kick in their own half, Chelsea lumped the ball forward, flicked it on and it landed to the feet of Anelka, who slotted the ball past Hart on 69 minutes, putting the visitors two goals ahead.

Terry was sent off for a professional foul on Jo, after the Brazilian had beaten the Chelsea skipper and was looking to race towards Cech's goal. But the Chelsea centre-back had other ideas, pulling him down.

Omonia Nicosia 1-2 Manchester City

UEFA Cup Round One, First Leg

Thursday 18 September, 2008 - 18:00 KO

City: Hart, Zabaleta, Richards, Dunne (c), Garrido, Kompany (Gelson 84), Ireland, Wright-Phillips, Elano (Hamann 85), Robinho, Jo (Sturridge 76)
Unused: Schmeichel, Ball, Ben-Haim, Evans

Goals: Jo (59, 72)
Booked: Garrido, Robinho
Man of the Match: Stephen Ireland

The first chance for City fell to the new signing Robinho, who cut inside from the left to receive a through ball, but his effort at the top corner was matched by goalkeeper Georgallides.

City should have taken the lead on 26 minutes, when Ireland stole the ball from Omonia's captain on the corner of the box, and bore down on goal. He squared it to Jo, who managed to produce a thin air shot facing an open goal.

City piled on the pressure at the end of the first half and Jo thought he had made up for his earlier mistake, but after a neat touch and a slide-rule finish, he watched as his shot bounced back off the inside of the post to safety.

Two minutes into the second half, Kompany mistimed a tackle on the edge of the box. Duro hit the free kick and it flew past Hart, taking a touch off his fingertips, into the top corner of the goal.

It looked like City were letting their heads drop and could end up getting nothing from the game, but on the hour, Wright-Phillips squared for Jo and this time the Brazilian made sure, getting off the mark for City.

Then, on 72 minutes, City finally grabbed the lead, and it had been coming. Zabaleta broke down the right and his deep cross fell to Jo at the back post. He took one touch with his thigh, before smashing the ball cleanly along the ground and into the back of the net.

Duro then had a go from distance, with his long range effort hitting the bar and going over with Hart struggling. City kept possession to see out a 2-1 away victory in the first round proper of the UEFA Cup.

Manchester City 6-0 Portsmouth
FA Premier League
Sunday 21 September, 2008 - 15:00 KO

City: Hart, Zabaleta, Richards, Dunne (c), Garrido, Kompany, Ireland (Gelson 77), Wright-Phillips, Elano, Robinho (Sturridge 85), Jo (Evans 72)
Unused: Schmeichel, Ball, Ben-Haim, Hamann
Goals: Jo (14), Dunne (20), Robinho (57), Wright-Phillips (68), Evans (78), Gelson (83)
Booked: -
Man of the Match: Stephen Ireland

The home side started the brighter, with Robinho testing James early on, after he found himself on the receiving end of a Jo flick. Then, just after the 10 minute mark, Wright-Phillips forced a great save from his former team-mate, after Robinho released him on the right.

Just before the quarter hour mark, Robinho sent a through ball to Jo. James raced out to try and cut it out, but the big Brazilian forward took a touch to take the ball away from the keeper and powered it into the empty net.

And it got better. On 20 minutes City extended their lead, after Elano spotted the near post was left unguarded and he had a shot directly from a corner. James got down to save, but he could only parry to Dunne, who forced the ball over the line on his 29th birthday.

Portsmouth looked like they might get it to 2-1 just before the break, as a free kick was lifted in and nodded back to Campbell by Crouch, but the Zabaleta was on hand to volley off the line.

On 53 minutes, Traore broke free in the box and looked set to score, until Ireland stole the ball with a superbly timed tackle. And it was Ireland who was instrumental in getting City's third, as he pinged a delightful ball over to Jo who appeared to miscontrol, but Robinho was there to collect. Robinho shot first time, sending it beyond James, and it was game over.

On 68 minutes, Zabaleta showed some skills by beating two men before finding Ireland, who in turn released Wright-Phillips. The little winger ran onto the ball and smashed it past James at the near post.

Kompany then spread a lovely ball out to Robinho, who crossed for Wright-Phillips. City's number eight back-heeled across goal for Ched Evans to drive the ball past James with his left foot to make it five.

With seven minutes remaining, Gelson got in on the act. Garrido's cross was met by neither James nor Wright-Phillips and it fell to the Swiss international, who poked the ball into the unguarded goal.

Brighton & Hove Albion 2-2 Manchester City (5-3 pens)
League Cup Second Round
Wednesday 24 September, 2008 - 19:45 KO

City: Schmeichel, Zabaleta, Ben-Haim, Dunne (c), Ball, Kompany, Ireland, Johnson (Elano 102), Gelson, Sturridge (Evans 61), Jo (Caicedo 91)
Unused: Hart, Garrido, Logan, Hamann
Goals: Gelson (64), Ireland (109)
Booked: -
Man of the Match: Stephen Ireland

Brighton started the game the better team, but it was City who had the opening chances in the match with Kompany firing wide and Sturridge hitting a drive straight at the goalkeeper.

After 20 minutes, Schmeichel was beaten but, fortunately for City, so was the goal, as Thomson's effort bounced off the post, after he had shot from the right side of City's box.

A last gasp clearance from Ball stopped Brighton's Thomson again and it seemed to wake City up, as they piled on the pressure towards the end of the first half.

After the break, City started where they left off, but still couldn't find the net. Gelson sent a diving header wide after a delightful Sturridge flick, and the home side had their keeper to thank once more, as Jo's effort from the left of the box was expertly tipped wide.

Just after the hour, City took the lead, and it had been coming. Brighton gave the ball away cheaply in their own half and Jo lobbed the ball over to Gelson, who slotted home from eight yards via a huge deflection.

But, just as City's minds were perhaps straying to a home tie with Derby, Brighton pulled level, after a rebound from a Schmeichel save was bundled in.

Five minutes into extra time, the home side were riding high and took the lead, as Cox crossed from the left, finding the head of on-loan Ayinsah to finish.

After 109 minutes the home side's defence looked tired and were caught in two minds over a Schmeichel clearance. The ball found its way to Ireland, who pulled the visitors back level when Brighton had their tails up.

City pressed for the rest of extra time, but they couldn't find a breakthrough, with both Dunne and Evans going close from corners. It was penalties.

David Livermore **scored**:	**1**-0
Ched Evans **scored**:	1-**1**
Tommy Elphick **scored**:	**2**-1
Elano **scored**:	2-**2**
Glenn Murray **scored**:	**3**-2
Vincent Kompany **scored**:	3-**3**
Adam Virgo **scored**:	**4**-3
Michael Ball *missed*:	4-3
Matt Richards **scored**:	**5**-3

Wigan Athletic 2-1 Manchester City
FA Premier League
Sunday 28 September, 2008 - 16:00 KO

City: Hart, Zabaleta, Richards, Dunne (c), Garrido, Kompany (Gelson 90), Ireland, Wright-Phillips, Elano (Sturridge 85), Robinho, Jo (Evans 73)
Unused: Schmeichel, Ball, Ben-Haim, Hamann
Goals: Kompany (22)
Booked: Garrido, Robinho, Kompany, Richards
Man of the Match: Richard Dunne

The first shot of the day came from Wigan's Zaki, but it flew over Hart's crossbar from range. It should have been the warning City needed, but they were undone a few minutes later by a stunning Valencia strike. Kompany was penalised on the right side of the City box and the resulting free kick was only half cleared to Valencia, who hit a thunderbolt past Hart and into the top corner.

City almost hit back immediately, with some neat interplay which left Robinho to swivel and shoot just outside the six-yard box but, somehow, the Brazilian poked the ball wide.

Five minutes later, City equalised, after Elano played a beauty of a ball into the area from a free kick on the right wing and Kompany stepped in to score his first goal of his City career.

But Wigan re-took the lead 11 minutes later as Palacios dived theatrically to win his side a penalty, when there was minimal contact with Garrido. The referee bought it and awarded the spot kick. Zaki sent Hart the wrong way.

City tried to hit back immediately. Dunne had what seemed to be a clear penalty turned down after he was clipped by Heskey, with the referee penalising the City skipper for handball – the offence committed as he fell to the ground.

A few minutes later, former City man Brown unfairly brought a halt to a Wright-Phillips winding run on the edge of the area, but the resulting free kick was blasted over by Jo, after it had been rolled to him by Elano.

Wright-Phillips produced an excellent save from Kirkland at his near post, after several City players were unable to get a shot away in the area. The Wigan keeper then appeared to be lucky not to concede a penalty, as he collided with City substitute Evans, not long after the youngster had come on.

City continued to try to break through Wigan's defence, but the closest they came was a Kompany shot from outside the area, which landed straight in Kirkland's hands. The home side could have made it worse for City, were it not for Hart's superb save from Zaki on one of Wigan's isolated chances.

HOW THE TIMES HAVE CHANGED

There used to be an old joke floating around in football. No matter how bad things were getting at Miscellaneous FC, no matter how low they sunk, at least they weren't Manchester City. We all know from experience how City can cock things up, so it's not especially a new concept.

But, times are changing. No longer have I heard the words "but at least we're not Manchester City", when fans are interviewed on TV. Newcastle are doing their best to steal the mantle of comedy club from our grasp and I, for one, can say that I'm not sad to see it go. They're welcome to it, if anything.

For years, we have watched as manager after manager has attempted to do something good with the team, only to fall at one of the many hurdles along the way. And then fall victim to the revolving door policy.

I watched at the end of last season (2007-08), as Sven persisted with the same tactics he had played all season. That, for me, was his only failing as City manager – he told the press he felt his squad had been found out and that the opposition had worked out how to play against his 4-5-1 formation. And yet, he kept it.

But, I expected him to make a flying start to this season. Instead, Hughes was brought in by our former chairman and I was sceptical, to say the least. Granted, he had Premier League experience, but it was on a shoe-string budget with a relatively small club.

Now, though, I am mystified as to why I was worried. He's turned Sven's squad into one that doesn't give up. Into a squad that will fight for each other.

Elano looks a better player, which I suspect is something to do with Hughes toughening him up. Maybe it's been the signings of Jo and Robinho that has helped. After all, the three of them have all been playing for Brazil together. Just watching the game against Portsmouth, the Brazilians always seemed to know where the others were without looking.

But, I think the most pleasing thing about the Portsmouth game (aside from the six goals, naturally), was the performance of Stephen Ireland. He ran the game, with some excellent tackles, some fantastic passes and awareness and some beautiful touches.

I think the most influential signings by Hughes have actually been the less well-known Kompany and the returning prodigal son in Wright-Phillips. The defensive frailties shown at Aston Villa were instantly wiped out when Kompany took up the defensive midfield role and it was clear we missed his presence in the away tie at Midtjylland.

Wright-Phillips hasn't just recaptured his old form for us, he's already surpassed it. I was concerned he wasn't the player that left us, and I was right, just not how I thought.

We're both firing well and defending well – we've scored in every Premier League game this season and that's not something to be sniffed at. We've scored the most at home, by far, the most in the league in total and have the second best goal difference overall.

So, hopefully, 2008-09 will be our season. And God knows it's been coming.

September 2008 Breakdown

Games (all competitions):
Won: 2   **Drawn:** 1   **Lost:** 2

Goals (all competitions):
For: 12   **Against:** 8

Progress:
Premier League: 8th
League Cup: Eliminated in Round Two
FA Cup: -
UEFA Cup: Leading in Round One

Premier League Table

		P	W	D	L	F	A	GD	Pts
6	Hull City	6	3	2	1	9	11	-2	11
7	Blackburn Rovers	6	3	1	2	8	12	-4	10
8	**Manchester City**	6	3	0	3	16	9	+7	9
9	Portsmouth	6	3	0	3	7	12	-5	9
10	Wigan Athletic	6	2	2	2	9	5	+4	8

October 2008

Manchester City 2-1 Omonia Nicosia
UEFA Cup Round One, Second Leg
Thursday 2 October, 2008 - 19:45 KO

City: Hart, Zabaleta, Richards (c), Ben-Haim, Garrido, Kompany (Hamann 67), Elano, Ireland, Wright-Phillips, Robinho (Petrov 70), Jo (Evans 67)
Unused: Schmeichel, Ball, Gelson, Sturridge
Goals: Elano (48), Wright-Phillips (55)
Booked: Ben-Haim
Man of the Match: Elano

The first real chance of the game came after 15 minutes and it was for the home side. After some quick feet from Robinho, the Brazilian flashed an effort across the goal, but it flew wide of the keeper's far post.

The second half began at a much higher tempo from the home side and Robinho latched onto a loose ball on the left and raced away from the Omonia defence. He slowed at the corner of the box and found his fellow Brazilian Elano, who volleyed home excellently from 25 yards.

And it was 2-0 shortly after, as some neat play by Zabaleta found Wright-Phillips in the area. The little winger battled his way through two challenges, before smashing the ball into the net, all but ending the tie.

Ireland should have grabbed himself a goal when he was played through by Zabaleta, but the Irishman's chip was miscalculated and dropped well wide of the mark.

With 12 minutes to go, the away side got themselves a goal, when Alabi gave his man the slip from a right wing corner and had a free header to beat Hart.

Three minutes from time, City broke and Wright-Phillips squared to Evans, who dummied a shot, before finding Petrov in space on the left. But the left-winger's shot was straight at Georgallides.

Manchester City 2-3 Liverpool
FA Premier League
Sunday 5 October, 2008 - 15:00 KO

City: Hart, Zabaleta, Richards, Dunne (c), Garrido, Kompany, Ireland, Wright-Phillips, Elano (Petrov 85), Robinho (Evans 80), Jo (Gelson 70)
Unused: Schmeichel, Sturridge, Ben-Haim, Hamann
Goals: Ireland (19), Garrido (42)
Booked: Dunne
Sent Off: Zabaleta
Man of the Match: Vincent Kompany

The game began with ex-City man Riera causing some trouble to the home side's defence, with him chipping in a cross just behind Kuyt and then firing off a volley which was spilled by Hart for a corner.

Kuyt blazed over when it seemed easier to score on 16 minutes before, down at the other end, Robinho somehow managed to keep the ball in play after beating three Liverpool men, but his low drive was gobbled up by Reina.

On 19 minutes, the ball broke kindly for Wright-Phillips, who broke into the area at pace. He squared for Jo, who was able to hold up the ball and find Robinho. Despite falling, he was able to block the defender's clearance into the path of Ireland, who volleyed home from 10 yards.

City began to get a foothold on the ball and were knocking it around nicely, when Wright-Phillips was barged cynically as he knocked it into the area, resulting in a free kick on the right side of the box. Up stepped left back Garrido and he curled into the top right corner.

Ten minutes into the second half, the England international Gerrard nutmegged Garrido and found Arbeloa, who crossed for Torres to poke the ball home, halving the deficit.

The referee then, to the disgust of the home fans, decided that a tackle by Zabaleta was worthy of a sending off. It was tough and he did catch the man, but it was a harsh decision to show a straight red card.

The 10 men couldn't hold on and, on 73 minutes, Spanish international Torres equalised as he nodded in a corner that Hart had got nowhere near.

Skrtel was forced off with a horrid injury after he was lucky not to see a red card for a karate kick on Jo. The Liverpool man was stretchered off as added time began.

Liverpool stole the points, as Torres saw his effort deflect kindly off Keane and fall to the onrushing Kuyt, who hit the ball into the roof of the net.

Newcastle United 2-2 Manchester City

FA Premier League
Monday 20 October, 2008 - 20:00 KO

City: Hart, Richards (Onuoha 58), Ben-Haim, Dunne (c), Garrido (Sturridge 83), Kompany, Ireland, Wright-Phillips, Hamann (Evans 64), Robinho, Jo
Unused: Schmeichel, Elano, Gelson, Berti
Goals: Robinho (pen 14), Ireland (86)
Booked: Garrido, Kompany
Man of the Match: Stephen Ireland

City fired themselves out of the starting blocks and looked to be swarming all over their hosts early on, aiming for a quick goal. With 12 minutes gone, some lovely interplay sent an over the top pass to Robinho who, after a touch to control, was clean through until the tackle of Beye. He was harshly sent off and

City had a penalty. Robinho sent Given the wrong way and put City 0-1 up.

Just after the half hour, Hart missed his punch, instead making contact with his captain, who also managed to clear the ball. With Dunne receiving treatment, Duff should have taken advantage, but his weak, left-footed shot was easily gobbled up by the City keeper.

Seconds before half time, Newcastle managed to claw themselves level, after a large slice of good fortune. A Dunne clearance smashed straight into the back of Hamann, and Ben-Haim was unable to react quickly enough to clear. The ball was deflected over Dunne's head into the path of the onrushing Ameobi, whose shot was mis-hit, but sliced past Hart.

Newcastle had their second slice of good fortune on 64 minutes, when Geremi's right wing corner was missed by the first challenge, before it smashed into Dunne. The skipper reacted as quickly as he could, but it wasn't enough to stop the ball flying off his boot and into Hart's top corner.

With just four minutes left to play, Ireland earned City a point after Kompany had found Robinho, who slid in the Irishman to poke it past Given. Ireland nearly took all three points for City when his flicked cross-shot spun just wide of Given's despairing dive, but it also spun wide of the post.

Manchester City 3-0 Stoke City
FA Premier League
Sunday 26 October, 2008 - 15:00 KO

City: Hart, Richards, Ben-Haim, Dunne (c) (Gelson 76), Garrido (Onuoha 70), Kompany, Ireland, Wright-Phillips, Elano, Robinho, Evans (Sturridge 42)
Unused: Schmeichel, Berti, Hamann, Caicedo
Goals: Robinho (14, 47, 72)
Booked: Kompany
Man of the Match: Robinho

The home side got off to the better start, testing Stoke's goalkeeper Sorensen immediately, but he was equal to Robinho's effort. City fans didn't have to wait long to see their side score, though, as Wright-Phillips crossed for Elano, who nodded the ball back for Evans. He played the ball to Robinho, who took a touch and slid the ball in the near post.

City were well in control of the match, but looked like they might throw away their lead when Ben-Haim under-hit a pass across the box for Fuller to steal in, but skipper Dunne deflected the shot and Hart was able to save.

A minute after the restart, Robinho doubled his tally and City's lead, after some good work by Sturridge. He cut in from the right and slid a neat pass through to the Brazilian, who was able to drive the ball low and hard into Sorensen's bottom right corner.

The home side broke with less than 20 minutes to go, and Wright-Phillips tapped the ball back to Sturridge, who slid the ball across the edge of the box for the unmarked Robinho, who sealed his and City's third of the game.

Kitson should have grabbed the away side a consolation on 85 minutes, but his header from a corner was straight at Hart, who held the ball well. No player had a bad game, but Robinho will take the headlines with his City first hat-trick.

Middlesbrough 2-0 Manchester City
FA Premier League
Wednesday 29 October 2008 - 20:00 KO

City: Hart, Onuoha, Dunne (c), Ben-Haim, Richards, Kompany, Ireland, Wright-Phillips, Elano (Gelson 67), Robinho, Sturridge (Evans 77)
Unused: Schmeichel, Garrido, Hamann, Berti, Jo
Goals: -
Booked: Kompany, Ireland
Man of the Match: Shaun Wright-Phillips

On 10 minutes, a Downing cross deflected off Onuoha and landed for Alves, but the Middlesbrough forward could only direct his header straight at Hart in the City goal.

Alves was denied by a superb last ditch tackle from Onuoha, before City had the chance to go in front, but it was spurned by Wright-Phillips. Seconds later, an excellent run by Richards ended with a driven shot straight at Turnbull.

Tuncay fired a volley well wide of the goal, before City went back on the attack. Sturridge missed a good chance, hitting his shot straight at the goalkeeper, before Alves was unable to connect to a cross after climbing above Onuoha.

The first action of the second half saw a Ben-Haim clearance fall straight to Ireland, whose shot looked destined to break the deadlock, before Turnbull saved brilliantly again.

The home side had their keeper to thank once again shortly after, when Sturridge back-heeled excellently for Wright-Phillips, but the little winger's first time effort was blocked by the feet of Turnbull.

Middlesbrough broke and got themselves a controversial penalty, as Wheater went down under a definite foul from Sturridge. The referee pointed to the spot, despite the City players being adamant the foul was committed outside the area, and Alves sent Hart the wrong way.

The home side were hanging on, but their defence was solid, as City tried and failed to grab an equaliser. And then came the sucker punch for the travelling fans: Tuncay's snapshot rebounded off Hart and to O'Neil to slot home.

It was the first time City failed to score in the Premier League this season and it was another disappointing away performance. It looks like the roller-coaster is set to continue, as City slumped to defeat in a game they really should have won.

WHO'S THE WANKER IN THE BLACK?

Since Graham Poll elevated the role of referee in a football match to 'centre of attention', there have been numerous attempts to steal each weekend's headlines by the neutral man with the cards and whistle. I know you're thinking immediately that it's easy for me to say this, sitting at my shiny computer desk, with my internet connection, access to YouTube and numerous slow motion replays from various angles.

And you'd be right, it's very easy for me to say that and I certainly wouldn't want to be the guy who has to make each and every split second decision in front of thousands of people. After all, I might get it wrong. Then I'd look a right fool.

But the thing is, some people do want to do it and they get paid a very healthy sum of money for it, too. So it's only fair that we expect a high standard of decision, right? And that's where I have a problem. I want it to be as simple as that, but, somewhere along that line of thought, it gets very complicated and more than a little bit messy.

Referees don't turn up to football matches in favour of one team over another. They are allowed to support teams and it's natural that they would, but they aren't allowed to referee matches that would influence something to do with their team.

But, once more, it's not quite that simple.

By supporting a team, the referees will surely have that natural, subconscious opinion on other teams. For example, if I was a referee, I couldn't referee a game involving or affecting City. But I could referee one that would affect Middlesbrough, and I have no good feelings towards them. Never have. I have no cause to hate them, there is no City-connection that makes me not like them, but the fact remains that I just don't like them. Maybe it's the kit or something.

But I'd still have to referee them.

So, I actually have quite a bit of respect for the officials – they have to put aside their personal prejudices to be objective. And objectivity is something that is virtually impossible to achieve anywhere, let alone when you have 30,000 biased people watching you.

But, then again, they are getting paid a good salary. Clearly, that should help them strive to do the best job they can. Or does it? When it comes down to it, everyone goes to work with the intention of doing the best job they can – after all, there's other people waiting in the wings to do your job if you continue to make mistakes. And I'm sure no referee goes out with the intention of getting decision after decision wrong.

However, the pressure they receive is much more than you or me. They make a mistake in their line of work and it's publicised in the media – they know if they get the decision wrong, then it'll splashed about Match of the Day as another 'big blunder from the referee'.

And I'm not for turning referees into robots, because, as we know, there are still sometimes disagreements over decisions with TV replays. There are some judgement calls that can be disputed and this is potentially a reason why we're heading down the path we are right now. The FA is attempting to tell referees how to govern by making them adhere to strict rules and removing all forms of common sense from the game.

What they should be doing is helping their officials. Take a couple of examples from recent weeks: Rob Styles incorrectly awards a penalty at Old Trafford, so he apologises to Bolton and referees a Premier League tie the weekend after. But, Mark Halsey correctly (in my view, of course) sends off John Terry at Eastlands and he is punished by a spell in League Two.

There's hardly a week goes by without a controversial decision and, of course, more TV cameras around the grounds are helping in bringing them to light – and I think that's exactly where the FA can help their own employees in reducing the number of contentious decisions that they make.

Video replays should be available, but not for each incident on the pitch. If a referee, for example, is unsure whether the ball has crossed the line, there's a simple solution – play on. Continue until the ball goes out of play, then take a look at the video. From there, we can go back and give the goal, if it crossed, and restart with a kick-off (and adding on the time that was played) or we can play on from where the ball went out.

The same works for penalty decisions and potential red cards. But this is clearly a power that could be used too often by officials and should be there with limitations – I don't think it would be wise to have referees relying on the video to make their decisions.

But, video technology isn't as foolproof as I've just made it out. A study based in the German Bundesliga showed that stadiums where the home crowd were louder tended to get more favourable decisions for the home side.

But this leads me on to my next point nicely. Singing "the referee's a wanker", or "you're not fit to referee" when he has made a call (potentially a correct one – remembering objectivity here) isn't likely to get him on your side.

Just as 40,000 fans shouting "handball!" might influence the referee to give the decision, a large quantity of that number shouting abuse at him is likely to work in the other direction – I certainly wouldn't help someone who had just called me a wanker. Would you?

The point is, the problem is not currently with the officials. In fact, there are numerous occasions that I've seen on City's message boards where both sets of fans have criticised the referee and both sides think he was biased towards the other. If anything, that probably tells you he *hasn't* been biased *at all*.

If the FA gave the officials more support – and actually accepted that bad decisions will happen, and not deny that decisions were wrong or publicly undermine the referee by demoting one, but not another – then perhaps we might see the standard increase with more consistency.

And if the referees commented in post-match interviews and explained certain decisions, then I'm sure most of us would have a hell of a lot more respect for them.

I know I would.

October 2008 Breakdown

<u>Games (all competitions):</u>
Won: 2   **Drawn:** 1   **Lost:** 2

<u>Goals (all competitions):</u>
For: 9   **Against:** 8

<u>Progress:</u>
Premier League: 8th
League Cup: Eliminated in Round Two
FA Cup: -
UEFA Cup: Qualified for Group Stage

<u>Premier League Table</u>

		P	W	D	L	F	A	GD	Pts
6	Manchester United	9	5	3	1	15	5	+10	18
7	Portsmouth	10	4	2	4	10	15	-5	14
8	**Manchester City**	**10**	**4**	**1**	**5**	**23**	**16**	**+7**	**13**
9	Middlesbrough	10	4	1	5	10	15	-5	13
10	Sunderland	10	3	3	4	9	11	-2	12

November 2008

Bolton Wanderers 2-0 Manchester City

FA Premier League

Sunday 2 November, 2008 - 16:00 KO

City: Hart, Zabaleta, Dunne (c), Ben-Haim, Richards, Kompany, Ireland, Wright-Phillips, Elano (Hamann 68), Robinho, Evans (Sturridge 68)
Unused: Schmeichel, Onuoha, Garrido, Gelson, Caicedo
Goals: -
Booked: Zabaleta
Man of the Match: Richard Dunne

City started the game brightly and, on six minutes, Robinho fired a warning shot across Bolton's bows, with a long range effort that flew narrowly over the crossbar.

Dunne produced the tackle of the game on 38 minutes when Riga thought he was away, but the big skipper had other ideas and slid in to prevent the break.

Minutes before half time, Evans picked up a bouncing ball in the middle of the pitch, brought it under control and began to drive at the Bolton defence. He slipped Ireland through superbly, but he could only hit Jaaskelainen.

The away side looked more likely to take the lead after the break, too: Wright-Phillips carried the ball past three Bolton defenders, but was losing his balance as he fired a left-footed shot well over.

But the hosts went in front on 77 minutes, when Nolan knocked a driven ball out to Steinsson on the break. He crossed low for Gardner to smash home off the bar, with the visiting defence stretched.

Gardner was freed down the left, as Bolton looked to finish the game off by hitting City on the counter. The Bolton man drove into the area and fired the ball across for Davies, but Dunne got there first and was unlucky to see the ball ricochet off his leg and into the net.

Manchester City 3-2 FC Twente

UEFA Cup Group A

Thursday 6 November, 2008 - 19:45 KO

City: Hart, Zabaleta, Dunne (c), Richards, Garrido, Gelson, Ireland, Wright-Phillips, Vassell (Elano 65), Robinho, Jo (Benjani 59)
Unused: Schmeichel, Ben-Haim, Onuoha, Hamann, Evans
Goals: Wright-Phillips (2), Robinho (57), Benjani (62)
Booked: Zabaleta
Man of the Match: Stephen Ireland

With just two minutes on the clock, Wright-Phillips picked the ball up in the

Twente half. A one-two with Jo later, and the tricky winger fired the ball past the away team's goalkeeper, giving City an early lead.

City looked to be well in control of the game, until Twente snatched themselves level. A ball over the top was left by Dunne and Richards after it appeared to be aimed to an offside man, but he left it and Elia stole in to score.

But, on 57 minutes, City got back in front. Ireland broke into the Twente half, before laying the ball left to Robinho. City's record signing cut inside and curled a beautiful, dipping shot around the goalkeeper and into the top corner, to the delight of the home crowd.

Jo then made way and Benjani came on for his first appearance of the season after injury. And the Zimbabwean didn't have to wait long for his first goal as, on 62 minutes, he broke into the Twente area and his shot deflected off the defender's feet and into the corner of the goal.

But the home fans had barely taken their seats, when they ended up back on the edge of them. Wielaert broke free of his man at a corner and, despite a last-ditch attempt by Dunne to challenge, he headed home.

On 75 minutes, the City fans thought they had a two goal cushion again, after Robinho snapped a shot across goal, only to see it rebound back to the keeper's arms after hitting the post.

Benjani, Robinho and Zabaleta then combined, and Robinho found himself free in the box. He shot across goal, only to see the ball rebound back off the very same post he had hit 10 minutes earlier.

Manchester City 1-2 Tottenham Hotspur
FA Premier League
Sunday 9 November, 2008 - 15:00 KO

City: Hart, Zabaleta, Dunne (c), Richards, Garrido, Gelson, Ireland, Wright-Phillips, Vassell (Hamann 31), Robinho, Benjani
Unused: Schmeichel, Onuoha, Elano, Ben-Haim, Jo, Evans
Goals: Robinho (16)
Booked: Gelson
Sent Off: Gelson, Dunne
Man of the Match: Pablo Zabaleta

The away side had the better of the opening exchanges, with Modric almost giving them the lead on 10 minutes, with a curling effort that just missed Hart's post. Vassell broke into the Spurs box, but he couldn't find Benjani with a cross and the away side were able to clear the danger.

And it was Vassell who worked the opening for City to take the lead on 16 minutes. Wright-Phillips found the pacey forward and Vassell's shot was only parried by Gomes. Robinho was there to slot the ball past Woodgate on the line.

Then came the game's turning point: Gelson picked up his second yellow, after a late tackle on Bentley. The Swiss international protested, the home fans weren't pleased, but he was given his marching orders.

Hart then pulled off the save of the day to preserve the one goal advantage. Modric produced a great bit of skill to beat Dunne, but his fired shot across the goal was expertly tipped wide by the City keeper.

But Hart was unable to stop the away side's equaliser on 29 minutes. Bent latched onto a through ball after a mistake from Dunne and drove the ball into the net, despite challenges from Garrido and Hart.

After the hour Spurs went ahead. Bent broke into the City area after a period of pressure from the hosts, and managed to slide the ball past Hart and in off the post, largely against the run of play.

With seven minutes to go, City's day got worse. A missed interception by the midfield headed towards Bent, and Dunne was there to clear. But his clearance hit Bent and fell kindly for the forward, who raced through on goal. Dunne fouled the Spurs man and was also sent for an early bath.

As the clock hit 90, the away side were reduced to 10 men, after Assou-Ekotto lunged in with a dangerous tackle on Zabaleta, which won the Spurs man a second yellow card, when it could have been a straight red.

Hull City 2-2 Manchester City
FA Premier League
Sunday 16 November, 2008 - 16:00 KO

City: Hart (Schmeichel 18), Zabaleta, Ben-Haim, Richards, Garrido, Kompany, Ireland, Wright-Phillips, Vassell, Robinho (c), Benjani (Jo 75)
Unused: Ball, Onuoha, Elano, Hamann, Evans
Goals: Ireland (38, 44)
Booked: Ben-Haim, Ireland, Wright-Phillips
Man of the Match: Stephen Ireland

Both teams had had a poor run of results in the league and both must have been looking at this game as one they could win. Ben-Haim got himself an early booking for a rash challenge on Geovanni. And the Israeli's day got much worse when, on 14 minutes, he received a square pass from Richards and it should have been a comfortable pass back. But it was much too short, allowing Cousin in to slot home. Hart was injured in the process and could only last another minute.

City were gifted their equaliser on 38 minutes. Zayatte stepped in as the ball was over-run by Benjani and, with Myhill looking to collect, strangely rolled the ball across his own goal for Ireland to score in the open net.

With just a minute of the first half remaining, City took the lead. Garrido burst down the left wing and, when the Hull defence expected a cross, he squared it low to the on-coming Ireland. He took a touch before placing it superbly around Myhill.

On the hour mark, City old boy Geovanni levelled the count. Hull were awarded a free kick and the Brazilian stepped up to take a shot. His curler deflected off Kompany, wrong-footed Schmeichel and sent the ball into the net.

Vassell could and should have won the game for City, after a bouncing ball fell to his feet in the box, but he couldn't direct the ball past Myhill, who made himself big enough to pull off the save.

Manchester City 3-0 Arsenal
FA Premier League
Saturday 22 November, 2008 - 15:00 KO

City: Hart, Zabaleta, Dunne (c), Richards, Garrido, Kompany, Ireland, Wright-Phillips, Vassell (Elano 70), Robinho (Hamann 82), Benjani (Sturridge 88)
Unused: Schmeichel, Onuoha, Ben-Haim, Evans
Goals: Ireland (45), Robinho (56), Sturridge (pen 90+1)
Booked: -
Man of the Match: Stephen Ireland

City started brightly and could have opened the scoring in the second minute, when a mistake in front of the Arsenal goal allowed Ireland to stab the ball on to Vassell, but he delayed and Zabaleta blazed wide.

On 33 minutes, van Persie was clipped in the ribs by Richards and got himself a free kick about 30 yards out. With the Dutchman off for treatment, Nasri took it. Hart saved, but didn't manage to get the ball behind and Bendtner back-heeled for Song, but his shot was well wide.

Seconds before half time, City had the lead. Benjani knocked the ball to Ireland, who took on the Arsenal defence. A Silvestre and Clichy mix-up presented the ball back to the Irishman, who made no mistake in slotting the ball past Almunia into the top left corner.

City were able to withstand the early second half pressure and, on 56 minutes, Wright-Phillips won the ball and broke quickly. He slid a perfectly weighted pass for Robinho to latch onto and, with the Arsenal keeper rushing off his line, the Brazilian expertly chipped over Almunia and into the net.

Arsenal could have hit back on the hour, when substitute Ramsey found Bendtner, but the big Dane was denied by Hart. Robinho thought he'd scored again, but it was wrongly ruled out for offside.

Van Persie had the ball in City's net with a minute to go, but it too was ruled out. Hart had thrown the ball up to kick it and the Dutchman touched it away and slotted home. In stoppage time, Sturridge ran onto a long pass into the Arsenal box and he wound his way along the by-line before being brought down by Djourou. He took the resulting penalty and beat Almunia.

Schalke 04 0-2 Manchester City
UEFA Cup Group A
Thursday 27 November, 2008 - 18:00 KO

City: Hart, Richards, Dunne (c), Kompany, Garrido (Ball 45), Ireland, Hamann, Wright-Phillips, Vassell, Sturridge, Benjani (Jo 84)
Unused: Schmeichel, Ben-Haim, Logan, Berti, Evans
Goals: Benjani (32), Ireland (66)
Booked: Richards, Ireland, Benjani
Man of the Match: Stephen Ireland

City were able to soak up the home side's early pressure, and went on to take the lead on 32 minutes. Kompany produced a well timed tackle and found Sturridge with a lovely through ball. He worked his way forward and fired a low cross through the box. It was missed by everyone but Benjani, who popped up at the back post to smash the ball into the net.

The second half began in much the same way as the first, with Schalke dominating possession, but doing nothing to worry the City defence. The away side broke on 55 minutes, and after some excellent hold up play from the youngster Sturridge, Wright-Phillips unleashed a thunderous drive from 25 yards that Neuer did well to push over.

The home fans were even more upset with their team's performance just after the hour, when City doubled their lead. Ireland set Benjani free on the left and the Zimbabwean's shot was deflected straight up into the air. Out came the keeper, but he didn't deal with it and Ireland was able to slide the ball under him to get the goal his performance deserved.

Schalke could have pulled a goal back with 15 minutes to play, when a free kick was whipped in and Asamoah headed towards goal. But Hart deflected the ball wide, making it six points from a possible six for the group.

Manchester City 0-1 Manchester United
FA Premier League
Sunday 30 November, 2008 - 13:30 KO

City: Hart, Richards (Sturridge 76), Dunne (c), Kompany, Garrido, Hamann (Zabaleta 45), Ireland, Wright-Phillips, Vassell (Elano 45), Robinho, Benjani
Unused: Schmeichel, Ball, Ben-Haim, Jo
Goals: -
Booked: Ireland, Vassell
Man of the Match: Vincent Kompany

The 151st Manchester derby got off to a quiet start, with the first real chance falling to the visitors. Rooney turned and shot at Hart's goal and it seemed a comfortable enough save, but the City keeper spilled the ball. Dunne, though, was on hand to clear the danger.

Hart then made up for his earlier error with a superb stop from a Berbatov header. Rafael crossed for the Bulgarian who must have already been celebrating before Hart, somehow, clawed it around the post for a corner.

City should have taken the lead on 32 minutes, when a right wing free kick wasn't dealt with by van der Sar, whose weak punch fell to Ireland. But his bobbling effort was missed by Richards and struck the post on its way behind.

Ireland then found his name in the book for what turned out to be a costly foul, as United took the lead. City couldn't clear and Carrick's low shot could only be pushed out by Hart, straight to Rooney a yard from goal. He was never going to miss.

Early in the second half, Kompany almost grabbed his second City goal with a thunderous drive from range, but it whistled just the wrong side of van der Sar's post, with the Dutchman scrambling. Benjani had the next chance to equalise, after a breakaway from the home side, but his drive hit the side netting.

Ronaldo collected a yellow card for a foul on Wright-Phillips, before he bizarrely palmed the ball away at a United corner and picked up his second, this one for handball.

City almost grabbed a point in the closing stages, when Dunne's header was well saved on the line by van der Sar. As the last roll of the dice, City sent Hart forward for a corner, but they couldn't force a shot and nearly conceded another, when Rooney attempted to lob the keeper from just inside the City half. Hart, though, was able to get back superbly to save.

> **"I don't think enough is done about it. By that I mean the systematic fouling of Ronaldo. One player fouls him, then another player fouls him, then someone else does."**

I would like to offer my congratulations to Sir Alex Ferguson: You've won.

Over the summer, City had to respond to claims that they had ruined football due to the amount of money the club's new owners had. But I'd like to put it to all those who made that claim that there is someone else we need to look at first.

Irony doesn't seem to hold much weight with Mr. Ferguson. He was the man who made the above statement and then, this month, won the Manchester derby by instructing his players to 'systematically' foul Shaun Wright-Phillips.

Fletcher could have walked for his hacking down of our number eight. Evra could have walked for his hacking down of our number eight. Carrick *should* have walked for his hacking down of our number eight… a pattern emerges.

If Mark Hughes spoke to the press after this game and told the reporters that the referee was out of order, gave everything to United and allowed them to 'systematically' foul Shaun Wright-Phillips, then he would get a fine and a ban.

But who gets off with saying the same things, of Ronaldo, after his team exit the FA Cup at the hands of, say, Portsmouth? You already know the answer. The next time Mr. Ferguson has the cheek to claim that Ronaldo didn't get the protection he should deserve, I would urge every single City fan that hears it to remind him what happened to Wright-Phillips in the 151st Manchester derby.

So, well done, Sir Alex. Your constant moaning, chirping away at, and mind games with the FA and referees have won you their favour. They won't make many major decisions against you, more subconsciously than consciously of course, but either way, you've achieved your aim. They won't stand in your way. And even then you'll be able to tell us that someone else cheated or played unfairly or looked at you in a funny way or blah blah blah…

There were so many United players that could and should have been sent off in that match, some for two yellows, and at least one for a straight red. But only one walked, and it was a soft second yellow at that. United's game plan was to stop Wright-Phillips from playing by kicking him up and down the pitch. And it worked, in no small part because the referee allowed it to work.

I'm not normally one to criticise a referee. I often think that we need to look at ourselves before we look at the referee. But this was an exception. This match was one of the few times that I will agree that it felt like playing against 12 men for the majority of the game.

So, well done Sir Alex. You've got it all your own way from here on in.

And an even bigger well done to Wright-Phillips. Well done for getting on with the game; well done for not complaining when you could have easily been carried off, and well done for not lowering yourself to Ronaldo's standards of rolling around the floor.

November 2008 Breakdown

Games (all competitions):
Won: 3   **Drawn:** 1   **Lost:** 3

Goals (all competitions):
For: 11   **Against:** 9

Progress:
Premier League: 14th
League Cup: Eliminated in Round Two
FA Cup: -
UEFA Cup: 1st in Group A

Premier League Table

		P	W	D	L	F	A	GD	Pts
12	Middlesbrough	15	5	4	6	15	21	-6	19
13	Stoke City	15	5	3	7	15	25	-10	18
14	**Manchester City**	15	5	2	8	29	23	+6	17
15	West Ham United	14	5	2	7	17	22	-5	17
16	Tottenham Hotspur	15	4	3	8	17	21	-4	15

UEFA Cup Group A Table

		P	W	D	L	F	A	GD	Pts
1	**Manchester City**	2	2	0	0	5	2	+3	6
2	Schalke 04	3	1	1	1	4	4	0	4
3	FC Twente	2	1	0	1	3	3	0	3
4	Racing Santander	3	0	2	1	3	4	-1	2
5	Paris Saint-Germain	2	0	1	1	3	5	-2	1

December 2008

Manchester City 0-0 Paris Saint-Germain

UEFA Cup Group A

Wednesday 3 December, 2008 - 19:45 KO

City: Hart, Zabaleta, Dunne (c), Ben-Haim, Garrido, Kompany, Ireland, Elano (Benjani 47), Vassell (Hamann 76), Sturridge, Jo (Evans 65)
Unused: Schmeichel, Berti, Logan, Caicedo
Goals: -
Booked: -
Man of the Match: Vincent Kompany

This was a game between a team who had qualified for the next round and a team that was virtually out, and boy did it show. Kezman found himself in the book after a series of questionable challenges. First, City skipper Dunne wasn't happy with Kezman's use of an elbow in challenging him, then Hart had some angry words for the Serbian after he caught the home keeper late.

With just three minutes to the break, Jo had the chance to head at goal, but he could only put Zabaleta's cross over the bar. The Argentinian right back forced Landreau into a good save, after Vassell had knocked the ball back.

Ben-Haim put in a terrific tackle to deny what looked like a certain goal, as the City defence were caught napping and the ball was driven low and hard across the area towards Luyindula. But the Israeli timed his tackle to perfection and Dunne was there to clear.

But the neat patches of play were few and far between, with neither side able to keep the ball for long. Hoarau placed a shot well wide of Hart's goal, when he should have done better, before Luyindula fired over from inside the box.

Fulham 1-1 Manchester City

FA Premier League

Saturday 6 December, 2008 - 12:45 KO

City: Hart, Zabaleta, Dunne (c), Ben-Haim, Ball, Hamann, Kompany, Ireland, Wright-Phillips, Vassell, Benjani (Evans 77)
Unused: Schmeichel, Onuoha, Berti, Logan, Jo, Caicedo
Goals: Benjani (6)
Booked: Ireland
Man of the Match: Pablo Zabaleta

The game started brightly and City had the lead inside six minutes. Some neat play down the right wing saw Zabaleta just manage to keep the ball in play, before he delivered a good looking left foot cross for Benjani to head home.

A minute later, City could have made it two. Schwarzer failed to deal with another Zabaleta cross, with his weak punch falling to Ireland. But the City midfielder volleyed wide, with the Fulham keeper off limits.

But just before the half-hour, Bullard equalised for the home side. He managed to lose Kompany and found himself free in the box, receiving a pass from Zamora, and he slammed the ball past Hart.

City could have re-taken the lead immediately, when Dunne found Vassell with a long ball. He took it down well, but his volley from the edge of the box was straight at the goalkeeper.

On 54 minutes, Zabaleta was very unlucky to have not made it 2-1, when his low, powerful drive from a Benjani lay off was flicked around the post. Then, just before the hour, centre-back Ben-Haim volleyed slightly over the bar.

A wrongly awarded Fulham free kick from 30 yards took a wonderful save from Hart to deny Bullard his second. Ball then nearly caught the home keeper out, with a cheeky effort that Schwarzer flapped onto his near post.

Manchester City 0-1 Everton
FA Premier League
Saturday 13 December, 2008 - 15:00 KO

City: Hart, Zabaleta, Dunne (c), Richards, Ball, Kompany, Ireland, Wright-Phillips, Robinho (Vassell 82), Elano, Benjani (Jo 45)
Unused: Schmeichel, Onuoha, Ben-Haim, Hamann, Gelson
Goals: -
Booked: -
Man of the Match: Elano

Everton started brightly. An Arteta free kick had the home support breathing a sigh of relief when it hit the bar and bounced clear. Their hearts were right back in their mouths, though, as the rebound fell to Fellaini, but his header hit the top of the bar, with Hart scrambling back to try and cover it.

City should have taken the lead shortly after through the move of the match. Elano took the ball forward and, after a one-two with Robinho, found Benjani, who knocked it to Ireland in the box. The Irishman, though, fired over. Four minutes before the half, Wright-Phillips was inches away from scoring, when his drive from inside the box crashed against the top of the bar.

Wright-Phillips got a good bounce of the ball on 64 minutes allowing him to break into the Everton box. But his low cross missed everyone.

On 72 minutes, Hart claimed the ball in the box and sent it quickly to Jo's head. The big Brazilian flicked on to Ireland, who took a low shot from just inside the box, only to find Howard's fingertips in the way again.

As the game entered stoppage time, a misplaced header by Dunne went for a corner. Cahill lost Richards in the box and was able to nod past Hart, from four yards out, stealing the points for Everton.

Racing Santander 3-1 Manchester City
UEFA Cup Group A
Thursday 18 December, 2008 - 19:45 KO

City: Schmeichel, Garrido, Ben-Haim, Richards, Zabaleta, Hamann (c), Gelson, Elano (Kompany 60), Vassell, Robinho (Ireland 45), Evans (Caicedo 76)
Unused: Hart, Ball, Onuoha, Logan
Goals: Caicedo (90)
Booked: Ben-Haim, Hamann, Elano, Zabaleta, Kompany
Man of the Match: Stephen Ireland

Ben-Haim earned a booking on 17 minutes for a needless foul and it was a costly free kick to concede. From it, Santander fired a low cross into the area, Schmeichel could only parry it and Pereira passed it into the empty net.

City couldn't get a foot on the ball and, mid-way into the first half, Santander doubled their lead. Serrano finished off a neat move after he had exchanged passes with Pereira, slotting the ball past Schmeichel coolly.

City were poor in defending a corner on 54 minutes and Valera took full advantage. After the first clearance, the visitors didn't deal with the second ball and a free header at the back post allowed Valera to slide the ball home.

Tchite could have made it more embarrassing for the away side on 64 minutes, when he rounded Schmeichel, but he sliced the ball wide when facing an open goal.

Hamann hit one over the bar from outside the area, before City did manage to grab themselves a consolation goal: Zabaleta whipped a ball into the box and Caicedo swept it into the bottom right corner.

West Bromwich Albion 2-1 Manchester City
FA Premier League
Sunday 21 December, 2008 - 13:30 KO

City: Hart, Zabaleta, Dunne (c), Richards, Ball, Kompany, Gelson, Ireland, Wright-Phillips, Vassell, Benjani (Caicedo 57)
Unused: Schmeichel, Onuoha, Garrido, Hamann, Clayton, Evans
Goals: Caicedo (86)
Booked: Dunne
Man of the Match: Stephen Ireland

City should have been in front after just seven minutes, when Ireland's shot was fired straight at Carson, before Wright-Phillips had a shot deflected over after a lay off from Vassell.

Morrison had the home side's first real chance on 21 minutes, as his shot from the near post was blocked wide by Kompany, after Dunne had blocked the initial effort.

The home side hit the post on 31 minutes, after Bednar turned Gelson and fired a snap shot towards Hart. The City keeper threw his body at it, but couldn't get a touch and the ball rebounded out for Zabaleta to clear.

With just over 20 minutes to go, Dunne and Zabaleta found themselves three on two at the back. Morrison drew Zabaleta, knocked a through ball for Moore and he slid it past Joe Hart.

Caicedo grabbed his first Premier League goal, after Ball threw the ball into the box and it found its way to the Ecuadorian, with his back to goal. He lifted his leg and back-heeled it into the net, off the post.

But with just one minute of stoppage time remaining, West Brom stole the points as, from a cross from deep, Bednar got himself inbetween Richards and Zabaleta. Hart came for the ball, but stopped, and the Albion man headed into the top corner.

City remain in the bottom three for Christmas.

Manchester City 5-1 Hull City
FA Premier League
Friday 26 December, 2008 - 15:00 KO

City: Hart, Zabaleta, Dunne (c), Richards (Onuoha 45), Ball, Kompany, Elano, Ireland (Gelson 85), Robinho, Wright-Phillips, Caicedo (Jo 45)
Unused: Schmeichel, Garrido, Vassell, Sturridge
Goals: Caicedo (15, 27), Robinho (28, 36), Ireland (82)
Booked: -
Man of the Match: Stephen Ireland

City could have taken the lead within 60 seconds, as Zayatte failed to clear the ball in his own penalty area, finding only Ireland. City's number seven then found Caicedo who, when perhaps the shot was a better option, squared for Robinho, and the Brazilian's effort didn't trouble Myhill.

Dunne stole the ball in defence and carried it 40 yards up the pitch, before finding Robinho on the left wing. He then sent an inch-perfect pass over the top to Ireland and the Irishman fired the ball low and hard across the box. Caicedo was on hand to smash it into the roof of the net.

With 27 minutes on the clock, Ireland latched on to a poor clearance and broke down the right. As with the first goal, he fired the ball across the six-yard box and Caicedo was, once again, in the right place to score.

A minute later, Ireland robbed the ball in the midfield and released Robinho. He was closed down by the Hull defence, but he cut the ball onto his right foot and bent it around Myhill into the bottom corner of the goal for City's third.

With 10 minutes of the first half remaining, Elano lobbed the ball over to

Wright-Phillips and his cross found Robinho in the area, with the Brazilian able to knock the ball past Myhill, as City dominated. The Hull manager then made his feelings known, giving his side a talking to and taking the team-talk on the pitch, right in front of the visiting fans.

With 11 minutes to go, Myhill was left flat-footed as Elano's free kick smacked into the Hull wall, before clipping the post. Cousin then fired a shot across City's goal, and Hart parried. The ball rebounded off Onuoha at speed, before landing to the feet of Fagan, who slotted home.

But it hardly mattered as, two minutes later, Ireland found Robinho on the left and the Brazilian tricked his way into the area. With everybody hoping he would get his hat-trick goal, he unselfishly squared to Ireland, who swept the ball into the net.

Blackburn Rovers 2-2 Manchester City
FA Premier League
Sunday 28 December, 2008 - 16:15 KO

City: Hart, Zabaleta, Dunne (c), Onuoha (Richards 64), Ball, Kompany, Elano (Vassell 71), Ireland, Robinho, Wright-Phillips, Caicedo (Sturridge 71)
Unused: Schmeichel, Garrido, Gelson, Jo
Goals: Sturridge (88), Robinho (90+4)
Booked: Ireland
Man of the Match: Daniel Sturridge

City nearly made a wonderful start to the game, after Kompany won a header from an Ireland corner and it fell to Caicedo in the box, but the Ecuadorian could only get his toe on the ball and send it over the bar.

The home side got a rather fortunate free kick in a promising position. Emerton took it, only for the ball to rebound off Ireland and into Hart's hands. The hosts wanted a penalty for a handball, but it was accidental and would certainly have been harsh.

It was City's turn to be denied a penalty on 10 minutes, when Robinho broke into the box and was clearly tripped by Ooijer, but the linesman's flag stayed down, with the visiting fans furious.

The home fans were expecting a goal on 25 minutes when a long ball found McCarthy on the edge of City's box, but just as he was about to pull the trigger, Dunne came out of nowhere to provide a crucial block. And just as it looked like the teams would go in at 0-0, McCarthy turned in the box, latching on to a cross and placing the ball past Hart.

The away side began to get their act together as the second half progressed, as Wright-Phillips flicked a header backwards onto the post, before Ireland curled a shot just wide from range.

Richards went close to equalising, but his cross-shot from a Ball corner needed a touch that never came to send it into the net. But, as City pushed forward for their leveller, Blackburn hit them on the break. Richards lost his man as the ball was floated into the box and it fell to the unmarked Roberts, who nodded the ball over Hart's despairing dive with just four minutes to go.

Robinho followed a series of step-overs with a high ball towards Kompany. Ooijer could only clear to Sturridge, who volleyed the ball past Robinson on 88 minutes, for what looked like a consolation.

But Sturridge then rode one challenge excellently, before working the ball onto his left foot and sending a perfectly weighted pass through the area to Robinho, who was unmarked at the back post. He took a touch and slid the ball past Robinson, earning City a point with just 20 seconds left on the clock.

December 2008 Breakdown

Games (all competitions):
Won: 1   **Drawn:** 3   **Lost:** 3

Goals (all competitions):
For: 10   **Against:** 10

Progress:
Premier League: 13th
League Cup: Eliminated in Round Two
FA Cup: -
UEFA Cup: Winner of Group A, qualified for the Round of 32

Premier League Table

		P	W	D	L	F	A	GD	Pts
11	Bolton Wanderers	20	7	2	11	22	28	-6	23
12	Portsmouth	20	6	5	9	21	33	-12	23
13	**Manchester City**	**20**	**6**	**4**	**10**	**38**	**30**	**+8**	**22**
14	Newcastle United	20	5	7	8	26	32	-6	22
15	Sunderland	20	6	4	10	21	29	-8	22

UEFA Cup Group A Table

		P	W	D	L	F	A	GD	Pts
1	**Manchester City**	4	2	1	1	6	5	+1	7
2	FC Twente	4	2	0	2	5	8	-3	6
3	Paris Saint-Germain	4	1	2	1	7	5	+2	5
4	Racing Santander	4	1	2	1	6	5	+1	5
5	Schalke 04	4	1	1	2	5	6	-1	4

January 2009

Manchester City 0-3 Nottingham Forest

FA Cup Third Round
Saturday 3 January, 2009 - 15:00 KO

City: Hart, Zabaleta, Dunne (c), Richards, Ball, Kompany, Wright-Phillips (Vassell 24), Elano, Gelson (Hamann 60), Sturridge, Caicedo (Jo 70)
Unused: Schmeichel, Garrido, Berti, Clayton
Goals: -
Booked: Dunne
Man of the Match: Vincent Kompany

Forest had the first chance, when Tyson crossed from the left and found McGugan free inside the six-yard box. Luckily for City, he headed wide.

On 37 minutes, Sturridge came closest to opening the scoring, when Vassell kept the ball in play and knocked it back to the youngster, whose turn and shot forced a good save.

Less than a minute later, Forest had the lead. Richards could only nod a header out to the edge of the box where Tyson was waiting. He volleyed it back in, straight past Hart and into the bottom corner.

And things got worse for the home side just before half time, when Zabaleta was caught in possession by the box and the ball was squared to Thornhill. His shot was well off target, but was diverted into the net by Earnshaw.

Dunne tried to spur City on when he rode two tackles before breaking down the left flank. He then skipped past a third tackle, before cutting inside and squaring for Vassell. With the crowd baying for him to shoot, he held it up before finding Elano, whose low cross was put behind for a corner.

With 15 minutes to go, Forest wrapped the game up and secured their place in the Fourth Round draw, when Hamann took a poor throw-in from the left. The ball didn't reach Dunne and Garner nipped in to score with his first touch.

Manchester City 1-0 Wigan Athletic

FA Premier League
Saturday 17 January, 2009 - 15:00 KO

City: Hart, Richards, Dunne (c), Onuoha, Bridge, Zabaleta, Kompany, Elano, Robinho, Wright-Phillips, Sturridge (Garrido 60)
Unused: Schmeichel, Vassell, Gelson, Weiss, Jo, Caicedo
Goals: Zabaleta (52)
Booked: Robinho
Sent Off: Dunne
Man of the Match: Pablo Zabaleta

Robinho should have scored on 12 minutes, after an Elano through ball sent him towards goal but, as he tried to sidestep Kirkland, he passed the ball well wide of the goal. With 20 minutes gone, Elano knocked a ball through for Robinho, who chipped Kirkland, but Bramble was there to volley it off the line.

Sturridge crossed to the near post and Melchiot's clearance fell only to Zabaleta, who took a touch and volleyed the ball past Kirkland from 20 yards, for his first City goal.

Less than a minute later, though, Dunne reacted to a Zaki elbow by kicking out and earned himself a red card, leaving City facing being a man short for over half an hour. The first, of what seemed like too many, goalmouth scrambles finished with Melchiot firing a fierce drive into Zabaleta.

Cattermole then headed towards goal, with Hart tipping the ball onto the bar. The rebound fell to Zaki who nodded over from three yards with an open goal to aim at.

The travelling fans wanted a penalty for a foul on Cattermole, but the referee judged that there was no infringement, before Cattermole himself shot well wide and Hart produced a wonderful save to deny Melchiot an equaliser.

Manchester City 2-1 Newcastle United
FA Premier League
Wednesday 28 January, 2009 - 19:45 KO

City: Hart, Richards, Kompany (c), Onuoha, Bridge, Zabaleta (Gelson 81), de Jong (Elano 77), Ireland, Wright-Phillips (Caicedo 90), Robinho, Bellamy
Unused: Schmeichel, Vassell, Garrido
Goals: Wright-Phillips (16), Bellamy (76)
Booked: Wright-Phillips
Man of the Match: Craig Bellamy

The first action of the game saw the opening goal. Zabaleta fired the ball across to the wing for Bridge and his cross into the middle was scuffed, but picked up by Robinho, who found Wright-Phillips and he slotted it home.

Barton tried an effort from range on his old stomping ground, but it was well over the bar and not troubling Hart, as the visitors just couldn't get to grips with the game in the opening 45 minutes.

Duff broke into the City box, wide on the left, and had room to run into. He crossed low towards the six-yard box as he was closed down by Hart. His ball across beat the City keeper but not Bridge, who was excellently placed to clear before Lovenkrands could get the vital touch.

Kompany swept a neat pass out to the right for Zabaleta, who centred for Bellamy on the edge of the box. With his back to goal, Bellamy took a touch, rolled his man and slotted the ball into the bottom corner of the goal, leaving Harper standing and scoring on his debut for his new club.

David Edgar stole the ball from Bridge on the left side of City's area, before delivering a low cross into the six-yard box that was too inviting for Carroll to turn down. He touched it into the net and halved the deficit, with Hart and Kompany sliding in. But it was too little too late and City took the points.

Stoke City 1-0 Manchester City
FA Premier League
Saturday 31 January, 2009 - 12:45 KO

City: Hart, Richards, Kompany (c), Onuoha, Bridge, Zabaleta (Elano 55), de Jong (Caicedo 72), Ireland, Wright-Phillips, Robinho, Bellamy
Unused: Schmeichel, Vassell, Garrido, Jo, Gelson
Goals: -
Booked: Elano
Man of the Match: Craig Bellamy

The game began with City in control of the ball for long spells, but never really looked threatening. Stoke flattered to deceive with a few long throw-ins from Delap.

In fact, City's first chance of the half came from a Delap throw-in. The ball was nodded clear and fell to Ireland down the right wing. He knocked the ball on to Bellamy, who squared for Robinho in acres of space. But the Brazilian decided not to take a touch and hit it first time, straight at Sorensen.

Stoke then lost their main weapon. Seconds after Wright-Phillips went in on him strongly, Delap felled the winger from behind. After a fracas involving most of both teams, the long throw expert was sent off for an early bath.

Just when it looked like City would be able to mount the offensive, Stoke took the lead, mere seconds before the break. A cross from their left which could have been blocked by Richards, fell to Beattie. The striker had given Bridge the slip, freeing himself to head past Hart at his near post.

With a man down and a goal in front, it's hardly a surprise that the home side sat in front of their own box and presented City with a sizeable obstacle to break down. Robinho fired a shot just wide from about 25 yards, before Ireland almost got his head on an Elano cross-shot, but his dive left him inches away from making a connection.

City's unbeaten run petered to an end at the Britannia Stadium, in a match where they dominated possession, but never actually looked like they were going to score.

SEEING THINGS IN BLACK & WHITE

"You're not fit to referee!" Several thousand City fans shouted past me, during City's 2-3 defeat against Liverpool. We had been in a great position – two goals in front at half time and Liverpool not looking like they were going to score, every City fan was bouncing. But then the game changed, just after Liverpool had pulled a goal back. Pablo Zabaleta was sent off for a foul that left the football pundits worldwide torn between whether it was or wasn't a red card.

Now, you might be wondering why I've taken you all the way back to the start of October, but there is method in my madness. Apart from the fact that it was quite a snappy opening, it illustrates the point in the title. The referee saw Zabaleta's tackle as dangerous and worthy of a red card and the FA backed him.

Meanwhile, everyone else in the country wasn't really sure. But the FA was, and that's what matters, when it comes down to it.

I don't get to a lot of away games, but I made the trip down the M6 to Stoke's Britannia Stadium. There, I witnessed a team who forgot to shoot when they had the chance play against a team who were happy to concede possession in return for not facing any shots, especially after they'd grabbed a goal when being a man down.

If that makes any sense at all.

And now, because of the incident that caused the national press to be preparing puns like *Delap thrown by Wright-Phillips challenge*, *Delap hurled off early*, *Delap launched into tackle*, or any other long throw based pun, City will be without Shaun Wright-Phillips for three matches.

Don't get me wrong, he shouldn't have kicked out at Delap after the Stoke man had chopped him down, and he's right to be punished for it. But what has me riled, is the clear and blatant double standards on show at the FA.

If anybody saw Chelsea's defeat to Liverpool last weekend, then you'll probably have seen an incident in the corner when Benayoun was wasting a bit of time and Bosingwa found a cute way to stop him doing it. It involved Benayoun's back, Bosingwa's foot and the Chelsea full back taking it upon himself to introduce them to each other. And, after the incident was looked at by the FA's video panel, they decided no further action should be taken and the player wouldn't be punished.

In the same game, Gerrard got away with a two-footed lunge on Kalou and, as far as I'm aware, the FA didn't even look at the incident, when most agreed he was lucky to stay on the pitch.

A few weeks ago, Tottenham played Manchester United and Ronaldo kicked out at Dawson. At the time, the referee didn't see it and it was reviewed by the FA panel. It was a petulant kick out, granted, but the pundit world was agreed that he was lucky to have stayed on the pitch. And, after the incident was looked at by the FA's video panel, they decided no further action should be taken and the player wouldn't be punished.

Just after Christmas, Rooney hurled Stoke's Faye to the ground by his neck and wasn't punished at the match, despite the incident being in full view of the assistant, three yards away. And, after the incident was looked at by the FA's video panel, they decided no further action should be taken and the player wouldn't be punished.

Spotted the connection yet? I could go on.

Basically, when you take the incident that Shaun Wright-Phillips has been punished for on its own, then the FA is correct to punish him. He kicked out at an opponent and it's not allowed. Had the referee seen it, he would have been sent off at the time. But, when it's put into context with the other incidents that have been left retrospectively unpunished, then it's nothing other than double-standards across the board.

I actually think the argument that the people at the FA 'haven't ever played the game and so their decisions could be excused' is utter rubbish. I've played football, but not to any decent standard – ok, so I might not understand everything about the game, but I know that wrestling someone to the ground, karate-kicking someone in the back and diving in with two feet is just as much of a red card or retrospective ban as kicking out because you've been chopped down.

The trouble is, the referees have to play by the rules in the book. And I know that sounds like a completely daft sentence, but there's absolutely no flexibility for common sense.

With the referees having an assessor in the stands who can't help meddling every time there's a minor decision the man in the middle has got wrong, resulting in said man in the middle being dropped a division for a few weeks, then the referees are going to stick to the rules as they are written.

There just isn't room for common sense in the rules. But the FA don't seem to see this and they are too preoccupied in trying to apply hard set, inflexible and abstract sentences to an entity that changes constantly and is about as predictable as a Manchester City form book.

But we don't live in such a black and white world. If we did, then there would be a very clear boundary between right and wrong, there would be no grey areas causing confusion, Frank Lampard wouldn't have been sent off for winning the ball and there would be absolutely no heavy metal music. I don't care what anybody says, it is just noise.

I think the ironic part of this is that each of the incidents I listed earlier, including the Wright-Phillips one, has no grey area. Each player is in the wrong and each should have been punished. But somehow, the video review panel has found the grey area, camped in it, before delivering a brutal right hook to Manchester City.

Part of the problem is that these decisions aren't usually made in the first place. Granted, some of them have been missed because they're subtle, but Bosingwa's kick was about as obvious as an alligator in a tutu trying to get into the Royal Ballet performance of Swan Lake just so it can have a tasty snack.

If the referee had taken action against the kick, then I doubt the FA would have overturned the decision. But, since he didn't – and the assistant didn't even flag for a foul on this one – then they can hide away and say he deserves no further action.

Since September people have been doing their best to blame City for ruining football because of the money the club can spend. But, if you want to truly find out what is causing the most problems in football, then I think there's wider issues to be looked at first, starting with consistency.

January 2009 Breakdown

Games (all competitions):
Won: 2   **Drawn:** 0   **Lost:** 2

Goals (all competitions):
For: 3   **Against:** 5

Progress:
Premier League: 10th
League Cup: Eliminated in Round Two
FA Cup: Eliminated in Round Three
UEFA Cup: Qualified for the Round of 32

Premier League Table

		P	W	D	L	F	A	GD	Pts
8	West Ham United	24	9	6	9	31	31	0	33
9	Fulham	22	7	8	7	22	19	+3	29
10	**Manchester City**	**23**	**8**	**4**	**11**	**41**	**32**	**+9**	**28**
11	Hull City	24	7	7	10	31	46	-15	28
12	Bolton Wanderers	24	8	3	13	27	34	-7	27

February 2009

Manchester City 1-0 Middlesbrough
FA Premier League
Saturday 7 February, 2009 - 12:45 KO

City: Given, Richards, Kompany (c), Onuoha, Bridge, Zabaleta, de Jong, Ireland, Wright-Phillips, Robinho (Caicedo 83), Bellamy
Unused: Hart, Garrido, Gelson, Elano, Vassell, Evans
Goals: Bellamy (51)
Booked: -
Man of the Match: Shay Given

City were up for this game from the off, with Bellamy chasing a ball down the left, after good work from Ireland and Robinho, but Jones was out to clear. Kompany showed his ball-juggling skills before volleying wide from a corner.

Middlesbrough should have taken the lead on 28 minutes, when the City defence was caught off guard. The ball was whipped in and Alves had slipped his marker to fire at goal first time, but Given made himself big and was able to push the ball away to safety, with Richards completing the clearance.

It had become end-to-end for the final few minutes of the first half, as Given produced a good stop when wrong-footed and City attacked with Ireland. The Irishman broke into the box for a cross, clipping the bar with a header.

The first action of the second half saw City score what turned out to be the only goal of the game. De Jong found Ireland in the midfield and he swept the ball out to Bellamy on the right. The Welshman cut inside onto his wrong foot and sent off a low, hard shot into the bottom left corner of the goal.

With just over an hour gone, Robinho could have made it 2-0. He found himself running one-on-one with Jones and attempted to go around the Middlesbrough keeper, but he got a hand on the ball and knocked it from him.

Portsmouth 2-0 Manchester City
FA Premier League
Saturday 14 February, 2009 - 15:00 KO

City: Given, Logan, Kompany (c), Onuoha, Bridge, Zabaleta (Evans 79), de Jong, Ireland, Elano, Robinho (Caicedo 66), Bellamy
Unused: Hart, Garrido, Berti, Gelson, Weiss
Goals: -
Booked: de Jong, Ireland, Bellamy
Man of the Match: Shay Given

City never really got going in the opening stages, with Portsmouth having most of the possession. Their first opportunity came on eight minutes, when a corner eventually found its way to Pennant, who found Crouch in the middle, but the tall centre-forward's shot was straight at Given.

With 53 minutes gone, Nugent was played onside and broke away for a one-on-one with Given. With the keeper to beat, the striker scuffed his shot wide.

And with 20 minutes of the game left, Johnson cut in from the right hand side and forced a good save from Given, before he smashed the rebound past the City keeper and into the top left corner of the goal.

Five minutes later, it got worse for City. Hreidarsson slipped Kompany at a corner and rose better than the acting City captain to power a header into the net, leaving Given with no chance.

FC Copenhagen 2-2 Manchester City
UEFA Cup Round of 32, First Leg
Thursday 19 February, 2009 - 19:00 KO

City: Given, Richards, Dunne (c), Onuoha, Bridge, Zabaleta, Kompany, Ireland, Robinho (Caicedo 89), Wright-Phillips, Bellamy
Unused: Hart, Garrido, Weiss, Vassell, Elano, Evans
Goals: Onuoha (28), Ireland (61)
Booked: Bellamy, Richards
Man of the Match: Stephen Ireland

The opening action saw Kvist head the ball weakly towards goal for Copenhagen, but Given was able to catch and immediately, at the other end, Wright-Phillips had a shot saved by Christiansen's legs.

Copenhagen looked to have cleared the danger from a cross on 28 minutes, but the ball was won back in midfield by Ireland. With one touch he sent Onuoha free in the box, whose shot was weak and straight at the keeper. But a howler saw it end up in the net, gifting City a vital away goal.

City could have doubled their lead on the half hour, but Ireland couldn't quite get his toe on a deflected Bellamy free kick. Christiansen cleared a Bellamy cross out of the box, but it landed to the feet of Zabaleta. The Argentinian had a go with his wrong foot, but it didn't have the power to curl around the keeper.

Shortly after half time, all of City's hard work was undone with one moment of defensive slackness. A free header from a corner on 56 minutes resulted in a goal for Almeida and an equaliser for the Danish side.

City, however, weren't on equal terms long. Wright-Phillips chased a lost cause on the right wing and fired in a low cross from just by the corner flag. Ireland, who found himself free in the box, didn't need telling twice and he fired a low, hard shot first time past the goalkeeper, leaving Christiansen standing.

Then, in the first of three added minutes, City were dealt another sucker punch. N'Doye crossed from the right and Richards had dropped off his man, leaving Vingaard with a free header, which he planted into the corner.

Liverpool 1-1 Manchester City
FA Premier League
Sunday 22 February, 2009 - 15:00 KO

City: Given, Richards, Dunne (c), Onuoha, Bridge, Kompany, Zabaleta, de Jong, Ireland, Robinho (Caicedo 90), Bellamy
Unused: Hart, Garrido, Evans, Elano, Weiss
Goals: Bellamy (50)
Booked: Dunne, Kompany
Man of the Match: Stephen Ireland

In the opening stages, Kuyt dragged a shot wide of Given's goal, before Torres won a free kick, though Benayoun could only hit the wall. A goalmouth scramble followed a Liverpool corner at the half's midway point, but a combination of Dunne, Richards and Onuoha got the ball away.

City had played with their backs against the wall, but should have taken the lead, when Ireland superbly found Robinho with a long, diagonal ball. But he could only hit Reina with his shot and he put the rebound into the side netting.

The second half began with the visitors putting themselves into a shock lead. Robinho was released down the left and he slotted a nice ball into the feet of Kompany, who knocked it back to Bellamy. His deflected shot found the net.

Dunne put in an excellent challenge on Torres to concede a corner on 66 minutes, and City were able to clear and break away. From that break, Ireland had the ball in the net, but he was flagged offside from Richards' cross.

City were growing in confidence, but they couldn't quite keep it tight at the back, and Kuyt took advantage. A cross from the left found Torres in the box, but his attempt on goal was completely mis-hit and fell to the Dutchman, who couldn't miss from five yards.

Given superbly denied Kuyt from a long range effort, before bettering himself when Benayoun volleyed, leaving Dunne and Onuoha to clear the danger. Onuoha, with just a minute to go, beat three Liverpool defenders but his left footed effort was straight down the throat of Reina.

Manchester City 2-1 FC Copenhagen
UEFA Cup Round of 32, Leg Two
Thursday 26 February, 2009 - 19:45 KO

City: Given, Richards, Dunne (c), Onuoha, Bridge, Zabaleta (Elano 82), Kompany, Ireland, Robinho, Wright-Phillips, Bellamy
Unused: Hart, Garrido, Vassell, Evans, Berti, Caicedo
Goals: Bellamy (73, 80)
Booked: -

Man of the Match: Robinho

Bellamy began by breaking down the right and his deflected cross sat up for Robinho to head at goal. The Brazilian was all ready to celebrate, but Christiansen had other ideas, getting both hands up to claw it off the line.

Zabaleta and Robinho both had shots from range that were easily swallowed up by Christiansen, before Robinho played Bellamy through on goal and the Welsh forward's chip beat the keeper and looked to be on its way in. But it clipped the inside of the post and bounced clear.

Copenhagen started the second half the stronger, with Almeida curling an effort just over Given's crossbar after some neat build-up play, before Bellamy had a free kick from 20 yards comfortably saved by Christiansen.

With 73 minutes on the clock, City took the lead. Zabaleta dinked the ball over the top towards Bellamy and the striker's pace allowed him to get around the defender, who couldn't get enough on the ball, and slot it into the net.

And soon after, Given played a quick ball downfield to Robinho, who managed to take it down and work his way into the box. He squared it to Bellamy, who found the top corner with his left foot to put City two clear on the night, and on aggregate.

City could have had a third, when Robinho clipped the outside of the post from six yards. With just seconds to go, City lost their clean sheet. Vingaard found himself with time and space outside City's box and drove a shot past Given.

THE SECOND DEATH OF FOOTBALL

Since the first destruction of football when Thaksin Shinawatra took over Manchester City, and the subsequent second destruction of football when Sheikh Mansour bin Zayed Al Nahyan bought the club from him, I am genuinely confused as to when this country's national sport was actually going to disappear down the Manchester City shaped black hole.

Sven Goran Eriksson became manager in the summer of 2007, and immediately set about spending some money to improve the quality of City's squad. But for a former England manager not to buy any English players was, apparently, criminal. Nevermind that Stewart Downing was, at the time, three times the price yet half the player that Martin Petrov was. Nevermind that he regularly included Englishmen in the squad, anyway. That was all conveniently overlooked.

And now the same is being said of Mark Hughes. I'm assured that Manchester City's new found wealth will, at some point soon, destroy football. And English football at that, because, as we all know, before City got money the Premier League had only one or two foreign players.

What about the youngsters? With City's money, they must all be out of the door to be immediately replaced by multi-million pound superstars, mustn't they? Surely that's the only way it works?

Well, no. Five of City's regular starting 11 this season has graduated from the academy, four of them English. Add to that the infrequent appearance of Daniel Sturridge (and the regular contributions from Hart earlier this season) and, suddenly, this notion of football's last days becomes daft.

And, if City apparently have a lot to answer for, why don't Arsenal? Their academy produces a lot of excellent players, but how many of them have represented England? And how many of them have represented *other* countries? Aren't *they* endangering the English game?

Apparently not.

Take a look at the Youth Cup. Manchester City won last season's, beating Chelsea in the final. Nothing was said about the lack of English players in the team for the runners up, or the potential English talent in the victorious team. And City's academy, this season, face Arsenal for a place in the final for the second year running.

In the last England squad, Manchester City had more players feature than Arsenal (none), Liverpool (none) and Manchester United (two). And they had the same number of call-ups as Chelsea (three). And over the last 10 years or so, those four clubs have spent much, much more than City have.

So, this impending doom of football caused by the club I support had better come soon, because I'm getting pretty hacked off with having to defend our corner. Especially when we're being attacked for doing something that hasn't happened yet and, I guarantee, will never happen.

Now, move along. Nothing to see here.

£14M FOR JUST WHAT CITY NEEDED

Okay. I have a confession to make. And I have to do it now before I'm embarrassed any further. And no, this one doesn't involve Take That, East-17 or Westlife. This time, anyway.

Nevertheless, it has to be said – I was wrong about Craig Bellamy.

Before he joined City, I thought Bellamy was all running, grit and tough man. I thought his main objective in being in the team was to be a nuisance first, get opposition players in trouble second and then score goals third. But only now, since I've watched him play regularly over 90 minutes, can I see that there's more to his game than that. He's quicker than I thought. He runs much more than I thought. He has a much better touch than I thought. And he can't half shoot.

Since the departure of, probably, Nicolas Anelka, City haven't had a striker that could be described as prolific. But our Craig's now hit five goals in six.

He's been vital to City's surge in form, in my opinion. He's provided an outlet that will always chase the ball when it's in the opposition half and he's also very useful with the ball played into his feet.

I was disappointed that Mark Hughes bought him for the price he did; I certainly didn't think he was worth £14m. But the more I think about it, the more it makes sense. Hughes sees the players everyday, so knew exactly what the squad was missing. He had also worked with Bellamy at Blackburn and Wales.

Signing Robinho was fantastic. Signing Kaka would have been beyond fantastic. But, in all fairness to Hughes, they're not the players we need right now. Although I wouldn't say no if they were to accept a transfer.

Hughes has taken over a side that finished ninth last season and just escaped relegation the season before with a sequence of wins at Easter time. No matter how much money you throw at a club like that, it can't be expected that they would be challenging for the top four almost immediately.

If City are to become a force in the Premier League, it will take hundreds of millions of pounds. I would like to see it happen with the kids as much as the next man, but we all know that won't happen – talented kids will get into the first team, but no team will ever break the current top four dominance with seven or eight of their academy products in the side.

And it needs to be a gradual change. Right now, Craig Bellamy is the player we need – someone who will score goals, chase the ball all over the place, never say die and be the tough man. If we want to attract the biggest players in Europe, we have to be playing European football regularly.

Money can talk, but it doesn't always. Change needs to be in stages, and we're still in Operation Keep Playing European Football. When that's complete, we can begin on Operation Break Into The Top Four.

And from the evidence I've seen so far, Craig Bellamy will help us greatly to completing part one of this project. So thank you, Craig. Thanks for signing and thanks for your goals so far.

You have my sincere apologies for judging you before you'd pulled on the blue shirt.

February 2009 Breakdown

Games (all competitions):
Won: 2   **Drawn:** 2   **Lost:** 1

Goals (all competitions):
For: 6   **Against:** 6

Progress:
Premier League: 10th
League Cup: Eliminated in Round Two
FA Cup: Eliminated in Round Three
UEFA Cup: Qualified for the Round of 16

Premier League Table

		P	W	D	L	F	A	GD	Pts
8	Fulham	26	8	10	8	24	22	+2	34
9	West Ham United	26	9	6	11	32	34	-2	33
10	**Manchester City**	**26**	**9**	**5**	**12**	**43**	**35**	**+8**	**32**
11	Sunderland	26	8	7	11	27	33	-6	31
12	Bolton Wanderers	26	9	3	14	29	38	-9	30

March 2009

West Ham United 1-0 Manchester City

FA Premier League

Sunday 1 March, 2009 - 12:30 KO

City: Given, Richards (Caicedo 15), Dunne (c), Onuoha, Bridge, Kompany, Zabaleta, de Jong (Bojinov 88), Ireland, Robinho, Bellamy (Elano 65)
Unused: Hart, Garrido, Berti, Vassell
Goals: -
Booked: Kompany, Ireland
Man of the Match: Richard Dunne

It was West Ham who began the game the brighter, but, at the quarter hour mark, Kompany had a volley on goal backheeled towards the corner by Robinho, who looked to be well offside. Yet the flag didn't go up and Green was forced into a superb fingertip save to put the ball behind for a corner.

Bellamy found himself on the left flank, where he was able to work the best chance of the match. He took the ball around Neill and played it into the box. Caicedo missed it, but it fell to Robinho who, somehow, put it wide.

Dunne was earning his corn two minutes into the second half, nipping in to deny Collison a strike on goal. Minutes later, Cole turned in the box and was ready to fire a shot, but Dunne again arrived with a superb sliding tackle.

But then, with 20 minutes to go, West Ham took the lead. Given produced a good save to deny Savio, but the rebound fell to Collison who lobbed the ball over the despairing dive of the goalkeeper and into the net.

City took the game to West Ham, trying to force an equaliser. Robinho dragged a shot wide from the edge of the box, when he received a back-heel from Elano, before Neill touched a Robinho effort wide.

As the clock hit the final minute, Elano hit a free kick, and it looked to be curling in, until Neill again touched the ball onto the post and behind.

Manchester City 2-0 Aston Villa

FA Premier League

Wednesday 4 March, 2009 - 19:45 KO

City: Given, Zabaleta, Dunne (c), Onuoha, Bridge, Kompany, de Jong (Gelson 46), Ireland, Elano (Bojinov 82), Wright-Phillips, Caicedo (Evans 73)
Unused: Hart, Vassell, Garrido, Berti
Goals: Elano (pen 24), Wright-Phillips (88)
Booked: Caicedo
Man of the Match: Shaun Wright-Phillips

The home side set their initiative from the off, with Elano getting into the thick of the action, sending Ireland through on goal on 10 minutes. Ireland, though, elected to square the ball to Caicedo and it was cleared by Knight.

On 21 minutes, City should have taken the lead. Ireland played a delightful first time ball to Wright-Phillips, sending him through in the area. The little winger, though, could only slide it wide, under pressure from Young.

On 24 minutes, some good possession football from City around Villa's box, set Wright-Phillips through on goal. As he moved his foot back, ready to pull the trigger, he was brought down by Milner. Elano stepped up and smashed the penalty into the net.

Villa came out for the second half desperate for their equaliser, but the closest they came was a Barry volley, that required Given to dive low to his right to push around the post.

Elano deserved a second goal for his volley, after Evans chested it down to him from a Bridge cross, but the Villa keeper superbly tipped the ball around the post, keeping his side in the game.

The City fans were incensed when Aston Villa contested a drop ball after a clash of heads, but City won it back and Evans steamed away down the right flank. He found Ireland, who laid it off to Wright-Phillips and the winger played a one-two with the Irishman, before sliding the ball past Friedel and into the net.

Manchester City 2-0 Aalborg BK
UEFA Cup Round of 16, First Leg
Thursday 12 March, 2009 - 19:45 KO

City: Given, Richards, Dunne (c), Onuoha, Bridge, Zabaleta, Ireland, Elano, Wright-Phillips (Etuhu 87), Robinho, Caicedo (Evans 60)
Unused: Hart, Berti, Garrido, Vassell, Gelson
Goals: Caicedo (8), Wright-Phillips (29)
Booked: Elano
Man of the Match: Shaun Wright-Phillips

City showed their intent from the off; Robinho fed the ball to Caicedo on the edge of the box and he showed great strength to work his way past the defender for a one-on-one. He gave the keeper the eyes, and rolled the ball into the near post for the opening goal.

The visitors were on top for a few minutes, trying to get their equaliser and an away goal. First, Richards slid to block a shot wide from inside the box and, second, Given stood up well to save a one-on-one.

But then, on 29 minutes, City sublimely doubled their lead. Elano found Wright-Phillips on the break, and the little winger picked the ball up on the halfway line. Running at the Aalborg defence, he beat three men to fire off a shot from just outside the box that flew into the top right corner of the goal.

Just two minutes later, though, Aalborg should have had an away goal. Elano put in a block on a long range shot and the rebound fell to the unmarked Shelton, but he slid the ball wide of Given's far post.

Seconds before half time and City should have had a penalty. Robinho had the ball inside the box and appeared to have been hacked down whilst doing his step-overs, but the referee awarded a goal kick and waved the claims away.

City had taken their foot off the pedal in the second half, but were still comfortably on top. On 74 minutes, Wright-Phillips missed from just inside the box after a great ball from Elano, before Dunne put in a cracking block to stop a free header from troubling Given.

Chelsea 1-0 Manchester City
FA Premier League
Sunday 15 March, 2009 - 13:30 KO

City: Given, Richards, Dunne (c), Onuoha, Bridge, Zabaleta, Ireland, Elano (Etuhu 65), Wright-Phillips, Robinho (Bojinov 81), Caicedo (Evans 54)
Unused: Hart, Garrido, Berti, Gelson
Goals: -
Booked: Elano, Evans
Man of the Match: Nedum Onuoha

Chelsea had the ball in City's net in under a minute, but Lampard was a good two yards offside when he scored. The officials correctly disallowed the goal. Onuoha slid wonderfully to deny Anelka a shot on goal and Chelsea were dominating with a succession of corners, but City were able to keep them out.

But not for long, as a Lampard free kick delivered into the box from deep found Essien, who had slipped his marker, and he hit it first time over Given and into the net.

On the other side of the half, only a superb tackle by Onuoha stopped Chelsea getting a second goal. Essien played Drogba in, but Dunne and Onuoha sandwiched him in the box and Onuoha slid in to poke the ball away. Given denied Drogba with an excellent save from a one-on-one.

On 63 minutes, Belletti hit the post from just outside the box on the left and the ball was eventually put behind for a corner. Lampard fired a free kick from 45 yards straight into the City wall, and some neat skill from Ireland allowed City to break, but it came to nothing.

Ballack had a header on goal blocked by Onuoha, before the substitute Bojinov was able to take a good touch on his chest, swivel and volley at goal, but it was straight down Cech's throat.

Dunne stooped to head out a Belletti cross, before Terry headed over from the resulting corner. Malouda then took advantage of a slip by Richards and had an attempt on goal. It beat Given, but not Dunne, who was able to clear from behind his own goalkeeper.

Aalborg BK 2-0 Manchester City (3-4 pens)

UEFA Cup Round of 16, Second Leg

Thursday 19 March, 2009 - 20:00 KO

City: Given, Richards, Dunne (c), Onuoha, Bridge (Garrido 54), Zabaleta, Kompany (Elano 107), Ireland, Wright-Phillips, Robinho (Caicedo 96), Evans
Unused: Hart, Gelson, Etuhu, Berti
Goals: -
Booked: Kompany, Wright-Phillips
Man of the Match: Pablo Zabaleta

City started the game the brighter, seemingly able to put their foot on the ball and play it around much better than their hosts. Ireland had a first minute shot charged down, while an Evans cross just evaded Ireland and Robinho after 11 minutes.

But after that, the game stalled. On 42 minutes, Robinho was selfish, after he shot from a narrow angle, trying to beat the keeper at his near post.

The second half couldn't have been more in contrast. The hosts came out with a passion, knowing they needed two goals to force extra time. Garrido was lucky not to have conceded a penalty after an hour, when he dived in and looked to have got all of the man and none of the ball.

With 10 minutes to go, a fantastic save from Given denied Shelton after he latched on to a blast out of the Aalborg defence. Minutes later, City were back up the other end and, from a short corner, Ireland gave the ball to Robinho, who got into the box after a one-two, and fired a shot against the crossbar.

Five minutes later, Aalborg were back in the tie. The ball was crossed in from the right and it was flicked to Shelton, who took it down and volleyed home.

But as the game entered time added on, a flicked on corner hit Evans on the arm and, despite him not being able to get it out of the way, the referee pointed to the spot, with Jakobsen sending Given the wrong way.

The chances in extra time were few and far between, with Richards making an excellent break down the right, but giving the ball straight to the defenders, and Wright-Phillips running straight into trouble in the box before Ireland's shot from the edge of the area was blocked.

Michael Jakobsen **scored**:	**1-0**
Ched Evans **scored**:	**1-1**
Andreas Johansson **scored**:	**2-1**
Elano **scored**:	**2-2**
Thomas Augustinussen *missed*:	2-2
Shaun Wright-Phillips **scored**:	**2-3**
Siyabonga Nomvethe **scored**:	**3-3**
Richard Dunne **scored**:	**3-4**
Luton Shelton *missed*:	3-4

Manchester City 1-0 Sunderland
FA Premier League
Sunday 22 March, 2009 - 15:00 KO

City: Given, Richards (Garrido 82), Dunne (c), Onuoha, Zabaleta, Elano, Kompany (Gelson 84), de Jong, Wright-Phillips, Robinho, Bojinov (Bellamy 65)
Unused: Hart, Garrido, Berti, Gelson
Goals: Richards (56)
Booked: Bojinov, Gelson, Wright-Phillips
Man of the Match: Nigel de Jong

Bojinov, on his first start since the Manchester derby in 2007, was in the thick of the action after just seven minutes, as he jinked the ball into Wright-Phillips, whose lob fell the wrong side of the post.

On 15 minutes, the visitors lost a man. McCartney was harshly sent off for pulling back Wright-Phillips and Bojinov put the resulting free kick just over the bar. Two minutes later, Richards broke free in the area and was chopped down by Malbranque. Robinho stepped up and, after a stop-start run up, he passed the ball into Fulop's hands with a terrible effort.

Malbranque was then felled by Dunne on the edge of the box, but Leadbitter smashed the free kick into the wall, before Elano had a go from range, but found only Fulop's gloves.

Some good work by Bojinov and Richards on the right wing early in the second half carved a chance for Wright-Phillips to shoot from just inside the area, but his first time effort was well over the bar.

The goal finally came a minute later. Bojinov was brought down on the right and Elano floated a cross into the box. Richards connected and headed past Fulop, with Robinho putting his foot on it and making sure it was in the net.

With 15 minutes to go, City had de Jong to thank for keeping their lead, as Cisse's header was acrobatically cleared off the line by the Dutchman from a corner.

City were under a lot of pressure, but were easing it with breakaways. First Bellamy found Elano, who smashed a shot from range, forcing a great save from Fulop. Robinho was then played through and was running free on goal. With just the keeper to beat, and Bellamy square, he elected to shoot, but Fulop pushed the ball over the bar.

DREAM A LITTLE DREAM

I've been having some weird dreams lately. I never normally remember my dreams, but for some reason, for the past three nights I have done. The first one worried me more than the second or third, I'll be honest, and it's the first and third ones I'm going to tell you because they do involve a City connection.

Just to give some context, before I dropped off, I was lying in bed – to be expected, really – and I was listening to a show by Eddie Izzard on my iPod and a certain section about Jesus speaking to the dinosaurs like he did to man.

So, imagine my confusion when my next memory is facing four entities in a completely bare room. The first was a woman, whose identity I don't know, the second was a tyrannosaurus rex, the third was Pablo Zabaleta, and the fourth, rather bizarrely, was a flying, blue, miniature hippopotamus.

It turned out, each of these were, quite naturally, God of a different species – it seems, in my head at least, Pablo Zabaleta is a superior form of human – and each had replaced one of the others, with the hippos currently on top.

Basically, what I'm saying here is that I suspect my dreams are influenced by what I'm listening to at the time. This probably goes some way to explaining why I've had dreams that involve a first-person shooter head-up display.

But last night, I dropped off whilst listening to Five Live. And, throughout the night, they were reporting on that night's UEFA Cup match – Aalborg vs. Manchester City – and I was hearing the same piece again and again.

Suffice to say, City won their first cup competition since my birth that night. It doesn't matter that the UEFA Cup final was staged on my local park or that we were playing the traditional FIFA nondescript 11, who aren't real players. It matters not that, for some reason, the referee was Danny Mills, nor that, despite me being in the crowd, there was match commentary from Martin Tyler and Andy Gray. That night, Manchester City won the UEFA Cup.

And, bizarrely, none of those things tipped me off as to that it wasn't reality. So, when I rejoined the conscious world, I was happy. It took me a few minutes to realise what had happened. But the happiness didn't go away.

I think there's a simple reason for that. And that is that I'm actually now quietly confident that City can go on and win the bloody thing. I quite fancy us to go to Hamburg and do a job on them. We'll have to play a lot better than we did against Aalborg, though. But what will be in our favour for the Germany trip is that we are not already winning by two goals and scoring whilst over there would put us in a good position. In fact, I'd take a 2-1 defeat and anything better we can get is a bonus.

Add to that the fact that we could so easily have gone out to Midtjylland in August. We even nearly threw it away again on Thursday, again in Denmark.

I'm just starting to wonder if we're going to be able to ride our luck to the end. We just have three more ties. Five games. And we don't even need to win all the games. We've played 14 already. Another five can't be too much, can they?

Can they?

March 2009 Breakdown

<u>Games (all competitions):</u>
Won: 3   **Drawn:** 0   **Lost:** 3

<u>Goals (all competitions):</u>
For: 5   **Against:** 4

<u>Progress:</u>
Premier League: 10th
League Cup: Eliminated in Round Two
FA Cup: Eliminated in Round Three
UEFA Cup: Qualified for the Quarter Final

<u>Premier League Table</u>

		P	W	D	L	F	A	GD	Pts
8	West Ham United	30	11	8	11	35	35	0	41
9	Fulham	30	10	10	10	30	26	+4	40
10	**Manchester City**	**30**	**11**	**5**	**14**	**46**	**37**	**+9**	**38**
11	Tottenham Hotspur	30	10	8	12	36	34	+2	38
12	Bolton Wanderers	30	10	4	16	32	44	-12	34

April 2009

Arsenal 2-0 Manchester City
FA Premier League
Saturday 4 April, 2009 - 15:00 KO

City: Given, Richards, Dunne (c), Onuoha, Bridge (Gelson 17), Zabaleta, Kompany (Elano 37), de Jong, Wright-Phillips, Robinho (Sturridge 75), Bellamy
Unused: Hart, Bojinov, Benjani, Garrido
Goals: -
Booked: Dunne, Zabaleta
Man of the Match: Nedum Onuoha

Arsenal had most of the possession in the opening minutes, but it was City who could have been in front but for a great Almunia save. Bellamy beat the offside trap and de Jong fired towards goal, but it was tipped away.

But it turned out to be a bad start for the visitors, when Adebayor was gifted a free header in the box and he put the home side in front after just nine minutes.

Wright-Phillips produced a moment of brilliance when he turned Clichy on the halfway line, before breaking towards the Arsenal box. He slipped the ball into Richards, who was free in the area and only an excellent save denied him.

City were taking the game to the hosts and should have been level after Wright-Phillips found Gelson unmarked, with acres of space in the area. The Swiss international turned and shot, rattling the outside of Almunia's post.

But, despite City's response, it was the home side who scored next. Just after half time, a fantastic ball over the top by Fabregas found Adebayor in the box, who took it down and around Given, before slotting it into the net.

And the goal turned the game on its head completely, as Arsenal were in full control. Walcott broke down the right flank and his low cross bobbled past Given, but Dunne was on the line to clear.

Hamburg 3-1 Manchester City
UEFA Cup Quarter Final, First Leg
Thursday 9 April, 2009 - 19:45 KO

City: Given, Richards, Dunne (c), Onuoha, Bridge (Garrido 45), Zabaleta, Ireland, Wright-Phillips (Gelson 83), Bellamy, Robinho, Sturridge (Benjani 61)
Unused: Hart, Berti, Elano, Petrov
Goals: Ireland (1)
Booked: Bellamy, Given
Man of the Match: Shay Given

City couldn't have wished for a better start in Germany. Ireland fed a long pass out to the left wing for Robinho, who controlled it expertly and ran at the Hamburg defence. Once he had cut inside, he found Ireland again, who had made up half the length of the pitch to support the Brazilian. He slotted it into the net for an away goal inside the opening 30 seconds.

Given then protected City's lead minutes later, as he blocked point-blank from a header from Petric and dived on the rebound, before he produced an even better save from a rifled effort in the six-yard box, after the home side had drilled a free kick into the box.

But, from the resulting corner, there was nothing Given could do about Mathijsen's bullet header. He rose up to divert the kick towards the back post. The City keeper got a hand on it, but could only help it into the far corner.

Pitroipa hit the crossbar with a looping header, before Jansen touched the ball over Richards neatly and set himself up to smash a shot at the City goal, which, again, took a great save from Given to keep out.

And it got worse for City after the break, again from a Hamburg corner. Richards had both arms in the air when making a block in the box and the ball struck them, leaving the referee no choice but to award the penalty. Trochowski smashed the ball past Given, in off the post, giving the keeper no chance.

With just over 10 minutes to play, City gave themselves some serious work to do in the return leg. Guerrero was left unmarked at the back post and was able to slot home a low cross.

Manchester City 1-3 Fulham
FA Premier League
Sunday 12 April, 2009 - 16:10 KO

City: Given, Richards, Dunne (c), Onuoha, Garrido, Zabaleta, de Jong, Ireland, Petrov (Robinho 63), Etuhu (Sturridge 63), Bojinov (Evans 55)
Unused: Hart, Elano, Gelson, McGivern
Goals: Ireland (27)
Booked: -
Man of the Match: Stephen Ireland

The first real action saw Zamora flash a shot at Given, after Dunne misjudged the bounce of a high ball, before slipping as he attempted to clear it. Given, though, was able to divert the shot over the bar.

And with City's first meaningful attack of the game came the first goal. Bojinov held the ball up on the halfway line, before finding Ireland breaking forward. He carried it all the way to the edge of the box and had an effort on goal. And, with the aid of a deflection, it looped over Schwarzer and into the net.

The second half couldn't have started worse for the home side. Zabaleta gave the ball away inside his own half, with the ricochet falling to Zamora. Richards got in a last-gasp tackle, but it fell to Dempsy who found the net.

City weren't able to recover and, just 10 minutes later, they were a goal down. Konchesky crossed the ball into the box and it was only half cleared. Former City player Etuhu collected it and volleyed in his first Fulham goal.

Robinho replaced Petrov, and he could have immediately gotten City back on terms. He was sent through on a one-on-one, but couldn't finish.

With just five minutes to go, Dunne gambled on the through ball and missed the tackle on Zamora. The forward ran at goal, drew Onuoha out before finding Dempsey, who slid the ball into the net, ending the contest.

Manchester City 2-1 Hamburg
UEFA Cup Quarter Final, Second Leg
Thursday 16 April, 2009 - 19:45 KO

City: Given, Richards, Dunne (c), Onuoha, Bridge, Zabaleta (Gelson 75), Kompany, Ireland, Elano (Sturridge 84), Robinho, Caicedo
Unused: Hart, Garrido, Logan, Petrov, Evans
Goals: Elano (pen 17), Caicedo (50)
Booked: Dunne, Kompany
Sent Off: Dunne
Man of the Match: Elano

City began the game with a packed stadium of fans waving flags and inflatable bananas. But City's task became immediately harder when the visitors got an away goal. Pitroipa crossed to Olic and he found Guerrero, who slid the ball past Given, as the keeper rushed out and Kompany slipped.

City, though, responded well. Five minutes later, Elano picked up the ball on the edge of the box and sent a cross in. It struck Trochowski on the arm and the referee pointed straight to the spot. Elano himself stepped up and coolly scored.

On 41 minutes, Robinho was hauled down about 30 yards out and Elano was first on the scene to plant the ball down for the free kick. The Brazilian was unfortunate not to have had his second of the night, crashing it into the crossbar.

The first action of the second half saw City get themselves their second goal. A through ball landed at Ireland's feet and he played it in to Caicedo. He switched it from his right to his left foot, before slotting it past Rost.

On 54 minutes, Elano hit another free kick from the left hand side of the box, beating Rost again, only to see it rebound off the post and be cleared for a corner. From the resulting kick, he shot directly at the goal. Rost flapped and Caicedo skied it when it seemed easier to score.

With 15 minutes to go, City's task got harder. Dunne was shown a second yellow card for a foul by the right side of City's box.

In the final minute, substitute Sturridge shot wide and, in added time, Richards worked hard to win a corner that saw Given join the attack. Robinho's cross, however, missed everyone, before Caicedo shot over.

Manchester City 4-2 West Bromwich Albion

FA Premier League

Sunday 19 April, 2009 - 15:00 KO

City: Given, Zabaleta, Dunne (c), Onuoha, Bridge, Kompany, de Jong, Ireland, Elano (Gelson 74), Robinho (Petrov 83), Caicedo (Sturridge 57)
Unused: Hart, Richards, Garrido, Evans
Goals: Robinho (7), Onuoha (20), Elano (pen 55), Sturridge (90+4)
Booked: Kompany
Man of the Match: Nedum Onuoha

The game looked to begin in a nervy manner, with the first chance of the game falling to Fortune, but his shot was comfortably wide of Given's right hand post. Dorrans skewed a shot wide, before Morrison curled one around the far post, with the City fans wondering where the home side were.

And it was down to Robinho to show them. City had their first real spell of possession, knocking the ball around the midfield before it fell to Ireland. It was his perfect ball over the top to Robinho that just needed touching in and the Brazilian didn't disappoint.

On 20 minutes, City extended their lead in somewhat controversial style. A right wing corner was headed straight up into the air and Onuoha scored his second of the season, heading past the oncoming Carson. Caicedo, though, looked to have fouled the West Brom goalkeeper in the process.

West Brom weren't finished yet, as City were finally punished for slack defending, when Brunt was found unmarked in the box. He didn't need a second invitation to slide the ball past the on coming City keeper.

53 minutes in, Brunt scored his second of the game and West Brom's equaliser directly from a free kick on the right hand side of the box. It was a low half cross, half shot that missed everybody.

But the game wasn't even for long. From the restart, City worked the ball to the box, where Elano weaved his way across and was felled by Olsson. Elano got up to score his second penalty in as many games.

In the final seconds of the game, Ireland broke from midfield as West Brom pushed forward. He was one-on-one with Carson, but chose to square to Sturridge, who scuffed his shot, but managed to find the net.

Everton 1-2 Manchester City

FA Premier League

Saturday 25 April, 2009 - 15:00 KO

City: Given, Richards (Gelson 57), Dunne (c), Onuoha, Bridge, Kompany, de Jong, Ireland, Elano (Evans 88), Robinho, Caicedo (Petrov 84)

Unused: Hart, Bojinov, Garrido, Berti
Goals: Robinho (35), Ireland (53)
Booked: Onuoha, Elano
Man of the Match: Robinho

City were without an away win since August and even the most optimistic of City fans wouldn't have been expecting to leave fifth placed Everton with more than a point. But City aren't ever likely to do what's expected.

The first action of the game saw Robinho finding his feet, and working his way into the box, with a series of stopovers. He skipped past Hibbert and then looked to be felled by Osman, but the referee said play on.

Howard was the busier of the two keepers in the first half, with him having to save a Robinho shot that was fiercely hit towards his goal. The chance came after a pull back was poorly cleared to Elano on the penalty spot and his shot deflected to his Brazilian team-mate, but he wasn't able to capitalise.

On 35 minutes, City took the lead. Everton were given a free kick, midway in City's half and, after Dunne headed clear, Robinho raced on to a long pass over the top, took the ball into the box and slid it through Howard's legs.

Given made the save of the day from Fellaini, after the ball was fed into the big Belgian's feet and he flicked it up and volleyed on the turn. Somehow Given was able to push the ball over the bar.

City stunned the home crowd into silence, not long after. A ball out of defence found Caicedo on the break and the Ecuadorian gave it to Robinho on the left, who expertly found Ireland racing into the Everton box. The Irishman took a touch, before placing the ball past the onrushing Howard for 0-2.

Dunne rose well to flick an Everton free kick just wide of Given's goal and, on the breakaway, Ireland found Robinho, whose left-footed shot clipped the outside of the post, with Howard grasping at thin air.

Hughes was furious to see the referee award seven minutes of added time, and in the fifth of those added minutes, Gosling left City hearts in mouths as he beat Given with a left-footed drive into the top right corner of the goal. But Everton couldn't muster another shot on target and the game finished 2-1, City finding a cure for their travel sickness at Goodison Park.

HOME AND AWAY

It's a long time since I read Stevenson's novella, but I was always under the impression that Dr Jekyll (or Mr Hyde, if you prefer) was a man and not a football club.

How can it be possible for a team to have such varying degrees of form at home and on the road? I mean, it's consistent on each, at least. But consistently good at home and consistently poor away isn't quite what the doctor ordered.

And with, at the time of writing, trips to Everton, United and Tottenham to go, I can't see the number of our away wins leaping above the one we have already.

Sunderland is going to be the only team we have doubled this season. We've already lost to the teams in the three remaining away fixtures, so it's only Sunderland we can double. What is it about our travel sickness that two managers have failed to crack?

Pearce was able to get us some wins on the road, but he couldn't get a bloody league goal at our place. And with the players currently at our disposal, how can we wipe away Arsenal at home, but fail to bother the Stoke keeper, when they have been a man down for about an hour? The longer we go without another win away from home, the harder it will become. We've already reached the stage where people (and City fans included) are saying: "Well, you know what we're like away from home…"

And that's quite a dangerous thing to be saying. We've hit the point where we have the mental attitude where we think we're going to lose, just because of our recent run. I'm not one who believes in that positive energy crap, but to go into a game thinking everything is going to go wrong, is to play like everything is going wrong. Suddenly, choices are made that wouldn't normally be made – strange passes, refraining from shooting, stupid goals being given away.

Something needs to be done about the away form, and I guess if I had the answer then I probably wouldn't be writing this. It's our home form, clearly, that has sent us to our league position, just as it was for the most of last season. So imagine where would could have been in the league had we got more than eight points on the road. We've got 30 points from our home games and a measly eight away.

But what's the big difference – the game's still 90 minutes in length, still between two teams of varying abilities, still on a pitch that's roughly the same size, with the same referees? Home and away fans do have some influence, I'm sure, but we have some of the best away support in the league – so that must count for something?

One of the ways that has been suggested by several people as a way to cure our travel sickness is to drop Robinho. I can see their argument, since he's not done a great deal away from Eastlands, but he's one of the best players in the world. The fact is, he can be missing for 80 minutes, then pop up with a moment of brilliance. The same was said of Kinkladze when Joe Royle had just taken charge of the club.

Robinho's also capable of doing some grafting – I know he is, I've seen him do it. The question, in my mind then, shouldn't be 'do we start without Robinho when away from home?' but 'how can we get him to play as well as he does at home?'

I think, first of all, he needs a goal. At home or away, he just needs to get his name on the scoresheet – whether that's be ploughing in a 40 yarder, a stunning solo run where he beats seven or eight players, or deflecting one in with his arse on the goal-line. He's not scored for us in 2009, so that needs to change for his confidence to pick up.

There's no reason for us to play differently away than we do at home. Perhaps a bit of luck might be the order of the day? If we can get three points from somewhere, whether by design or complete and total fluke, then maybe we can start reproducing the home form on the road?

SUPERBIA IN PROELIO

Back in 1999, I was 11. City were 2-0 down at Wembley and I was crying. I had travelled from a school trip in Anglesey to London, before knowing I was going to have to return to a tent full of United fans. United had, a week earlier, won the European Cup, coming back from a goal down against Bayern Munich, and I was getting myself ready to face the taunts. As usual.

But Kevin Horlock scored on 90 minutes. And suddenly, those tears started more. Why did he have to go and do that? City were never going to come back from two goals down. All he had done, the selfish sod, was put more false hope into the crowd's hearts.

But then, from a long punt forward, the ball landed to Dickov, via a blocked Goater shot. Dickov set his sights and he found the top corner. And the tears carried on. 2-2.

Ten years later, give or take, and City were 1-0 down... 4-1 on aggregate. But, on 17 minutes, they were handed a lifeline – a penalty – that Elano dispatched. There was about 70 minutes to get two more goals to force extra time. Backs couldn't have been further against the wall.

That night against Hamburg was the best atmosphere that The City of Manchester Stadium has ever seen. The team battled hard and played football that was miles better than most of the football I've seen in that stadium. They deserved to win the match that night. They deserved to win the tie. But they just missed.

Not one player on that pitch didn't give all they had. Elano was a force I don't think I've seen since October 2007. Zabaleta was fierce, Richards was running on empty at the end. Onuoha was a beast in the air. Kompany was strong in the tackle and played some superb passes. Bridge lost a tooth.

Realistically, few of us City fans expected us to get a semi final place. Yet, we were one goal away from forcing a team who are three points from the top of their league into extra time.

In fact, it wasn't even one goal. It was two inches, twice, from Elano free kicks and one yard on a Caicedo offside goal. And then a whole host of chances that could (should) have been goals. On another night, they would have been.

Ten seasons ago, we were 30 seconds away from another season in Division Two. Had we stayed in Division Two, I'm pretty certain we wouldn't be where we are now.

'Pride in Battle' is the club's motto. 'Superbia in Proelio'. If that night wasn't pride in battle, then I don't know what is. Hamburg hadn't lost away from home in Europe all season. And City were twice inches away from not just beating them away from home, but dumping them out of the competition.

City may well be out of the UEFA Cup, and it doesn't look like they'll qualify for it next season. But I don't care. Normally, after a cup defeat, I usually feel let down. But not this time. We went down fighting and I'm proud, this morning, to call myself a City fan.

I fucking love this club.

April 2009 Breakdown

Games (all competitions):
Won: 3   Drawn: 0   Lost: 3

Goals (all competitions):
For: 10   Against: 12

Progress:
Premier League: 9th
League Cup: Eliminated in Round Two
FA Cup: Eliminated in Round Three
UEFA Cup: Eliminated in the Quarter Final

Premier League Table

		P	W	D	L	F	A	GD	Pts
7	Fulham	34	12	11	11	34	28	+6	47
8	West Ham United	34	12	9	13	38	38	0	45
9	**Manchester City**	**34**	**13**	**5**	**16**	**53**	**45**	**+8**	**44**
10	Tottenham Hotspur	34	12	8	14	41	41	0	44
11	Wigan Athletic	33	11	8	14	31	38	-7	41

May 2009

Manchester City 3-1 Blackburn Rovers

FA Premier League

Saturday 2 May, 2009 - 15:00 KO

City: Given, Richards, Dunne (c), Onuoha, Bridge, Kompany, de Jong, Ireland, Elano (Petrov 78), Robinho, Caicedo (Bojinov 61)
Unused: Hart, Garrido, Gelson, Berti, Evans
Goals: Caicedo (26), Robinho (33), Elano (pen 45)
Booked: Caicedo, de Jong
Man of the Match: Vincent Kompany

With 20 minutes on the clock and the game looking like it was going to be a stalemate, Grella curled an effort on Given's goal, but the Irish goalkeeper was alert and able to hold the shot under pressure from McCarthy.

It seemed to give City a kick up the backside and the home side began to get their foot on the ball. The home fans were wondering what both Tugay and Diouf had to do to be shown a yellow card, when both flattened Ireland just four minutes apart, after the ball had gone.

After 26 minutes, an Elano corner caused havoc in the Rovers box. The ball fell to Kompany's feet, who slid the ball wide to Onuoha. The big centre-back's shot was deflected to Caicedo, who slotted the ball into the corner. He picked up a booking for taking off his shirt, but, at this stage in the season, it wouldn't count for much.

And just as Blackburn were hoping to get back into the game, Robinho put them further behind. Kompany nodded the ball down to him, and, after a touch, he curled the ball past Robinson, with the former England keeper left standing. Blackburn were looking dead on their feet.

And just as the City fans were preparing for a 2-0 half time lead, it got better. Givet accidentally handled the ball when tackling Ireland in the box and, after three yellow cards for dissent from various Blackburn players, Elano stepped up to confidently slot the penalty home.

Early in the second half, Samba had a shot blocked by de Jong when he was free in the box, before a Villanueva free kick deflected off Richards and looped onto the roof of the net. The visitors were asking questions.

Blackburn were given a ray of hope after Onuoha was adjudged to have brought down Pedersen in the box. Given saved the penalty from Diouf, and the rebound, but he could only present an unmissable opportunity to Andrews from two yards. The visitors, though, couldn't muster another chance.

Manchester United 2-0 Manchester City

FA Premier League

Sunday 10 May, 2009 - 13:30 KO

City: Given, Richards, Dunne (c), Onuoha, Bridge, Kompany, de Jong (Petrov 73), Ireland, Elano, Robinho (Evans 89), Caicedo (Bojinov 63)
Unused: Hart, Berti, Gelson, Zabaleta
Goals: -
Booked: Ireland
Man of the Match: Vincent Kompany

City started the brighter, forcing the game's first corner from a through ball aimed towards Onuoha, who had broken out of defence and carried on into the box. The flag-kick, though, came to nothing and it turned out to set the pattern for City's attacks.

Shortly after, Ireland was chasing Berbatov back after City lost the ball in attack and his sliding challenge won the ball, but a free kick was given. Ronaldo's effort deflected off the wall and wrong-footed Given, finding the net. City were left cursing their luck.

Soon, City were fortunate not to be two goals behind, as the ball fell to Tevez on the edge of the box and, with Given out of position, the Argentine curled the ball around City's keeper, beating him, but not beating the post.

But that didn't matter, as, from a long punt out of defence, Berbatov showed an excellent touch to take the ball down and find Tevez, who finished from range, in off Given's left hand post. The City keeper didn't stand a chance and City were sinking with a whimper.

City's next chance didn't come until the second half. Petrov hit a shot from 30 yards, curling towards van der Sar's post, but the United keeper was equal to it, tipping it away.

Fletcher was the next United player to hit the post with a header from a corner. Had it gone in, it would have been very harsh on City after their second half performance. And with that, City pressed for the closing minutes, but were unable to force a goal. For the first time since returning to the Premier League, City had lost both Manchester derbies in the season.

Tottenham Hotspur 2-1 Manchester City

FA Premier League
Saturday 16 May, 2009 - 15:00 KO

City: Given, Richards, Dunne (c), Onuoha, Bridge, Kompany, de Jong, Ireland, Elano (Zabaleta 30), Petrov (Bojinov 60), Caicedo (Benjani 60)
Unused: Hart, Berti, Gelson, Sturridge
Goals: Bojinov (64)
Booked: Zabaleta
Man of the Match: Nigel de Jong

It was all or nothing for City's European ambitions. A victory would put City two points ahead of Tottenham, but a Tottenham win and it was all over for the visitors' season – with the away side unable to catch their hosts even if they were to win on the final day of the season.

Despite this, City just never got started. It took two wonderful saves from Given, from Defoe, to keep the scores level. It was all one-way traffic and the only real surprise was that the home side didn't take the lead sooner.

A long ball from the back was taken down well by Huddlestone, who crossed into the box. Defoe had gotten around the back of the City defence, stayed onside and was able to flick the ball past Given from five yards. To say it had been coming would have been an understatement.

Just a few minutes before half time, Defoe was lucky to have escaped a yellow card for an over the top tackle... on the linesman. Onuoha won the ball and brought the Spurs striker down, who then appeared to take out the official on the line.

The second half started with City looking much brighter. Bojinov and Benjani joined the match and, four minutes later, a ball to the right was headed down by Benjani. Bojinov was there to half-volley the ball into the net for his first ever City goal.

Five minutes from time, though, and the home side were gifted a golden chance to put City out of the running for European football next season. Both Campbell and Richards went down after coming together in the City box, as a harmless cross bounced to Given. The referee, though, had seen an infringement and awarded the home side a more than generous penalty.

Keane stepped up and sent Given the wrong way. City should have equalised from a corner two minutes later, when de Jong's header fell to Benjani in acres of space, but the Zimbabwean headed over.

The Blues wouldn't be finishing in the European places.

Manchester City 1-0 Bolton Wanderers
FA Premier League
Sunday 24 May, 2009 - 16:00 KO

City: Given, Richards, Dunne (c), Onuoha, Bridge (Berti 83), Kompany (Zabaleta 82), de Jong, Ireland (Weiss 70), Wright-Phillips, Robinho, Caicedo
Unused: Hart, Petrov, Bojinov, Benjani
Goals: Caicedo (8)
Booked: -
Man of the Match: Nedum Onuoha

The game started brightly, when Robinho was felled outside the area and his run up to the resulting free kick suggested a shot. But instead, he passed to Ireland, who chipped for Richards and the full back pulled out the acrobatics to cross for Caicedo, who slotted the ball into the empty net.

Ireland then picked up the ball just to the right side of the box and set up Robinho, who smashed a shot against the post. Robinho pulled out a backheel from a lying down position to set up Richards, but the full back was denied by Jaaskelainen, minutes before the City defender cleared from Cahill off the line.

It was beginning to feel like an end-of-season game with two sides who had nothing to play for, as the chances were becoming few and far between.

With 12 minutes to go, Jaaskelainen had to be alert to tip a dipping and deflected Wright-Phillips effort over the bar. Then, the City fans got to see their new cult hero. The biggest cheer of the day was saved for Berti joining the action in place of Bridge. Every one of his touches on his debut was greeted with a massive roar from the crowd.

But, as far as highlights went, that was it.

It was a solid win on the last day of the season, which saw City finish tenth.

May 2009 Breakdown

Games (all competitions):
Won: 2   **Drawn:** 0   **Lost:** 2

Goals (all competitions):
For: 5   **Against:** 5

Progress:
Premier League: 10th
League Cup: Eliminated in Round Two
FA Cup: Eliminated in Round Three
UEFA Cup: Eliminated in the Quarter Final

Final Premier League Table

		P	W	D	L	F	A	GD	Pts
1	Manchester United	38	28	6	4	68	24	+44	90
2	Liverpool	38	25	11	2	77	27	+50	86
3	Chelsea	38	25	8	5	68	24	+44	83
4	Arsenal	38	20	12	6	68	37	+31	72
5	Everton	38	17	12	9	55	37	+18	63
6	Aston Villa	38	17	11	10	54	48	+6	62
7	Fulham	38	14	11	13	39	34	+5	53
8	Tottenham Hotspur	38	14	9	15	45	45	0	51
9	West Ham United	38	14	9	15	42	45	-3	51
10	**Manchester City**	**38**	**15**	**5**	**18**	**58**	**50**	**+8**	**50**
11	Wigan Athletic	38	12	9	17	34	45	-11	45
12	Stoke City	38	12	9	17	38	55	-17	45
13	Bolton Wanderers	38	11	8	19	41	53	-12	41
14	Portsmouth	38	10	11	17	38	57	-19	41
15	Blackburn Rovers	38	10	11	17	40	60	-20	41
16	Sunderland	38	9	9	20	34	54	-20	36
17	Hull City	38	8	11	19	39	64	-25	35
18	Newcastle United	38	7	13	18	40	59	-19	34
19	Middlesbrough	38	7	11	20	28	57	-29	32
20	West Bromwich Albion	38	8	8	22	36	67	-31	32

Summer 2009

A STEP IN THE *WRONG* DIRECTION?

Well, I wasn't expecting that. When I woke up this morning… okay, early afternoon… okay – afternoon… I certainly didn't expect the day to finish like it has done.

As I sit here typing with my sunburnt face, I am in a state of shock. Well, I'm not actually typing with my sunburnt face. That would be silly; I'm using my hands, obviously. It probably wouldn't be this coherent if this was written with my face. It'd probably be more like this: \zp93w \p983jsd dsgn#'

But this is all beside the point. I'm quite shocked, and that's as far as we've got in this article and we're already three paragraphs in. At this rate, it's going to take two sittings to read this.

Anyway, Manchester City have signed Gareth Barry. I figured the Villa player was going to leave them this summer, but I expected it to be a top four team. Not the team I support. Not City. Us.

I got a text message from a friend this morning, saying *"Ahhh! Need to upgrade to Sky for a week. Is it still the Hoff?'* Then I realised he'd sent that message to the wrong person, before he sent another one saying *"Gareth Barry in talks with City"*. And I'll be honest, I didn't believe him. He gets quite excitable during the summer and during January, and so we have to keep him away from the rumour mill websites for the good of his health. And ours.

I read his text message and I thought: *'I'll believe it when I see it'*. Then I saw it on Sky Sports News and thought: *'Well, they did think we were virtually sure of signing Kaka, so I'll give it a while longer'*.

I turned off Sky Sports News shortly after, because there's only so long you can watch a 24-hour rolling news channel without being able to recite the headlines and that can't be a good thing. In fact, I forgot about the story, busying myself with looking for a Father's Day present, watching re-runs of old TV classics, and getting my glasses mended, until I logged on to a particular internet forum to find he'd signed. Incidentally, we can all agree I live a rock 'n' roll lifestyle.

I'll be honest, I was a little giddy. It's the first big move of the summer and it signals City's intent. Barry was wanted by Liverpool last summer and now he's a Manchester City player. Mark Hughes is building something at this club and if we can sort this bloody away form out, we'd be one heck of a decent team. After all, we've made two top 10 finishes in consecutive seasons and have won six – of a possible 38 – away from home in that time. That says more about our home form than you'd think.

Adding Barry to the midfield should make City a better prospect going forward. I'm not sure who he's going to take the place of: Kompany, de Jong, Zabaleta, Ireland, Robinho, Petrov, Wright-Phillips, and now Barry, are all competing for places. But I guess it's a good headache to have and should make it a more competitive squad.

I might upset a few Villa fans with this next bit, too. Most of them, from my experience – and without wishing to make any sweeping generalisations here –

seemed to have accepted that he was going to leave the club this summer. But the fact that it was to City and not to a side in the Champions League seems to have had the same effect as a man jabbing a stick repeatedly into a wasps' nest – on the surface, it's something you'd not immediately expect to see, but the overall result is that a lot of people get upset. And a man gets stung quite a bit.

I can understand why they're a tad annoyed with him, especially after he said he wanted to play in the Champions League then came to us, but I don't quite see why it's being considered as this enormous leap backwards for him.

Okay, so City aren't in Europe next season and Villa are. But what's the point in being in Europe if you're perfectly happy to throw your kids in the first team for a crucial match and leave the competition with a whimper? City just missed out on seventh place, and we also only just missed out on a UEFA Cup semi final place. Villa made their intentions towards the competition very clear, early in the season.

And that Villa's squad was thin and their season started early with the Intertoto Cup caught up with them, come the end of the campaign. Their late season form was disastrous, making their push for fifth place seem like they were trying to gift it to Everton. But they hobbled into sixth place thanks to their early season victories, nonetheless.

So, whether or not Barry joined City because he saw the pound signs is for only the player to know. But clearly, Hughes and Cook sold City as a much better prospect in the long run than Villa – and whether or not that is true will remain to be seen.

But, somehow, I think it's going to be a lot of fun finding out.

THE FUEL OF THE DISCONTENT

A wise man once said: *"Fear leads to anger. Anger leads to hate. Hate leads to suffering."* I'd say, just at this moment in time, we're in stage two, the penultimate stage, smack bang in the centre, of Jedi Master Yoda's chain. Let me explain what I mean in more simple terms. No, I haven't been drinking.

A lot of people – fans, managers, chairmen and officials (I'm looking at you, Messrs Platini and Blatter, by the way) – seem to think that because Manchester City have virtually unlimited funds, they're going to buy absolutely every player they can. Not because they need or want to, but because they can.

Well, they're not going to. Trust me.

Now, the signing of Gareth Barry was a shock for me. But clearly, Mark Hughes sold the club to Barry and clearly Barry liked the idea of where the club wants to be, otherwise he'd never had signed his contract.

It's a mark of the level of footballer City are trying (and succeeding) to attract. Kaka was never a realistic option; we succeeded in tempting Milan with the money, but the man wasn't for budging and that was fair enough.

City are building a team – signing Barry is building on a strong platform with some quality players. The club are likely to be taken for a ride on some transfers – Santa Cruz being the prime example: We tried throughout January and Allardyce wouldn't bite the bait, but now he has for perhaps more than anyone else would have had to have paid. But while we might have to pay a bit more than necessary because of our spending power, we're not just buying players to stop other teams from buying them. We're buying them because we want them and they will do a job for us.

But that doesn't stop the accusations being fired towards the club virtually every day – that City are ruining football. Do me a lemon – Real Madrid can buy one player for £80m and nobody cares a jot; City bid (note – not buy, but bid) £100m for a player and the national sport of England is minutes away from being sucked into the abyss by some unnatural money-hating extra-terrestrial beast. £20m more and it'd tip the scales, quite clearly.

Tevez to City? I'd love it – he'd be a brilliant signing for the club. But he wouldn't be coming to City for the money, as one Manchester United fan suggested on Sky Sports News – he'd be coming for the assurance of first team football and the lure of turning a traditional 'shoot yourself in the foot' club into a club capable of challenging for major honours.

Why didn't he want to stay at United? I don't know – perhaps he was fed up with being messed around by the manager in the whole 'is he going to get a contact?' scenario. Maybe he was sick of being on the bench every week. Maybe he didn't like the food in the canteen, I don't know.

And isn't it odd how there are now so many United fans who 'never wanted him anyway' despite the thousands chanting for their manager to 'sign him up'? Hypocrisy is something that seems ever so common in football, eh?

But I think that fact that City are now aiming for the likes of Tevez or Barry, compared to a few years ago of snapping up aged freebies like McManaman or

Corradi, is what has led to this outcry. City have been away from the top of the league come season's end for decades; it's been decades since we last won a cup competition. And the fact of the matter is, attracting players of that ilk are likely to go some way to challenging the top four of this country – the immovable object that was formally the four teams who could outbid anybody else for anyone they wanted to.

But now somebody can outbid them, they don't like it. The stupid thing is, City don't have the pull that the top four have – we aren't currently challenging for major honours, so we have to try harder than the likes of Liverpool, Chelsea, Manchester United, Arsenal to acquire signatures. But because we're slowly building a team and proving to be an attractive prospect for the likes of Barry, it seems to have upset a lot of people.

There's the fear that City might just upset the balance of the Premier League. That the top four might not be the same top four it is now in a few years' time. The other teams up there are starting to run scared.

I mean, how can City justify trying to buy players that will make them better? It really isn't on. But losing in the quarter-finals of cups or to lower division teams and finishing tenth or below is getting quite tiresome now.

Hopefully, if Mark Hughes can build the team properly, strengthening weaknesses and adding quality, the rest of the Premier League will be suffering at the hands of Manchester City FC in years to come. Fear leads to anger. Anger leads to hate. And hate leads to suffering.

MEGA MONEY MORALITY TALES

So, now that Wimbledon's over, the whole country can remember that they never really liked Andy Murray anyway and that he was never realistically going to win it, and we can get back to the proper order of the day: Football.

In true 'just after Wimbledon' style, me and a few friends played tennis on Monday – it's fair to say that, while we all might have more of a personality than he does, Andy Murray is a bit better than we are. But only a bit – after all, one of us managed not to double fault for a whole game.

Anyway, while I was picking everyone up the radio was on and the discussion on the station I was listening to was of John Terry transferring to Manchester City. Potentially, at least. It's controversial and easy radio.

But here's the thing – the transfer of Terry isn't particularly controversial. I doubt there's a City fan alive who expects this to happen. City's bids haven't been controversial – cheeky, yes; audacious, definitely; controversial, hardly.

You see, my gripe is that a lot of the pundits on such radio shows suggest that players are moving to City for the money. Whether or not this is true can only be determined by one person – the player himself – so it's a bit of a pointless debate to be having. But what irks me most about this line of argument is the idea that they're moving to a club with no history who just happen to have got a bit of money.

City are a brilliant club. Just because we have won no major honours in the last three decades does not indicate a lack of history. Hadrian's Wall hasn't been up to much lately, but it's certainly got something significant going on in its past. City have been league champions. City have won cups. Ok, not as many as other clubs, but the sole reason why the four at the top keep finishing there is the fact that there has been so much money available to them recently.

It's a vicious circle – you qualify for the Champions League and get a ton of cash, so you can buy players to qualify for the Champions League. Everyone else has to feed off the scraps that are left, but that's ok because the top four can keep qualifying for the Champions League.

Up until 2007, City had a pittance to spend. If they spent it wrong, as they usually did, then there isn't a stream of funds available to correct the error. For years, the top four have had this ability that nobody else has. It's not City's fault that transfer fees are as high as they are for mediocre players, it's those that have gone before them.

Debating the morality of City's transfer bids, but not doing so for any other team in the past is wrong. AC Milan have smashed the world record transfer fee more than any other club and they've been propped up sugar daddy style for years. The English transfer record has been smashed by Manchester United several times.

City can bid high money for Terry. And if Chelsea accept, then it's up to Terry to choose. If Chelsea or he refuses, then it won't happen. Simple, really, but that won't stop people making it much more complicated than it actually is.

August 2009

Blackburn Rovers 0-2 Manchester City

FA Premier League

Saturday 15 August, 2009 - 15:00 KO

City: Given, Richards, Dunne (c), Toure, Bridge, Barry, Ireland, Wright-Phillips, Robinho (Tevez 68), Bellamy, Adebayor
Unused: Taylor, Zabaleta, Onuoha, de Jong, Petrov, Weiss
Goals: Adebayor (3), Ireland (90+1)
Booked: Richards
Man of the Match: Craig Bellamy

The season started quickly for City: Dunne did well to clear off the line with his thigh, before City worked the ball to Wright-Phillips, midway into the Blackburn half. After carrying the ball towards the area, he slid it into Adebayor's path, and the Togolese forward slammed the ball past Robinson from the edge of the box, scoring on his debut for the club.

A goalmouth scramble in the City area finished with Samba thinking he must have scored, but his effort from close range was superbly saved by Given. And it was the home side doing the pressing, looking for that equaliser, but they were struggling to create any clear cut chances.

Ten minutes until the break and Robinson had to be alert. City broke well with Adebayor knocking the ball to Bridge, who found Robinho. The Brazilian took the ball into the box and had a curling effort finger-tipped over, when it looked destined for the top corner.

On the hour mark, the City fans were pleased to see their side knocking the ball around well, with the home side unable to get a kick. A lovely passing move was almost finished off by Robinho, who, after breaking into the box, forced Robinson to flick the ball around the post.

A Wright-Phillips cross bounced out to Bellamy, with just five minutes to go, but his left foot volley was well over the bar. It didn't matter, though, because, as stoppage time began, City broke with speed and Ireland was set free with a one-on-one with Robinson. It looked like he had taken too long and allowed the defence to get back to cover, but, with options square, he squeezed the ball past the Blackburn keeper and the defenders on the line to secure the opening day victory for City.

Manchester City 1-0 Wolverhampton Wanderers

FA Premier League

Saturday 22 August, 2009 - 15:00 KO

City: Given, Richards, Dunne (c), Toure, Bridge, Wright-Phillips, Ireland, Barry, Robinho (de Jong 83), Tevez (Bellamy 72), Adebayor

Unused: Taylor, Zabaleta, Onuoha, Petrov, Weiss
Goals: Adebayor (17)
Booked: -
Man of the Match: Gareth Barry

The first chance of the game wasn't forthcoming, and it was City's first shot of the game, in fact, that put them into the lead. After a Bridge cross was flicked on by the Wolves defence, Tevez knocked down a superbly cushioned pass to Adebayor, and he smashed the ball first time past Hennessey at his near post.

Just before the break, Jarvis steamed towards the City goal and his curling effort was superbly pushed over the bar by Given. On the stroke of half time, it should have been two, when Tevez was found by Barry from the left, but his header from six yards was just wide.

On 66 minutes, Adebayor had a chance to put City further ahead, as he rounded the keeper, but took it too wide and it was on his weaker foot. His shot hit the side netting, to the frustration of the home crowd.

With 20 minutes to go, Wolves were almost level. Hennessey smashed the ball upfield and Toure didn't get enough on his header. The ball fell to Doyle, whose shot slammed into the crossbar, with Given beaten. It was then all Wolves pressure, as Given saved well from an Elokobi shot and Dunne got up to clear the resulting corner. From looking dominant in the game, the Blues suddenly had their backs against the wall.

A huge punt downfield from Hennessey, with minutes to go, forced Dunne to head behind for a corner, before a cross from the Wolves left bounced through City's box with nobody connecting and the fans breathed a sigh of relief.

City were hanging on at the final whistle, but they should have been miles ahead after the chances they had missed in the first hour of the game. Though, traditionally, City have never done things the easy way.

Crystal Palace 0-2 Manchester City
League Cup Second Round
Thursday 27 August, 2009 - 20:00 KO

City: Given, Richards, Lescott, Toure (c), Bridge, Wright-Phillips, Ireland, Barry, Robinho (Bellamy 72), Tevez (de Jong 86), Adebayor
Unused: Taylor, Zabaleta, Onuoha, Petrov, Weiss
Goals: Wright-Phillips (50), Tevez (70)
Booked: Richards
Man of the Match: Stephen Ireland

The second round of the League Cup has been a stumbling block for City in recent seasons, with the Blues going out at this stage to Doncaster, Colchester and Brighton in three of the last four campaigns. So Mark Hughes fielded a full strength side to make sure it didn't happen again.

Sears wasted an excellent chance for Palace, when he broke the offside trap and faced Given in a one-on-one. But the Irish keeper stood up well and blocked his shot with his chest. City were slow out of the blocks.

But they were on top, as the half came to a close, with Speroni in the Palace goal pulling off a fine save from Adebayor to keep the scores level. He then stopped a Tevez shot with a brave save, after the little Argentinian had played a neat one-two with Ireland.

Palace had the most of the early second-half possession, but it was City who used the ball best. Neat play from Robinho and Ireland found Wright-Phillips unmarked and he was able to lash a shot into the back of the net.

It could have been two and then three almost instantly, as first Speroni denied Adebayor and then the crossbar denied Wright-Phillips, as City began to take control of the game. The home side needed something to get back into the tie and they were leaving gaps as they took more chances pushing forward.

City added a second to their total 20 minutes from the end from a corner. New signing Lescott made a run to the near post, dragging two defenders out of the way for Tevez to get his first goal for City, neatly nodding the ball home from close range.

Portsmouth 0-1 Manchester City
FA Premier League
Sunday 30 August, 2009 - 13:30 KO

City: Given, Richards (Zabaleta 59), Lescott, Toure (c), Bridge, Wright-Phillips, Ireland (de Jong 75), Barry, Bellamy, Tevez, Adebayor
Unused: Taylor, Onuoha, Petrov, Weiss, Robinho
Goals: Adebayor (30)
Booked: Zabaleta
Man of the Match: Gareth Barry

City's visit to the south coast started well, with Tevez chasing down the ball across the Portsmouth back line. He won it and it fell to Wright-Phillips, but the winger's cross was cut out.

On 10 minutes, Portsmouth wasted the best chance of the game, as Piquionne beat City's offside trap and went one-on-one with Given. But the Irish keeper didn't even need to make the save, as the Portsmouth man hit the side netting with a volley. He should have done much better.

Four minutes later, Begovic flapped at a cross and Richards looked like he was going to knock it into the empty net, but the goalkeeper recovered his mistake well to get a hand on the ball. From a corner just after the midway point of the half, though, Barry's cross was met by the head of Adebayor and the ball powered its way past Begovic, into the net.

Nine minutes later, and it should have been two. Barry was flagged offside from a Bellamy low smash across goal, but the ball didn't reach him as Richards put it in first, with his England colleague not interfering with play. The linesman, though, was unmoved and the goal didn't stand.

Just after the hour mark, Adebayor nipped past three players right in front of the City fans and his shot was well saved by Begovic from a tight angle. The City fans wanted a penalty for a foul by Vanden Borre on Tevez shortly after, but the referee waved away the appeals.

With minutes to go, David Nugent had an excellent chance to level the count. But the one-time capped Englishman fired the ball into the ground and Given pulled off a match-winning save to preserve City's unbeaten start and run of consecutive clean sheets.

HOW ARE CITY THE BAD GUYS HERE?

We do love a good bit of outrage in this country. Outrage at MPs' expenses; at the Tory MEP's comments on the NHS; at the Lockerbie bomber's release on compassionate grounds; at anything to do with immigration; at Joey Barton. So, it wouldn't be a proper Premier League transfer if it didn't include a bit of furore, would it?

For several weeks, I've been successful in ignoring the Joleon Lescott saga, but since it's been gaining momentum like a complaint to Ofcom about the offensive comedian of the week, I've found myself dragged kicking and screaming into the debate.

As far as my understanding goes, City put in a bid for Lescott in private and Everton said no, before releasing the information on their website. City bid again, Everton said no, and the press latched onto it, asking Mark Hughes if he wanted to sign a player he'd bid twice on and he told them he did. Then David Moyes is asked about it and he says that the player isn't for sale, City have no class or respect, before adding that he'd like to sign some player or other from Valencia, completely ignoring the irony of the situation.

Interestingly, Moyes said he wouldn't sell anyone this close to the transfer window closing, anyway. Yet he expects other clubs to sell or loan him players this close to the deadline. Slightly hypocritical, but I'll let that one go.

A few radio station phone ins then tried to get City fans annoyed and get them to call in by saying that City are tactless and the newspapers then tried to get more people to buy their product by reporting a graceless City. Before you know it, City are not just rude, but also responsible for global warming, forest fires and swine flu. Pesky bleeders.

I heard, at one point, Stan Collymore delightfully whipping up some more furore by suggesting that Mark Hughes should have simply called David Moyes and asked him to sell Lescott – at which point, Hughes, rightly, pointed out that if he had done that, Moyes would have said no and they'd have both hung up.

The point is, City's first transfer enquiry was through the correct channels and was rejected through the correct channels, too. It was then Everton who released the story on their website, so, naturally, sports journalists ask both Hughes and Moyes what's going on. Hughes says he's interested in signing Lescott and Moyes says he's not for sale.

So, what's wrong there?

City have conducted themselves no differently in this transfer saga than they have with Arsenal over Toure and Adebayor, with Blackburn over Santa Cruz, with Newcastle over Given, with Hamburg over Kompany... Yet it's only Everton who seem to have a problem with it.

Moyes is the one who has hit out to the press, kept Lescott from training with the first team and left him out of the side. The only one of them actions I can understand is the last one, since the player had put in a transfer request. But Moyes turned that down as well.

I understand that any team wants to keep their best players, but if their best players don't want to stay, then they're hardly going to perform. Hughes might ask himself if he really needs a new defender, and Everton could be left with an unhappy player.

As I remember with the Rooney transfer, Everton did something similar and ended up with a big wad of cash and no time left in the transfer window to spend it. And then it went towards the club's debts, never to be seen by the manager again.

I don't really understand why it's become acceptable to knock City for doing nothing wrong. They put in a transfer bid and it was rejected. Lescott got wind of it and decided to ask to leave because he wanted to make a go of it at City.

I find it amusing that the accusation is that City have never contacted Moyes, when the club have had two bids turned down. If it is indeed Moyes who makes the decisions at Everton, like he says, then to have had those bids turned down, it must have been done by him. That's a strange definition of 'no contact' if it actually means 'plenty of contact, but we don't want to make people think we're the bad guys'.

Hughes has spoken to the media about it, true. But he has in the same way that Gordon Brown spoke about that Susan woman off Britain's Got Talent – he didn't call a press conference to talk about Lescott, the press asked him about the transfer and he responded.

So if that's being disrespectful in the eyes of David Moyes, then I guess every football manager in the country is disrespectful. What a shoddy state the game has gotten itself into, eh?

August 2009 Breakdown

Games (all competitions):
Won: 4   **Drawn:** 0   **Lost:** 0

Goals (all competitions):
For: 6   **Against:** 0

Progress:
Premier League: 4th
League Cup: Qualified for Round Three
FA Cup: -

Premier League Table

		P	W	D	L	F	A	GD	Pts
2	Tottenham Hotspur	4	4	0	0	11	4	+7	12
3	Manchester United	4	3	0	1	8	2	+6	9
4	**Manchester City**	**3**	**3**	**0**	**0**	**4**	**0**	**+4**	**9**
5	Stoke City	4	2	1	1	3	4	-1	7
6	Arsenal	3	2	0	1	11	4	+7	6

September 2009

Manchester City 4-2 Arsenal

FA Premier League
Saturday 12 September, 2009 - 15:00 KO

City: Given, Richards, Lescott, Toure (c), Bridge, Wright-Phillips, Ireland (Petrov 73), Barry, de Jong, Bellamy, Adebayor
Unused: Taylor, Onuoha, Zabaleta, Vidal, Weiss, Sylvinho
Goals: Richards (20), Bellamy (74), Adebayor (81), Wright-Phillips (83)
Booked: Lescott, Adebayor, de Jong
Man of the Match: Craig Bellamy

Early in the game, Gallas missed a golden opportunity to give the visitors the lead – heading over from a corner, when he found himself unmarked at the back post. It was a let off for the hosts.

Barry then whipped in a cracking cross from a deep free kick and Richards met it beautifully. His header smashed against the post, hit the back of Almunia and dropped into the net, giving the home side the lead.

Arsenal took control in the second half. From an Arsenal corner from the right, Vermaelen headed with power and Given's reactions prevented it from crossing the line, while Bridge was able to clear.

On the hour, the ball was in the back of the City net, courtesy of van Persie, as Lescott dived in and missed the ball. The Dutchman smashed it home and never looked like missing.

It didn't stay level for long. Richards skipped past a weak challenge from Song and into the Arsenal box. From there, he got his head up and found Bellamy, who lashed the ball into the net.

And then, the former Arsenal forward Adebayor got what he wanted. A good advantage let Wright-Phillips break free down the right side and his cross was perfect for the unmarked striker to head into the net with power.

But it got even better. Arsenal pushed forward, and, after winning back possession, Bellamy carried the ball up the pitch and found Wright-Phillips free. He dinked the ball over Almunia to put City in full control of the game.

Four minutes later, Rosicky pulled a goal back for the visitors, slotting the ball past Given with the City defence asking for offside. It wasn't, and the goal was given. And it could have been a tense finish, when the City defence switched off a minute later and van Persie flashed a shot across goal, hitting the post.

Manchester United 4-3 Manchester City

FA Premier League
Sunday 20 September, 2009 - 13:30 KO

City: Given, Richards, Lescott, Toure (c), Bridge, Wright-Phillips, Ireland, Barry,

de Jong (Petrov 82), Bellamy, Tevez
Unused: Taylor, Zabaleta, Weiss, Sylvinho, Garrido, Ball
Goals: Barry (15), Bellamy (51, 90)
Booked: Tevez, Bellamy
Man of the Match: Nigel de Jong

City couldn't have gotten off to a worse start and had barely touched the ball when Given was forced to pick it out of the net. From a United throw in, the ball found its way to Rooney in the box and he poked it past the City keeper.

But as City found their feet, they found an equaliser. A long ball forward was chased by Tevez, who caught Foster in possession outside his area. The former United man laid the ball to Barry who slotted it into the empty net.

It was an end-to-end game. The next real chance fell for Tevez at the Stretford End, when a fine break from defence by Toure found the Argentine in the box. His shot beat Foster, but hit the post and bounced behind.

But as well as they ended the first half, City began the second in the same manner as they started the game. Fletcher beat Barry in the air from a Giggs cross and nodded the ball past Given.

City, though, were in no mood to roll over. Bellamy found himself on the left side of the United box. He cut inside and fired in an unstoppable, right-footed effort that found the top corner superbly to equalise again.

The visitors had Given to thank just after the hour mark, when he made two world class saves from two Berbatov headers. The first, from a corner, was point blank and the second was as the Bulgarian headed towards an empty net.

But then, with 15 minutes to go, a dubious free kick was crossed into the City box and Fletcher got his second goal, as Barry failed to challenge.

Then, as Ferdinand looked to try and flick a pass wide, Petrov intercepted and set Bellamy free. The Welshman carried the ball past Ferdinand, around Foster and slotted it in from a very tight angle in the first of four added minutes.

City's delight, though, suddenly turned to anger, as the referee played on for longer than he had added, giving Owen the chance to score from close range, as he gave the City defence the slip.

Manchester City 2-1 Fulham (AET)
League Cup Third Round
Wednesday 23 September, 2009 - 20:00 KO

City: Given, Zabaleta, Lescott, Toure (c), Bridge, Wright-Phillips, Ireland (Petrov 75), Barry, de Jong (Weiss 91), Bellamy, Tevez
Unused: Taylor, Sylvinho, Vidal, Garrido, Ball
Goals: Barry (51), Toure (110)
Booked: -
Man of the Match: Craig Bellamy

Despite City's side being strong, Fulham worked hard from the off and the game took a very long time to get going. The first two chances fell to City, with Barry heading directly at the keeper and Wright-Phillips firing wide from range.

And while Given was a spectator for most of the first half, he had no chance when Gera fired Fulham into the lead. It was the visitors' first shot of the game and it was a sublime volley from range.

While the first half petered out with City behind, the home side pulled level shortly after the break. Bellamy worked hard to win a left wing corner and then the striker found Barry from the resulting kick, who nodded the ball into the empty net when Stockdale came for it and missed.

Despite their possession, City couldn't force a chance to avoid extra time.

With 10 minutes until penalties, Toure was left unmarked at a corner and Petrov planted the ball on his head. The skipper headed the ball into the net off the bar, giving City a much deserved lead.

Manchester City 3-1 West Ham
FA Premier League
Monday 28 September, 2009 - 20:00 KO

City: Given, Zabaleta, Lescott, Toure (c), Bridge, Wright-Phillips (Santa Cruz 80), Barry (Johnson 88), de Jong, Petrov, Bellamy, Tevez
Unused: Taylor, Weiss, Sylvinho, Richards, Garrido
Goals: Tevez (4, 60) Petrov (31)
Booked: Bridge
Man of the Match: Nigel de Jong

Before West Ham could settle into the match they were behind. Petrov was released down the left wing and, when he got to the by-line, he found Tevez. The Argentine slammed the ball into the net as Green dived for the low cross.

But, with their first chance of the game, the visitors equalised. Diamanti's free kick wasn't cleared by the City defence and Kovac put in a weak shot. It didn't look too threatening until it flicked off the heels of Cole and beat Given.

Seven minutes later, the home side had the lead again. De Jong was fouled outside the area and Petrov took it, beating Green low to the bottom left corner.

On 60 minutes, City were given a free kick on the left flank. Bellamy floated it in and there were City players queuing up at the back post to put it in. It was Tevez who got the header and beat the despairing dive of Green.

With 20 minutes left, Given earned his corn with three top class saves. The first, from Diamanti on the break, was an excellent fingertip stop to his left and, moments later, the same player forced Given to push the ball over the bar.

With minutes to go, Petrov found himself through on goal, but decided to cut back onto his right foot and his curling effort was just over the bar.

PROPORTION AND DISTORTION

There have been some terrible scenes throughout the UK over the past few days. Protest marches, effigies burnt, witty slogans on banners, pins in the eyes of voodoo dolls… All because of two separate incidents in one football match.

Adebayor's stamp on Robin van Persie deserves a ban, that isn't in question. As a football fan, I'm supposed to be shocked. And I am: His behaviour was shocking, I'm shocked. There. He was wrong to do it and will be punished for it.

But, the thing is, I don't believe for one minute City's forward began the game with the aim of stamping on one of his former team-mates, with the aim of injuring one of the opposition players or with the aim of doing somebody some damage. Robin van Persie, on the other hand, disagrees, as his statement on the official Arsenal website confirms:

> "We are both professional footballers and I know that the game is physical, I too have made hard and sometimes miss-timed challenges but never with the intention of hurting an opponent. He set out to hurt me today.

> "He had his own agenda today and that is bad for football. It's bad for the game we all love."

The statement suggests that van Persie thinks that Adebayor began the game wanting to kick either him or his fellow team-mates. From what I witnessed, Adebayor started the game with the aim of helping his side to victory.

Then what happened was as follows: City were on the back foot and the ball was cleared to half-way. Adebayor was on his own and in possession. As he tried to skip past one tackle, he knocked the ball too far and lost it. At that same moment, van Persie came flying in with two feet recklessly, failing to win the ball and ends up in front of Adebayor. Who then, in my opinion, decides stupidly to kick out at him – not in some pre-meditated attack, but because of an ill timed and two-footed challenge. A reaction.

That, by no means, makes Adebayor's actions right or above punishment, he deserves whatever punishment he gets – I don't want to be accused of condoning his actions or the injury to van Persie's face. But neither am I condoning a witch hunt of somebody who looks to have reacted in the spur of the moment and who probably now regrets what he did.

It's not as if Robin van Persie has never lashed out in the heat of the moment, or been a bit careless with his elbows. I don't recall other victims of such incidents issuing statements on club websites. Thomas Sorensen didn't feel the need to when he was stamped on and shouldered by the very man who has "made hard and sometimes miss-timed challenges but never with the intention of hurting an opponent".

Neither Robin van Persie nor Arsenal needed to bring this incident to the media's attention – it was already there. They could have complained to the FA

117

in private, who would probably have looked at the incident anyway: The referee clearly didn't see it, otherwise he would have punished Adebayor.

The second incident, on the other hand, has been blown out of all proportion. And because it was from the same man as the first, then needless to say, the gallows are being prepared and the black cap dusted.

So then, Adebayor scored. Then he proceeded to run 90m down to the other end of the ground to celebrate with the opposition fans. Fans of his former club. Fans who hadn't a good word to say about him beforehand. Fans who had booed and jeered every touch of the ball he had.

A lot has been made of Adebayor's celebration, but not a lot has been made of the behaviour of some of the Arsenal fans. Now I know most Arsenal fans are like most City fans and most fans of other teams – sensible, enjoy chocolate and hate Manchester United – but the minority who hurled themselves at the stewards, threw coins and hot dogs, and tried to burst onto the pitch shouldn't go blameless here.

Adebayor was ill-advised to celebrate how he did, but if the Arsenal fans that reacted can't take a bit of banter from an ex-player when they had been perfectly willing to dish it out to that ex-player throughout the game, then football probably isn't the sport for them.

If we as people can't rise above retaliating with violence to a counter-taunt, then we should be taking a long, hard look at ourselves. Not at the man who simply celebrated a goal, handing back what he had been given throughout the game. Why should the fans be allowed to be offensive, but not be offended?

As far as I'm concerned, the matter should be finished. He was booked for the celebration and, as Graham Poll explained on Sky Sports News, that's the punishment that applies in the rules for what he did. Other players have done it in the past – even van Persie turned and ran towards the City fans when he equalised to celebrate in front of them, shouting a few obscenities.

It was heat of the moment stuff. He was booked and he's apologised for doing it. Players have done it in the past and been booked, they'll do it in the future and get booked. There's no need to punish them on the pitch with a yellow card, then off it with a ban.

Adebayor did exactly what the vast majority of us in that position would have wanted to do. He knows what he did was wrong in the circumstances and was punished accordingly with a yellow card – they add up over the season and result in bans. Try and tell managers with key players banned for receiving one or more of five yellow cards for celebrating by taking their shirt off that cautions don't mean much post-match.

And in this entire furore, most people have forgotten the stern defensive display that City put in and their excellent finishing on the break. You'd have thought that these two incidents happened and then some football broke out, not the other way round.

"THE FOURTH OFFICIAL HAS INDICATED THREE ADDITIONAL MINUTES, THAT'S FIVE ADDITIONAL MINUTES..."

So, a couple of days have passed since 'Time-gate' and I've calmed down enough to write a coherent article. Well, one that doesn't include swear words over and over and over again, anyway. What angered me about the Manchester derby's last minute winner wasn't that United won – because, being honest here, they dominated the half and looked more likely than City to win it – but the manner in which it was won.

Time was added to the match for the celebrations after the equaliser five seconds before stoppage time. Bellamy's goal celebration took about 50 seconds. And a minute of time was added because it was, according to Alan Wiley, the fourth official, 'excessive'. Most goal celebrations, last minute or not, tend to take about that time, but most goal celebrations aren't 'excessive'. Michael Owen's goal celebration took about 50 seconds, but that wasn't 'excessive'.

My problem, though, isn't that this time was added on in this match. Well, it is, but that's not the reason City lost. The City players knew they had to play until the final whistle and to leave Michael Owen with time and space in the box was asking for trouble. My problem is that you won't see time added on for stoppages in stoppage time again for a long while.

How many times does a team equalise in stoppage time and celebrate wildly, but the referee blows for full time when his three original, four original, five original minutes have passed? How many times is a free kick awarded in stoppage time and players spend a minute arguing with the referee or each other, but full time still comes at the end of what the fourth official's board said? If what happened in the Manchester derby was the norm, then fine. But while it's not the norm, I'll have a problem with it happening.

If we flip the situation over – and City were winning 3-2, having dominated the half when United equalised – would the referee have re-added time? I don't imagine so. Would United have settled for a 3-3, just like City were doing? I think they would.

And to say City had the same amount of time to score a winner as United is a bit of a churlish argument. Yes, they did. But they were the away team at Old Trafford who have been under pressure for most of the second half. Just how likely was a City winner? If we played on, would a United winner be more likely? Being the home side, with 70,000 fans behind them, I'd say it was.

If the Manchester derby proved anything, it's that City are capable of competing with the top four clubs. Three away goals at Old Trafford, added to four goals at home to Arsenal, is not something a City team would have been capable of in recent years. There's still a few defensive lapses, but Hughes will be well aware of them and will be working to cut them out.

This season should be anything but dull.

September 2009 Breakdown

Games (all competitions):
Won: 2   Drawn: 1   Lost: 1

Goals (all competitions):
For: 12   Against: 8

Progress:
Premier League: 5th
League Cup: Qualified for Round Four
FA Cup: -

Premier League Table

		P	W	D	L	F	A	GD	Pts
3	Liverpool	7	5	0	2	22	10	+12	15
4	Tottenham Hotspur	7	5	0	2	17	10	+7	15
5	**Manchester City**	**6**	**5**	**0**	**1**	**14**	**7**	**+7**	**15**
6	Arsenal	6	4	0	2	18	8	+10	12
7	Aston Villa	6	4	0	2	9	5	+4	12

October 2009

Aston Villa 1-1 Manchester City

FA Premier League

Monday 5 October, 2009 - 20:00 KO

City: Given, Zabaleta, Lescott, Toure (c), Bridge, Wright-Phillips, Barry, de Jong (Ireland 50), Bellamy, Tevez (Santa Cruz 68), Adebayor
Unused: Taylor, Johnson, Sylvinho, Richards, Petrov
Goals: Bellamy (66)
Booked: de Jong, Wright-Phillips
Man of the Match: Wayne Bridge

The match was started at break-neck speed as Barry stopped Carew with a crunching tackle, and a Petrov shot flew just wide of Given's post. The City goalkeeper, though, knew where the shot was heading.

With the game moving as quickly as it was, something was bound to give. Unfortunately, from City's point of view, it was at their end and it was the former captain who nodded Villa into an early lead from a corner. Dunne didn't celebrate his first Villa goal out of respect to his former employers, but the damage was done and City were behind at Villa Park.

Halfway into the first half and Tevez was on a one-man mission to find an equaliser. First, his long range effort was just over the bar, before a second effort from distance was miles wide, with Wright-Phillips free to his right.

Just before the hour mark, Tevez played a nicely weighted pass inside the fullback for Wright-Phillips, but the little winger had to stretch for his first touch and it allowed enough time for Milner to get back and get a vital touch away from the City man. City were beginning to grow into the game and the pressure was starting to build on the home side.

Then City got what they had been pressing for. Wright-Phillips knocked the ball to Ireland, who sent Adebayor free in the box. With the angle narrow, the City front-man pulled it back to the unmarked Bellamy, who smashed his shot into the back of the net. It was no more than City deserved and it appeared to change Mark Hughes' mind, who had previously been preparing Petrov to join the action for the visitors.

And, with the clock nearing 90, Bellamy called on his endless supplies of energy to set off down the left. His cross-shot was comfortable for Friedel at his near post, but the American had to be alert to make sure that the visitors didn't steal the three points in the closing stages.

Wigan Athletic 1-1 Manchester City

FA Premier League

Sunday 18 October, 2009 - 16:00 KO

City: Given (c), Zabaleta, Lescott, Richards, Bridge, Wright-Phillips (Ireland 82), Barry, de Jong, Petrov, Tevez (Santa Cruz 82), Adebayor (Kompany 69)
Unused: Taylor, Johnson, Sylvinho, Weiss
Goals: Petrov (47)
Booked: Zabaleta
Sent Off: Zabaleta
Man of the Match: Nigel de Jong

Despite the early shots coming from the home side, it was City who started the stronger. Adebayor had the visitors' best chance of the game in the opening minutes, as he was set free in the area. But a combination of Kirkland and Bramble prevented the big forward from finding the net.

Zabaleta showed what he was made off, not even flinching when he took a Rodallega scissor-kick shot to the face. The Argentinian was then wrongly booked when he barely caught Figueroa, who made a meal of the challenge. City were frustrated.

Just before half time, Given, not tested much in the first half, was alert to palm Rodallega's long range drive to safety. Wigan had a goal disallowed for a foul on Barry, as N'Zogbia raced onto a Scotland knock-down.

And, as the teams were preparing to go in level, Wigan got the break they, perhaps, didn't deserve. City switched off at the back, leaving room for a low, driven cross from the left. Given could only parry to N'Zogbia, who beat Bridge and slid the ball into the net.

But shortly into the second half, City were level. In fact, Wigan had had the early possession, but just over a minute in, Tevez worked hard down the right and knocked the ball inside. Wright-Phillips let it go and Petrov opened up his body and curled the shot past Kirkland.

Adebayor was then through in the area, but an excellent tackle from Bramble stopped him from getting a shot in. The ball fell to Wright-Phillips, who was unmarked, but he saw his shot deflect off Adebayor and over the bar. City appeared to be getting themselves on top.

But then the game turned in favour of the hosts. An ill-advised and mistimed challenge from Zabaleta saw him shown a red card, via a second yellow, and Mark Hughes was left furious at the Argentine's first booking.

Wright-Phillips was denied a clear penalty when N'Zogbia went to ground and took none of the ball and all of the man. Given then secured a point for City, after a good save at his near post, before quickly closing down Scotland and deflecting his shot wide.

Manchester City 2-2 Fulham
FA Premier League
Sunday 25 October, 2009 - 15:00 KO

City: Given, Richards, Lescott, Toure (c) (Kompany 90+2), Bridge, Barry, de Jong (Ireland 72), Bellamy, Petrov (Wright-Phillips 67), Tevez, Adebayor
Unused: Taylor, Johnson, Sylvinho, Weiss
Goals: Lescott (53), Petrov (59)
Booked: -
Man of the Match: Gareth Barry

The first action of the game saw Petrov try a new corner routine, firing it wide from the flank to the edge of the box, but the waiting Bellamy could only volley well over the bar as the Fulham defence rushed out towards him. City were looking for the early breakthrough against a team that had been stubborn in this fixture in the League Cup earlier in the campaign.

The best chance of the half then fell to the visitors. The City defence were at sixes and sevens as the ball was played over the top to Kamara. The back four wanted offside, but the linesman's flag stayed down and Given dived to smother the ball at the forward's feet to snuff out the danger. It was a let off for the home side.

Minutes before half time, City scored... only to see it ruled out for a foul in the box. Richards got up well to head in from a corner, but the referee judged that Barry had blocked the run of Richards' marker unfairly. It was proving to be hard work for the Blues.

Just after the break, City were fortunate not to be behind from Zamora and they used that to their advantage, as a right wing corner was cleared only as far as Bridge. After taking a touch, he curled an effort around a group of players in the box and it was a fine save from Schwarzer that denied him goal.

From the resulting corner, though, City took the lead. As the ball came into the box, it was nodded into the middle from the back post, where Adebayor thought he'd put it over the line, but it was Lescott got the final touch – though both were trying to award it to the other!

City soon doubled their lead. Bellamy's corner was cleared out to Toure, who played the ball wide to Petrov, the winger having dropped deep. He fed it wide again to Barry, who returned a pass to the Bulgarian and he slammed it into the corner of the net.

But two minutes later, the City confidence took a dent. Fulham came straight on the attack and Duff was able to fire past Given from outside the box, after receiving a chest-down from Zamora, to make it 2-1.

And with 20 minutes to go, City received a double blow. First, the on-form Petrov had to leave the action with injury and, seconds later, the visitors equalised. A free kick from the left flank was curled into the box and Dempsey got above Lescott to head past the despairing dive of Given.

City had thrown away their lead and, after a good start to the season, were beginning to leak points. It was the club's third draw on the bounce and something needed to change.

Manchester City 5-1 Scunthorpe United

League Cup Fourth Round
Wednesday 28 October, 2009 - 19:45 KO

City: Given, Zabaleta, Lescott, Kompany, Sylvinho, Wright-Phillips, Ireland (Weiss 59), Barry (Johnson 73), de Jong (c), Santa Cruz, Tevez (Benjani 79)
Unused: Taylor, Richards, Bridge, Bellamy
Goals: Ireland (2), Santa Cruz (37), Lescott (55), Tevez (71), Johnson (77)
Booked: de Jong, Zabaleta
Man of the Match: Roque Santa Cruz

With a quarter final place at stake, City stuck to their guns and named another strong League Cup side, taking the competition very seriously. The Blues were going all out for their first piece of silverware in three decades.

And it was City who took the initiative, and, after Wright-Phillips had played him in, Ireland scored a beauty from the edge of the box, leaving the keeper standing. A good start nearly got better for City, as, from kick-off, Ireland stole the ball and sent Wright-Phillips in. But the little winger's effort from range was just inches over the bar, as the visitors couldn't get out of the starting blocks and could have been overrun.

But while City controlled possession, they weren't able to test the visiting goalkeeper. And Scunthorpe punished the Blues after 25 minutes. Defensive midfielder de Jong gave the ball away in the centre and it was played past Kompany into Williams' feet. Lescott wasn't sure whether to close the ball or mark the man square and, in the end did neither, leaving himself in no man's land as the low cross found Forte to tap home.

It was somewhat against the run of play.

With half time approaching, City re-took the lead. Zabaleta crossed to the back post and Santa Cruz peeled off his man to meet it with a powerful header. It found the bottom corner of the goal and City were able to take an advantage into the break, the Paraguayan scoring his first in a blue shirt.

Ten minutes into the second half, City got their third. A corner from the left was crossed by Wright-Phillips and Lescott found himself unmarked on the penalty spot. He didn't need asking twice and he powered home a header for his second goal in as many games. It made up for his error of judgement in the first half and had appeared to put the game beyond the visitors.

Ireland's last action of the game was to beat the goalkeeper on a one-on-one, but his touch wasn't heavy enough to earn himself his second goal of the night, as Canavan was able to get back and clear from the line, as the ball trickled towards the empty net.

Tevez then joined in on the fun, as he was quickest to react to a low Weiss cross after a short corner, and City found themselves in complete control of the game at 4-1. Scunthorpe had all but thrown in the towel and the game took on the feel of a training exercise.

With just over 10 minutes to go, Michael Johnson wriggled free from two challenges, before he smashed a left footed shot into the top corner from over 20 yards out. As he celebrated with the team, there wasn't a City fan in the ground who wasn't pleased for him, after his torrid time with injuries.

IT COULD HAVE BEEN WORSE

From a winning position, Manchester City dropped two points. 2-0 up, at home, against a side that had played a tough game in Europe only three days earlier and any Premier League team should be able to see the game out. The biggest disappointment, though, was that it was a weekend when the club's closest rivals – Tottenham, Villa, Arsenal – all dropped points and City didn't take advantage. But... there are two sides to every story. The way I'm looking at this weekend's events is: *'well, it could have been worse'*.

This fixture with Fulham is one City have, classically, struggled with. In the 2005-06 season, City were winning 1-0 with a minute (plus added time) to go... and lost. A year later, City beat Fulham 3-1, but Fulham had two goals disallowed and were always threatening. And one of City's was a bit dodgy.

In the 2008-09 season, Fulham famously came back from a 2-0 half time deficit to win 3-2, and it was one of the games they needed to win to stay in the Premier League. Then last season, despite being a goal up, City could only muster a 3-1 defeat, much to my annoyance as it is (so far) the only home game they have lost in the whole of 2009.

City were poor, there's no getting away from that. If anything, they were perhaps a little fortunate to have been two goals in front when they were, but having gotten into that position, they should not have drawn the game.

But two soft goals later, and they had. This defence, compared to this time last season, has changed significantly. Starting against Stoke last season were: Hart, Richards, Dunne, Ben-Haim and Garrido. Only Richards is still at the club (though I hope we'll see Hart back here in a few seasons' time with a ton of Premier League experience) and he's not exactly been hitting the heights of form.

And all this isn't being disrespectful towards Fulham, either... the visitors would have been hard done to had they not had a point from the game. If anything, they shouldn't have found themselves two goals down. But, having gotten two goals to the good, I'd expect any team looking to finish in the top four to be able to see out the game and take all three points no matter their opposition. Though it does happen, it's not a hard and fast rule.

The point I'm trying to make is that one bad performance and a disappointing result doesn't make a season. Any top team drops points unexpectedly – who, aside from the most optimistic fans, thought Burnley would beat Manchester United? Having lost that game, did the wheels come off their season? Of course not.

City's coming games are all very winnable. So, City fans, instead of getting hung up over only a point gained, let's focus on taking maximum points from Birmingham, Burnley, Hull and, hopefully, Liverpool. The only way to show this league what we're made of, is to move on from disappointments and make sure those disappointments are few and far between.

October 2009 Breakdown

Games (all competitions):
Won: 1   **Drawn:** 3   **Lost:** 0

Goals (all competitions):
For: 9   **Against:** 5

Progress:
Premier League: 6th
League Cup: Qualified for Quarter Final
FA Cup: -

Premier League Table

		P	W	D	L	F	A	GD	Pts
4	Tottenham	11	6	1	4	21	17	+4	19
5	Liverpool	11	6	0	5	25	16	+9	18
6	**Manchester City**	**9**	**5**	**3**	**1**	**18**	**11**	**+7**	**18**
7	Aston Villa	10	5	3	2	14	9	+5	18
8	Sunderland	11	5	2	4	20	17	+3	17

November 2009

Birmingham City 0-0 Manchester City
FA Premier League
Sunday 1 November, 2009 - 16:00 KO

City: Given, Zabaleta, Lescott, Kompany, Bridge, Barry, de Jong (c) (Ireland 59), Bellamy, Wright-Phillips, Tevez, Santa Cruz (Petrov 66)
Unused: Taylor, Richards, Johnson, Sylvinho, Weiss
Goals: -
Booked: Bridge, Santa Cruz
Man of the Match: Shay Given

The home side started quickly. Benitez wriggled his way free and fired a shot through Kompany's legs as the Belgian attempted to close him down. Given, though, got the slightest of touches and forced it onto the post, leaving his defence to clear the danger.

Shortly after, Birmingham stand-in keeper Taylor struggled with a long range effort from Wright-Phillips and could only spoon it back into the box. His centre-backs, though, combined to clear before Santa Cruz could connect.

The first chance of the second half fell to Tevez, but his effort went well over the bar. De Jong was then harshly punished for handball in the area and the referee awarded a spot kick to the home side. But it was Given to the rescue, as he made a great save from the penalty to deny McFadden.

On 70 minutes, Bowyer fired a low cross into the City box and Zabaleta did tremendously well not to put it through his own goal as he cleared the danger from just in front of his own goalkeeper.

With five minutes left, Bridge made a run into the box and his shot was blocked by Johnson. The game had to be stopped for a bad injury to the defender, who looked like he was struggling to breathe after blocking the City full back's effort and colliding with one of his own players.

The last action, though, was a very silly and truly bizarre second yellow card for Birmingham's Ferguson, booked for handball, when he stopped Zabaleta from taking a throw-in midway in the City half by raising his hands to block the ball in.

Manchester City 3-3 Burnley
FA Premier League
Saturday 7 November, 2009 - 15:00 KO

City: Given, Zabaleta, Lescott, Toure (c), Bridge, Barry, Ireland, Bellamy, Wright-Phillips, Tevez (Petrov 75), Adebayor
Unused: Taylor, Richards, Johnson, Sylvinho, Weiss, de Jong
Goals: Wright-Phillips (42), Toure (54), Bellamy (57)

Booked: Bellamy
Man of the Match: Craig Bellamy

City struggled to get going and Burnley took full advantage. Mears fired in a point blank centre at Lescott and it appeared to strike his arm in front of his face, but the assistant referee was in no doubt and Alexander left Given with no chance from the spot. Burnley then punished the home side further. Eagles knocked the ball into the middle and Fletcher tapped in, with Given stranded.

But City were back in the game just before half time. Wright-Phillips had a pop from wide right and it flicked off ex-blue Jordan, curling around Jensen.

Barry took a second half free kick towards the back post, where Lescott was able to get a foot on the ball and divert it back across goal. There, City captain Toure was on hand to side-foot home and pull City back level.

Three minutes later, just before the hour mark, City took the lead. Ireland knocked the ball to Wright-Phillips, who fired in a low cross towards Tevez. It was behind the Argentine, but Bellamy was there to hammer the ball home.

Burnley were thankful to substitute Nugent as he used his thigh to clear the ball off the line to prevent a Carlisle own goal from a well hit Petrov corner.

And with two minutes to go, City were hit with a sucker punch. After having created the better chances of the half, and with Given having been much of a spectator for the latter stages of the game, Burnley found the net. Lescott lost the ball to Nugent too cheaply, who crossed for Fletcher to nod back into the box and McDonald slotted the ball past the despairing dive of Given.

Liverpool 2-2 Manchester City
FA Premier League
Saturday 21 November, 2009 - 12:45 KO

City: Given, Zabaleta, Lescott, Toure (c) (Onuoha 45), Bridge, Barry (Tevez 60), Ireland, de Jong, Bellamy, Wright-Phillips, Bellamy, Adebayor
Unused: Taylor, Johnson, Kompany, Weiss, Santa Cruz
Goals: Adebayor (68), Ireland (75)
Booked: -
Man of the Match: Stephen Ireland

Liverpool started on top. Gerrard fired a volley wide, before Bridge deflected a Kuyt shot around the post. Bellamy knocked the ball inside for Ireland, whose beautifully disguised step over let the pass reach Wright-Phillips but the little winger could only slice the ball wide from 18 yards.

The first action of the second half saw the home side take the lead. Zabaleta grabbed too much of N'Gog for Phil Dowd's liking and gave away a free kick on Liverpool's wide left. The ball was swung in by Gerrard and Skrtel lost Adebayor in the box to touch it past Given.

The goal, though, seemed to spur City on. Bellamy's superb corner delivery found Adebayor on the penalty spot. He'd lost Skrtel, roles reversed from the last set piece, and he nodded it down past Reina. City were on top and good value for their goal.

And, minutes later, City were ahead. The ball was fed into Wright-Phillips in the box and he wriggled away from the defender to fire across to Ireland. The Irishman was unmarked and couldn't miss.

But just as City would have wanted to keep it tight, Liverpool hit them straight back. N'Gog was given a second chance to volley and his shot deflected off Lescott, spinning across goal. Benayoun slid in to knock it home.

With a minute to go, Wright-Phillips saved City a point, when he got up on the back post ahead of Kyrgiakos to concede a corner, before Lucas could have won it for the home side, but his free header on the six-yard box was well wide.

Manchester City 1-1 Hull City

FA Premier League
Saturday 28 November, 2009 - 15:00 KO

City: Given, Richards, Lescott, Toure (c), Bridge, Ireland, de Jong, Robinho (Bellamy 75), Wright-Phillips, Tevez, Adebayor (Santa Cruz 67)
Unused: Taylor, Johnson, Onuoha, Kompany, Weiss,
Goals: Wright-Phillips (45+1)
Booked: de Jong
Man of the Match: Wayne Bridge

The game started with the home side the better. Robinho was close to scoring on his return from injury, as he cut inside from the left and, after turning McShane inside out, he fired a low effort at the back post. It was inches wide.

Tevez should have scored, after some neat play from Robinho, de Jong and Adebayor, but his one-on-one from the left side of the box was saved. With half an hour gone, Wright-Phillips hit the side netting with a cracking acrobatic volley – it just wouldn't go in for the home side.

But, just as the teams were preparing for the interval, Wright-Phillips gave City the lead. He had the ball on the edge of the box and decided to have a go. And, via a flick off Gardner's head, it beat Duke and found the net.

Five minutes into the second half and there was a scare for the home side. Garcia beat Given with his dinked shot, but Lescott was behind his goalkeeper to clear off the line, preserving the lead.

Some good work from Wright-Phillips in the Hull half saw him break into the box, but his pull back was just short of Adebayor and was intercepted. Making almost the same move two minutes later, he was unlucky not to have won a penalty, when Hunt appeared to pull him down.

With eight minutes to play, there was controversy. The referee indicated a foul by Toure on Vennegoor of Hesselink in the area, despite little contact. Nevertheless, the penalty was duly dispatched by Bullard, despite Given's hand.

It was another game City had dominated, but failed to take chances in.

It was City's seventh draw on the run, a new club record.

IS THERE A CASE FOR THE DEFENCE?

Goals haven't been so much of a problem for Manchester City this season. Well, they have, but not goals scored, anyway. It's the soft goals going in at the back that have been something of a problem. And for a defence that has a fair amount of Premier League experience and has cost what a good defence costs, it's beginning to concern me.

Okay, we're 11 Premier League games in and 11 games is no time for a team to click. Except, at the start of the season the defence looked solid: Clean sheets to Blackburn at Ewood Park, Wolves at Eastlands, Crystal Palace at Selhurst Park, and Portsmouth at Fratton Park saw a month of fixtures when a first team defence looked faultless.

But, as the season has worn on, a few mistakes have crept in to the game. Lescott dived in at van Persie for Arsenal's equaliser and, then, after we had fought to get back in front and extend the lead for the emphatic 4-1 scoreline, the back four switched off totally and conceded a late consolation. And even that nearly became an edge of the seat job as van Persie hit the post in stoppage time.

We then went to Old Trafford and played well. But, while Sir Alex may bang on about City's goals being terrible defensive errors, I look at United's and see mistakes of our own. Switching off from a throw-in, while Richards berates Toure... failing to put up a challenge for two headers in the six-yard box is criminal... leaving Michael Owen – injury prone or not – time to turn and shoot in the box is even more criminal.

Then, a couple of weeks ago, City let a two goal lead slip to Fulham. No matter what team you play in the Premier League (or any league for that matter), you should not let a two goal lead slip and not be disappointed. Even the goal conceded against Scunthorpe didn't cover anybody in glory, as de Jong gave it away, and Lescott didn't cut the cross out leaving Kompany stranded.

But how can a back four go from looking solid to looking so shaky in the space of a couple of months? I don't for a moment profess to have the answers, but I do have a few thoughts.

Lescott, for example, has looked nothing like the player he was at Everton. But £22m is a lot of money and to know that you cost that much and have been wanted for so long by a manager willing to spend that much money, then it can go one of two ways: It could boost your ego and you could have the feeling of being unbeatable. Or it could have, as I think might have happened here, put a lot of pressure on Lescott to perform immediately and the harder he tries to make it work, the more things go wrong for him.

We have seen that he is a great defender at Everton, but he's far from that man at City and, in my opinion, he needs to relax. He needs to calm down and focus on what he can do, and not try to impress and put in that amazing sliding tackle when it perhaps isn't on. We've seen his ability in the air, but that's no use if his man has gotten away from him, a la Dempsey against Fulham.

Then there's Micah Richards, who has been dropped recently, but started the season as part of that solid defence. His positioning has been questionable at times and he seems to be nothing like the player that broke into the first team a few years ago or even the player that started the season under Sven.

It's almost as if he doesn't know where he is supposed to be, but to have played Premier League football for as long as he has now, and to have started for England, surely that can't be the case? I'd like to think he's just in bad form, but this is bad form that's been with him for almost 18 months.

He can tackle; we've seen his ability to do that. He can beat most players in a head-to-head sprint. He can get up in the air and head the ball with power. But it's his position that lets him down – if he can hold his position, then he'd be easily be in contention for an England place.

Wayne Bridge: he's possibly the most improved player for City in comparison to last season. Last season he looked like a rabbit in the headlights far too much and this season he's been blocking crosses, making inch perfect tackles and getting down the line.

But, along with Pablo Zabaleta – who has come in for Richards – I wonder if there's too much emphasis being made on getting forward to help Wright-Phillips or Bellamy/Petrov? I mean, looking at Burnley's second goal, as Barry gave the ball away, Bridge was one of the players furthest forward…

Even Toure hasn't looked that solid since his injury, but I suspect that's because he's still not fully fit. Kompany is coming back from injury too, and looked a bit uncomfortable in the 0-0 with Birmingham. Onuoha hasn't yet had a look in, partly because of injury, but he was solid at the end of last season.

The team has shown that it can score goals – four against Arsenal and three at Old Trafford speak for themselves. But what I worry about is, on the days that the strike force has an off-day (just like when visiting St. Andrews), what if the defence give away another sloppy goal?

A lot of City's conceded goals this season could have been prevented. There's nothing we can do about them now, but what we can do is learn from mistakes and not make them in the future. But that doesn't seem to be happening and it's something the team needs to sort quickly if they've any ambitions of unseating Liverpool.

This season is perhaps the best chance to do that: Liverpool are struggling to pick up points at the moment, but that won't last forever. We have to make the best of their bad recent form.

November 2009 Breakdown

<u>Games (all competitions):</u>
Won: 0   **Drawn:** 4   **Lost:** 0

<u>Goals (all competitions):</u>
For: 6   **Against:** 6

<u>Progress:</u>
Premier League: 7th
League Cup: Qualified for Quarter Final
FA Cup: -

<u>Premier League Table</u>

		P	W	D	L	F	A	GD	Pts
5	Liverpool	14	7	2	5	31	20	+11	23
6	Aston Villa	14	6	5	3	22	14	+8	23
7	**Manchester City**	**13**	**5**	**7**	**1**	**24**	**17**	**+7**	**22**
8	Sunderland	14	6	2	6	21	20	+1	20
9	Stoke City	14	5	5	4	13	15	-2	20

December 2009

Manchester City 3-0 Arsenal
League Cup Quarter Final
Wednesday 2 December, 2009 - 19:45 KO

City: Given, Richards, Lescott, Toure (c), Bridge, Wright-Phillips (Weiss 77), Ireland, Barry, Bellamy, Adebayor, Tevez (Kompany 74)
Unused: Taylor, Onuoha, Johnson, Santa Cruz, Robinho
Goals: Tevez (49), Wright-Phillips (69), Weiss (89)
Booked: Bellamy, Kompany
Man of the Match: Craig Bellamy

The first action of the game saw Barry take a right wing corner towards the former Arsenal man Adebayor. From his powerful header, Fabianski had to save and hold, with Lescott closing in for the rebound.

With 23 minutes on the clock, Vela spurned Arsenal's best chance, firing over the bar under pressure from Lescott from eight yards, before Tevez brought a decent save out of Fabianski after running from the half-way line.

The second half saw City take the lead. Good work by Bellamy and Tevez saw the Argentine emerge with the ball on the left. He stepped inside, around two challenges and fired towards the top corner. Leaving Fabianski stranded, the ball cannoned in off the underside of the bar.

Soon after, Bellamy bolted out of the midfield to chase onto a Lescott clearing header and squared for an unmarked Adebayor, but Fabianski did enough to make sure that he fired over on the stretch.

On 68 minutes, Wright-Phillips doubled City's lead. He broke with the ball and on the corner of the box, fired a vicious drive straight into the top corner.

In the closing stages, City sealed the game. Bellamy held up the ball on the half-way line, waiting for the Arsenal challenge. When it came, he skipped through two men to go through, before finding Weiss for his first goal in a blue shirt. It was in off the crossbar and he rounded off an excellent night for City.

Manchester City 2-1 Chelsea
FA Premier League
Saturday 5 December, 2009 - 17:30 KO

City: Given, Richards (Onuoha 69), Lescott, Toure (c), Bridge (Kompany 76), Barry, de Jong, Robinho (Zabaleta 90), Wright-Phillips, Tevez, Adebayor
Unused: Taylor, Johnson, Petrov, Santa Cruz
Goals: Adebayor (36), Tevez (55)
Booked: Barry
Man of the Match: Nigel de Jong

It all looked to be going wrong for the home side after just 10 minutes. Given first saved brilliantly from Drogba, before Chelsea won a dubious corner. Drogba had a go, but it was saved by Given. Anelka hit the rebound and City were unlucky to see the keeper's save bounce into the net off Adebayor.

From a corner after 36 minutes, City pulled level. The ball was driven in from the edge by Wright-Phillips and a spot of pinball left Adebayor with a tap-in. Chelsea wanted a handball by Richards, but the referee said no.

On the stroke of half time, City had a scare. A Drogba free kick on the edge of the box flashed by Given's post, with the Irish keeper throwing himself at it.

The second half began very cagily. Carvalho was booked for kicking Tevez in the back as the two challenged for a header. It proved costly, as the Argentinian put the resulting free kick into the back of the net, low around Cech's wall.

With six minutes to go, Chelsea were awarded a penalty. Onuoha caught Drogba in the box, after the City man had lost him on a cross, and there was no doubt about it. Up stepped Lampard, who rarely missed a spot kick, but Given saved low to his right, with de Jong completing the clearance.

With two minutes to go, Drogba was through on goal and did everything but score, sliding the ball wide of the goal when he should have found the net.

Bolton Wanderers 3-3 Manchester City
FA Premier League
Saturday 12 December, 2009 - 15:00 KO

City: Given, Richards, Lescott, Toure (c), Sylvinho, Barry, Kompany (Robinho 72), Bellamy, Wright-Phillips (Ireland 20), Tevez, Adebayor (Santa Cruz 81)
Unused: Taylor, Onuoha, Zabaleta, Petrov
Goals: Tevez (27, 76), Richards (45)
Booked: Sylvinho, Bellamy
Sent Off: Bellamy
Man of the Match: Carlos Tevez

City got off to a poor start: With 12 minutes gone, Lee had a shot deflected off Sylvinho and it fell to Klasnic, who couldn't miss from a yard out. But it was a bad decision to award the goal – Klasnic was a yard offside.

Cohen tried to double Bolton's lead with an overhead kick from inside the six-yard box, but it flew over the bar, with Given helpless. Jaaskelainen saved well from Tevez, but nobody was there to follow up and put the rebound in.

With just under half an hour gone, City did pull level. A Bellamy cross was half cleared and Tevez put it in - via a deflection - from the edge of the area.

But then, as City looked most likely to take the lead, the home side did exactly that. Cahill lost the ball under his feet on the edge of the City box, but managed to get it under control before the defence could recover and he put a peach of a shot past Given, leaving the keeper with no chance.

But City were able to respond immediately. Some neat play from Bellamy and Adebayor sent Richards through and the full back finished like a striker, beating Jaaskelainen at his near post.

Ten minutes into the second half, Bolton struck again. Klasnic beat Lescott to the ball and volleyed straight past Given, before the City keeper could react.

Robinson clearly fouled Bellamy, but the referee thought otherwise and gave the City frontman his second yellow card for diving... leaving both Bellamy and his manager mystified.

With 15 minutes to go, Bolton substitute Elmander should have done better when he was free at the back post, but his cut back was nodded behind by Toure and City got the corner clear.

Then, with just over 10 minutes to go, Tevez fired a shot straight past Jaaskelainen from the left side of the box. It beat the Bolton keeper, finding the bottom corner and the visitors were back on terms.

Tottenham Hotspur 3-0 Manchester City
FA Premier League
Wednesday 16 December, 2009 - 20:00 KO

City: Given, Richards, Onuoha, Toure (c), Sylvinho, Barry, Ireland, de Jong (Petrov 71), Robinho (Santa Cruz 59), Tevez, Adebayor
Unused: Taylor, Zabaleta, Weiss, Kompany, Benjani
Goals: -
Booked: Sylvinho, de Jong, Tevez
Man of the Match: Stephen Ireland

The game never really got started and, with 20 minutes gone, a bad back-header by Barry nearly let Defoe in to open the scoring, but Toure and Onuoha were there to clear the danger.

Just before half time, Spurs found the breakthrough. A Defoe shot was blocked by Ireland from close range and the rebound fell to Kranjcar, who tapped the ball in, with Given helpless after reacting to the first shot.

Shortly before the hour mark, the hosts doubled their lead. A free kick given against Adebayor was pumped long by Gomes, where a flick on from Crouch left Defoe to toe-poke into the roof of the net. It was too easy.

With 70 minutes on the clock, Adebayor had a great chance to pull a goal back, but his effort from the edge of the box was over the bar and it didn't look like it was going to be City's night.

Two minutes from time, Gomes punched away a Petrov free kick after Tevez was felled on the edge of the box, before Santa Cruz was astonished that the officials missed a handball back to his keeper by Dawson.

Kranjcar added insult to injury, rounding off the scoring in the final minute of added time, toe-poking through Given's legs.

Manchester City 4-3 Sunderland

FA Premier League

Saturday 19 December, 2009 - 15:00 KO

City: Given, Richards (Zabaleta 22), Onuoha, Toure (c), Sylvinho, Barry, Ireland, Wright-Phillips (Kompany 53), Bellamy (Petrov 86), Tevez, Santa Cruz
Unused: Taylor, Adebayor, Weiss, Robinho
Goals: Santa Cruz (3, 69), Tevez (pen 11), Bellamy (34)
Booked: Zabaleta, Given
Man of the Match: Craig Bellamy

Mark Hughes dropped two of his big names, Robinho and Adebayor, after their no-show performances at White Hart Lane, showing his displeasure in a bold move to motivate the team.

And it was a great start for the home side, with Bellamy reaching the by-line and crossing low for Santa Cruz to knock home inside three minutes, leaving the defence and goalkeeper stranded and putting City ahead.

Eight minutes were on the clock when City got the chance for their second. Bellamy was bundled over in the box as he tried to cut inside and, after a delay while the referee cut out any encroaching, Tevez slotted the penalty away.

It should have been an easy task for City to go on to win from this position. But is that ever the case? Sunderland got themselves back into the game with two quick corners – the second being their most dangerous, as Mensah was gifted a free header and found the net.

Sunderland continued to press and got their reward in the 25th minute. City failed to clear another corner from the visitors and, after everybody missed it, Henderson smashed it in from 10 yards to make it 2-2.

But, 10 minutes later, City were back in front. Zabaleta chipped the ball over the Sunderland defence for Wright-Phillips, who checked back superbly and crossed low into the box. Santa Cruz left it and Bellamy smashed it into the net.

However, Sunderland pulled level once again. Given cleared out of play and, after a delay for an injury, the throw in was taken and a low cross into the box was met by Jones, who found the net.

On 68 minutes, City were back in front once again. The ball broke for Barry in the box and his cut-back past Fulop left Santa Cruz with the easiest of finishes, getting his second and City's fourth of the game.

As the game moved into stoppage time, Turner clashed with Barry in challenging for a header and caught him with a flailing arm. The referee produced a straight red and sent the Sunderland defender for an early bath.

It turned out to be City's last win with Mark Hughes in charge, with the City manager waving a goodbye to the fans at the end of the game, as news broke that he had been sacked in favour of Roberto Mancini.

Manchester City 2-0 Stoke City

FA Premier League

Saturday 26 December, 2009 - 15:00 KO

City: Given, Zabaleta, Kompany, Toure (c), Sylvinho (Richards 65), de Jong, Barry, Ireland, Petrov, Robinho (Bellamy 69), Tevez (Garrido 89)
Unused: Taylor, Vidal, Weiss, Boyata
Goals: Petrov (27), Tevez (45+2)
Booked: -
Man of the Match: Pablo Zabaleta

Roberto Mancini's first game in charge got off to a very slow start. On 21 minutes, Given pulled off a fantastic save to keep the scores level. Tuncay broke into the box and was one-on-one, but his fierce shot was well blocked.

City took the lead after 27 minutes. Ireland and Tevez combined well on the left side, with the latter then breaking into the box and knocking it square to Robinho. The Brazilian's mis-hit shot fell straight into the path of Petrov, who slotted home with his right peg from a yard out.

Just before half time, Petrov had the chance to double his goal tally for the game, but the low, driven cross fell to his right foot and he sliced it well over and well wide of the visitors' goal.

As the teams were preparing to go in at 1-0, City doubled their lead. Zabaleta crossed from deep and found the head of Barry, who nodded the ball towards goal. It was an effort on goal and would have been a simple save for Sorensen, were it not for Tevez in the six-yard box. The Argentinian got his studs on the effort and flicked it past the Stoke keeper.

In the opening seconds of the second half, City could have been three goals to the good. Robinho broke into the box, but the ball was cleared after a bad touch. It fell straight to Petrov, who hit it first time and it need a great double save from Sorensen to keep it out.

With nine minutes to go, Bellamy was denied a penalty when it looked like Huth brought him down. But because the forward tried to keep his feet and got away a somewhat hindered shot, the referee said no.

Wolverhampton Wanderers 0-3 Manchester City

FA Premier League

Monday 28 December, 2009 - 19:45 KO

City: Given, Richards, Kompany, Toure (c), Zabaleta, de Jong, Barry, Ireland (Garrido 55), Petrov (Robinho 85), Bellamy, Tevez (Sylvinho 90+2)
Unused: Taylor, Weiss, Vidal, Boyata
Goals: Tevez (33, 85), Garrido (68)

Booked: Zabaleta, Tevez
Man of the Match: Carlos Tevez

The game opened with Wolves pressure. Given was called into action to make a fine save from a long, driven shot from Henry. It was bending away from the Irishman, who got down well to hold.

Just before the half hour, Tevez screwed a shot well wide of the goal after some neat play from Bellamy, before the Welshman should have given City the lead, but he volleyed the ball over from inside the six-yard box. It seemed easier to score.

But then City did take the lead, thanks to a deflection on a Tevez effort and the little Argentinian had his seventh goal in as many games. Bellamy crossed and the forward scuffed his shot, but it hit Berra and sent Hahnemann the wrong way. It was a stroke of luck, but City had gotten themselves on top.

Wolves had the first chance of the second half, as Henry hit the ball over the bar from the edge of the box. City should have doubled their lead seconds later, after Petrov's excellent pass sent Bellamy through, but he could only poke the ball wide.

City then added their second from an unlikely source. Mancienne bodychecked Barry and, from the resulting free kick, Garrido curled the ball around the wall and into the net, leaving Hahnemann standing.

City should have made it three soon after, as some fantastic one-touch football produced the move of the match, with Petrov finding Bellamy. He, in turn, found Tevez, who tried to chip Hahnemann, but it landed just wide. Had it gone in, it would have been one of the goals of the season.

Robinho then joined the action and will have done his case for a place in the starting line-up no harm when he crossed for Tevez to double his tally and score City's third. The Brazilian fired it in low to the Argentinian's feet and he skipped to the left and fired it into the bottom corner.

A solid start for Roberto Mancini.

KEEPING A COOL HEAD

"Handball!" roughly three thousand Chelsea fans screamed a second or so before Emmanuel Adebayor slotted the ball just inside the post, beating Petr Cech for the first time in over eight Premier League hours. The Chelsea captain, John Terry, proceeded to remonstrate with referee Howard Webb while the home players celebrated. But did those three thousand or so have a point?

As Petr Cech punched the left wing corner away, the ball fell to Shaun Wright-Phillips, who drilled it back into the box. His shot slammed into Micah Richards' right arm, which was in front of his stomach as he made an action, turning away, to try and avoid the blast. He couldn't, the ball hit his hand and fell to Adebayor, who promptly found the net.

Surely an infringement?

Well, I wouldn't be so quick to call Howard Webb's judgement on the award of that goal. First off, if it is an infringement, it could be seen as a slice of luck in City's favour, which balances out the slice of luck that went in Chelsea's favour – the award of the corner that should clearly have been a goal kick from which the visitors scored.

Then again, according to the official FIFA laws of the game, the referee at the City of Manchester Stadium got the decision correct. Law 12, Fouls and Misconduct, is what referees judge handball on and it says that a player is only guilty of handball when "handling the ball deliberately (except for the goalkeeper within his own penalty area)." And, when looking back at the contact between Micah Richards' arm and the ball (specifically the pace of the ball), the player's body motion, and the positions of his arms, it certainly wasn't deliberate and, therefore, could not have been handball.

Now, as a Manchester City fan, of course I'm going to be biased in this instance. Whether or not the rules are correct is a different matter; after all, few players will intentionally handle the ball when attacking (except for maybe a certain Argentinian or Frenchman), so that would surely mean the most blatant, yet accidental of handballs should go unpunished: Nigel de Jong didn't mean to handle the ball against Birmingham in the box a few weeks back, but his arms were above his head when the ball struck them. It wasn't intentional, so, strictly speaking, the penalty shouldn't be given. But, realistically, you have to ask why his hands were there in the first place; accidental, but it would surely be unreasonable to ignore it.

So, perhaps the handball rule shouldn't be decided upon by intent, but reasonability. If a player's hands are by his sides and the ball strikes them, I'd say it would be reasonable to play on, if accidental. But if his hands are over his head and the ball accidentally strikes them, it would be unreasonable for his hands to be there and, as such, unreasonable not to award the foul.

But, either way, punishing Richards would have been harsh. And wrong.

It was this incident that showed why Chelsea lost the game and City won it. The difference in attitude between the teams when something happened that they believe went against them was clear. Chelsea chased the referee screaming

"Handball!" and lost their heads, while City set-up (albeit badly) to defend the wrongfully awarded corner and got on with the game.

But, for the rest of the match, Chelsea seemed to feel that they were being harshly done to with every decision – each foul against them was hotly contested; met with a reaction that suggested the call was unjust. It was as if they had convinced themselves they were fighting an uphill battle, when in fact they weren't. Had the visiting players kept their cool, I'd have thought they would have been able to come back at City, instead of losing it and blaming the ref.

Then came the award of the free kick for City, from which Tevez scored the winner (with 35 minutes and a missed penalty still to go to recover, I might add). Carvalho was the 'victim' of a bad decision because he won the ball, right?

Wrong.

Just because a player wins the ball, it doesn't give him licence to stud another player in the back. Carvalho wasn't penalised for a high boot, otherwise Tevez's free kick would have been indirect and it wasn't. He was penalised because he kicked an opponent, which is an offence resulting in a direct free kick.

The Chelsea fans, players and manager all said it was an incorrect decision because it was part of Carvalho's follow through and Tevez jumped into him. But it just wasn't, as I saw it. I think that the Chelsea centre-back knew exactly what he was doing; after making contact with the ball, his leg extended towards the City player in an entirely separate movement to the one in which he played the ball and he planted his foot in his back intentionally.

You could argue that Tevez jumping into Carvalho was a foul against Chelsea and there would be a case for that. But, as Graham Poll noted on Monday, when two simultaneous offences occur together, the more serious one is punished – in this case Carvalho's. And, to be honest, I'd be looking more at the non-save by Petr Cech than the decision in itself, because he didn't cover himself in glory from the not-so-fantastic shot that beat him.

John Terry also complained that he wasn't given a penalty for Lescott hauling him to the ground. I actually think it's a bit rich coming from the man who man-handles attackers when defending corners in exactly the same manner as Lescott did. And that's ignoring the fact that Terry was fouling Lescott (holding his shirt and pulling his neck) just as much as Lescott was Terry (holding his shoulder and pulling his shirt): Six of one and half a dozen of the other is the phrase.

Now then, on to the penalty save. I don't really have much defence on this one – Given was off his line as the penalty was taken and it should, therefore, be retaken. It wasn't and 99% of others where this happens aren't either, so if the referee punished Given all other referees should punish every other goalkeeper that has, does and will do it, too. You can't punish one and not another, so I assume Chelsea will be complaining next time Cech saves a penalty when starting off his line? Obviously not. But, if Given had been punished, you could guarantee they'd complain if Cech was punished in the same way.

The one thing that struck me about the match was the canny tactics by Mark

Hughes. Leaving Robinho on the pitch until the 90th minute was a brave move – he's just back from injury and not at full fitness, so it was natural he'd be tired, if not burnt out, by then. But by leaving him on the pitch, it meant that Ivanovic couldn't leave him alone on the halfway line and push forward; it's suicidal to give Robinho that much time and space, tired or not. And with Wright-Phillips being dogged on the other side, Cole's movements forward were restricted too.

It forced Chelsea through the middle and right down the throat of the man of the match, Nigel de Jong, as well as, later on, the equally solid and dependable, Vincent Kompany.

City were back at their best and put in, perhaps, their best performance of the season. It was nail-biting, but it was good to see. The team didn't sit back on a one goal lead and invite pressure, they pushed forward and tried to get the (as it turned out, not-needed) third goal, before defending stoutly during the final onslaught in the last 10 minutes. I'm glad to see that the team got what they deserved, despite Chelsea's grievances.

Sometimes it's all too easy to blame a referee for a defeat or the concession of a goal, when the problems are players losing their heads, not performing to their best or making mistakes. In fact, the refereeing decisions can be quite a convenient excuse that can paper over the cracks of a poor performance.

Chelsea didn't lose because of the referee. They lost because they didn't take their chances and City did; they lost their cool, while City didn't. Over the entire game, City were the better team and deserved their victory.

THE ITALIAN JOB

When it happened on Saturday, I couldn't really put my feelings into words. But being somebody who commentates on a lot of the goings on at Manchester City, I knew that the sacking of Mark Hughes and the appointment of Roberto Mancini was something that I couldn't ignore. But as I sat down on Saturday evening, nothing came from my keyboard and I found I was browsing Facebook, using Windows Live Messenger and Tweeting more than I do normally.

So, I thought I'd try again on Sunday. And again, nothing happened. Microsoft Word remained well and truly Microsoft Wordless.

And then it occurred to me why I was finding it so difficult to put my feelings down in an article such as this one. It was because it was something I didn't have any strong feelings on either way – unlike with topics such as Jeremy Clarkson, self-service checkouts or the BNP, I wasn't motivated to put pen to paper. Or finger to keyboard. Or whatever the modern day equivalent of that saying is.

I'm just struggling to actually have an opinion on this. Don't get me wrong, I was in favour of Mark Hughes keeping his position, but I wasn't completely shocked to hear the news that he had been sacked. He wasn't sacked for losing games, but rather for not winning them; a return of eight draws in 17 games didn't do him any favours, especially when they were coming against teams City should be beating if they have any ambition of a top four finish – Burnley, Hull, Birmingham, Bolton… and for a team with such aspirations to need to score three against Bolton and Burnley just to get a point, it's quite disappointing.

See, part of my problem is that I have no prior knowledge about Roberto Mancini. I'm sorry if that seems absurd, but it's the truth – I have no real interest in Italian football and he's spent a large portion of his career (ie. all of it except four games) over there. For me, Italian football is very much like Lily Allen's music; I know it exists and a lot of people like it, but I've never actually gone looking for it because I tend to find it quite dull.

All I know about Mancini is that he used to manage Inter Milan and spent a bit of time at Leicester City when they weren't hanging around the second division or whatever it's called this season, but apart from that I've only got Wikipedia to go off. And Wikipedia once told me Titus Bramble was attracting the attention of Barcelona to the tune of £100m after being voted World Player of the Year… and I didn't make that up.

It seems he won a few honours in Italy – the cup with Fiorentina, Lazio and Inter Milan. Along with the league title three times with the latter, as well. Which, if anything, must bode well for City's upcoming League Cup semi final with Manchester United. And, yes, I suppose that's more than "a few honours in Italy".

But are those statistics slightly skewed? A bit of reading around the subject tells me that the first title was won by default; Juventus originally won the league, but it later became clear that the results of several games could have been handed to the newswires before they had actually kicked off. Inter Milan were simply the highest placed team after points deductions.

Though the following season, all that was immaterial. Inter went on a massive winning streak and the points deductions of rivals (Lazio lost three points, AC Milan eight points, Reggina 11 points, Fiorentina 15 points, while Juventus were relegated to Serie B) weren't influential in the outcome of the season. Inter finished an enormous 22 points ahead of second placed Roma and 36 points ahead of city rivals AC Milan.

I wouldn't grumble about that.

Though I won't be expecting us to finish 36 points ahead of Manchester United just yet. Give it a season or two, though… not that I'm setting my sights too high, naturally.

What might be something to grumble about is the manner in which the managerial change has been conducted. It's been floating around the press for a while that Mark Hughes hasn't been far from the sack, but for it to have been announced directly after a 4-3 victory and a wave goodbye to the crowd suggests that the decision had been made some time ago and Hughes himself knew before the match kicked off. Whether he had been told in an official capacity or not is unclear, especially after his statement to the press on Sunday, but as he left the pitch he certainly looked like he was well aware that he wouldn't be taking another training session.

But, some would argue that City have never been good at sacking managers.

I'm just not sure I see the logic in swapping a manager who is untried and unproven at the top level in England for a manager who is untried and unproven at the top level in England. Especially when the club isn't yet at the top level in England.

Don't get me wrong, I'm as fickle as the next football fan and when success comes to City – be it with Mancini with Hughes' players, Mancini with his own players, whoever takes over from the new man, or whoever takes over from whoever takes over from the new man, using whatever players are still around from any scenario I've painted in this rather long and unnecessary paragraph – I'll be as happy as a man who's just discovered that his 4.00pm meeting on a Friday has been cancelled.

I suppose I just feel a bit sorry for Mark Hughes, who was on course for what a lot of City fans would have seen as a successful season – a top six finish and a cup win. Ok, neither is guaranteed, but with two cup games against Manchester United coming up and their unease at using first team players for the competition, and with a game in hand while already sitting in sixth position, both outcomes were, and still are, certainly possible.

But I suppose the biggest reason why this article has been totally underwhelming is, when it comes down to it, what's done is done. Mark Hughes has been sacked, Roberto Mancini is the manager, Manchester City is my football club and I'll be cheering them come rain, snow, sleet, hail, or shine next Saturday.

Forza Mancini. A new chapter begins.

THE KOMPANY THAT MANCINI KEEPS

The biggest and most notable change in City in the last two games is how much more solid the defence has looked. It recent weeks it's been about as stable as a toddler taking their first steps on a high piece of scaffolding balanced precariously on several plates of jelly standing unsecured on a mound of ball bearings. In a wind tunnel. During an earthquake.

The point is, it's been shaky. And, more importantly, it's been leaking goals easily and more frequently than a government department can leak personal details. And sometimes government departments can't half leak them quickly.

I'm not entirely convinced if it's been through merit that he's been picked or if the situation has been a lack of match-fit players, but since Mr. Mancini arrived there's been a big Belgian at the back for City, who had previously been overlooked in favour of two summer signings as the centre-back pairing.

And before Mancini took charge, City's last clean sheet in the league came against Birmingham. Before Mancini took charge, that was Vincent Kompany's last start in the centre of defence. In the league, the Lescott and Toure partnership has produced just one clean sheet. Back in August.

That's not to say that Lescott and Toure are bad players. What it is to say is that something was clearly not working at the heart of City's defence and that pairing had conceded 20 goals in 11 games, which, let's face it, is rubbish.

And from what I saw of him last season – bearing in mind he played most of the campaign injured and played well despite that – I think Kompany should be battling with Lescott and Toure for one of those centre-back positions, especially since Nigel de Jong is going from strength to strength in the middle of the pitch. Not only does he look assured and comfortable on the ball, but he brings to the defence confidence and leadership.

And a six foot four, 13 stone frame that doesn't shirk away from a challenge.

The defence needed to be tightened; that was one of Mancini's first jobs. There have been far too many games this season where it's looked like all the opposition have to do is send the ball into City's box and it would cause the red alert alarms to sound, panic to spread, arms to be waved around like crazy and, soon enough, a goal be scored. But in the space of two games, the new manager has kept two clean sheets and not had one moment of tension in the City box from a cross or long ball and, personally, I think that this has happened when Kompany has started has been no coincidence.

Having lost his place in midfield through a combination of injury and the subsequent top quality form of de Jong, Kompany now being available to play at the centre of defence is like having a new signing. With his eagerness to get his head on every cross coming in, his willingness to throw himself in front of the ball, his bravery to go in for a tackle when he knows he might get hurt and that odd swagger he has when he's just crunched an opposition player in winning the ball (fairly, too), he should be staking a claim for a regular place at centre-back.

December 2009 Breakdown

Games (all competitions):
Won: 5   **Drawn:** 1   **Lost:** 1

Goals (all competitions):
For: 17   **Against:** 10

Progress:
Premier League: 5th
League Cup: Qualified for Semi Final
FA Cup: -

Premier League Table

		P	W	D	L	F	A	GD	Pts
3	Arsenal	19	13	2	4	51	21	+30	41
4	Tottenham Hotspur	20	11	4	5	42	22	+20	37
5	**Manchester City**	**19**	**9**	**8**	**2**	**38**	**27**	**+11**	**35**
6	Aston Villa	20	10	5	5	29	18	+11	35
7	Liverpool	20	10	3	7	37	25	+12	33

January 2010

Middlesbrough 0-1 Manchester City

FA Cup Third Round

Saturday 2 January, 2010 - 15:00 KO

City: Given (c), Richards (Barry 45), Kompany, Boyata, Sylvinho, de Jong (Tevez 45), Zabaleta, Garrido, Petrov, Weiss (Bellamy 73), Benjani
Unused: Taylor, Vidal, Trippier, Tutte
Goals: Benjani (45)
Booked: Garrido, Barry
Man of the Match: Vincent Kompany

With the snow falling heavily, the game got off to a very slow start. From the first corner of the match, City caused havoc in the Middlesbrough penalty area, when Kompany and Boyata both challenged for headers, though the defence were able to clear. It fell to Zabaleta on the edge of the box, his first effort was blocked and his second looked destined for the back of the net before it hit the defender and dropped wide.

The home side then should have done better when Wheater nodded a free kick back into the box and Boyata cleared, before the young Belgian put in an excellent tackle to deny Emnes.

With 40 minutes on the clock, Petrov had an excellent chance to give the visitors the lead, but his right foot shot curled wide of Coyne's post. Then, just as it looked like the sides would go in all square, Petrov ran at the Middlesbrough defence and slipped Benjani in. He made no mistake and slotted the ball calmly past keeper and into the back of the net.

The first action of the second half saw O'Neil booked for a blatant dive in the area, before Tevez had an effort that needed a comfortable save from the Middlesbrough keeper from just inside the box.

Kompany pulled off a great saving header to clear an effort off the line with 15 minutes to go, before Williams skied the rebound as the home side looked for an equaliser.

It wasn't the best performance of City's season, but they got the job done in difficult conditions and they made it three wins and three clean sheets in three games for Roberto Mancini.

Manchester City 4-1 Blackburn Rovers

FA Premier League

Monday 11 January, 2010 - 20:00 KO

City: Given (c), Garrido, Richards, Kompany, Zabaleta, de Jong, Barry, Petrov (Boyata 87), Bellamy (Robinho 69), Tevez, Benjani (Santa Cruz 81)
Unused: Taylor, Sylvinho, Wright-Phillips, Ibrahim

Goals: Tevez (6, 48, 90+1), Richards (39)
Booked: Zabaleta
Man of the Match: Carlos Tevez

City started the game on the front foot, with Tevez, workmanlike as ever, forcing a corner in the opening minute. Blackburn managed to clear, but they were soon architects of their own downfall as Samba needlessly nodded the ball behind, under pressure from Benjani. From that corner, Petrov aimed at the front post and Robinson flapped, dropping the ball to Benjani. The Zimbabwean smashed back towards goal, past Robinson and Tevez was on hand to turn the ball home with his knee.

But then the game became scrappy. That was until Richards took it by the scruff of the neck. He won the ball mid-way into his own half and carried it 80 yards, before sending Benjani through. The Zimbabwean's first time shot beat Robinson, but not the post, though Richards had carried on his run to get there first and guide it into the net.

The first real action of the second half was the goal that put the game beyond doubt. The ball broke for Benjani on the right wing and he got his head up and knocked it inside to Petrov. The Bulgarian couldn't connect, but Tevez was behind him to finish with a superb curling effort, straight into the top corner.

With an hour gone, Tevez should have had his hat-trick, after Zabaleta swung a left-footed ball straight onto his head, while he was unmarked on the edge of the six-yard box. Somehow, though, the little Argentinian nodded the ball past Robinson and past the far post and straight to the nearby ball boy.

N'Zonzi shouldered the ball well wide of the goal from six yards out, after Given was caught in no man's land, before Pedersen grabbed an unlikely goal for the visitors, giving them some brief hope of a comeback.

Tevez then managed to get his first Premier League hat-trick, as Robinho picked him out on the edge of the box and he was able to turn. With no backlift, he curled the ball around Robinson and into the corner of the net.

Everton 2-0 Manchester City
FA Premier League
Saturday 16 January, 2010 - 17:30 KO

City: Given (c), Garrido, Richards, Kompany, Zabaleta, de Jong, Barry, Petrov (Benjani 45), Bellamy, Tevez, Santa Cruz (Robinho 9 (Wright-Phillips 61))
Unused: Taylor, Sylvinho, Onuoha, Boyata
Goals: -
Booked: -
Man of the Match: Shay Given

Petrov had City's first effort on target, with a shot from range after cutting in from the right and curling it towards the far post. Howard could only parry, but Tevez couldn't get to the rebound first and it was cleared. City then lost Santa Cruz to injury. Robinho should have given City the lead after 14 minutes, when a quick throw-in from Petrov was whipped into the box and flicked on to the Brazilian by Tevez, but he volleyed over from eight yards.

After 36 minutes, Pienaar put Everton ahead. A soft free kick given away by Zabaleta on the edge of the box was punished, as the Everton winger curled the ball over the wall and into Given's near post. And it had been coming.

The pressure didn't stop there. City were struggling to get any foothold into the game and Bilyaletdinov nearly hit the visitors further, but his effort was inches over the bar from a Cahill flick. City then conceded a penalty for a Richards shirt pull. Saha took it and scored, putting Everton into pole position.

In the second half, City were fortunate to escape conceding a third when Bilyaletdinov flicked on a corner that was cheaply given away by Richards, before Kompany was in place to block an effort from the edge of the box. Cahill then hit the bar shortly after, with Given beaten.

City just never turned up.

Manchester City 2-1 Manchester United
League Cup Semi Final, First Leg
Tuesday 19 January, 2010 - 20:00 KO

City: Given (c), Richards, Kompany, Boyata (Onuoha 69), Garrido, Barry, de Jong, Zabaleta, Bellamy, Wright-Phillips (Sylvinho 84), Tevez (Benjani 79)
Unused: Taylor, Robinho, Petrov, Ireland
Goals: Tevez (pen 41, 64)
Booked: de Jong
Man of the Match: Carlos Tevez

After one failed attempt to set the ball rolling on this tie due to the weather, City had a point to prove after a horror show at Everton, while United were on a roll after a comfortable victory against Burnley.

It was the visitors who got off to the better start, with a fair amount of possession in the City half. With 20 minutes on the clock, United got themselves a goal. Valencia cut inside, beat Garrido with his cross and, despite Given saving from Rooney, Giggs was able to put the rebound into the open net. Not only did it put City behind, it gave United an away goal and neither side had come back from behind to win a Manchester derby in a long time.

On the half hour, a Zabaleta effort was deflected wide and, from the resulting corner, a Richards header hit Boyata and fell harmlessly into the goalkeeper's hands. De Jong then had an effort well saved by the keeper, after he smashed it at the top corner from 25 yards.

But then, Bellamy was pulled back by Rafael just outside the box. A combination of his fall and momentum took him over in the area and the referee controversially awarded a penalty. Tevez stepped up and belted it into the net with feeling, against his former employers.

On the hour, a Rooney cross fell perfectly for Giggs at the back post and it took an excellent save from Given to deny the Salford-born Welshman only his second Manchester derby goal in 14 years.

With 64 minutes on the clock, Tevez did some more damage to his old club. A Wright-Phillips run won City a corner and, despite the initial cross being cleared, Zabaleta nodded to Kompany, who coolly squared and Tevez was on hand to head home from three yards. His celebration right in front of the Manchester United bench went down well with the City crowd, too.

City were then thankful for substitute Onuoha's defending. Given did well to save from a Rooney one-on-one, but the rebound fell to Owen, who took a touch and shot at goal. It was deflected past Given and was going in, until Onuoha put his foot through it and cleared.

City will, of course, be pleased with their lead in the tie and with the victory, especially after falling behind. Although Roberto Mancini would have preferred a clean sheet, City have the advantage. Even if it's a very narrow one.

Scunthorpe United 2-4 Manchester City
FA Cup Fourth Round
Sunday 24 January, 2010 - 16:00 KO

City: Taylor, Onuoha, Boyata, Kompany, Sylvinho, de Jong (c) (Cunningham 45), Ireland (Zabaleta 66), Ibrahim, Robinho (Bellamy 85), Petrov, Benjani
Unused: Nielsen, Richards, Barry, Wright-Phillips
Goals: Petrov (3), Onuoha (45), Sylvinho (57), Robinho (84)
Booked: Sylvinho, Cunningham
Man of the Match: Martin Petrov

The game opened with Taylor collecting a loose ball in the area. Following his distribution, City kept the ball well and worked it via Benjani and Ireland to Robinho. After a step-over, he found Petrov, who ran into the box and thumped it into the top corner, giving the visitors the lead.

Williams broke from midfield and received the pass from Woolford, just before the quarter of the hour mark, and Ibrahim put it out for a corner with an excellent tackle. There was chaos in the City box as first Scunthorpe hit the bar and then knocked the ball wide from three yards.

A poor decision from the linesman then allowed the hosts back into the game. Hayes, standing in an offside position, received a high ball over the defence and finished excellently past Taylor. On the balance of play, it was deserved, but the flag should have gone up.

Seconds before the half time whistle, an Ibrahim cross was nodded as far as de Jong, who found Ireland. He played a delightful ball over to Onuoha. The academy graduate slotted the ball coolly under Murphy and gave City the lead, with a deft finish.

The first action of the second half saw the youngster Cunningham, on for de Jong, see yellow for a misjudged challenge – jumping to head the ball, but missing – and it seemed very harsh. Boyata was at hand to clear the resulting free kick.

With 57 minutes played, City extended their lead. Ireland set Petrov racing free and, at the second attempt, he found Sylvinho in some space in the centre of the pitch. He unleashed an unstoppable drive from 30 yards, straight over Murphy and into the back of the net.

Just after the hour mark, a mistake in the Scunthorpe defence allowed Petrov in to shoot, but he dragged his shot wide of the post, before a goalmouth scramble saw Ibrahim's shot blocked on the line, and Murphy was able to save both rebounds fired in by Robinho.

Just before the clock ticked to 70 minutes, a long throw into the City box was flicked on and bounced onto Boyata. It wrong-footed Taylor and rolled into the far corner and Scunthorpe were back in the game.

With six minutes left to go, though, Robinho popped up with his first goal of the season. A neat passing move left Sylvinho to find Petrov who flicked the ball on to the Brazilian and he slotted the ball over Murphy and into the net, ending the game as a contest.

Manchester United 3-1 Manchester City
League Cup Semi Final, Second Leg
Wednesday 27 January, 2010 - 20:00 KO

City: Given (c), Richards, Kompany, Boyata, Garrido (Ireland 64), Barry, de Jong, Zabaleta, Bellamy, Wright-Phillips (Adebayor 72), Tevez
Unused: Taylor, Onuoha, Sylvinho, Petrov, Ibrahim
Goals: Tevez (76)
Booked: Tevez
Man of the Match: Vincent Kompany

It was the hosts who got off to the better start. A series of corners came to nothing, as Fletcher headed a tame effort well wide of Given's goal. Scholes had an effort that beat the crossbar, after Kompany had done well to clear, before Boyata was in the right place at the right time to beat Rooney to the ball and concede the corner.

Ferdinand was in the thick of the action as Tevez, all alone in the United half, ran at goal and broke into the box. He tried to take on the England centre-back, but he couldn't get round him and the ball ended up in van der Sar's gloves. Though the defender had fouled the forward and was lucky not to concede a penalty.

City were on the front foot as the second half began. Richards drove out of the defence with the ball, switched it on to his left foot and had a go for the top corner. It was curling in until van der Sar came across with a fantastic save to keep the scores level.

Bellamy was then hit by a coin thrown from the crowd and the game stopped while the referee reported the incident. In truth, the stoppage helped the home side, who cleared the Welshman's corner and hit City on the break. Scholes had an effort from the edge of the box, finding the the net and pulling them level on aggregate.

With 70 minutes on the clock, it got worse for City. Carrick slid the ball back across the goal, with Given going the other way and the back of the net bulged once again. Rooney should have immediately made it three, but he somehow missed from two yards, knocking the ball wide.

Just as United were starting to put their minds to Arsenal at the weekend, City got themselves back on aggregate terms. Tevez superbly flicked the ball into the net with his heel from a Bellamy cross and City were back in the game.

But then, in stoppage time, came the sucker punch for City again. With three minutes held up on the board, and two minutes played, a fantastic Given save meant nothing as, from the resulting corner, Rooney was left unmarked and he headed to win the tie for United.

Manchester City 2-0 Portsmouth
FA Premier League
Sunday 31 January, 2010 - 13:30 KO

City: Given, Garrido, Toure (c), Kompany (Boyata 59), Zabaleta (Onuoha 38), de Jong, Barry, Ireland, Petrov (Bellamy 73), Tevez, Adebayor
Unused: Taylor, Sylvinho, Ibrahim, Wright-Phillips
Goals: Adebayor (40), Kompany (45+1)
Booked: de Jong
Man of the Match: Kolo Toure

After a draining game in midweek, it's hardly surprising that City didn't get off to a quick start. Utaka had their first chance, skewing an effort high and wide after Given couldn't get more than a fingertip on a Webber cross. O'Hara had an effort on goal after an initial corner cross was cleared, but Given held it comfortably.

City lost Zabaleta to injury and, while temporarily down to 10 men, Vanden Borre broke into the City box, hitting his effort straight at his fellow Belgian, Kompany. It deflected off the City man, beat Given, but struck the crossbar, with the follow-up belted clear by Kompany, as Ireland and Toure guarded the line.

Ireland then played an excellent ball over the top for Adebayor, who was just onside, and his first touch was perfect, allowing him to volley past James with his second and put City a goal to the good.

Then, as the board went up for added time, it got better for the home side. Kompany was left unchallenged from a left wing corner and he didn't need asking twice, powering a header straight past the Portsmouth keeper.

With just over 20 minutes to go, Webber was left embarrassed as he fell over his own feet when trying to slot the ball past Given, after the City keeper had parried an effort across the box.

Tevez was then unlucky not to have added to City's lead, after receiving an excellent pull back from Bellamy. He kept his cool, stepped around the challenge of Ben-Haim and shot past James, but the ball hit the outside of the post and went behind.

Barry should have done better with a free header from a Bellamy corner with just six minutes to go, before Toure put in a fantastic tackle on Utaka, preserving City's clean sheet.

UNEXPECTED ITEM IN THE NET

What do Manchester City and self-service checkouts have in common? Apart from the fact that you can never tell if they're operating perfectly until you have to experience them, they also might stop working in the last minute because of an unexpected item in the bagging area. Or net, if we're talking about City.

You see, while I was trying to scan a bag of a popular brand of half-priced extra-large home cook oven chips with 50% extra free for the fifth time at my local supermarket, I suddenly realised, as the greasy goods slowly defrosted in my hands, how the machine that I was trying my hardest not to rip from its housing and send through the window in front of me was the perfect metaphor for the football team I support.

I said, this time last week, that City went into the League Cup Semi Final return leg at Old Trafford with a very slender advantage. That, this week, City are now out of the competition entirely goes to prove my point, though the defeat actually says a lot more about City than you would think at first glance.

Like any self-service checkout I have ever used, City were working perfectly until just over the halfway point – the time when you think you might make it to the end successfully. But then you hear the dreaded words: "Unexpected item in the bagging area." Or, as they were pronounced on Wednesday night: "And Scholes finds the back of the City net."

That United scored in the last minute is no great surprise to me. City had several attempts to get the ball away and failed, and slack marking cost them. But that it was another 4-3 in stoppage time shows that City are getting closer to United; in previous seasons this could quite easily have not been a contest by the final minute.

I could bleat on at you here about how Scholes was lucky not to have been sent off for his 'tackles', or the fact that Bellamy was hit by some coins and that changed his game, or that miscellaneous event A affected City in non-specific manner B and the outcome was a goal from Manchester United player C but, when it comes down to it, I don't think I need to. While I have my grievances over United's goals, it's more to do with the fact that City should have defended better than they did.

City have, throughout the competition, showed that they had the intention of finishing the season as its victor. The team selections from both Mark Hughes and Roberto Mancini have demonstrated that: Full strength against Crystal Palace, full strength against Fulham, full strength against Scunthorpe, full strength against Arsenal and then full strength in both legs against Manchester United.

Manchester United, on the other hand, haven't: A weakened side against Wolves, a weakened side against Barnsley, a weakened side against Tottenham and then full strength in both legs against Manchester City.

What does that say to the football world? Does it say: "We would like to win this competition because it is important to us"? Or does it say: "We're not too bothered if we get knocked out of this cup because we have more important things to be thinking about"? Well, actually, to me, it says something that's in between the two: "We're not too bothered if we get knocked out of this cup, but since we've drawn City, it's important that we don't allow them to win it."

That United felt they needed to put City in their place says a lot more about how United are feeling about City's potential than anything else. City fans are excited about the progress the club is making: That they are currently among the favourites to displace Liverpool in the top four, that they have an excellent chance of winning the FA Cup and that only a collapse of England batting proportions could stop there being some sort of European football next season.

United are still top dogs in Manchester, of that there's no question. But they are no longer as far in front of City as they used to be and it is certainly looking like their fans and management are getting very uncomfortable about the little club from down the road. After all, that little club aren't so little any more.

Ferguson insisted he would stick with his youth policy for the League Cup, yet his team selection over the two semi final legs was anything but junior. Of course, I'm not complaining that he did that – after all, it's his right to renege on what he's said; he's done it before and, by Jove, he'll do it again! – but it tells us that he was much more preoccupied with stopping City from winning a competition than actually winning it himself.

In fact, that Rio Ferdinand appealed against his ban, knowing its extension by one match was as certain as the self-service checkout not liking or accepting your £20 note, just so that he could play in this match tells you that Ferguson wanted his strongest possible side to dampen the City spirit. Except, it appears he forgot that that would put him in a lose-lose situation: Either City won the tie against United's best team or he inadvertently told the world just how concerned with City's progress he was.

Unfortunately, it was the latter. And Rio Ferdinand will now miss four games because of it and I have had to find another way to pay the bloody self-service checkout because that was the only £20 note I had.

I've seen a lot of United fans so desperate to remind City fans that they still hold the power in the city, by way of text messages, joining Facebook groups or by sending mass emails. Why? Is there some underlying concern that these opportunities could become few and far between over the coming years? Perhaps so, and I think City fans need to remember, too, that City aren't there yet; that there's still a lot of work to be done.

The difference, though, between City now and City in the past is that some of the work has already been done and that there are now resources to back it up. Historically, empires rise and fall. United won't be top dogs forever and it's up to City to make sure that when the Manchester United Death Star blows up (the second one, obviously; the one that was half built and had the Emperor on it), that it's Sheikh Mansour and Roberto Mancini who are piloting the Millennium Falcon out of the reactor core ventilation shaft.

In terms of the League Cup Semi Finals, United may well have won this little battle, but the Manchester Civil War is far from over.

INTERVIEW: VINCENT KOMPANY

You'd expect the mood around a football club to be very sluggish the morning after a night match. Especially when that night match had been a derby game and it had been won by a goal in second half stoppage time by the opposition. And, as I drove up to City's Carrington training complex, that was certainly how I was feeling, the 'hangover' from the League Cup exit the night before still very fresh in my mind.

Sitting in the press room, I didn't really know what to say. It's difficult to make small conversation when your cup run has just come crashing to a last minute end to your rivals, especially when it was the nearest thing to a final City had seen in decades. But all of that awkwardness and bad feeling was blown away when the man of the match from the evening before entered the room.

As he did, I naturally did what everyone else would do: I stood up and shook his hand. When I did, you'd never have thought that I was only 18 months Vincent Kompany's junior. He was a man who was confident and, despite what had happened the evening before, wasn't going to lie down and be beaten.

Of course, we couldn't avoid the issue of the League Cup: "It's not enjoyable to concede a last minute goal in such an important game. But I don't think it's going to be bad for us in the long term.

"You could see today the lads were shocked by the fact that we're out of the cup so close to the final, but everybody's really motivated now to get in there and have this top four finish and maybe even go to Wembley in the FA Cup.

"It's definitely not something we see as the end of the road, more something that will bring us closer to what we want to achieve. If you look to the future, there's so many exciting things to come."

Kompany arrived at City before Sheikh Mansour took control on the final day of the summer transfer window in 2008. He's turned out to have been a snip at a mere £6m, brought in at a time when City were struggling for cash, and if there's one man at the club that's seen a lot of change, it's him.

"We never seem to be beaten, really," he says, comparing this season to the last. "Even yesterday at Old Trafford, we were 2-0 down and we got that one goal that brought us back in the game [making it 3-3 on aggregate]. We never seem to be beaten until the last minute, but that doesn't happen that often.

"There's no reason for us not to be happy about what we've done so far [this season], especially knowing that, if you look at United or other top four teams, they've been playing together for a while. And we've all just come together at one time and been asked to do a job.

"Surprisingly, because it's not always like that, there seems to be a team on the pitch," he says, commenting on the quick turnover of players that City have seen in recent years. "There seems to be a great connection already between the players and the fans, and I'd say that's maybe thanks to the fact that there's been so much negative press about us."

Kompany gives off the air of a natural leader. He's one of those characters that every dressing room needs; someone who can be counted on not to go missing when things aren't going according to plan. But even he points out that there are things that motivate him.

"I kind of love people hating on us," he says. "I think if anything has helped us to become more of a team quickly and to feel like we're part of Manchester City, if anything has brought us closer together, it will be probably be what people have been saying outside of the club. We're all in it together."

Perhaps one of the reasons why Kompany is mature beyond his years is due to his upbringing. While coming through the ranks at Anderlecht, he was attracting the attentions of some of the biggest clubs in England: Chelsea, Manchester United. But he stayed with the Belgian club and stayed in education.

"It was an important decision, but for me it was never a question," he says, thinking back to his growing up in Brussels. "My mother and my father really insisted that I finished my studies and I wasn't really excited about this club or that club, I just wanted to play as much as I could. I was playing in a league where we had about six or eight big games in a year.

"I was playing lots of games, I was playing Champions League and national team games, too, and I was gaining lots of experience. So, for me it was a really good development and, so far, it's proven to have been the right choice."

It was clear, though, that Kompany was going to be something special. Despite his young age, he was receiving the plaudits: He took the Golden Shoe (best player in Belgium) in 2004 and the Young Professional Footballer of the Year in 2004 and 2005, all before he turned twenty. With Anderlecht, he won the Belgian first division in 2004 and 2006, too.

But Kompany didn't let the plaudits, including comparisons to the French international Marcel Desailly, get in the way of his development: "I didn't ask myself too many questions about it, it just happened. It was the result of the work I put in. It was, for me, just the beginning of what I was hoping would become a great career.

"It was special [to be compared to Desailly], because my first official national team game was against France. And at that time I played against Desailly, Zidane, Vieira, and a lot of other players from that generation.

"I always looked up to him as a player and as someone off the field," he says. "I guess maybe why people have compared me to him is because he started off playing in defensive midfield and so did I, I can play centre-back as well and so can he.

"It's not something I think was deserved, but it was something nice to hear."

In 2006, Kompany moved from his home country to Germany and Hamburg, where he was brought in to replace the departing Daniel van Buyten. But, not long after he made his debut, just six games into his career with his new club, he was ruled out with a long term Achilles injury. At just twenty years old, did that affect him?

"People will call it pressure," he says. "But I don't because I don't really experience pressure, as such. But I was the most expensive transfer in the history of the club and a lot of people were expecting a lot from me. After the first games, I'd given a good impression to everyone, but then I was out for almost a year.

"People sometimes forget the fact that you are a human being and you can be injured, and they'll think that you're expensive and haven't performed yet because of your injury.

"I put in a lot of hard work and after a bit of adaptation and time to come back, I started building up again from there. It was a good experience for me, because I learned a lot and it was a hard time for me as well because I was going to lose my mother at that time, too. It wasn't easy, but it's made me the man I am today."

Kompany was only at Hamburg for two years. In the summer of 2008, he and the club fell out over his ambitions to represent Belgium at the Olympic Games in Beijing. He wanted to stay and play for his country as they progressed through the tournament, but the club wanted him to return and prepare for the Bundesliga season.

Initially, Kompany planned to defy the call to return to Germany, but Hamburg threatened the Belgian FA with legal action and, against his wishes, he went back. It was a matter of weeks until he signed for City and he says the club's stubbornness played a big part in his decision to leave.

"I always wanted to play in the Premier League," he says. "But, I was comfortable at Hamburg. It's a great club with great fans and I was really happy there. But it [the decision to recall him] decided everything.

"I wanted to play for my country, that's all I was asking for. And that right had been taken away from me. From that moment on, the relationship changed.

"I'm someone who speaks his mind and, without being disrespectful, I gave my opinion about it and we realised we couldn't come together about that. Then City came in for me and the way the manager spoke to me at that time, I felt that it was going to be the perfect place for me to get to the next level."

At City, he quickly became one of the first names on the team sheet. Originally playing in defensive midfield under Mark Hughes, he controlled games and became one of the most important players of that season. Now, under Roberto Mancini, he's dropped back to the centre of defence and has been one of the most consistent performers in the league.

His leadership on the pitch has had him touted as a future club captain, but the Belgian's keeping his feet firmly on the ground: "It would be a great honour someday to fill in that role," he says. "But everything in its time. At the moment, I'm still learning a lot.

"I'll always command on the pitch. It's always been in my character since the age of six. Whether I'm captain or not, it won't change how I am around the ground or on the pitch and my team-mates know that.

"We have a great captain at the moment, though."

January 2010 Breakdown

Games (all competitions):
Won: 5   **Drawn:** 0   **Lost:** 2

Goals (all competitions):
For: 14   **Against:** 9

Progress:
Premier League: 6th
League Cup: Eliminated in the Semi Final
FA Cup: Qualified for Round Five

Premier League Table

		P	W	D	L	F	A	GD	Pts
4	Tottenham Hotspur	24	12	6	6	45	25	+20	42
5	Liverpool	24	12	5	7	42	26	+16	41
6	**Manchester City**	**22**	**11**	**8**	**3**	**44**	**30**	**+14**	**41**
7	Aston Villa	23	11	7	5	31	18	+13	40
8	Birmingham City	23	9	7	7	22	23	-1	34

February 2010

Hull City 2-1 Manchester City
FA Premier League
Saturday 6 February, 2010 - 15:00 KO

City: Given, Zabaleta, Bridge (Petrov 85), Toure (c), Boyata, de Jong, Barry, Ireland (A Johnson 56), Bellamy (Vieira 61), Tevez, Adebayor
Unused: Taylor, Onuoha, Sylvinho, Wright-Phillips
Goals: Adebayor (59)
Booked: Toure, Boyata, Zabaleta, Vieira
Man of the Match: Nigel de Jong

Hull started the game the stronger, dominating the possession inside City's half, without really causing the visitors any problems. But, with 28 minutes on the clock, the home side made their domination pay. The ball was knocked into the feet of Vennegoor of Hesselink and he held off Boyata to tee up Altidore. The Hull man's first time shot curled around both Toure and Given and the hosts had themselves the lead.

Some patient play in stoppage time forged City's best chance of the half, as Barry, Bellamy and Bridge combined to find Ireland, who slotted the ball past Tevez and back into the path of City's left back, who had continued his run. His shot, though, was parried by Myhill and Adebayor hit the rebound over.

Ten minutes into the second half and Altidore hit the deck in the box under pressure from de Jong and Zabaleta, but the referee ruled it was a fair tackle and awarded the corner. From the kick, Boyata cleared as far as Boateng on the edge of the box and he lashed the ball back, straight past Given and into the net.

City had a mountain to climb and, with Myhill still yet to make a save, it looked like it would end badly for the visitors. But, just five minutes later, City were back within a goal of their hosts. Toure and Adebayor tried to force the ball into the net from City's first corner of the day and it fell to the big Togolese forward, who gave Myhill no chance with a driven shot.

Despite City's pressure, they couldn't force another chance until a minute to go, when substitute Johnson curled a cross into the box from the right wing and Myhill let it slip through his hands, nearly dropping into the net. Unfortunately for the visitors, though, it didn't end up in the net.

Manchester City 2-0 Bolton Wanderers
FA Premier League
Tuesday 9 February, 2010 - 19:45 KO

City: Given, Zabaleta, Bridge (Wright-Phillips 69), Toure (c) (Lescott 55), Kompany, de Jong, Barry, Vieira, A Johnson (Sylvinho 85), Tevez, Adebayor
Unused: Taylor, Onuoha, Ireland, Petrov

Goals: Tevez (pen 32), Adebayor (73)
Booked: -
Man of the Match: Adam Johnson

After the disappointment of the KC Stadium, City needed a good performance to bounce back. In truth it never looked like coming, though Bolton seemed content to contain the home side for large spells. City began the brighter, with Kompany cutting out a pass to Davies and an Adebayor bicycle kick landing just wide of the post.

Just after the half hour, Johnson was central to City taking the lead. He skipped into the box by the right by-line and was brought down by Ricketts. Tevez stepped up and blasted the penalty down the middle. It hit Jaaskelainen, who will feel he should have saved it, and it just about found the back of the net to put City in front.

Right on half time, Bolton had the chance to equalise after a dubious handball decision against Barry. Almost all of the City side were in Given's man wall and it was enough to block the ball to safety.

With 73 minutes gone, two former Gunners combined to give City a two goal cushion. Vieira played a neat pass over the top to Adebayor, who was just onside, and he brought it down superbly, before volleying straight past the onrushing Jaaskelainen.

Davies headed over for the visitors, before Elmander poked a Bolton free kick onto the post. Knight then wasted the chance to pull a goal back from a corner, well into stoppage time and City cruised to victory.

Manchester City 1-1 Stoke City
FA Cup Fifth Round
Saturday 13 February, 2010 - 17:15 KO

City: Given, Zabaleta, Toure (c), Lescott, Bridge, de Jong, Barry, Ireland (Vieira 73), Wright-Phillips, Petrov (Santa Cruz 62), Adebayor
Unused: Taylor, Garrido, Sylvinho, Onuoha, Boyata
Goals: Wright-Phillips (11)
Booked: -
Man of the Match: Shaun Wright-Phillips

It didn't take long for City to get in front. Ireland played a nice ball over the top for Wright-Phillips, who lifted it over the onrushing Sorensen. It was dropping wide of the goal until Shawcross, lying on the floor, tried to head it back to his defensive partner and didn't get enough on it, leaving Wright-Phillips with an open goal and a simple tap in. But, despite the early goal, the game didn't get started from there.

Just before the hour, Delap sent one of his trademark long throw-ins into the box and the unmarked Fuller nodded it straight past Given. It was more questionable defending from the home side, who let the front man in without a challenge.

With 10 minutes to go, Diao gave away a needless corner and Barry's header was expertly touched over by Sorensen. Wright-Phillips hit the side netting before Santa Cruz was able to chest the ball down and turn in the area. He smashed it across the goal and it was blocked on the line by Shawcross, with Sorensen diving on it before Adebayor could pounce.

Tuncay had the final effort of the game, firing wide on the counter attack as the visitors looked to avoid a replay. They couldn't and it'll be another trip to the Britannia Stadium for City.

Stoke City 1-1 Manchester City
FA Premier League
Tuesday 16 February, 2010 - 19:45 KO

City: Given, Garrido (Wright-Phillips 60), Toure (c), Lescott, Richards (Zabaleta 82), de Jong, Barry, Vieira, Johnson (Petrov 87), Santa Cruz, Adebayor
Unused: Taylor, Onuoha, Bridge, Ireland
Goals: Barry (86)
Booked: Vieira, de Jong, Barry
Man of the Match: Joleon Lescott

It started badly for the visitors, when Garrido missed a Barry pass and presented Delap the chance to hurl the ball into the box. He did and Robert Huth headed it just over the bar, when he probably should have done better. Vieira was lucky not to have been sent off as he threw a leg out at Whelan, after the former City man had challenged for the ball, and caught him in the stomach.

Five minutes before the break, Johnson whipped a free kick into the box and some excellent defending from Faye saw the ball ricochet off Santa Cruz and just wide of the post. It was an isolated chance for the visitors.

City began the second half much better than they had begun the first, but they weren't able to fashion a shooting chance. That was until 10 minutes into the half, when Faye missed his control under pressure from Adebayor and the City man nipped in behind and stole the ball. Through on goal, Faye hauled the forward down and earned himself a red card.

With 72 minutes on the clock, Stoke had an isolated attack, working the ball to the left wing with Delap and his cross was missed by everybody. It was sliced badly by Johnson on the edge of City's box and hit first time by Whelan. It was a good strike that Given should have saved, but it went straight through the City keeper and found the back of the net.

City responded with the lion's share of possession, but every ball into the box was swallowed up by Sorensen or the Stoke defence, leaving Adebayor and

Santa Cruz frustrated. After a period of pressure, though, Wright-Phillips forced a corner.

From that corner, the little Englishman swung the ball into the box. Adebayor got up well to flick the ball on and Barry, arriving late, touched it past Sorensen and onto the post. The City man, though, reacted before everyone else and was able to poke it into the net from close range.

In time added on, Stoke should have won the game. Delap threw long and Shawcross got up well before Given, flicking the ball into the net. The referee, though, wrongly ruled it out for a foul on the goalkeeper and City were, in the end, fortunate to leave the Potteries with the point that took them into fourth.

Manchester City 0-0 Liverpool

FA Premier League
Sunday 21 February, 2010 - 15:00 KO

City: Given (c), Bridge, Kompany, Lescott, Zabaleta, de Jong, Barry, Ireland (Ibrahim 76), Wright-Phillips (Bellamy 69), Johnson, Adebayor
Unused: Taylor, Richards, Sylvinho, Toure, Santa Cruz
Goals: -
Booked: Barry
Man of the Match: Joleon Lescott

The game started cagily and the best either side could offer was a cross from Gerrard that was well cleared by Kompany, before Wright-Phillips was marginally offside as Zabaleta tried to play him through. It looked like two teams who were more afraid to lose the game than having the initiative to win it, so both were reluctant to open it up.

With 28 minutes gone, Gerrard cleared the bar with a left-footed effort from the edge of the box. Reina then comfortably caught a Johnson free kick, after the left winger had been fouled by Mascherano, who earned himself a yellow card.

That was the most work the visiting keeper had had to do in the first half.

City started the second period the brighter, with Johnson winning a series of corners after Reina had punched the ball away. Johnson then left Babel wondering what day of the week it was, blasting a driven cross straight into the Dutchman's face from close range.

But that was about the best the game could offer, as the two sides continued to play safe. With chances at a premium, it was hardly surprising that, when opportunities did come, they were being squandered.

Minutes from the end, Adebayor should have scored after he robbed Skrtel of the ball in the box, but the defender was able to recover to get in a last ditch tackle as the big centre-forward was about to pull the trigger.

The game ended with Liverpool on the front foot, pressing the home side, after Lescott was dispossessed in midfield, but they couldn't force another shot on Given's goal.

A no score draw summed up the performances from both teams.

Stoke City 3-1 Manchester City (AET)
FA Cup Fifth Round Replay
Wednesday 24 February, 2010 - 19:45 KO

City: Given (c), Richards, Onuoha, Lescott, Bridge (Santa Cruz 87), Zabaleta, Kompany, Bellamy, Ireland (Wright-Phillips 62), Barry (Sylvinho 108), Adebayor
Unused: Taylor, Garrido, Boyata, de Jong
Goals: Bellamy (81)
Booked: Richards, Zabaleta, Bellamy
Sent Off: Adebayor
Man of the Match: Vincent Kompany

City returned to the Britannia Stadium with ambitions of beating Stoke at the third attempt, and it was the visitors who started the brighter. With nine minutes gone, both Adebayor and Bellamy had almost caught Sorensen in possession, before the former forced the goalkeeper into a good save with a shot from range.

Soon after, Adebayor squared for Bellamy, but his first touch was too heavy and Sorenson was out quickly to block. City will have been regretting their wasted chances as the half wore on, though, as Stoke got back into the game as the break approached. Several Delap long throws were a little close for comfort, before a series of corners ended with an excellent block by Richards.

In the second half, Bellamy had a volley deflected for a corner, before Onuoha was in the right place to put in an excellent tackle on Fuller as he tried to break. City had lost the initiative they had begun the game with.

With 79 minutes on the clock, Kitson played a neat one-two with Tuncay and rolled the return pass into the net and past Given, handing the advantage to the home side with just over 10 minutes to go.

But, two minutes later, any thoughts of a trip to Stamford Bridge in the next round for the hosts were cut short, as City levelled. Adebayor did well to chest down a cross and Bellamy found the back of the net with a volley.

Though, having gotten themselves back into the game, City handed the initiative right back to the home side. Adebayor saw a straight red card for throwing an arm at Shawcross and the 10 men would have to work hard to stay in the competition.

The visitors could have won it at the end of normal time as Santa Cruz was sent through, but Sorensen was out quickly to head it clear. And then Stoke could have done the same through Shawcross, who headed just wide after a scramble in the City box.

In extra time, City failed to deal with one of Stoke's main weapons: The Rory Delap throw-in. The Stoke man hurled the ball into the box and Given came and missed it, as Shawcross nodded the ball into the net.

Three minutes later, Tuncay sealed the tie for the home side. Kitson broke away from the City defence, found the forward, who cut inside and slotted the ball home, with Lescott diving in to try and stop it on the line.

Chelsea 2-4 Manchester City
FA Premier League
Saturday 27 February, 2010 - 12:45 KO

City: Given (c), Richards, Kompany, Lescott, Bridge (Santa Cruz 78), A Johnson (Wright-Phillips 61), Zabaleta, Barry, de Jong, Bellamy, Tevez (Sylvinho 90+5)
Unused: Taylor, Toure, Onuoha, Ibrahim
Goals: Tevez (45, pen 76), Bellamy (51, 87)
Booked: Zabaleta
Man of the Match: Craig Bellamy

With all the television cameras pointed at Terry and Bridge, perhaps a lot of people had forgotten that there was a football match happening at Stamford Bridge and what a game it was. The City left back refused to shake the Chelsea captain's hand and it could be one of the reasons why Terry's performance was below par.

While there was the off the field drama, the game struggled to get going. Lampard fired high and wide, Johnson found touch instead of Tevez and Kompany could only nod a header wide from a free kick, all in the opening 10 minutes.

But, after that, Chelsea pressed and City struggled to get a foothold on the game. Drogba hit an effort over the bar, before Anelka fired a shot straight at Lampard and the City defence cleared. Just before half time, Lampard found the net, after breaking the offside trap and rolling it past Given, in off the post.

But, three minutes later, it didn't matter. In first half stoppage time, a clearance for City was misjudged by Terry and Tevez nipped in to win the ball. Running at the two centre-backs, he worked his way into the box and mis-hit his shot. But, some poor defending and poor goalkeeping let the effort trickle into the net via the glove of Hilario, and City went in level at the break.

The visitors started the second half the stronger, and soon they had the lead. The ball was played over the top for Bellamy, who raced at the Chelsea goal. He was showed outside by the defence and onto his left foot, but that wasn't going to stop him as he fired it low and hard past Hilario and into the bottom corner.

Given was right behind an effort from Ballack from range, before City had the chance to extend their lead. Barry broke into the box after some poor defending from Belletti and then went down under the Chelsea man's challenge. It was a penalty and a red card.

Tevez smashed the spot kick into the bottom left corner.

Wright-Phillips had an effort well wide, before a stupid tackle from Ballack from behind on Tevez earned the German his second yellow card and the home side had a mountain to climb with just nine men.

And, with three minutes left on the clock, a City breakaway sent Wright-Phillips clean through on the right. His low cross found Bellamy on the back post and the Welshman couldn't miss, side-footing home from three yards out.

As the clock ticked over to 90, Barry got his legs tangled up with those of Anelka in the box and the referee gave the penalty. Lampard had missed in the reverse fixture earlier in the season, but Given couldn't stop him this time, as he rolled it into the bottom corner.

ANOTHER TROPHYLESS SEASON

We found out this month that Manchester City are going to be 35 years without a trophy, and the victims of the recent Haitian earthquake, which devastated hundreds of thousands of lives, took time out of their busy rebuilding schedule to send their condolences to the club in a heartfelt gesture. A hotline has been set up for their donations to the club's fans and Simon Cowell is beginning work on his CupAid song. Of course, I'm being facetious, but now that I've calmed down from City's FA Cup exit I feel I need to remind some City fans that worse things happen and, as disappointing as the result was, there are people without a roof over their head or clean water to drink.

Worse things happen in football, too. We could be Portsmouth, bottom of the Premier League and looking at a nine point deduction thanks to calamitous business deals that saw the club without enough money to pay players. A club that, after a relegation that looks virtually nailed on without a points deduction, might never get themselves back into the top division for many a year. We could even be Chester City, a football club on a par with Enron at the top of the Badly Run Businesses League.

We only lost a game of football we shouldn't have done.

The point is, all is clearly not well at City. With all due respect to Stoke, a team of City's position – one that is aiming to break into the top four – should have won more than none of the last three games against them.

In truth, City haven't looked the same since the second last minute winner at Old Trafford. The shaky defence that had been transformed into a solid one at the start of Roberto Mancini's tenure has, to some extent, slipped into their old ways; they haven't been making the same basic errors that they were when shipping three goals to Burnley or to Bolton, but simple mistakes are starting to lead to simple goals. The worry, though, is that City aren't looking as dangerous in attack and, while you shouldn't have to score four times to beat Sunderland at home or three times to draw with Burnley at home, City were at least creating enough chances to do that.

That being said, if you're going to Stoke and can't defend set pieces, you're in trouble – how can one team concede three goals from long throw ins (albeit one that was wrongly disallowed) and not learn from their mistakes, especially when the games have come in such close proximity? It's not as if Delap's throws have been a secret weapon and taken us by surprise; we knew it was in their arsenal.

It's as if that Rooney goal in the League Cup completely destroyed any confidence at the club. It was understandable that the performance against Portsmouth – the weekend straight after that game - wasn't good, but the win was what was most important. The confidence finally seemed to have returned in the first half at Stoke, but chances were missed, the home side got themselves into the game and, suddenly, in the space of four extra time minutes, any talk of Wembley for this season had gone the way of Ron Atkinson's punditry career.

The reaction of a lot of fans, though, has been a bit over the top. And I'll admit that, straight after the game I wasn't thinking rationally and that's why I didn't write this back then, otherwise you'd have spent the last 10 minutes reading line after line of hysterical to the point of pitchfork carrying, over-reactionary gobbledygook.

The defeat was frustrating, especially given that it was City's best performance in a tie with Stoke this season, but we lost to a Premier League team... not Nottingham Forest, or Brighton, or Sheffield United, or Colchester, or Doncaster. It was only 2007 when cries of you're not fit to wear the shirt greeted an abject FA Cup defeat to a 10-man Blackburn side. That was a hard defeat to take. While the defeat at Stoke wasn't a pleasant experience, it's an improvement on what we've been served in the past. It's like going to Little Chef after eating at McDonalds; you're able to appreciate the taste more, if only slightly.

City is a work in progress. A work in progress that still has a game in hand on and is on level points with fourth place; the good news is that, if this is a crisis, then I can't wait until the crisis is over. Progress doesn't happen overnight; we're not pretending City are the finished article yet. That's an unfinished article in joint fourth place with games against nearby rivals to come.

Since the incredible level of investment from Sheikh Mansour, there seems to have been a change in attitude with a large proportion of the fans. Just because there's limitless funds doesn't mean that everything will fall into place instantaneously. We have to be patient – it's a bit like mashed potato, in that respect. Buy the cheap, instant mash and it tastes powdery. But, buy quality King Edwards, peel them, boil them and mash them yourself and, while it costs a bit more and takes longer, it tastes nice and creamy. City are just being peeled now.

If we're going to get any sort result from this season, then we need to draw a line under the cup disappointments and under the recent league form and start again. Forget about them. They're done with. We have to focus on finishing fourth; if we carry on feeling sorry for ourselves, then that fourth spot will slip further and further out of reach.

We need to find a combination of the two teams of this season; we need to find the balance between Hughes' offensiveness and Mancini's defensiveness to create a team with is going to compete. And the players could probably do with a kick up the backside to get them going again.

This season is far from over. But if we're going to wallow in self-pity and forget to get behind the team for the final push for fourth, it might as well be. A lot of fans seem to have forgotten that we're not simply aiming to hit 40 points with a good cup run anymore and that we've still got something to play for.

So let's cut the crap and bloody well play for it.

A MISGUIDED SENSE OF MORALITY

I have previously written that I had been ignoring the Wayne Bridge and John Terry situation. But the events of the past week mean that it's something that I don't think I can ignore any longer. Every man/woman/child/other has had their say on it, whether they qualified to or not, so why shouldn't I?

I missed the handshakes at Stamford Bridge on Saturday because I was just parking my car roughly 220 miles away in Preston. I didn't get lost on my way to Chelsea and end up in Preston; I just didn't go to the game because of a social gathering. I did, however, make it to the pub in time to witness one delightfully charming Chelsea fan give Bridge a lovely and heartfelt greeting as he went to take a throw-in on his return to his old stomping ground... it went something like: "You fucking prick."

It has to be said, though, that a large number of Chelsea fans applauded Bridge when he was substituted. But there were still a lot who seemed to think that he had done something wrong... y'know, when his close friend and former team-mate had that extra-marital affair with his ex-girlfriend and mother of his child, that was, somehow, the City left back's fault.

Wayne Bridge has done nothing but conduct himself with dignity of the past month. The fact that he has decided to give up his England career over what has happened has shown not only how strongly he feels about this situation, but it has shown him to be a true gentleman. While Terry is in the England team, Bridge's presence at the camp will, ultimately, be divisive. But, I have to ask, if that's the case – and, of course, it is going to be – why is it Bridge, the man who has done nothing wrong, that has to lose his chance to represent his country? If somebody should fall on their sword, why is it up to Bridge to do it and, more importantly, why has 95% of the country decided that it's fine?

I'll tell you why – it's because Terry is the more important for the England team. He's the first choice centre-back and Bridge is the second choice left back. This is the combination that gives England the best chance of winning the World Cup, so of course that's why people aren't that fussed that an innocent and wronged man has given up his opportunity. It just goes to show that football stinks where morals are concerned.

To have journalists, television hosts, radio presenters and both sporting and non-sporting commentators criticise his decision for being selfish is, perhaps, one of the biggest insults they can deliver. I had the (mis)fortune of channel hopping into the segment of the deep thinking and heavy politics based discussion programme Loose Women, where they took time out of discussing the important issues like doing funny voices for kids or snoring to comment on Bridge's retirement. Not only did the panel with no football background (and little football interest, from what I could gather) decide that his decision was wrong, but they also concluded that he was acting like a small child, because a couple of them had had disagreements with colleagues in the past and had to carry on working with them.

But nevermind because, after the break, there's a nice little table discussion about whether beards are sexy and a very cosy interview with somebody off Coronation Street. Honestly, it would be like getting me in to talk about plumbing...

This decision was to give the team the best chance; effectively, Bridge has said he can't work with Terry and, if the team is going to function properly, one of them has to go. Since Terry wasn't going anywhere, Bridge decided he had to give up his international career. And that deserves respect, not criticism. It's not like giving up crisps or stopping wearing hats, it's a very big decision. I'm not the best (or in a squad of the best) in my country at anything, but, if I was, it would have to be something very serious to make me want to give that up.

It wasn't a decision he took lightly. Bridge hasn't given up his England career on a whim. My personal opinion is that it wasn't a decision that Bridge should have had to make; if only one of Bridge and Terry could stay in the England squad, it shouldn't be the one who has done nothing wrong that leaves.

Whether or not Bridge should have an overriding desire to win the World Cup isn't an issue. If he had gone to South Africa, he would have been in close quarters with a man whose guts he now hates for four weeks – what would that do for team morale? For Bridge's own morale? For John Terry?

Clearly, from his reaction to his former team-mate at the start of the match on Saturday, Bridge isn't in the right frame of mind to be around Terry. If he can't bring himself to shake the Chelsea man's hand, then how can he possibly be a positive influence on the England squad in the summer?

It's nothing short of disrespectful and insulting for commentators to suggest that the left-back's decision is through a lack of desire to win the World Cup. He should just put his personal issues behind him? Really? Most people would struggle to do that in the office, let alone on the world stage with millions of people watching.

And, as for Terry...

He was right to have been stripped of the captaincy. While what has happened off the pitch doesn't change his ability, it does change his credibility. He's not this squeaky clean character that has authority over the team; knowing your leader has behaved immorally is going to make you wonder why they should be your leader over somebody else. The level of respect in the dressing room for him, no matter what anybody says to the press, will not be the same.

I'm glad that Bridge decided not to shake Terry's hand. Partly because of what Terry had done, but mainly because I'm a Manchester City fan. And, personally, I think from that moment on, John Terry's head just wasn't on the game, which made City's task easier. Not easy, mind you, winning at Stamford Bridge is never easy (especially if you've not even scored there in the last 10 years), but easier.

What's more, I'm glad City's equalising goal came from a Bridge clearance that was defended calamitously. And the word 'calamitously' is still putting a positive spin on it, bearing in mind Tevez had to run a long way with the ball against two defenders faster than him, before he ended up mis-hitting it completely and the goalkeeper forgot to dive, choosing to fall over instead.

In the midst of all this Terry-Bridge stand-off, we seem to have forgotten that a football match happened last Saturday. One where a City victory looked about as likely as finding a man with no eyes wearing prescription glasses, thanks to recent performances by Mancini's side. But a tough performance in defence and some lethal breakaways (and comedy defending, of course) saw the unlikely happen.

And on Saturday night, Bridge will have felt better than he had for weeks.

February 2010 Breakdown

Games (all competitions):
Won: 2   **Drawn:** 4   **Lost:** 1

Goals (all competitions):
For: 9   **Against:** 9

Progress:
Premier League: 5th
League Cup: Eliminated in the Semi Final
FA Cup: Eliminated in Round Five

Premier League Table

		P	W	D	L	F	A	GD	Pts
3	Arsenal	28	18	4	6	66	31	+35	58
4	Tottenham Hotspur	28	14	7	7	50	27	+23	49
5	**Manchester City**	**27**	**13**	**10**	**4**	**52**	**35**	**+17**	**49**
6	Liverpool	28	14	6	8	45	28	+17	48
7	Aston Villa	26	12	9	5	37	21	+16	45

March 2010

Sunderland 1-1 Manchester City

FA Premier League

Sunday 14 March, 2010 - 16:00 KO

City: Given (c), Richards (Vieira 63), Kompany, Lescott, Bridge (Santa Cruz 32), Zabaleta, de Jong, Barry, Wright-Phillips (A Johnson 72), Bellamy, Tevez
Unused: Taylor, Toure, Sylvinho, Ireland
Goals: Johnson (90+2)
Booked: Tevez, Richards, Wright-Phillips, Barry
Man of the Match: Adam Johnson

It was the home side that started the brighter, with Jones hitting the first effort of the game straight at Given. But, with eight minutes gone, he got up well to meet a Malbranque cross and his second effort of the game found the bottom corner, leaving Given standing. It was a bad start for City.

City were under pressure throughout the first half and Campbell should have done better when he picked up the ball from a Lescott header, but he scuffed his shot wide. Richards then got across well to block from Malbranque.

If Gordon had an easy first half, his second half was anything but.

Just before the hour, Barry was booked for reacting to Meyler's words after the City man had given away a free kick for handball, before Vieira came on to replace Richards. That change nearly had an instant impact, as Wright-Phillips' cross was cleared to the edge of the box, but Vieira's effort was blocked on the line by Mensah.

Johnson then fed the ball through to Santa Cruz. He was given a golden chance to cross, but he sent it over the bar from the right wing, when he should have found a blue shirt. It looked like it was going to be one of those days.

When it looked like City were going to come away with nothing because of a dour first half display, a corner from the right wing was cleared only to Johnson. He took a touch to get it under control and, after looking up, curled a beautiful effort into the top corner, over the man on the post, leaving Gordon helpless and grabbing a draw for the visitors.

Fulham 1-2 Manchester City

FA Premier League

Sunday 21 March, 2010 - 15:00 KO

City: Given, Zabaleta, Toure (c), Kompany, Garrido, Barry, Vieira, A Johnson (Wright-Phillips 83), Bellamy (Onuoha 90), Tevez, Santa Cruz (de Jong 81)
Unused: Taylor, Sylvinho, Richards, Ireland
Goals: Santa Cruz (7), Tevez (36)
Booked: -

Man of the Match: Adam Johnson

With Liverpool and Aston Villa dropping points and Tottenham beating Stoke earlier in the weekend, City went into this game knowing that three points would certainly be very useful in the race for fourth spot. And they started the brighter. Toure was on hand to clear off the line, before Bellamy found himself in a shooting position and fired an effort towards goal. It took a deflection and crashed into the post, leaving Santa Cruz to tap home the rebound.

City began to dominate possession and it paid off on 36 minutes. Bellamy and Tevez played a neat one-two and the Argentinian stepped inside the defender and slotted it straight past Schwarzer for City's second.

The second half began with City looking content to hold on to the ball and soak up any Fulham pressure. Johnson was instrumental in creating a good chance for Santa Cruz, just before the hour mark, as he weaved into the box and found the Paraguayan. He forced a save from Schwarzer, but should have scored. Johnson then fired in an effort from range and hit the post, as City looked for the third.

With 15 minutes to go, Duff sent a low ball into the box and it appeared to hit Barry on the arm. The linesman awarded the penalty, with the City players feeling it was harsh, and Murphy stepped up to send Given the wrong way. De Jong could have finished the game as he was found by Tevez, but he hit his effort straight at the goalkeeper from just inside the box, although ultimately it didn't matter to the outcome.

Manchester City 0-2 Everton
FA Premier League
Wednesday 24 March, 2010 - 19:45 KO

City: Given, Richards (Vieira 75), Toure (c), Kompany, Zabaleta, Barry, de Jong, Ireland (Wright-Phillips 41) A Johnson (Santa Cruz 57), Bellamy, Tevez
Unused: Taylor, Sylvinho, Garrido, Onuoha
Goals: -
Booked: Tevez, Given, de Jong
Man of the Match: Craig Bellamy

The game got off to a lively start, with Tevez and Bellamy hassling the Everton back line. Tevez had a good shout for a penalty turned down when it looked like Howard was fortunate to have been adjudged to have won the ball.

Just before the half hour, Heitinga went straight through the back of Ireland and picked up a yellow card. It ended the game for the Irishman, who had to be substituted later in the half, unable to run the knock off.

Cahill won a free kick on the edge of the City box on 33 minutes, and he picked himself up to get the last touch on a Baines shot, after the left back had got it from the dead ball. It sent the ball into the net and City were left wondering where the defence had gone.

With 64 minutes on the clock, Tevez had a good chance to find the back of the net with a free kick from 25 yards out. He got it up and over the wall, but could only plant it into Howard's hands, who didn't even need to move his feet to claim it.

And just when it looked like City might get into second gear and get themselves back into the game, Everton effectively ended it as a contest. Rodwell brought the ball inside from the right wing and found Arteta on the edge of the box, who fired the ball past Given with just four minutes to go.

Manchester City 3-0 Wigan Athletic
FA Premier League
Monday 29 March, 2010 - 19:45 KO

City: Given, Zabaleta, Toure (c), Kompany, Garrido (Onuoha 87), de Jong, Vieira, Wright-Phillips (Bellamy 46), A Johnson, Adebayor, Tevez (Sylvinho 87)
Unused: Richards, Taylor, Santa Cruz, Barry
Goals: Tevez (71, 74, 83)
Booked: Garrido, Zabaleta, Tevez
Man of the Match: Carlos Tevez

It was the home side who started the brighter, when a superb reflex stop from Wigan's goalkeeper prevented the home side from taking the lead after 12 minutes, as Tevez connected to a Wright-Phillips cross inside the six-yard box, but Stojkovic was there to deny him.

Moreno shot wide of Given's goal, leaving the home fans with their hearts in their mouths, before Tevez nearly added to his tally for the season, cutting in from the left, but his shot curled agonisingly wide of the upright.

City wanted a penalty for handball early in the second half, as Tevez weaved his way into the box. The ball broke towards Zabaleta, whose first time cross appeared to strike the arm of Caldwell, but the referee waved the appeals away.

On 55 minutes, the game changed in City's favour. Tevez held the ball up well on the edge of the Wigan penalty area, wriggling away from several challenges, before contesting a 50-50 with Caldwell. The visiting player dived into the tackle, catching the City man, and the referee deemed it worthy of a straight red card.

Wigan initially responded to the sending off well. They weren't able to hold on, though, as Vieira's lobbed pass caused confusion in the box between Stojkovic and Scharner, leaving Tevez to tap the ball into the empty net from close range.

Two minutes later, Tevez was lurking at the back post as Kompany expertly flicked a Garrido cross towards him with his heel, and he slotted it home. Tevez was then played in on the right side of the penalty area. Adebayor wanted it at the back post, but Tevez, on a hat-trick, was always going to take the shot on and he found the back of the net, with the keeper grasping at thin air.

It was three for Tevez and three for City and a hard fought victory.

FROM HUMBLE BEGINNINGS

Well then, that defeat to Everton's gone and made it interesting. After all, it wouldn't be City if there wasn't some foot shooting involved when things were looking good. In fact, City don't just shoot themselves in the foot; before they do, they tend to bayonet it a few times first, ram a grenade up their backside and search out a landmine to stand on seconds after they've pulled the trigger.

I often look back over the foot shooting with fondness. Like the time we needed Kevin Horlock and Paul Dickov to rescue a situation that should never have needed rescuing at the rear end of 1999. Or when a penalty conversion in the last minute of the last game of 2004-05 would ensure European football for the following season, only for it to be missed. Or when Ireland scored after 20-odd seconds at Hamburg last season, only for City to return to Eastlands with a two goal deficit.

City are often referred to as the rollercoaster club because of this tendency to have unbelievable highs followed by desperate lows. But, of course, if City were a rollercoaster, they'd have been shut down by health and safety long ago after numerous complaints of whiplash. I don't recall many complaints of whiplash from the City of Manchester Stadium, though I have seen many a fan turn a strange purple colour because of the various horror shows on the pitch down the years.

As for me, I should probably shut up about who I think is going to finish where because, whenever I say what I think, the opposite tends to happen, usually starting a few hours after my opinion has been published. So, I'm going to try some reverse psychology to try and catch fate's ass unawares: Manchester City will not win the Premier League next season.

That'll show me when we do. Mooney 1, Pre-Determinism Theory 0.

City didn't play too well against Everton. It wasn't the worst performance of the season – congratulations to Tottenham away, that's going to take some beating in this category for the end of season awards – and, in all fairness, City should probably have won the game. In fact, before the end of the season, City will play worse than that and win… and deserve to win.

Enough chances were created, but Howard wasn't tested enough, and two sloppy, against-the-run-of-play goals were conceded – and, City fans, whether you think the referee was right to award the free kick for the first goal or not, it still had to be scored and, if you think it wasn't a free kick, you still have to blame an unmarked Baines and a Cahill free header before Peter Walton's decision. The referee's decisions were inconsistent and occasionally a bit strange, but that wasn't the reason for the defeat.

And because of those two goals, City went from two points behind fourth place with a game in hand to two points behind fourth place with no games in hand. And, judging by the general (over)reaction, you'd think the club was on the verge of being wound up or something.

Don't get me wrong, it was a missed opportunity. But I'd be greatly surprised if one of Aston Villa, Liverpool, or the current fourth placers Tottenham finished the season without dropping another point. And if they did, you'd have to say they probably deserved to finish in the Champions League spots.

It's not as if City have to cross their fingers and wait for those teams to slip up, either – the fact that there are games with Aston Villa and Tottenham coming up, at home, means that City's fate is still in their own hands. Two victories in those two games and, providing there's no other silly results, City could well be in the Champions League next season.

It won't be easy. Not because it never is; we're talking about City, of course it never is – that's as predictable as the plot of a Schwarzenegger film. But because the defeat to Everton has done two things – knock City's confidence, because it's the season-long unbeaten home record gone, and boost Tottenham's, because they are now in the driving seat.

City have never been this close to the top of the top division in England at this stage of the season since I was born. It's a new experience for a lot of our fans, so I can understand where the impatience comes from: We really want to finish fourth because that would be the biggest achievement for the club in our young lifetimes. But, all things considered, does it truly, honestly, matter if it happens this season or next season?

No, it doesn't. It would be nice – very, very nice, if we can clinch it this season – but, not the end of the world if we missed out. I'd be surprised if there was no European football at all next season, looking at the current table. There's been a marked improvement on this City team from that of last season, and the season before. Just imagine what next season's team will be like if there's another vast improvement during the summer.

There's still a big difference between this City team and the best teams in the country – consistency being the key factor. City have followed up their two victories against Chelsea this season with a 3-3 draw against Bolton and a 1-1 draw against Sunderland. With the greatest respect, would Arsenal or Manchester United have drawn those two games having just beaten Chelsea?

That said, I still think City will finish fourth. Despite the consistency of City's inconsistency, with the exception of Everton, they have often been unplayable at home. And even when they have been playable, they've usually got something from the game. That five of City's last eight games are at Eastlands could be the narrow divide between fourth, fifth or sixth.

It's now down to City to knuckle down and pull their socks up. This is potentially the most exciting end to a season I've ever seen – we're in late March and I'm not content that we'll be playing Premier League football next season after just having reached the 40 point mark.

The foundations are in place for a successful future. It just needs patience, time and discipline. City are far from being the finished package and look where they are: Talking as if not finishing fourth would be a disastrous season. This is a club that has never finished above eighth in the Premier League.

I really can't wait to see the final product.

THE LEAGUE'S BEST BOTTLERS

Manchester City fans, I bring good news: Manchester City, mathematically, can't finish bottom of the Premier League (and that's also not allowing for any points deductions Portsmouth may incur). And, if Arsenal beat Hull and Wolves get nothing at Turf Moor, then a victory at the Stadium of Light will ensure Premier League football for the Citizens next season, too.

We could be safe by Sunday evening. Fingers crossed, eh?

See, there's a certain oddity about City fans I've noticed that doesn't seem to be present with any other set of supporters. I don't know many grounds in the country where the phrase "come on, one more just to be safe" can be heard when the team is five goals to the good and there would be no hint of irony in the tone of voice. It says it all when, for the first nine years of my life, I was convinced we were called Fucking Hell City.

City have done stupid things for years – in 1938 they became the first (and are currently still the only) team ever to be relegated whilst being reigning league champions; in the 1957-58 season they scored over 100 goals and also conceded over 100 goals; then there's always being 2-0 in front at half time in the final home game of 2008-09 to Fulham (who had been without an away win all season)… and finishing the game as the losing side, with the 2-3 final score being the springboard for Fulham's survival that season.

I suppose City fans have to have some wry sense of humour to be able to deal with turns of events like that. The same sense of humour is shared by the club itself: The rumour has it that, on one occasion, when a City fan was so disgusted with what he had seen, he ran onto the pitch and tore up his season ticket. Later in the week, he received a replacement, accompanied with the note 'If we have to suffer this rubbish, then so do you.' Though I fear we're heading into urban myth territory, there.

This stupidity must be something ingrained into the club's DNA, because managers, coaches, directors, chairmen, players and even stadiums have been and gone, yet the stupidity remains. Outside of football, I'm a firm believer that no amount of positive or negative thinking can influence an outcome one way or another; I have no belief that fate exists or plays a part in how life transpires and I don't believe in anything of the supernatural. But, when City are playing, that doesn't stop me sending daggers from my eyes into Frank Lampard's back as he stepped up to take a penalty, thinking 'miss miss miss', during City's 2-1 win over Chelsea or asking a God I don't believe in to use powers I don't believe he has to help us on derby day.

Of course, none of that superstitious rubbish actually works. It just makes me feel better when I'm in the stands and unable to change anything going on on the pitch...

But can that stupidity be vanquished? Can it be locked away somewhere, never to see the light of day again, like an unwanted Christmas present or Katie Price's dignity? After all, even after large investments City aren't immune to creating little to no chances in a series of dire displays, which culminated in a 2-4 victory at Chelsea and the completion of their first league double over the London club since 1957. Predictably unpredictable.

It's at this point in articles like this one where the columnist would start looking at the form book as some sort of guide to working out who would be favourites to get fourth spot. But with City's ability to throw anything away, Tottenham and Villa's notoriety in bottling their position better than Coca Cola could ever bottle tap water and Liverpool's somewhat haphazard displays all season, it would probably be better to study the Lord of the Rings books for clues than it would be to study any of the form books.

I still think City are in the best position to grab fourth, but it's all going to come down to whose capacity to bottle it wins out – whoever bottles fourth place the least will get there and that's not going to be easy for experienced bottlers such as Manchester City Football Club. The bright side, though, is that Aston Villa, Tottenham and Liverpool have all bottled finishing fourth in the past, while this is new territory for City.

I'd quite like City to get fourth place. I've never seen the club win something; I've never even seen the club do better than has been expected of them, with the possible exception of the Kevin Keegan promotion season. I'm sick to the back teeth of being every cabbie's second favourite club – ask any supporter of a successful club if they'd rather be less successful and more popular and they'll look at you like you've just handed them a bag of hedgehogs and said: "Here, have a bag of hedgehogs."

It's going to be an interesting end of season, whatever happens.

At any rate, it should be more interesting than a Lily Allen album.

Though, that's not especially hard.

March 2010 Breakdown

Games (all competitions):
Won: 2   **Drawn:** 1   **Lost:** 1

Goals (all competitions):
For: 6   **Against:** 4

Progress:
Premier League: 5th
League Cup: Eliminated in the Semi Final
FA Cup: Eliminated in Round Five

Premier League Table

		P	W	D	L	F	A	GD	Pts
3	Arsenal	32	21	5	6	74	34	+40	68
4	Tottenham Hotspur	31	17	7	7	57	29	+28	58
5	**Manchester City**	**31**	**15**	**11**	**5**	**58**	**39**	**+19**	**56**
6	Liverpool	32	16	6	10	53	32	+21	54
7	Aston Villa	31	13	12	6	43	32	+11	51

April 2010

Burnley 1-6 Manchester City

FA Premier League

Saturday 3 April, 2010 - 17:30 KO

City: Given, Onuoha, Toure (c), Kompany, Sylvinho (de Jong 68), Barry, Vieira, A Johnson, Bellamy, Adebayor (Santa Cruz 80), Tevez (Nimely 83)
Unused: Nielsen, Wright-Phillips, Garrido, Boyata
Goals: Adebayor (4, 45), Bellamy (5), Tevez (7), Vieira (20), Kompany (58)
Booked: -
Man of the Match: Carlos Tevez

Having seen Tottenham lose to Sunderland earlier in the day, City knew that they needed to win to go back into the driving seat for fourth place. And it couldn't have started better for the visitors.

In the opening minutes, Johnson sent a warning shot across Burnley's bows, when his deflected effort struck the foot of the post, with Jensen left standing. It wasn't a warning that Burnley took note of, though, and from a fourth minute corner, the ball broke for Adebayor at the back post. He fired it low and hard and into the net.

A minute later, it got better for the travelling fans. Johnson fed the ball into Tevez and his slide-rule pass found Bellamy breaking unmarked into the box. The Welshman slotted the ball past Jensen coolly, doubling City's tally.

Two minutes later, City broke the record for the fastest Premier League three goal lead. Adebayor's smashed shot was too much for Jensen to hold on to and he spooned it to the feet of Tevez, who was never going to miss the tap in.

With 18 minutes played, Johnson flashed a shot wide, before Adebayor dallied on the ball for too long and wasn't able to find a shot. But, soon after, Vieira was on hand to finish with a fierce header, straight from a Johnson corner.

Just before the half hour, Alexander shot wide from range as Burnley looked for an unlikely way back into the game. Duff then fired a shot straight at Given, but the City keeper was able to hold on.

It was all the visitors and it could have been five when City broke with a three-on-one. Tevez sent the ball wide to Johnson and broke into the box with Adebayor, but the winger's pull back was superbly intercepted and cleared.

Soon after, Tevez was inches away from connecting with a Bellamy shot to turn it into the empty net after a Barry cut-back, but the Argentine could only hit the post.

As the board went up for stoppage time, Adebayor increased City's lead. Tevez played a sublime pass into the big centre-forward's path and he needed no second invitation to slot the ball past Jensen on a one-on-one.

Despite being 5-0 up at half time, the City fans weren't feeling comfortable about the game. During the interval, the pitch was left open to the Lancashire elements and looked to be heavily waterlogged. The referee, though, allowed the game to continue, though the home side wouldn't have complained if he didn't!

With 57 minutes gone, Bellamy received a pass from the right from Onuoha and had an effort on goal deflected wide. The first corner came to nothing, but the second was met by the unmarked Kompany and he bagged his second goal of the season, and City's sixth of the game.

The home side got themselves a consolation goal with 15 minutes to play. Fletcher was sent through on the left and he fired a cracking shot past Given and into the top corner of the net, but it wasn't going to count for much.

As the game entered stoppage time, City nearly grabbed a bizarre seventh goal. Toure cleared from just inside the Burnley half and the bounce completely defeated Jensen, but fortunately for the home side's goalkeeper, it bounced just wide of his goal.

Manchester City 5-1 Birmingham City
FA Premier League
Sunday 11 April, 2010 - 16:00 KO

City: Given, Onuoha, Toure (c), Kompany, Garrido, Barry, de Jong, A Johnson (Cunningham 90+3), Bellamy (Wright-Phillips 81), Adebayor, Tevez (Santa Cruz 87)
Unused: Nielsen, Boyata, Ibrahim, Kay
Goals: Tevez (pen 38, 41), Onuoha (76), Adebayor (43, 88)
Booked: -
Man of the Match: Nedum Onuoha

It was the home side that started the brighter, when Adebayor found the side netting after Tevez had slotted him through, before Tevez himself fired a shot over the bar. With 15 minutes gone, Adebayor poked an effort just wide of the far post as Taylor had come out to meet him.

On the half hour, some neat one-twos from Tevez and Adebayor sliced Birmingham open, but City still couldn't find a shot on target to trouble the goalkeeper. But Dann then gave City the perfect opportunity to open the scoring – by bringing down Adebayor in the box. Tevez stepped up and didn't disappoint.

Three minutes later and City were further in front. A superb corner delivery from Johnson was just over Kompany, but Onuoha was there to dive and connect with his head. Tevez got the final touch, grazing the centre-back's header into the net for his second of the game.

Birmingham responded immediately. Jerome was left unmarked at the back post and, after he was picked out by McFadden, he was able to nod into the net, past the despairing dive of Given.

But, another minute later, City had their two goal cushion back. Barry lifted an excellent ball over the top for Bellamy, who opened the taps to catch it before it went behind. His first time, low cross was met by Adebayor and he poked it into the empty net to round off a crazy five minutes. City went in at the break good value for their lead.

The home fans' frustration with Birmingham's stout second half defending ended in the most unlikely of ways. Onuoha picked up the ball mid-way into the Birmingham half and carried it forward. He looked for Adebayor with a short pass, but nobody responded and Onuoha himself was able to get on the end of it, hitting his shot into the bottom corner, with his left foot.

With two minutes to go, Adebayor latched onto a City clearance after letting the ball bounce over his head. Just like with Burnley last week, he slotted the ball past the goalkeeper and it was City's fifth of the game.

Manchester City 0-1 Manchester United
FA Premier League
Saturday 17 April, 2010 - 12:45 KO

City: Given, Onuoha, Toure (c), Kompany, Bridge, Barry, de Jong (Ireland 79), A Johnson (Vieira 66), Bellamy, Adebayor (Wright-Phillips 75), Tevez
Unused: Nielsen, Boyata, Santa Cruz, Zabaleta
Goals: -
Booked: Kompany, A Johnson
Man of the Match: Nigel de Jong

It was the visitors that started the game the brighter, with some early pressure culminating in a Fletcher shot from range. Given threw himself at it and couldn't get there, but it was just wide of the post. City responded: Tevez was felled on the edge of the box by Gibson. The Argentinian picked himself up to take the free kick and it took an excellent catch from van der Sar to stop the home side taking the lead.

Just before the break, Tevez wanted a penalty for a challenge by Vidic in the area, but the referee didn't agree and awarded City a corner. Rooney found some space in the box and pulled the trigger from roughly the penalty spot. It was low and hard and had Given scrambling, but it was wide of the far post.

Kompany received a yellow card for a foul on Rooney – after the forward had rolled over a few times, though, he was able to jump back up to his feet when the card had been produced, with the home fans incensed.

Nani should have done better on 70 minutes, as he connected with a Giggs low cross. He had the entire goal to aim at, but he stabbed it well wide of the near post. Barry then wriggled free in the United box and went down under a challenge – both the City fans and the City players wanted a penalty, but there was nothing doing again from the referee.

An almighty goalmouth scramble from a corner could have had City in front in the closing stages. United keeper van der Sar came for the cross and got nowhere, leaving Vieira to fire at the goal. Vidic blocked it and Tevez couldn't turn to shoot in time, before it was scrambled away by Neville.

With a minute to play, Wright-Phillips flashed a shot past van der Sar's post, before Bridge fired an effort straight at the big goalkeeper as he found himself free in the box. If either side was going to score, it looked like it would be City.

But, with two and a half of the three added minutes played, true to recent history, United stole the points. City switched off and left Scholes unmarked in the area and he connected with Nani's cross, nodding it past a helpless Given.

Arsenal 0-0 Manchester City
FA Premier League
Saturday 24 April, 2010 - 17:30 KO

City: Given (Nielsen 76), Zabaleta, Toure (c), Kompany, Bridge (Richards 27), Barry, Vieira (Adebayor 53), de Jong, A Johnson, Bellamy, Tevez
Unused: Onuoha, Ireland, Wright-Phillips, Santa Cruz
Goals: -
Booked: Bellamy, Zabaleta
Man of the Match: Vincent Kompany

The game didn't start at all well – both sides were unable to get a hold of the ball and nobody seemed capable of forcing a goal scoring chance. City lost Bridge to injury, while Toure cut out a van Persie cross and that was as lively as it got in the opening stages.

With half time fast approaching, the game saw its first effort on target. Nasri wriggled free in the box and fired a shot past Kompany. Given, though, was on hand to save and pounce on the rebound.

A minute before half time, Vieira had the chance to give City the lead back at his old club. Zabaleta found Bellamy, who turned and played it in for the ex-Gunner, but his first touch was too heavy and the ball was cleared by Campbell. To round off a much-improved end to the half, van Persie hit the side netting from a tight angle.

Deep into the second half, Adebayor nutmegged Silvestre as the defender slipped in midfield. He then stepped around a challenge from Song and raced for the by-line. He managed to cross, but it was too long and came to nothing.

Diaby hit an effort from outside the box on 72 minutes and it took a good save from Given to turn it around the post. The Irish keeper, though, appeared to land badly on his shoulder and, after lengthy treatment on the pitch, he was stretchered off with a suspected dislocation. Nielsen came on for his first appearance for City, becoming the first Faroe Islander to play in the Premier League at the same time.

Three minutes from time, van Persie had an effort that went just wide from a free kick outside the box. With 90 minutes on the clock, Bellamy tried to make the breakthrough at the other end, but his shot was comfortable for Fabianski.

A PREDICTABLE SUCKER PUNCH

What's the worst thing you could hear at a football match? "Ladies and gentlemen, please welcome to the pitch, performing her new single, Lily Allen," is right up there in my hit list of terrible, soul destroying sounds, but alas, this time, it's not that. So is: "Hello, I'm Graeme, I've just bought this seat next to you for the season and I love steam trains." But, again, it's not that.

The most awful noise at a football match follows the point when your SODDING football team leaves a player from your BLOODY closest rivals totally and utterly unmarked in the BLEEDING centre of your own penalty area, 17 seconds from the end of the BUGGERING game.

Sorry. You'd think I'd have grown acclimatised to it by now, what with it having happened for the THIRD TITTING TIME this season, but, clearly, it seems not. Clearly, I'm still quite irritated by City's inability to defend when there's only seconds to go. In truth, though, the more painful part of the day was watching Tottenham not lose to Chelsea – the saving grace post City derby defeat was that Tottenham probably wouldn't win, so everything would be okay.

That one turned out well, eh?

I mean, how do you not see Scholes, anyway? It's not as if he was hard to miss: He was wearing a bright red shirt in the middle of blue territory, he had to run past several City players and he has a rather distinctive hair colour.

It's almost as if there is some footballing god making City and Tottenham's seasons come crashing together in one, penultimate-game-of-the-season decider. Incidentally, I can only assume, as one does, that, if there is a God of football, someone at City did something awful a long, long time ago and the club is still having to face up to the consequences to this day. Maybe a former manager killed a man on the quiet or something.

I expect it's because the season isn't over with just four games to go that means I'm both more nervous and more terrified, yet at least 147% more excited than I have ever been before when watching City. I shouldn't be this nervous… this is a good thing; yet I'm falling to pieces because, feasibly, there are still four teams who might finish in the final Champions League place.

And there are only four games to go, this isn't right. Who cares about who's staying up or who's winning the league when there's this going on smack bang in the upper-middle region of the league?

I suppose the most surprising aspect of the last few weeks is that Tottenham have six points from two games – against Arsenal and Chelsea, following a disaster against Portsmouth. To be honest, they've gotten more points from those two games than I expected and they have deserved those points, too. That makes this Saturday one of the few legitimate times when I will have to support Manchester United – if Tottenham's run of victories extends to three despite their last three games, then they're going to be feeling unbeatable. And rightly so, really… you can't argue with that form.

I'm not confident that Tottenham will leave Old Trafford with nothing… Should they get something, that turn of events may well tip my anger at United to breaking point and I might have to smash something to compensate. Inanimate objects are often not safe in my vicinity when football is concerned, as various mugs, phones, PlayStation pads, DVD cases and light blue plastic seats can vouch for.

And from a City point of view, there could hardly be a better time for Tottenham to visit Old Trafford. Ironically, thanks respectively to Tottenham's success and City's defeat last weekend, United are right back in the title race and will have everything to play for as Spurs visit.

This has been a season for surprises, though – City doubled Chelsea, as unlikely as both results looked; relegation fodder Birmingham should finish in the top 10 after taking everyone on the blindside; and Charles N'Zogbia was released on bail after being arrested for allegedly cheating on his driving theory test. I often make things up for these columns, but even that's beyond me.

The most surprising thing about the Manchester derby last weekend, however, was probably not the last minute winner. Those have been something of a given this season, so I suppose no last minute winner would have actually been that unexpected. Indeed, the most surprising aspect was when a group of players, for argument's sake we'll called them Manchester United players, surrounded an official, we'll call him, say, the referee, in an attempt to get an opposition player, we'll call him, for argument's sake, Gareth Barry, booked – one of which, who we'd give a name to if he wasn't the wrong side of the referee from me and I could see who it was, waved an imaginary yellow card.

Then there's Nigel de Jong, who, aside from having a cracking game and being the best player on the pitch, discovered that he has healing powers to rival those of Jesus. I don't mean that to be offensive in any way, but I think he was the nearest player to the fifth or sixth roll of Wayne Rooney after Vincent Kompany's yellow card challenge. Once that yellow card was produced, though, Rooney was fine to leap into the air and sprint away.

Ferguson then pointed out that City targeted Rooney's injured ankle cynically, just as Bayern Munich had done in the Champions League tie. As an argument, it's flawless… that is, of course, until you take into consideration that, in the corresponding fixture from last season, Shaun Wright-Phillips wasn't able to run more than six yards before he was forcibly introduced to the ground by a United player that hadn't already been booked. It's give and take; you can't have cake and eat it. Unless you're a baker, I guess.

This is probably where City have been falling down all these years (aside from the various amounts of mismanagement both on and off the pitch, obviously). City have only just started to use Craig Bellamy to referee the match for them, in the same way that, for several years, United have used Rooney, Chelsea have used Terry and Liverpool have used Gerrard.

Not that I condone it, but sod it, everyone else does it.

As it stands, it's going to be very close. As much as I don't want it to, it looks like there's going to be no getting away from City vs. Tottenham for the decider.

Sarcasm alert: I just can't wait.

GOALKEEPING CRISIS

The weekend containing the first of City's two dreaded games approaches and, like a van tailgating a pensioner in a Micra, one can only assume that there's likely to be some sort of horrid collision in the very near future. And now the pensioner has pressed the brakes and it's going to take until tomorrow evening to find out which of Manchester City and Aston Villa are the van and Micra in another one of my needlessly over the top analogies.

If City beat Aston Villa this weekend, then the damaged City-esque van will be contemplating a head on collision with another road vehicle, this one more Tottenham shaped and more Hotspur fuelled. And I'll either be in a state of euphoria or despair – because I don't do any other setting, it would seem. And, by the same measure, should City not win against Aston Villa, then the wrangled Micra mess will have to try and hold itself together to survive the Tottenham related pileup.

After that sort of build-up, we're only every going to get two tight and horrible games, with neither side playing anything too dangerous for fear of losing. In fact, I suspect City's next two games could be settled by the odd goal; a situation that, as a City fan with experience of having seen leads thrown away, does worry me somewhat. I'm quite excited about the prospect of finishing fourth, but dreading the next two matches with equal proportion.

One of the biggest talking points for City fans this week has been whether Joe Hart could be recalled from his loan at Birmingham and, once the approach was rejected, whether Gunnar Nielsen should play ahead of the emergency loan goalkeeper, Marton Fulop.

Was anyone that surprised that Joe Hart wasn't allowed to return to City? As a City fan, I hoped it would happen, given his performances for the whole of this season, but I knew from the off that it would be an unlikely occurrence, at best. Then again, people buy music by Lily Allen, so I suppose anything is possible.

Hart has been on a season-long loan and, as part of the Premier League's rules with a season-long loan, City couldn't include a recall option in the contract. So, while the argument that Hart is a City player was, technically, true, he is contracted to Birmingham until the end of the season and this week isn't the end of the season. It would have needed permission from Birmingham and permission from the Premier League to break that contract and it was refused.

Why some City fans are getting so annoyed by that, I'm not sure. It's not exactly like the Premier League are being deliberately anti-City or as if Birmingham are being particularly obtuse about the situation. Both parties are within their rights to deny City the recall and the Premier League decided to invoke that right.

I can understand why the Premier League would turn such a request down, too. As far as I'm aware, there has been no precedent set in recalling season-long Premier League loans until now. So, should the Premier League have allowed it and Hart helped City finish fourth, there could be potential legal issues from Tottenham, Aston Villa and Liverpool, similar to the whole Carlos Tevez, West

Ham and Sheffield United mess of 2007.

And helping City to fourth is something Hart would have had the potential to do, had he returned. Having seen some of his performances for Birmingham, I suspect he's a lot closer to Given's standard than Mark Hughes thought at the start of the season; and with Given potentially injured for the start of next season – City will be playing some sort of European competition, so the season could be starting earlier and will contain plenty more games – Hart may well be keeping the Irishman out of the side.

The choice of Marton Fulop as the emergency loan goalkeeper is a strange one, too. He's not played a lot in the Premier League recently, so there is the possibility that he is a bit rusty and, with a lot of fans having seen neither him nor Gunnar Nielsen play, nobody knows who would be the better choice to start. Nielsen looked comfortable and competent in the final 17 minutes with Arsenal, but it was hardly like he was put under any real pressure. And Mancini has form when it comes to putting inexperienced fringe players in for big games – with the more senior Nedum Onuoha fit for the League Cup games with Manchester United, he stuck with the inexperienced Dedryck Boyata, who had been playing fairly well at the time.

I suppose it could be the catalyst for the rest of the defence to tighten themselves up in order to help or protect the inexperienced player and help him through his first few games. Not that the defence has been that fragile recently, anyway; with 180 minutes against two of the best sides and most potent attacks in the country, it was only a marking error in the final seconds of one the games that allowed one of them in to score.

As for fourth spot… who knows what will happen? I would say that it's going to be fun finding out, but I suspect the finding out bit will be one of the most nerve-wracking, nail-biting and horrid experiences of my football-watching life. Hopefully, the City van won't need too many repairs after tomorrow and can steam-roller through Wednesday evening in as best condition as possible.

April 2010 Breakdown

Games (all competitions):
Won: 2   **Drawn:** 1   **Lost:** 1

Goals (all competitions):
For: 11   **Against:** 3

Progress:
Premier League: 6th
League Cup: Eliminated in the Semi Final
FA Cup: Eliminated in Round Five

Premier League Table

		P	W	D	L	F	A	GD	Pts
4	Tottenham Hotspur	35	19	7	9	63	37	+26	64
5	Aston Villa	36	17	13	6	51	35	+16	64
6	**Manchester City**	**35**	**17**	**12**	**6**	**69**	**42**	**+27**	**63**
7	Liverpool	36	18	8	10	61	33	+28	62
8	Everton	36	15	12	9	59	49	+10	57

May 2010

Manchester City 3-1 Aston Villa

FA Premier League

Saturday 1 May, 2010 - 15:00 KO

City: Fulop, Zabaleta, Toure (c), Kompany, Bridge, de Jong, Vieira, A Johnson (Wright-Phillips 80), Bellamy, Adebayor, Tevez (Richards 88)
Unused: Nielsen, Garrido, Sylvinho, Onuoha, Santa Cruz
Goals: Tevez (pen 41), Adebayor (43), Bellamy (89)
Booked: Kompany
Man of the Match: Vincent Kompany

Despite City's pressure in the opening stages, it was the visitors who opened the scoring. Carew ran on to a through ball from Downing, getting away from Toure and getting his shot in. Toure should probably have blocked it, but he didn't and it went through Fulop's legs and into the net. It was a very soft goal for the home side to concede and exactly what they didn't need.

Just before the half hour, Zabaleta wanted a penalty when he went down in the box, but it was nothing doing from the referee. Three minutes later, City had more appeals for a penalty. Tevez ran with the ball towards the edge of the box, before sidestepping Warnock and firing in a right-footed shot. The full back blocked it with an arm, but the referee decided it was unintentional.

Soon enough, though, City were on level terms. Warnock floored Adam Johnson in the box as the winger looked to go around the defender and Tevez stepped up to smash the resulting penalty kick under Friedel.

Two minutes later, it got better. City broke, after Carew had hit the bar, and Johnson was played through on the right. He cut the ball back onto his left foot, rolled it back for Adebayor and the big forward found the net, via Friedel's hand, to give City the lead at the break. It was no less than what City deserved for a hard-fought first half performance after falling behind.

The start of the second half was a much different affair. For all City's domination in the first period, they couldn't get their foot on the ball and the game became quite scrappy. Tevez was caught in possession and it took a Toure interception on a Dunne run to stop the former City player getting a shot in on his old stomping ground.

With 10 minutes to go, Kompany nodded wide from a corner, as City tried to kill the game off. It was getting tense and the City fans were feeling it, especially when Zabaleta had to rescue a poor clearance from Fulop. The tie was balanced on a knife-edge.

Then, after a Villa corner where Fulop had had to come and punch, City got their winner. The ball found its way to Wright-Phillips on the left and he skipped past two challenges at full speed to find Bellamy unmarked in the box. He took a touch and bent it into the top corner, leaving Friedel standing.

Aston Villa were out of the running for a Champions League spot and City will go head-to-head with Tottenham for it in midweek.

Manchester City 0-1 Tottenham Hotspur

FA Premier League
Wednesday 5 May, 2010 - 15:00 KO

City: Fulop, Zabaleta, Toure (c), Kompany, Bridge, de Jong, Barry (Vieira 57), A Johnson (Wright-Phillips 72), Bellamy (Santa Cruz 84), Adebayor, Tevez
Unused: Nielsen, Richards, Sylvinho, Onuoha
Goals: -
Booked: -
Man of the Match: Gareth Barry

The noise in the City of Manchester Stadium was high as the teams emerged from the tunnel in the game that could decide who was to finish fourth. A win for City would leave them need to take all three points away from West Ham on the final day to be in the Champions League next season. However, a win for Tottenham would mean City definitely wouldn't be finishing in fourth position.

City started brightly, with Barry flicking an effort wide with his left foot in the opening exchanges, before Tevez forced a save from Gomes after wriggling his way into the box.

But Tottenham responded with some pressure of their own. With 16 minutes gone, City had their first warning shot as Crouch hit the post, rising above Toure to meet Bale's free kick. Three minutes later, King fired another shot across City's bows, heading home from a right wing corner, but the referee disallowed it for climbing. It was a let off.

On 25 minutes, Johnson forced Gomes into a superb stop, after a Bellamy corner was cleared to the young winger on the edge of the box. He took a touch to steady himself, before firing it through the crowd, but Gomes got down to palm it around the post.

Fulop then nearly made a hash of a clearance, kicking it straight at the oncoming Crouch, but, fortunately for the emergency loan keeper, it went straight into the air and he was able to catch it as it dropped. The nerves were obvious around the stadium and the atmosphere could have been cut with a knife.

In the second half, Fulop had to be alert to tip a Defoe effort around the post, before Huddlestone was lucky not to see red when he aimed a stamp in de Jong's direction after a scramble on the edge of City's box.

The game was becoming stretched and City were beginning to struggle to cope with their opponents as Barry was forced off the pitch through injury. Vieira came on to replace him, but he didn't have the same impact as the England midfielder, with Tottenham beginning to take control.

With eight minutes to go, Fulop made a vital save with his legs to deny Crouch from a yard out, before Fulop was unable to hold on to a Kaboul cross and Crouch was left with the easiest of headers to put the visitors in front. It was a difficult goal for the fans to take, but, in the closing stages, the visitors had looked the more likely to take the lead.

It turned out to be the last chance of the game and City were left ruing the missed chances in the first half, as Tottenham got the win they wanted to ensure a fourth place finish.

City will be in the Europa League next season.

West Ham United 1-1 Manchester City
FA Premier League
Sunday 9 May, 2010 – 16:00 KO

City: Fulop, Zabaleta, Toure (c), Kompany, Sylvinho (Richards 73), de Jong, Vieira, A Johnson (Cunningham 90), Wright-Phillips, Adebayor, Santa Cruz (Tevez 74)
Unused: Nielsen, Ibrahim, Boyata, Garrido
Goals: Wright-Phillips (21)
Booked: -
Man of the Match: Adam Johnson

The final day of the 2009-10 season left City with nothing to play for: They were certain to finish in the Europa League places and would achieve their highest ever Premier League finish whatever the result.

With 18 minutes on the clock, it was the home side who took the lead. A lovely flick from Diamanti let Boa Morte in on goal and he fired it, first time, straight past Fulop and into the corner of the net.

It didn't matter, though, because City responded almost immediately. Just three minutes later, Zabaleta found Johnson on the right. The England hopeful crossed to the back post where his fellow countryman, Wright-Phillips, leapt into the air and headed the ball back across Green and into the net. The smallest man on the pitch ghosted in to nod the ball into the far corner for the equaliser.

Just before the half hour, Johnson should have gotten the visitors a penalty when he was tripped in the box by Upson after one of his trademark runs, but the referee turned it down and waved away the protests. Adebayor had a goal disallowed for offside, before Diamanti nearly put the home side back in front – drilling a low shot at goal and hitting the post, as Fulop flung himself across to try and stop it.

Cole had the first chance of the second half, but, after rising well, he was only able to nod wide, before Wright-Phillips fired a shot over the bar. Diamanti then tried a scissor kick from a Cole header, but it lacked power and didn't trouble Fulop.

Sylvinho tried to sign off the season with a wonder goal, picking up the ball mid-way into the West Ham half and running it into the box. Upson, though, wasn't going to let him get that strike and got in an excellent block as the left back tried to finish.

On 78 minutes, ex-Hammer Tevez nearly scored at his old stomping ground when he got his toe on the end of an Adebayor through ball. But, under pressure from both Upson and Green, he was only able to poke it onto the roof of the net and the scores remained level.

It turned out to be the final chance of a game that had a distinct nothing-riding-on-it feel and City will be looking for a few new faces to boost the squad's push for Champions League football next time out.

DISAPPOINTING BEST EVER SEASON

It seems strange to be talking about Manchester City's greatest ever Premier League season as a disappointment. It's very much like being disappointed with your wife of just two hours or not being content with Belgian chocolate after years of that stuff your grandma always gives you that looks like a dog turd, smells like it went off in 1984 and crumbles under the weight of an ant.

Let me make it clear that I am, in no way, shape or form, linking my beloved football club to a dog turd.

But, like a man who's stepped in a dog turd, I'm currently feeling a mixture of anger and disappointment, and I can sense a bad smell hanging around. The defeat against Tottenham on Wednesday ended City's push for fourth place and, while I'm not especially surprised that Tottenham won the game, I feel justified in being angry and disappointed.

Disappointed that City couldn't raise their game and take on Tottenham on their home pitch and angry that I let myself think that City would probably win the game before kick-off. I'm a City fan; I've seen unexpected defeats snatched from the jaws of victory, I've cried at Wembley because of this team's obsession with putting its fans under the type of stresses and strains known only to astronauts, and I know better than to expect a victory in one important game.

Yet, despite the news that City will finish outside of the Champions League, I'm not as disappointed as I wrote that I would be. I can't say why exactly; I expected that I would be absolutely distraught, but I'm just not. This has been an excellent season, but it finishes on a low note because it could have been so much better. It's still something to be proud of, though.

I could have gone to bed last night salivating at potential ties with Barcelona or Real Madrid. You'd think that not getting to play the best in Europe would be totally earth shatteringly bad, but it's not. It's not ideal, either, but the positives to take are that City are in a competition they weren't in this season and they have a fair chance of winning it. It doesn't have the player-pull that the Champions League has, but I don't think it was a 'this season or never' situation for City and I do think that they will be in the competition sooner rather than later – I don't think any potential transfer targets would be too put off by that.

We can analyse until the cows come home a multitude of reasons why City didn't finish fourth this season. Had there not been daft home draws from leading positions to Fulham, Burnley and Hull… had there not been daft last minute goals against United… had we bothered to turn up against Tottenham twice. All of those arguments hold water as to why City didn't finish fourth, but when it comes down to it, they all count for nothing unless we improve on them next season. Other teams will have 'what if's, too.

But, to reiterate, while City haven't finished fourth, this has been a good season. City have finished above Liverpool for only the third time in the last 48 years. City, at the time of writing, have the same number of defeats as Manchester United. City have scored more Premier League goals than ever before. City have qualified for a European competition outright and haven't had to rely on not getting booked, sent off and being all round nice to everyone. City's season wasn't over when the points tally ticked to 40. City's points tally ticked to 40 well before March. City have three players in the goal scoring charts in double figures in the top flight for the first time in decades.

It shows how far City have come for all of that to be a disappointing, eh?

A lot of fans compared Wednesday night's match to the 1998-99 Division Two playoff final. While the reward two days ago was potentially bigger and better – the Champions League – personally, I don't feel that that game was as important. Should City have lost to Gillingham in 1999, where would they be now? Would they have found Division Two as hard to get out of as even the most uncomfortable of beds early in the morning when the alarm sounds, just like Leeds have done? It could be questionable as to whether they would have ever re-climbed the league ladder and it would certainly be questionable as to whether Sheikh Mansour would have bought the club.

And what has losing to Tottenham done? Nothing but make City have to try again next year, following on from their best ever Premier League position and with the added bonus of a hefty transfer budget. How awful is that?

It's all too easy to forget that, just over three seasons ago, City fans were contemplating a season of relegation struggle and financial oblivion, while crossing their fingers for a takeover. And, when that takeover came, it wasn't all sweetness and light as, at the end of the 2007-08 season, there was the rumoured fire-sale because of a lack of funds. Add to that several managerial changes for a nice bit of instability and it's a miracle that City are in as good a shape as they are.

For now, we have to say congratulations to Tottenham. It's hardly like they have finished fourth by accident – City haven't done enough and Tottenham have, it's as simple as that. It's not the end of the world; it's not like football won't exist after next season, it's not like the human race will cease to exist next May and it's not like Lily Allen's releasing any more albums.

It's just a matter of time and patience. It doesn't matter that City just missed out this season, especially if the club can improve and build on that next time around. Just imagine what City could be capable of, after a summer of spending and hard work, next season. It's exciting to say the least.

Though, as City fans, we must know by now to expect the unexpected.

Relegation battle here we come!

May 2010 Breakdown

Games (all competitions):
Won: 1   **Drawn:** 1   **Lost:** 1

Goals (all competitions):
For: 4   **Against:** 3

Progress:
Premier League: 5th
League Cup: Eliminated in the Semi Final
FA Cup: Eliminated in Round Five

Final Premier League Table

		P	W	D	L	F	A	GD	Pts
1	Chelsea	38	27	5	6	103	32	+71	86
2	Manchester United	38	27	4	7	86	28	+58	85
3	Arsenal	38	23	6	9	83	41	+42	75
4	Tottenham Hotspur	38	21	7	10	67	41	+26	70
5	**Manchester City**	**38**	**18**	**13**	**7**	**73**	**45**	**+28**	**67**
6	Aston Villa	38	17	13	8	52	39	+13	64
7	Liverpool	38	18	9	11	61	35	+26	63
8	Everton	38	16	13	9	60	49	+11	61
9	Birmingham City	38	13	11	14	38	47	-9	50
10	Blackburn Rovers	38	13	11	14	41	55	-14	50
11	Stoke City	38	11	14	13	34	48	-14	47
12	Fulham	38	12	10	16	39	46	-7	46
13	Sunderland	38	11	11	16	48	56	-8	44
14	Bolton Wanderers	38	10	9	19	42	67	-25	39
15	Wolverhampton Wanderers	38	9	11	18	32	56	-24	38
16	Wigan Athletic	38	9	9	20	37	79	-42	36
17	West Ham United	38	8	11	19	47	66	-19	35
18	Burnley	38	8	6	24	42	82	-40	30
19	Hull City	38	6	12	20	34	75	-41	30
20	Portsmouth	38	7	7	24	34	66	-32	19

Summer 2010

THE CITY LOVE AFFAIR GONE WRONG

At precisely just a few minutes before midnight on Sunday 31 August 2008, Manchester City sent a message to the entire footballing world. £32.5m later and they had acquired one of the biggest talents in world football in Robinho, and, this being Manchester City, of course it wasn't going to be anywhere near as simple a signing as everyone at the club would have hoped. It never is, is it?

Roll forward 22 months and Robinho puts in an excellent performance for Brazil in their opening game of the World Cup Finals in South Africa, after a turbulent time with City. He'd spent most of 2010 back home in Brazil on loan with Santos, the club where he started his career, after just 10 appearances in the first half of the season for his parent club.

The player that left for Santos in January was but a shadow of the player that City fans saw from September to December 2008, during which time he scored 12 goals in all competitions. From then on in, though, nothing looked like it would work for him: He seemingly lost his finishing ability, scoring just four more goals in the next calendar year, he struggled to beat players, he looked disinterested and then, to top it all off, he picked up an injury that would keep him out for three months.

It started well, but soon all went downhill and now he is the enigma that divides many of us Citizens. As, undoubtedly, one of the best players in the world, it's understandable that a lot of City fans want him to be a part of the squad for the coming season. But many others disagree, citing a poor work rate and overall poor form for the best part of a year.

He has been criticised for his lack of defensive hard work, with the counter-argument being that defending isn't his job. I can buy the second argument, providing he's being played as a centre-forward (or just behind). When playing wide-left, however, you have to give the left full back some help. I would never have expected him to chase back and put in a superbly executed tackle, but I would expect that he put up some resistance when the opposition are coming towards him with the ball.

That, though, is a minor part of what could be perceived as a big problem. With only five or six exceptions, since January 2009, Robinho looked like he just didn't care what was happening on the pitch both defensively and offensively. No matter how badly things are going, there's no excuse for coming off the pitch without having given it everything and a lot of fans often thought Robinho guilty of having done just that.

What the fans think, though, isn't really that important. Quite a strange statement for someone writing something that is all opinion from no qualified position other than being a fan, I admit, but it's true. My opinion doesn't matter.

The only opinions that do matter here are those of Roberto Mancini and Robinho. Will the manager want to take the player back and try and integrate him into his squad – after all, Mancini got no more than a matter of weeks with him before he left on loan? Will Robinho decide that he wants to fight for his place?

In March 2009 while at Santos, Robinho himself said: "Where I have to be happiest is within the four lines of the pitch, and this is happening. I intend to continue for long. I hope that the board is already addressing this issue. You just have to look at my face to see my desire to stay at the club."

Those aren't really the words of a man who wants to come back to Manchester. A cynic would say that the situation isn't too dissimilar to the one that he was in at Real Madrid.

But let's flip this whole situation on its head for a moment. Stephen Ireland hasn't looked the same player he was since Robinho's absence from the City team and, given that the two players worked very well together, that's not really a huge surprise. If City were to decide that there is no room for Robinho in the team, does it also mean that we will be hard pushed to see a return to form for Ireland?

There's just as much chance, however, that a spell back home in Brazil and a good World Cup will benefit City… and not in the sense that it will bump up his price for a sale, but rather that he'll have gotten his head screwed back on the right way and will be prepared to work hard and strut his stuff at Eastlands. Admittedly, that does feel like it could be something of a long shot.

City achieved their highest ever Premier League points tally and their highest ever Premier League finish last season without the influence of Robinho for most of it. The decision that Roberto Mancini now has to make is really quite simple: Is Robinho one of the additions to the team that will turn that fifth place finish into a finish in the top four?

In my totally unimportant, completely irrelevant, yet still written opinion, Robinho's time with City has been something like a love affair. It was good while it lasted, but it looks like it's time to call it a day and move on. Robinho's attitude has been questionable for quite a while and, unless he can change it, give everything for the team and do what the manager asks of him (whether he agrees or not), then I don't think he's right for City.

Someone once said that the whole is greater than the sum of its parts. But, for that to be true, all of the parts need to be working together and in harmony with each other. In the case of a football team, that's various players doing their jobs and doing them to the best of their ability. If Robinho's attitude is such that he isn't interested in the game being played, for whatever reason, then it means accommodating him into the team just in case he turns on the magic and that starts to become a problem when the magic doesn't happen.

My heart wants him to stay and prove me wrong. My heart wants him to return to City and be the missing link, recapture his late 2008 form and help City to their best ever Premier League finish again.

But my head says it's not the likely outcome this summer.

EXCUSES, EXCUSES

Excuses have been made since the dawn of time for all sorts of things. "I'm late because my sundial didn't go off" or "The bus was late because the wheel hasn't been invented yet" or even "A Stegosaurus ate my homework." Of course, I'm being silly – dinosaurs and man never came into contact with each other outside of Jurassic Park and, if the documentary series I saw about those islands is to be believed, there wasn't much homework-doing going on.

But excuses generally all have one thing in common – they're utter cowpats. "I'm sorry I'm late, the bus didn't turn up on time" is, 99% of the time, code for "I'm not actually sorry I'm interrupting your lecture, but I know I have to give a reason for doing it now that I have done it and I know that telling you I preferred to sleep in for another half an hour isn't going to go down well, so here's some rubbish I'm spouting out of my face to save both of us the embarrassment of me turning up late."

And, of course, turning up late isn't the only time you need excuses. Excuses are golden for when leaving early: For example, a party you didn't want to go to ("I have to get home because I'm working in London tomorrow"), a date that isn't going well ("My grandfather's not well, so I have to get back"), or even an international football competition where you didn't do as well as you and millions of others had expected ("Manchester City keep buying people from abroad, so the England team is rubbish").

Like I said, cowpats.

It has to be City's fault that Wayne Rooney had the control and agility of a combine harvester. Who else is there to blame that the defence looked as stable as a puddle of nitroglycerine near a fire? And it goes without saying that there's only one place to look as to the reason why Gerrard and Lampard looked like two people who'd not even spoken to each other for 10 years.

So, and this is a question aimed at a certain Brian Woolnough from the Daily Star (who argued that, with clubs like City spending money on foreign players, the England team will suffer), why have England not been much cop for the last 44 years? I mean, City were taken over in 2008 and Chelsea in 2003 – so that covers the last seven years, but what about the remaining 37? And why are City being blamed for the high finances of football and lack of English youth development when they are just the latest of many clubs to have spent big and, in the years just before the takeover, they were over reliant on academy products to be able to put out a team most weeks?

That transfer fees and wages are as high as they are isn't the fault of football's latest rich kids. Before City broke the English transfer record for Robinho, many others had broken it first, on such illustrious flops as Juan Sebastian Veron or Andriy Shevchenko. Money clearly not well spent at a time when the fees spent on those individual players were more than City's entire transfer budget.

I don't think there's a football fan in the world that wouldn't prefer a team to win their league by producing a squad of academy talents all at the same time, before spending money on foreign imports. There's always that romantic view of the team of kids showing the big boys in the league how it's done, most of them from the area around where the club is based.

Unfortunately, as much as that would be the desired method of competing with the best, it just isn't ever likely to happen. With the amount of prize money that has been earned by those at the top, it made them self-financing in that they were the only teams that could afford to price everybody else out of the market. They bring in better players, win more things, get more money and bring in better players. And on and on it goes.

The days when several academy graduates topple the establishment are going, if not already gone. So, when City are taken over and decide that they'd like to compete with the best, it's unfair to blame them for inflating transfer prices. The choice was to either spend little money and remain everybody's second favourite club or to try and compete. Competing, of course, involved bringing in better players; players whose value had previously soared, anyway.

England don't win the World Cup and City spend big. To say the first happened because the second happened is an inaccurate and ill considered conclusion; one that's far too easy and lazy to arrive at. For a start, at the time of writing, City's squad contains no less than nine Englishmen (four from the club's own academy) who have been regulars for the club in the past, with an additional three that are currently breaking into the first team. And that doesn't include the six non-English academy products that have represented the first team and are currently available for selection. Clearly, youth development is at an end because the chequebook has come out for Silva, Toure, Boateng, et al.

While it may be true that City can field a first team that contains no English players, it is also true that they can field one that contains no foreigners (though the formation would be a bit off, granted). It seems pretty churlish to point the finger at City for strengthening the squad from abroad, when there's a potential season of 64 matches (not including any FA Cup replays) coming up and when English players are as over-priced as they are.

If recent reports are to be believed, Aston Villa's valuation of James Milner is £30m. And, of course, should City decide to pay that amount, they would still be the bad guys, because, despite the promotion of English talent, it would be an obscene transfer fee. Should City decide it's too much and look overseas for a cheaper, equivalent player, then the club are ruining the chances of future England teams. Lose-lose, or what?

The only option for City to be the good guys is to promote academy products before they are ready... the very same system of providing first team players that nearly saw the club relegated in 2007. The club is now in the position where they don't need to rush young talent into the squad, where only the best of the best will make it through, and where those youngsters can learn from some of the best players the game will see.

Yet that is the wrong way to run a football club. Work that one out.

The problem isn't that the influx of foreigners is stopping English youth developing. Forcing teams to play x number of English players in their team won't increase the quality of the national team, but rather decrease the quality of the Premier League. If the youth isn't good enough to break into the first team for any reason other than being forced in there by the rules, then those players are never going to be good enough to help England to a World Cup win. But if the English youth is good enough, then those players will play.

If you want to look for excuses as to why England didn't win the World Cup, you could look at poor management, incorrect tactics, the fact that we're not as good as other teams that have gone further than us...

But the takeover of Manchester City and their transfers in isn't a valid excuse.

TIME TO THINK BIG

The Beatles once sang that money can't buy you love. That may well be true, but there are plenty of things that money can buy you – a castle or an island, for example. Or a luxury yacht. Or, indeed, a whole host of international footballers. But, then again they also sang that there were eight days in a week, so that could have been an indication that 1964 was the year they started losing their marbles.

With four high profile signings already this summer, the coming season should be something of an exciting one for us Manchester City fans. With a squad that finished just shy of fourth place and the money that has been spent so far this summer – and, if reports are to be believed, there'll be a lot more of it spent soon, too – the expectations must rise, too. It would be odd to have a strong squad strengthened by (at the current count) roughly £75m and four new faces to make up the gap of just three points. That sort of gap could be bridged for much less.

At the time of writing, in has come Aleksandar Kolarov, a left back with a thunderous free kick, Jerome Boateng, a defender who has a reputation for a tough tackle, David Silva, a midfielder known for link-up play and his ball skills, and Yaya Toure, a midfielder whose strength, technique and ball-playing abilities have looked superb.

Indeed, with those additions, while qualifying for the Champions League must be the ultimate aim for this coming campaign, I suspect privately, if not publicly, Roberto Mancini's targets will be more focused on closing the 19 point gap between his club and last season's league winners Chelsea.

In other words, a title challenge.

Call me optimistic (or deluded), but with the level of investment City have had these last two seasons and looking at where that investment took the club to last season, it can't be that much of an outrageous claim. I could make much more outrageous claims like Belgium doesn't exist, or Star Wars is a factually accurate documentary, or that Lily Allen made good music.

Last summer, Mark Hughes made several high profile signings. The likes of Adebayor, Tevez and Kolo Toure came in and pushed a squad that finished outside of all of the European qualification places to one that was one win away from playing in the Champions League this season. Now, while it would be foolish to expect such an improvement in the coming season, it isn't foolish to suggest that City can do better than to finish fourth.

Especially when you consider that, of all the squads in last season's top five, City's is by far and away the most improved. Even everybody's favourite pundit and computer game co-commentator thinks City have, man for man, the best squad in the league. It's all going to depend on how well the team can play together and whether they can get off to a flying start.

And that rather neatly, and conveniently, brings me onto pre-season. Since Sky Sports decided that pre-season was important a few years ago and presented it much in the same way they do when there's a round of league or cup matches ("And there's been a goal at Eastlands, which way has it gone…?", "It's finished with another defeat for a Premier League side… Manchester City fans, how are you feeling?"), far too much has been made of pre-season.

I don't want to sound unenthusiastic and bored by pre-season, but I am. So that's probably why I inevitably sound unenthusiastic and bored by pre-season whenever I have to comment on it. The problem is that the results don't actually matter and no teams play like the results matter. In fact, I think it's only Sky Sports that do think the results matter.

City have been somewhat unimpressive this pre-season. And I don't care one iota. I don't for a minute think that winning only two friendlies (one of which was a behind closed doors affair right at the start of the warm-up fixture list) matters when it comes to the two teams that walk out at White Hart Lane on Saturday lunchtime. What will matter is that the players are ready for competitive football – that they are fit to play, that they aren't still carrying a few pounds of summer holiday weight and that they are ready for a 38 match Premier League campaign. Winning pre-season games doesn't make that happen, but rather playing pre-season games does.

I've not decided if it's a good thing that City play Tottenham first, either. While traditionally Tottenham win this fixture, City have the strongest team they've had in decades. Still, the same could have been said last season and it wasn't exactly a classic performance from the visitors to the capital, was it?

But this time around, City will be going to White Hart Lane with ambitions of not finishing fourth. This will be a City team who will be looking towards finishing above fourth and who I will maintain (if optimistically/deluded-ly so) should be looking at challenging the Premier League title this season.

Will City win the league? Probably not; it would come as quite a surprise to me if they did. But that doesn't mean they won't be trying to and that doesn't mean it won't be one of Roberto Mancini's aims for this season. I spent years trying to dive into a swimming pool without making a massive splash, hurting my stomach and making spectators wince… I aimed to do that. I tried to do that. But I couldn't do it immediately.

Still can't, actually.

There's nothing wrong in aiming high. Should that mean at Christmas we have to reassess our aims, then we have to reassess our aims. But, right now, City's squad is the most improved in the Premier League. So you'd expect that to be reflected in the final table… and hopefully that squad can pick up a trophy, too – be it the Europa League, FA Cup or League Cup; I don't think any City fan cares which.

The football's back. Let's go.

August 2010

Tottenham Hotspur 0-0 Manchester City

FA Premier League
Saturday 14 August, 2010 – 12:45 KO

City: Hart, Richards, Kolarov (Zabaleta 45), Kompany, K Toure, Barry, de Jong, Y Toure, Wright-Phillips (A Johnson 68), Silva, Tevez (c) (Adebayor 84)
Unused: Given, Lescott, Vieira, Jo
Goals: -
Booked: Kompany, Zabaleta
Man of the Match: Joe Hart

With 10 minutes gone, it was all the home side. Hart hadn't been properly tested in the City goal, but the majority of the play was inside the visitors' box.

Soon, the City goalkeeper was showing why he has been tipped as a future England regular. First, from a Crouch nod down, he reacted superbly to push away a Defoe swivel and shot, as it looked destined for the net. A minute later, he was there to tip away a Huddlestone effort from range.

But the best was yet to come. From a Spurs corner, Assou-Ekotto fired it back in. It looked to be flying wide of Hart's goal until it hit the head of Wright-Phillips, which sent it looping towards the top corner. Hart, however, got up well and flicked it over the bar, producing what would surely be one of the saves of the season – and in the opening 20 minutes, too.

On the half hour, Spurs continued to press and it nearly paid off. Bale drove a low shot across goal that had Hart beaten, but it struck the foot of the post and bounced out, leaving Kompany to clear the danger. Kolarov then went to sleep and allowed Defoe a run at goal. Hart, though, was off his line quickly to stop the England forward.

The best chance of the second half came immediately after the kick-off. Wright-Phillips was sent clean through into the Spurs box, but Assou-Ekotto recovered to tackle as the England winger waited too long for the ball to drop.

Hart was called into action to deny Pavlyuchenko's effort from outside the box, before de Jong put in an excellent tackle to prevent Bale getting a run at goal. Kompany then bettered it, sliding in to take the ball off Pavyluchenko's toe as he was about to pull the trigger. Bale missed a sitter as the ball broke to him inside the box with Hart beaten, but on his right foot he blazed it wide.

FC Timisoara 0-1 Manchester City

UEFA Europa League Playoff Round, First Leg
Thursday 19 August, 2010 – 20:00 KO

City: Hart, Zabaleta, Kompany, K Toure, Lescott, Barry (Balotelli 55), de Jong, Y Toure, Silva (A Johnson 65), Tevez (c) (Jo 77), Adebayor

Unused: Given, Richards, Wright-Phillips, Vieira
Goals: Balotelli (71)
Booked: Balotelli
Man of the Match: Mario Balotelli

City began to get their foot on the ball as the game progressed, but weren't able to forge any chances, as a David Silva corner was easily swallowed up by the home side's goalkeeper. Timisoara had an appeal for a penalty turned down as Curtean went down under Zabaleta's tackle. The City right caught his trailing leg.

Just before the break, City put the ball into the Timisoara box from a free kick on the left, but it was comfortably headed clear. Yaya Toure produced a moment of inspiration, dancing into the area, beating four men, before drilling a cross into the six-yard box, but it was well blocked by Pantilimon.

The second half started where the first finished – with City in control of the game. Silva hit the bar, but was flagged offside, before Tevez tried an overhead kick after an Adebayor flick, but it was off target and fell to Balotelli at the back. It looked a tap-in, but he could only hit the side netting.

Two minutes later and City should have been in front. A Balotelli corner fell to Yaya Toure at the back post and he coolly controlled the ball on his chest, before lashing a right-footed volley at goal. It beat the keeper, but didn't beat the post and it bounced away.

But, soon after, it was a dream debut for Balotelli. Adebayor broke into the area and drilled the ball across the six-yard box for his team-mate, who couldn't miss and planted the ball into the net from close range.

The game finished on a sour note for the man of the match, however. After some sterling work by the City defence to stop two Timisoara free kicks, the Italian broke into the box and went down after winning a corner. He couldn't continue and City finished the game with 10 men.

Manchester City 3-0 Liverpool

FA Premier League
Monday 23 August, 2010 - 20:00 KO

City: Hart, Richards, Lescott, Kompany, K Toure, Barry, de Jong, Y Toure (Zabaleta 86), A Johnson, Milner, Tevez (c) (Jo 86)
Unused: Given, Silva, Vieira, Wright-Phillips, Adebayor
Goals: Barry (13), Tevez (53, pen 67)
Booked: Richards
Man of the Match: Gareth Barry

The game started cagily. Liverpool looked to have settled quicker than the hosts, but City soon sprang into life. Johnson flashed a shot just past Reina's post, before the Blues took the lead. Milner did well on the right, controlling a difficult ball and cutting inside. He rolled it to Barry, who planted the ball in the net. But that was the last of the first half action.

The second half started slowly and it was the home side who took the initiative once again. From a Milner corner on 53 minutes, Richards climbed highest to nod the ball at goal. Tevez touched it past Reina and Johnson couldn't keep it out from behind his goalkeeper.

Liverpool, looking to get back into the game, began to dominate as City looked like they might have relaxed too soon. Gerrard hit the post with a shot from range, before Hart parried from N'Gog from inside the six-yard box, and was then back up to dive at the feet of Torres to put it behind.

With just over 20 minutes to go, City sealed the game. Johnson broke into the box through two Liverpool challenges and, as he got to the ball, Skrtel hacked him down to concede the penalty. Tevez stepped up and buried it.

On 73 minutes, Torres reminded City that the game wasn't quite over, as he turned Richards in the box and sent a shot towards the top corner. But it was Hart in goal and he wasn't going to be beaten on his near post, as he touched it around for the corner. On this performance, City looked like they were the top four regulars of the past.

Manchester City 2-0 FC Timisoara
UEFA Europa League Playoff Round, Second Leg
Thursday 26 August, 2010 – 20:00 KO

City: Hart, Richards, Kompany (c), Boyata, Zabaleta, de Jong (Cunningham 62), Vieira, Wright-Phillips, Silva, Jo, Adebayor
Unused: Given, A Johnson, Barry, Lescott, Tevez, Y Toure
Goals: Wright-Phillips (42), Boyata (57)
Booked: -
Man of the Match: Dedryck Boyata

City dominated possession in the opening stages, but struggled to test the visiting goalkeeper, with Zabaleta having a close range shot blocked after Jo slipped him in and Pantilimon making a meal of a cross from Wright-Phillips, just getting enough on it to punch it away.

It felt like the second leg of a Europa League tie, with City content to keep the ball, making their opposition do the chasing and just waiting for the openings to appear. The veteran Vieira soon showed his skill and provided a through ball from which City took the lead. It was Wright-Phillips running into the box to collect the perfectly weighted pass and he touched it first time past the defenders and into the bottom corner.

Early in the second half, a perfect delivery from Silva at a right wing corner landed right on Boyata's head. The young Belgian nodded it back across goal and past the keeper, grabbing himself his first senior goal.

From the restart, it should have been three, as Adebayor latched onto a short passback in the box, but he could only poke the ball wide when it seemed easier to score. On the hour mark, Jo could have extended City's lead with a header from a corner, but it flashed just past the post and the fight appeared to have died from the visitors.

It was another game that finished like a training session for the Blues.

Sunderland 1-0 Manchester City
FA Premier League
Sunday 29 August, 2010 – 15:00 KO

City: Hart, Richards, Lescott (Adebayor 74), Kompany, K Toure, Barry, de Jong, Y Toure, A Johnson (Silva 80), Milner, Tevez (c) (Jo 90)
Unused: Given, Zabaleta, Vieira, Wright-Phillips
Goals: -
Booked: de Jong, Richards
Man of the Match: Yaya Toure

Sunderland started the game pressing the away side, who looked comfortable in possession, albeit in their own half. With 15 minutes gone, City should have been in front. On the break from a Sunderland free kick, Yaya Toure nicked the ball ahead of the covering defender and was bearing down on the box. As the Sunderland defence moved to close him down, he squared it to Tevez and, with an open goal in front of him, the striker somehow put the ball over.

Soon after, Campbell looked to have twisted his knee after a tangle with Richards and the home fans weren't happy that no cards were produced, though there wasn't a foul by either player.

Yaya Toure could have given City the lead in first half stoppage time as a Johnson free kick was flicked to him at the back post. Unmarked, he took a touch and tried to side-foot it into the goal, but Mignolet was out quickly.

Bent had an early shout for a second half penalty waved away, before Kompany miscued a header and Hart had to be off his line quickly to punch the ball clear.

City almost took the lead midway through the half, as Richards nodded the ball back across goal and Adebayor flicked it towards the net with the outside of his right foot. It looked destined to cross the line but for a world class save from Mignolet and City were left scratching their heads.

With a minute of stoppage time remaining, City threw away what would have been a point with a silly push in the box by Richards on Bent. The striker got up to score the penalty himself, under Hart as he stretched to his left hand post, leaving City to rue their missed first half chances.

HARDLY THE END OF THE WORLD

Some things in life will never change. As they say, the only things in life that are certain are death and tax collectors. What they don't say, however, that they probably should, is that, whatever you do, wherever you go and whatever your life brings up, Manchester City will always, but always, let you down by shooting themselves in the foot.

I was genuinely worried that, with the investment of Sheikh Mansour and some of the best talent that had signed for the club over this and last summer, the City team would lose touch with their roots and start doing normal, sensible things that normal, sensible football clubs do. I am delighted to see that, especially after the result at Sunderland, my fears were totally unfounded.

How could I possibly have thought that City might have stopped doing stupid things? There had only been two games of the season, but the warning signs were missing... there was a stout, if limited offensively, performance at Tottenham and a dominating and strong performance at home to Liverpool. Two strong teams and two good displays, leading to four points...

Maybe the warning sign of City's eventual "shoot-yourself-in-the-foot" moment was that there were no warning signs. It's a new one, I'll give them that. It's gone on the list, just after having a player sent off for licking an opponent's nose and just before being knocked out of the FA Cup by a balloon. And yes, Andy Morrison was once sent off for licking Stan Collymore's nose.

Missing an open goal, being denied by a world class save, dominating one half before being dominated the other, looking nailed on for a goalless draw, conceding a 94th minute penalty with a needless grapple on a player not likely to reach the cross that had gone into the box and losing doesn't quite hit the top spot of "shoot-yourself-in-the-foot" moments for City, but it's right up there with the best of them. Along with losing the replay of a game that was rained off when City were leading 6-1. And being the only club to score over 100 and concede over 100 goals in one season.

It doesn't quite match up to losing to Bolton, despite having hit the post and bar seven times (twice with the same header) and nor does it compete with losing at home to Middlesbrough, despite the visitors being camped in their own half and not having a single shot on target.

You'd think I'd react better to my team throwing away a game in the final minutes, bearing in mind it happened in three of the four Manchester derbies last season. But apparently I still get annoyed... no, frustrated... no, hysterically cheesed off by it. Nevermind, though, City will stop doing it soon when they start doing normal, sensible things, just like every other normal, sensible club.

What? A boy can dream.

While disappointing, annoying, frustrating and hysterically-cheesed-offing, the defeat at the Stadium of Light isn't such a terrible turn of events. Chelsea lost away at Wigan, Aston Villa, Everton and Tottenham (as well as two defeats to City) last season and they won the title. I don't think one defeat that, as a City fan, you would have expected as a victory before the game is any cause for concern... after just three matches. There are 105 more points to play for and I would dare to say that no team will win all 105 of them.

It's not panic stations just yet. It's not like it's eight draws in a row, or defeats at teams that end up being relegated, or being knocked out of the cup by a last minute goal to your nearest rivals, or being unable to beat Stoke in three attempts in a month, or losing your first choice goalkeeper with three vital games to go. They are the ingredients for a terrible season, after all.

I don't think many people will have expected a Sunderland victory, especially when the game got to half time. But I also don't think many people would have had Wigan down for winning at White Hart Lane; not after conceding 10 in their opening two games and conceding nine on their last visit to Tottenham. City will lose games most people expect them to win again this season, and Wigan will also lose games most people expect them to lose this season, too. And that wasn't a typo.

This season, City will play worse than they did at Sunderland and win. They will also concede a last minute goal again in the not too distant future. The season is decided over 38 games, not three. I don't think anybody should be too downhearted until it's mathematically impossible to win the league/finish fourth/finish sixth/finish in the top half/stay up/not finish bottom (delete as appropriate for your personal City ambitions).

And, anyway, City are two points up on the corresponding fixtures from last season. And I'm clutching at straws there, so I guess I should stop there before I mention that Darren Bent's big toe was offside in penalty incident or that Roberto Mancini was clearly the most stylish and best dressed manager on any touchline this weekend.

Oh.

Damn it.

CITY'S NATIONAL SERVICE

As I and many other Manchester City fans have taken great delight in telling others over the past few days, the club's spending power is far from damaging the England team, as had previously been decided in the tabloid kangaroo court based at Fleet Street. We'll be doing nothing but going over old ground to repeat that argument, but it was a point I felt needed reiterating.

Especially with all the English City players that have been the spine of the last two of Fabio Capello's teamsheets. You can insert here one of the many jokes that have been going around the web about hating international breaks but it being ok this time around because it was just like watching City. I was also disappointed with the number of my friends that told me the same Wayne Rooney joke over and over again. You can insert that here, too, if you like, just to get it out of the way.

With the introduction of the 25-man squad rule, a lot of the press were looking towards City as a team that would struggle to get their squad size down. But, in reality, the squad picked itself, there was more than enough of the home grown talent in there to meet the rules and the English players aren't just there to make up the numbers. The victory over Liverpool in August demonstrated this, with six Englishmen both starting and finishing the game, with a seventh on the bench should he be needed. I'm not quite sure where the vitriol against City came from, given that, either through the chequebook or club academy, English talent isn't being ignored.

Odd, how there hasn't been nearly as much backlash towards other squads. Take Arsenal's, for example, which doesn't contain one English player. How often will the English Arsenal under 21 players make first team appearances, especially now with Walcott out injured? It looks like it's going to be down to infrequent appearances from Wilshere and Ramsey.

Chelsea couldn't name a full 25 man squad because of the lack of home grown players – English or not. And, despite this, it's City who are in the wrong because they're the ones who have spent the money.

Speaking of spending money, I'm also perfectly willing to go back onto the record and state my belief that Adam Johnson will be the best value for money buy in the Premier League in the last five years. He's young, English (and therefore with added transfer premium), not afraid to take a player or four on and he's not afraid to have a shot when necessary. And, unlike a lot of footballers, he is comfortable and looks natural on both wings.

In fact, I'd go as far to say I've never been as excited about a City attacking player in the past. That he will, even though he is left footed, head for the by-line or cut inside whichever wing he is on, leaves full backs not knowing what to expect and makes City (and, as we've seen recently, England) a much more dangerous prospect attacking. After a World Cup where England were crying out for a left winger to offer service, it seems obvious (as, I suppose, everything does with the benefit of hindsight) that not taking Adam Johnson to the tournament was a mistake.

Middlesbrough's youth academy, like City's, is known for developing a large number of prospects and talents and, in recent years, has been noted as one of the most productive in the country. I was concerned, when Roberto Mancini signed Johnson from the north-east club in the winter transfer window, that he was going to be another player that was 'one-for-the-future'. That he would get maybe ten or fifteen minutes at the end of most games, providing the points were safely in the bag. That he would struggle in the Premier League at first and that it would take several years to see what sort of player he could be.

Having watched Johnson play regularly for City, it now stumps me how Stewart Downing was keeping him out of the Middlesbrough team. Out of the two left wingers transferred from the north-east, I don't think there can be much question that City got a better deal than Aston Villa.

City are going to play a very large part in the future of England's development, especially since Milner and Johnson joined the club. With Hart back from his loan at Birmingham and keeping Given out of the team, Barry putting in his usual solid and stern performances and Lescott proving he's comfortable at left back as well as centre-back, both City and England have bright futures ahead of them. And that's not including any potential call ups for Richards and Wright-Phillips, who, I think by most City fans' admissions, haven't exactly been on the tops of their games recently.

And, the second half display against Sunderland aside, if watching England in years to come is anything like watching the new City, then international breaks should make for much more pleasant viewing than they have lately.

August 2010 Breakdown

Games (all competitions):
Won: 3   **Drawn:** 1   **Lost:** 1

Goals (all competitions):
For: 6   **Against:** 1

Progress:
Premier League: 9th
League Cup: -
FA Cup: -
Europa League: Qualified for the Group Stage

Premier League Table

		P	W	D	L	F	A	GD	Pts
7	Wolverhampton Wanderers	3	1	2	0	4	3	+1	5
8	Newcastle United	3	1	1	1	7	4	+3	4
9	**Manchester City**	**3**	**1**	**1**	**1**	**3**	**1**	**+2**	**4**
10	Sunderland	3	1	1	1	3	3	0	4
11	Tottenham Hotspur	3	1	1	1	2	2	0	4

September 2010

Manchester City 1-1 Blackburn Rovers

FA Premier League

Saturday 11 September, 2010 – 15:00 KO

City: Hart, Richards, Lescott, Kompany, K Toure, Vieira (Barry 67), Y Toure, A Johnson (Silva 85), Milner, Wright-Phillips (Jo 57), Tevez (c)
Unused: Given, Zabaleta, Boyata, Santa Cruz
Goals: Vieira (56)
Booked: Vieira, Milner
Man of the Match: Adam Johnson

With 14 minutes gone, Johnson came close to giving City the lead after one of his trademark runs from the right. He cut inside onto his left foot and curled it towards the back post, but it was just wide.

But, while it was all City going forward, they were finding chances difficult to come by against a very stubborn visiting defence. It looked like the away side had come to Eastlands for a point, but soon they could have been heading away with more. A long ball out of the Blackburn defence and a mix-up between Hart and Kolo Toure, left Kalinic with an open goal. Hart, leaving his box to clear the ball, was beaten by a low bounce and Toure was left to chase, but Kalinic was never going to miss.

The second half started slowly, with City struggling to hold on to possession and Blackburn happy to sit on their lead. But, 10 minutes into the half, the hosts were level. Vieira knocked the ball wide to Tevez and broke into the box, finding himself in a perfect position to tap home as it was crossed back low and hard.

Ten minutes later, Tevez picked up a loose ball and ran towards the Blackburn goal. His shot took a flick off Samba and beat Robinson, but it hit the foot of the post and went behind for a corner. Shortly after, Barry was found in the middle by Johnson and his shot had to be turned around the post by the visiting goalkeeper.

As the game entered the final 10 minutes, Hart needed to be alert to deny Kalinic as he broke into the box, before he was out off his line quickly to steal a bouncing through ball aimed for Pedersen. City were denied a penalty for a foul on Johnson, after the winger had been felled after cutting inside from the left.

As the game entered stoppage time, City could have won it. Tevez went through and got to a Barry cross before Robinson, but his effort was blocked on the line. He picked up the loose ball and squared for Jo, but the Brazilian's shot was blocked over the bar by Samba.

Red Bull Salzburg 0-2 Manchester City

Europa League Group A

Thursday 16 September, 2010 – 18:00 KO

City: Hart, Zabaleta, Kompany, K Toure, Bridge (Boyata 67), de Jong, Barry, Y Toure, Silva (Wright-Phillips 83), Jo, Tevez (c) (Vieira 78)
Unused: Given, Richards, Milner, A Johnson
Goals: Silva (8), Jo (63)
Booked: Kolo Toure
Man of the Match: David Silva

With only eight minutes on the clock, Bridge picked the ball up on the left wing and crossed it in for Jo. He touched it back to Silva, who stroked the ball into the net with his right foot coolly. It was the perfect start for the visitors and put them in a commanding position in the game.

Just before the half hour, City had to be alert to defend well from two Salzburg corners. The first was nodded away by Jo, before the second allowed a miscued shot from Sekagya, who sliced the ball down into the ground and it bounced up and onto the top of Hart's crossbar.

Ten minutes before the break, Silva should have doubled his goals tally and City's lead. Tevez did well to hold the ball up while the Spaniard broke into the box unmarked. The Argentinian found him, but Silva chose not to shoot with his right foot and cut back inside, allowing the goalkeeper time to re-adjust and save.

With an hour gone, Jo doubled City's lead with his first goal since September 2008. Tevez worked an opening for himself from just outside the box and he fired a fierce shot at the Salzburg goal. Tremmel could only parry it and Jo was on hand to get to the rebound first and knock it home.

The goal virtually killed the game, with City continuing to dominate possession, playing keep-ball and the heads of the Salzburg players dropped. Though, the home side should have pulled a goal back almost immediately from a low cross across Hart's six-yard box, but nobody could get a touch.

City were content to see the game out with some neat possession and, with Juventus only able to draw with Lech Poznan at home, it is the Blues that top the Europa League Group A table.

Wigan Athletic 0-2 Manchester City
FA Premier League
Sunday 19 September, 2010 – 15:00 KO

City: Hart, Richards, Kompany, K Toure, Zabaleta, de Jong, Barry, Y Toure (Jo 75), Silva (A Johnson 72), Milner, Tevez (c) (Wright-Phillips 88)
Unused: Given, Boyata, Vieira, Santa Cruz
Goals: Tevez (43), Y Toure (70)
Booked: de Jong, Yaya Toure
Man of the Match: Pablo Zabaleta

The game got off to a very slow start, with a hanging cross from Richards on eight minutes knocked down for Silva to volley well wide the best that either side could manage early on. Tevez went close to opening the scoring on 13 minutes when he skipped three challenges in the midfield and flashed a low shot at goal, but it was just wide of the post.

And just as it looked like it would be level at the break, City went in front. Despite all of their possession play, it was a long punt from a Hart goal kick that took a flick from a Wigan head and sent Tevez clear. The City skipper looked up, chipped the ball over Al Habsi and watched it drop neatly into the net.

In the opening stages of the second half, it almost got better for City. Wigan looked comfortable in defence, but a short pass sent Tevez through on goal and the City striker could only find the gloves of Al-Habsi.

But, soon enough, City had doubled their lead. There were 20 minutes to go when a disastrous defensive header thanks to pressure from Silva fell to Tevez and he fired it across the box for Yaya Toure to slot home with his left foot.

There was a final push from the home side in the closing stages, with Rodallega firing just wide of Hart's goal, before Diame got up above the defence, but could only head the ball wide.

Johnson almost added to City's goal tally deep into stoppage time, as his left wing cross was deflected and needed a great save from Al-Habsi to touch it onto the bar. It turned out to be a comfortable day at the office for the Blues.

West Bromwich Albion 2-1 Manchester City
League Cup Third Round
Wednesday 22 September, 2010 – 20:00 KO

City: Given, Vidal (Zabaleta 53), Boyata, Mee, Cunningham, Vieira (c), Ibrahim (Milner 70), A Johnson, Jo, Santa Cruz (Silva 80), Guidetti
Unused: Taylor, Kompany, Kay, Veseli
Goals: Jo (20)
Booked: Vidal, Vieira
Man of the Match: Shay Given

With tough fixtures against Chelsea and Juventus coming up, it showed Roberto Mancini's intentions towards the League Cup when he made 11 changes to the side that started on Sunday at the DW Stadium. Given got his chance to impress, while debuts were handed to Vidal and Mee.

And it was the home side that had the early pressure. With three minutes on the clock, Reid shot well over the bar, before Tchoyi took on and beat Mee, curling an effort just wide of the post. Given was then alert to produce a smart save from Dorrans, pushing the ball away and Bednar was just inches away from the rebound.

Then, against the run of play, the visitors took the lead. A lovely ball from Vieira found Guidetti in the box, who knocked it to Jo. He rifled it into the net with his left foot on the spin.

Just before half time, a goalmouth scramble in the City box could have got the hosts level, but Given was there to push a header from Barnes onto the post. And, as the half entered stoppage time, Vieira gave the ball away and Boyata and Given had to combine to stop Bednar from finding the equalizer, as City hung on until the break.

The second half, though, began where the first ended – with West Brom pressure. Given produced another good save from a one-on-one with Barnes, as the Baggies' man tried to lift the ball over him, before the home side pulled themselves level. Zuiverloon drilled it low and hard across the City keeper from the right side of the box and, as good as the Irish international had been, he couldn't stop it.

And, two minutes later, it got worse for City. Virtually straight from the kick-off, Cox nipped in ahead of Given to slot the ball into the net. For a chance to visit Wembley, the Blues will have to wait for the FA Cup in January. West Brom never looked in danger of letting their lead slip.

Manchester City 1-0 Chelsea
FA Premier League
Saturday 25 September, 2010 – 12:45 KO

City: Hart, Boyata (Boateng 89), Kompany, K Toure, Zabaleta, de Jong, Barry, Y Toure, Silva (A Johnson 79), Milner, Tevez (c) (Adebayor 87)
Unused: Given, Lescott, Vieira, Jo
Goals: Tevez (59)
Booked: Zabaleta, Boyata
Man of the Match: Vincent Kompany

It was the home side who started the better, as de Jong released Tevez into the Chelsea half, but his shot flashed wide of Cech's post. Cech then had to be alert to pluck a Silva cross out of the air after the Spaniard had beaten the offside trap, before he was called into action to stop a Milner free kick from the left wing dropping just under his bar.

Boyata was then on hand to dispossess the former City striker Anelka, stepping across him to allow the ball to run behind, before Zabaleta swooped in to take the ball from Drogba, as the hosts showed they were no push-overs in defence.

Just before the half hour, Chelsea should have taken the lead. From a left wing corner, Ivanovic headed against Hart's crossbar and the rebound fell to a Chelsea shirt. Hart, however, was able to react and hold on, to keep City level.

It was Chelsea who came out of the blocks quickest for the second half. After some early pressure from the visitors, an Anelka shot from range needed Hart's fingertips to put it around the post, before de Jong tried his luck from range. His shooting is getting better, though – this was on target until it hit the Chelsea defender. He might earn a goal before the end of the season.

Chelsea won themselves a corner just before the hour, but it was City who took full advantage. Tevez latched onto the clearance and ran at the visitors' back four. Silva opened the space for him, he took it to his right and fired a shot between Cole's legs, past Cech, off the post and into the back of the net. It was the first time either side had been stretched and it resulted in a goal.

Alex should have done better from a Chelsea corner as he nodded wide with 15 minutes to go, before Tevez had the opportunity to put the game beyond Chelsea's reach with a free kick in exactly the spot where he scored the winner in the corresponding fixture last season, but his effort was wide of Cech's post.

Manchester City 1-1 Juventus
Europa League Group Stage, Group A
Thursday 30 September, 2010 – 20:05 KO

City: Hart, Zabaleta (Boyata 45), Kompany, K Toure, Boateng (Milner 85), Vieira, Barry, Y Toure, A Johnson, Adebayor (Silva 74), Tevez (c)
Unused: Given, Lescott, de Jong, Jo
Goals: A Johnson (37)
Booked: Barry
Man of the Match: Vincent Kompany

Juventus started the brighter, as City were sloppy in possession and couldn't hold on to the ball, gifting it back to the visiting side. And they were in no mood to let City off the hook, as Hart was needed to stop a speculative drive from the right. The City keeper was in action again, minutes later, scooping Del Piero's free kick away from danger.

But, just as it looked like City had ridden the early storm, the visitors took the lead. Iaquinta picked up the ball on the edge of the City area and curled an effort towards the far post. Hart couldn't reach it and it sneaked into the net. It had been coming, too.

City almost hit back immediately as Vieira got up to nod a Johnson corner towards goal, but it was cleared off the line by Marchisio. Barry then flicked a back-header from a Tevez cross onto the post and Johnson couldn't quite put the rebound in. The home side were growing into the match.

Then, with 37 minutes gone, Johnson cut inside from the right and latched on to a brilliant through ball from Yaya Toure. He took a touch to deceive the goalkeeper and was able to prod it into the net. City were good value for their equaliser.

On 65 minutes, it was still all City, as Barry chest-trapped a Johnson cross-field pass on the edge of the box and volleyed just over the bar under pressure. Yaya Toure picked up the ball midway into the Juventus half and carried it towards the box. He worked his way inside, beating three defenders and squared it to Adebayor on the penalty spot. But, under pressure from the Juventus defence, the big centre-forward couldn't get the ball out of his feet and it was cleared.

As the game entered stoppage time, Juventus could have won it with another Del Piero free kick. He powered it past the wall and straight past Hart, but it hit the underside of the bar, bounced down onto the line and out, with the officials deciding the whole of the ball wasn't in the net. It was a let off for the Blues, but it was a very good decision from the linesman.

CITY'S SILVA LINING IN MIDFIELD

Several things struck me during Manchester City's 0-2 Europa League Group A win in Austria. Having spent the day messing around on my Twitter page making up facts about Austria, I was in quite a jovial mood at kick-off, despite having watched a frustrating City performance recently at home against Blackburn.

A lot of City fans I know, after that Blackburn game, were none too happy with the tactics employed by Sam Allardyce in their visit to Eastlands – wasting time, long balls, sitting behind the ball, etc. – but that's a viewpoint I can't really subscribe to. Too often I heard the phrase "that's not football" or "it's anti-football" when the game was being discussed post-match, but when it comes down to it, I wouldn't have expected Blackburn to go to a side that is aiming for a top four finish, not to play to their strengths and, instead, to try to beat them with possession football. It wasn't as if City didn't create chances – the worrying part of the game was the stat of 20 attempts on goal, but only one scored.

City didn't play especially badly against Blackburn, they just failed to break their opposition down. Too often, the opportunity for a quick break was declined for a series of short passes in midfield or the opportunity for a first time pass was declined in favour of several touches. And that allowed Blackburn to get back behind the ball and regain their shape.

There were plenty of shots on goal from the home side, but it was frustrating to see them being largely, with one or two exceptions, of course, comfortable saves for Robinson or off target to begin with. It was doubly frustrating when it took so much work to get into a shooting position.

But then roll forward five days. What struck me in the game in Austria, albeit against different opposition with a different style of play, was that the Manchester City that turned up, as a weakened side, mark you, and didn't look the same Manchester City that passed and passed and passed the ball in front of Blackburn the weekend previous. There were penetrating runs, successful through balls, dangerous attacks, one-touch football, and two good goals to finish it all off.

The biggest reason I can see for this improvement was that David Silva was given his chance to start. From the kick-off, he was involved in virtually everything positive that City did until he was substituted five minutes from time. His vision and work rate were as good as ever, but his ability to execute the right pass at the right time looked second to none.

For someone his size, he didn't look too put off by a tough tackle here or there. He's not the bulkiest of players, which does aid his agility, but he isn't afraid to get stuck in, too.

It summed his entire night up when he broke his neck to support Tevez, who was battling his way into the Salzburg box, to end up with a shooting chance (though he did decide to cut back onto his left foot and consequently gave the goalkeeper time to adjust). Tevez, traditionally, isn't the most selfless of players and will normally take a shot on if he can, so Silva bust a gut knowing he mightn't have even gotten the chance to shoot.

Keeping our feet on the ground, for a moment, though, we should remember that Red Bull Salzburg aren't Arsenal or Chelsea or Manchester United. But, equally, they're not a poor side; last season, they won every one of their Europa League group stage games and were also the Austrian Bundesliga winners. Ok, so it's not the FA Premier League, but it's hardly the Northwest Counties League, either.

The second thing that struck me was my parents' ability to fall asleep at the drop of a hat. Not just a problem when hat shopping, but also a completely strange sight when, only seconds after the half time whistle had been blown, I was able to look across and see them snoozing away on the sofa, despite having been in full conversation with them virtually right up until the whistle.

Gareth Barry's return to the starting line-up and subsequent influence on the match was the third thing that struck me. Looking back to the Blackburn match, with Milner and Yaya Toure struggling to find form and Vieira as the third, deeper, central midfielder, there was little service to Tevez (and later, Jo). And it was no coincidence that it was Barry's introduction that made the home side more threatening.

I was genuinely quite worried for Barry at the start of the season, especially after he struggled, like most of the other England players, in the World Cup (though he was battling back from injury). With the midfield talent that Roberto Mancini brought in to City, Barry was one of the favourites among several fans to be starting more games on the bench than on the pitch, condemned to proving his worth in European or League Cup matches.

However, the man himself had no such thoughts of being a bit-part player. He's been nothing short of outstanding so far this season and last night was just another example. It's the hard work he does that goes unnoticed. He links the defence with the attack with simple passing.

It's a popular misconception, especially amongst television pundits who don't get to see matches in their entirety, that when City start with Nigel de Jong and Gareth Barry that they are starting with two defensive midfielders. And it's usually followed by a criticism, especially if City are at home.

While it may be true that de Jong won't give the side much on the attack, the same cannot be said of Barry. He is the player responsible for finding Yaya Toure in advanced positions or moving the ball wide to Milner or chipping it in to Johnson or making the late drive into the box.

In fact, here's me calling for Silva to join the starting eleven, but I can't for the life of me decide who I would drop – personally, I'd like to see all of them start. Though, I'm not on the same contract as Roberto Mancini, so I'll probably be left with that selection headache on Football Manager only.

CITY YOUNGSTER IN GOOD KOMPANY

If you had said to a Manchester City fan 10 years ago that they would beat the team that would go on to be champions of England and then, subsequently, reigning champions of England three times in three league games, scoring seven in the process, you would probably have been laughed out of the room. If you'd have gone on to say that there would be two Belgians in the back four of the team for the third match and that it would be a clean sheet without any real threat on goal from the reigning champions, you'd probably be told that there was more chance of David Haye becoming a jockey.

Back in January this year, I went to Carrington, where City train, to interview one of these Belgians for the BlueMoon Podcast, off the back of them both appearing at an Official Supporters' Club meeting. It was the day after the League Cup defeat to Manchester United and, for obvious reasons, the mood was quite downbeat. And after I had recorded the interview and triple checked my machine had saved it, I chatted to the then number 33, now number 4, Vincent Kompany – just small talk.

One thing he said to me struck a chord. He says he's a midfielder. And that he prefers to play in the centre of midfield rather than the centre of defence. At that time, that didn't really surprise me – he had played the majority of the season before in midfield, under Mark Hughes, and, with new signings Lescott and Toure taking the centre-back roles for the start of the 2009-10 season, combined with his injury, Kompany found himself out of the team. Especially with how well Nigel de Jong had started the season in his place.

When he moved to centre-back and began to get a run of games under his belt covering for injuries, it became clear that he was actually the best centre-back at the club. In fact, I'd go as far to say he's probably the best centre-back in the Premier League.

How many others have had room to fit both Anelka and Drogba in their back pocket at the same time? He had had Torres in there earlier in the season, also, but the Spaniard was still recovering from injury, so I had given him the benefit of the doubt.

Perhaps it's Roberto Mancini's influence on the City style of play, but this season more than any the team look comfortable keeping possession. That's one of the biggest changes between this current City side and City sides of years gone by. Part of this possession-keeping City comes from having two centre-backs who are perfectly willing and perfectly able to stroke the ball around quickly. Neither one of them is too fussed about stretching their legs and opening the taps going forward, either, as Toure has proved in the past with both City and Arsenal, and as Kompany has proved when nipping in to make one of his beautifully timed interceptions, before carrying the ball into the midfield.

Good teams start with a solid foundation and protecting perhaps the best goalkeeper in the league is perhaps the best central defensive partnership in the league. They don't come much more solid than that.

When he walked into the small press room where we did the interview, he carried the air of someone wise beyond his years. He is only actually 18 months older than I am, but you wouldn't know it to look at the way he plays and the way he conducts himself off the pitch. His reading of the game is that of someone you expect to be towards the end of their career; and the scary thing is, that at 24, he's still only going to get better.

I recently said that Adam Johnson would be the best value for money transfer in the Premier League in the last 10 years. But, given that Kompany set City back a mere £6m, I might have been wrong.

He will, I'm sure, be a future City captain. He's got leadership qualities, something that has, no doubt, helped his fellow countryman Dedryck Boyata graduate from City's academy and play a part in the first team. It was clear, from Boyata's debut and subsequent appearances in January 2010, that Kompany had taken him under his wing.

After all, it can't be easy to be thrown in at the deep end as he was and play as well as he did. Being a goalkeeper with hands as safe as a Northern Rock investment has restricted my football career somewhat, admittedly, but I've never had the chance to play in front of 48,000 people and I doubt I ever will. Though I don't imagine it's easy.

Bearing in mind that he played out of position at right back for the league fixture with Chelsea, that it was only his second Premier League start, and that he was facing the free-scoring, chance-creating Malouda he was unbelievably assured. Malouda didn't get a chance to have a shot on goal, while Cole's role in the game was about as significant as Jar-Jar Binks' role in the entire Star Wars saga (ok, so maybe Jar-Jar got Palpatine elected to the Chancellor position, but he wasn't the gunner on the Imperial ship that could have shot down the escape pod with C-3P0 and R2-D2 in before that got to Tatooine, stopping them finding Luke and subsequently Obi-Wan and therefore stopping any of them helping the Rebel Alliance overthrow the Empire... *ahem* Where was I?).

The Boyata that expertly stepped across Anelka and let the ball run out for a goal kick; the Boyata that slid in to dispossess Malouda, before blocking from Drogba; and the Boyata that scored a towering header against Timisoara wasn't the same Boyata that walked into the Supporters' Club meeting with Kompany.

In January, he was the shy guy who looked like he didn't really know what he was doing and like he was going to be found out as a fraud and an impostor any moment. It's clear, though, that the two have a good relationship – when asked who their heroes were at that meeting, Kompany responded with a series of players who were at their peak as he was growing up. While, just behind him, Boyata was amusing the kids by using his eyes to point out that his hero, his team-mate, was sitting next to him.

If Boyata continues to work with Kompany and take advice from him, then he's got the potential to be another great City academy product. He already reads the game well and knows when a good tackle is needed, so there's no reason why he can't become a first team regular of the future.

He's certainly learning from the right man.

September 2010 Breakdown

Games (all competitions):
Won: 3   **Drawn:** 2   **Lost:** 1

Goals (all competitions):
For: 8   **Against:** 4

Progress:
Premier League: 4th
League Cup: Eliminated in Round Three
FA Cup: -
Europa League: 2nd in Group A

Premier League Table

		P	W	D	L	F	A	GD	Pts
2	Manchester United	6	3	3	0	16	9	+7	12
3	Arsenal	6	3	2	1	16	7	+9	11
4	**Manchester City**	6	3	2	1	7	2	+5	11
5	Aston Villa	6	3	1	2	8	10	-2	10
6	West Bromwich Albion	6	3	1	2	8	11	-3	10

Europa League Group A Table

		P	W	D	L	F	A	GD	Pts
1	Lech Poznan	2	1	1	0	5	3	+2	4
2	**Manchester City**	2	1	1	0	3	1	+2	4
3	Juventus	2	0	2	0	4	4	0	2
4	Red Bull Salzburg	2	0	0	2	0	4	-4	0

October 2010

Manchester City 2-1 Newcastle United
FA Premier League
Sunday 3 October, 2010 – 13:30 KO

City: Hart, Boateng, Kompany, K Toure, Lescott, de Jong, Barry (A Johnson 73), Y Toure (Adebayor 58), Silva, Milner, Tevez (c) (Vieira 87)
Unused: Given, Boyata, Jo, Santa Cruz
Goals: Tevez (18 pen), A Johnson (75)
Booked: K Toure, Boateng, Tevez
Man of the Match: Vincent Kompany

City started the game knowing that a victory would take them up into second place in the Premier League table and above Manchester United. The match, however, started on something of a sour note, with Nigel de Jong going in very strongly in a challenge with Ben Arfa. The City man won the ball, but the Newcastle man was stretchered off with a suspected broken leg.

With 18 minutes on the clock, City benefited from a slice of good fortune as Tevez was given a penalty for a foul by Williamson. It looked unfortunate for the Newcastle defender, who appeared to win the ball, but that didn't stop the captain picking himself up and slamming the ball home from the spot.

With 24 minutes on the clock, Hart was called into action for the first time, tipping a Coloccini effort from just outside the box away for a corner. But, within a minute, the visitors were level. Kompany could only half clear a cross from the left and it was picked up by Gutierrez, who found the top corner, off the underside of the bar.

Newcastle threatened with an isolated second half attack. The goalscorer, Gutierrez, though, could only find the gloves of Hart, when he should probably have found the net.

Though, as it looked like it was going to be another frustrating afternoon at home for City, Johnson turned on the style to score the winner. He picked up the ball on the right wing and ran at the defence. Stepping inside the full back, he fired his shot low and into the bottom corner.

The visitors then could have had a penalty for what looked like a clear foul on Ameobi by Lescott, but the referee didn't see anything wrong with the challenge and waved play on.

Blackpool 2-3 Manchester City
FA Premier League
Sunday 17 October, 2010 – 16:00 KO

City: Hart, Boateng (Richards 75), Kompany, Lescott, Bridge, de Jong, Barry, Milner, A Johnson (Vieira 85), Adebayor (Silva 64), Tevez (c)

Unused: Given, Zabaleta, Wright-Phillips, Santa Cruz
Goals: Tevez (67, 78), Silva (90)
Booked: Tevez, Silva
Man of the Match: David Silva

The game got off to a ferocious start at the seaside. With two minutes gone, Tevez slid the ball across the box, looking for a touch into the net, but that didn't come, before a scathing Johnson shot needed touching over the bar by Gilks. Kompany headed into Gilks' hands, before Adam, who had seen a lot of the ball in the opening stages, fired a right-footed shot well wide of Hart's goal.

A diving header from Campbell should have at least found the target, but it was another wasted effort and well wide of the goal, before Hart took his time clearing a Lescott back-pass and was close to being embarrassed by Varney.

Early in the second half, Kompany and Lescott were both drawn towards the ball and Campbell was free in the centre. The ball found him, Hart came racing out and made it difficult, but the forward could only prod the ball wide.

A minute later, Blackpool did have the ball in the net, but it wasn't going to count. Taylor-Fletcher raced onto a long pass over the top from an onside position, but the swing for the ball by Grandin in an offside position caused the linesman to flag.

Milner fed Silva down the left and the Spaniard found Tevez in the box, who flicked the ball into the back of the net, hugely against the run of play. Then Milner twice almost doubled City's lead. First, he chipped the ball over Gilks as he dived for the ball, but it didn't have enough pace to beat Eardley on the line, before the City midfielder hit the underside of the bar from the edge of the box.

Eight minutes later, Blackpool were on terms. A superb delivery from a free kick by Adam left Harewood to flick the ball to the back post, beating Hart. But Blackpool were caught out still celebrating, perhaps, and Tevez put City straight back into the lead. He picked the ball up on the edge of the box and swung a shot at goal with his left foot. It took a deflection and beat Gilks, who couldn't react in time.

As the game entered the final minute, City looked to have secured the victory. Milner took a quick free kick to Silva on the right flank and the City midfielder cut into the box, beat three defenders, and curled the ball expertly to the back post and into the net for a goal of the season contender.

But, just as the City fans were relaxing and thinking about the tie with Lech Poznan in midweek, Blackpool pulled a goal back. A right wing corner found its way to the edge of the box and was powered back towards Hart's goal. Taylor-Fletcher couldn't have missed and he didn't.

Manchester City 3-1 Lech Poznan
Europa League Group A
Thursday 21 October, 2010 – 20:05 KO

City: Hart, Zabaleta (Bridge 85), Boyata, Lescott, Richards, Vieira, de Jong (c), Silva (Toure 75), Wright-Phillips (Jo 78), A Johnson, Adebayor
Unused: Given, Kompany, Milner, Tevez
Goals: Adebayor (14, 25, 73)
Booked: -
Man of the Match: David Silva

It was the visiting fans making all the noise, but their team started slowly and an early City goal was the key to silencing them. It came from a neat Vieira pass to Adebayor and a fantastic turn by the Togolese forward. He looked up and stroked it into the net to give City the lead.

The goal gave City a boost and they began to knock the ball around the pitch comfortably, keeping possession well. Chance creation, however, was at a minimum, until Adebayor doubled City's score and his tally for the evening. Silva found him with a beauty of a cross and the big man leapt up to nod home from inside the six-yard box, unmarked.

Bosacki picked up a yellow card for a late challenge on Zabaleta before de Jong put in one of his trademark tackles on Injac, winning the ball both toughly and fairly.

Before the break, Poznan earned a corner that allowed them one of their isolated shooting chances, but it was from the edge of the box and well over the bar, not troubling Hart. It had been fairly plain sailing for the Blues.

But it was the hosts who struggled to start the second half. The first action saw Poznan begin to dominate possession and it led to them pulling a goal back. Zabaleta dallied on the ball in the box and his clearance deflected off a Poznan forward and fell to the feet of Tshibamba, who had the simple task of sliding the ball past Hart.

With 54 minutes gone, Silva was unlucky not to add another cracking goal to his City collection, as he beat four Poznan defenders on his way into the box and fired off a low shot, which was flicked into the side netting by the keeper.

Two minutes later, a speculative free kick from Poznan whistled past Hart's post, before Vieira fired over as the ball broke to him on the edge of the area. Boyata put in a fantastic tackle on Tshibamba to stop an attack, before Silva dinked a beautiful pass over to Zabaleta, but the ball was just too much for him and it bounced behind.

Tshibamba had a great chance to equalise, but his effort was well off target when he was in the clear in the box, before City sealed the game. With 73 minutes gone, Silva played an early low cross to Adebayor in the middle and he grabbed his third of the game to win it for City.

Five minutes later, it could have been four, as Johnson beat three Poznan defenders to break into the box. With Adebayor waiting to tap his fourth into the net, the winger elected to shoot from a tight angle and clipped the top of the bar.

With seven minutes to go, a short backpass from Boyata almost spelled trouble for City. Hart came racing out, but could only clear into the shins of the oncoming forward. Fortunately, it lobbed Hart and the bar, before bouncing behind to safety.

Manchester City 0-3 Arsenal
FA Premier League
Sunday 24 October, 2010 – 16:00 KO

City: Hart, Boateng, Kompany, Boyata, Richards, de Jong, Barry (Balotelli 73), Milner, Y Toure (Bridge 45), Silva, Tevez (c) (Adebayor 53)
Unused: Given, Lescott, Vieira, A Johnson
Goals: -
Booked: Barry, Kompany
Sent Off: Boyata
Man of the Match: Joe Hart

City had been in good form against the Gunners at home in recent seasons, with three wins on the bounce. And it was the home side that almost took the lead with a minute on the clock. Tevez broke away well down the right flank and squared for Silva, whose deft flick towards goal produced a fine save.

But, just as City were getting into their stride, they were dealt a blow. With just five minutes on the clock, Chamakh broke away from the home defence and Boyata slid in to win the ball. He didn't and that foul left the referee with no option but to send him off for denying a clear goalscoring opportunity.

Fabianski had to be alert after 15 minutes to keep out Tevez's deflected shot, as the 10 men tried to hit their visitors on the break. But then, two minutes later, Arsenal's control of possession paid off. A neat one-two between Nasri and Arshavin sent the number eight free in the box and he powered the ball past Hart, giving the City keeper no chance.

A minute later, City were almost level. Richards broke into the Arsenal box after a lovely pass from Silva. He cut back inside onto his left foot and unleashed a shot at the top corner, but it was just wide of the post.

With the clock ticking down to half time, Arsenal had the chance to effectively seal the game after a foul by Kompany on Fabregas in the box. The Arsenal skipper stepped up, but Hart pulled off a fantastic penalty save.

City lost Tevez to injury in the second half, before Boateng was needed to clear the danger as Arsenal looked to secure the points. Fabianski's fingertips then preserved their lead at the other end, as Silva linked up well with Milner to get a shot in from a tight angle.

But, with 20 minutes to go, the inevitable happened with the disparity in personnel numbers. Bridge was unfortunate to deflect a tackle straight into the path of Song and he fired it into the roof of the net.

The game petered to a close with Arsenal content to keep possession, as City looked for a consolation through first Adebayor and then the substitute Balotelli.

241

It didn't come and Bendtner piled more misery on the home fans with a goal in added time that left the game with a scoreline that flattered the visitors.

Wolverhampton Wanderers 2-1 Manchester City

FA Premier League
Saturday 30 October, 2010 – 15:00 KO

City: Hart, Boateng, Kompany, K Toure (c), Richards (Jo 84), Barry (A Johnson 68), Milner, Y Toure, Silva, Balotelli, Adebayor (Zabaleta 77)
Unused: Given, Lescott, Wright-Phillips, Vieira
Goals: Adebayor (pen 23)
Booked: Zabaleta, Balotelli
Man of the Match: Adam Johnson

City got off to a flying start at Molineux and, with just two minutes gone, had had three great chances to take the lead. First, Adebayor ran the length of the Wolves half to get a low cross in towards Balotelli, but the Italian couldn't get the vital touch.

Then the same combination gave Balotelli a first time shot on the six-yard box, but he couldn't steer it into the net and, seconds later, Adebayor was inches away from connecting to a low cross.

A minute later, Balotelli was found neatly on the penalty spot by Silva and Barry, after another good run by Adebayor, but he was crowded out before he could shoot. He then got another chance from the edge of the box, but it was over the bar, as City stormed the Wolves goal.

Balotelli headed over from a Boateng cross, before Kompany had a header from a corner cleared off the line. Silva got to the ball and kept it in inside the box, while Edwards slid through him and took him down, leaving Mike Dean no choice but to award the penalty to the visitors. Adebayor stepped up and sent the keeper the wrong way.

A couple of minutes later, though, Wolves were level. Milijas latched onto a Jarvis cross that had been partially blocked by Milner and Kolo Toure couldn't get out quick enough at him, leaving him to fire beyond Hart. Jarvis nearly assisted another Wolves goal seconds later, as his low ball across the six-yard box missed everybody, despite the despairing dives of Doyle and Hunt.

City started the second half with all the pressure, but couldn't force a chance on goal. Then, a ball into the City box caught Kolo Toure out and he could only nod it down to the edge of the area. The shot was volleyed in and, as Hart dived to save, Toure blocked, leaving Edwards with a simple finish from the rebound.

With just over an hour gone, City tried to pull level through Silva, but his low drive lacked power and it was a simple save for Hahnemann to tip it around the post. Wolves were content with their lead and City looked toothless up front.

The golden chance came and went for City on 78 minutes, as a beautiful through ball from Yaya Toure found Johnson on the left. His first time pull back reached Adebayor in space, but his shot was well over the bar when it should have been in the net.

The final chance for the visitors was a shot from Yaya Toure as the game edged towards stoppage time. But, typical of City's luck in the match, it was twice deflected off Wolves defenders and fell kindly into Hahnemann's arms. After their start to the game, City shouldn't have lost, but once Wolves had gotten themselves in front, the equaliser never looked likely.

THE CHARACTER ASSASSINATION OF A CITY MIDFIELDER

I don't condone breaking legs. In fact, I don't know many people who do condone the breaking of legs, aside from maybe debt collectors in Hollywood films or perhaps your average Bond villain. Even though it was only 007's fingers that Mr. Big broke, it still doesn't change anything. I, and most other people on the planet, don't condone it. I'm a Manchester City fan, most of my articles are about Manchester City and I've just started this one about broken legs... I think you can see where this one's going.

Now, I didn't see the Nigel de Jong tackle on Hatem Ben Arfa live. I should have seen it live because I had arrived at the game in good time, but thanks to a mix-up involving the people I go with and our tickets, I didn't get in until 10 minutes into the game. And, as I took my seat, the people around me informed me of what I had missed (which, in the context of this game was absolutely nothing apart from the injury to Ben Arfa).

And not a lot was made of it by them, yet it happened right in front of them. None of them saw a foul, though all of them saw the stretcher and all of them saw the oxygen. The referee didn't see a foul. Neither did the linesman nor the Newcastle players nor even Kevin Keegan, Nicky Butt, Lee Dixon or Alan Hansen, who were all pundits covering the game that day.

Having seen numerous replays of the challenge and read thousands of column inches dedicated to crucifying de Jong (and, to be fair, several – not quite as many – column inches dedicated to defending him), I'm beginning to wonder where the calls for an extended punishment have come from. De Jong has been vilified on the Dutch Match of the Day and has even been dropped from the national team – why? For being anti-football and a vicious thug.

But that's all too easy to say. And wrong, obviously.

We'll start with the anti-football accusation. I don't believe there is such thing as anti-football to begin with. It is something that I have seen numerous times said by teams who enjoy playing quick passing football (Arsenal, Manchester United, Chelsea... now, in all fairness, City) when they have lost or drawn against a side that is working on a much stricter budget and has set their tactics accordingly. Stoke utilise a long throw-in; it's anti-football. Blackburn play a long ball from Robinson frequently; it's anti-football. You get the idea.

It's not. Anti-football is, in my opinion at least, a snobbish phrase coined by fans of clubs who have been bettered by a team they should, on paper, have beaten. Everybody plays to their strengths – if your team has a long throw-in or a goalkeeper with such a big kick, then use it. I wouldn't expect Stoke to ignore their long throw-in abilities when it can be effective. They're breaking no rules.

Now then, back to Nigel de Jong. He doesn't score many goals, granted, but that's not his strength. However, because a player doesn't score many doesn't make him part of this anti-football concept. Tackling and defending is just as much a part of football as shooting and scoring. That City have had one of the most frugal defences in the country this season tells you all you need to know about how well de Jong, Kompany, Toure et al have played.

A house isn't built on sand for the same reason a football team doesn't focus solely on attack. The foundations have to be right for anything to be a success; City's ability to concede very few goals will see them in good stead when the goals dry up. And de Jong is an important part of that defence, allowing the rest of the midfield to play further forward. It's a popular misconception that a midfield containing de Jong, Barry and Yaya Toure is one of three defensive players. Barry and Toure push forward well.

The challenge that broke Ben Arfa's leg was tough, but fair; no different to a large proportion of challenges that are made in every division in every league in every country in every round of fixtures. It's very, very unfortunate that the Newcastle player was so badly injured in the challenge and I, along with all other football fans, wish him a speedy recovery, but it was nothing more than an unlucky and freakish accident.

De Jong has previous form, however, so that must make him a thug. He broke Stuart Holden's leg whilst on international duty with the Netherlands. Quite famously, in the previous World Cup final, he karate kicked Xabi Alonso in the chest – and should have been sent off for it. The irony there, though, is that the entire Dutch team were doing their best to foul the Spanish at every given opportunity and the manager that had instructed his players to adopt these tactics – tactics they hadn't used throughout the rest of the tournament, mind – has now taken the moral high ground in dropping one of his own players for a fair tackle. In 20 months with City, this is the first time a tough de Jong tackle has caused an injury and he hasn't changed his style of play since he arrived.

For there to be calls for de Jong to be suspended for as long as Ben Arfa is injured is insanely ludicrous. The severity of the foul is the only condition on which a punishment should be decided, whether that is at the time by the referee or afterwards by a video panel. Never should the severity of an injury be taken into consideration in deciding a punishment; freak injuries can happen in the most innocuous of challenges or fouls.

After the match, the Newcastle manager Chris Hughton described the tackle as 'unnecessary'. I understand his disappointment with his player's long term injury, but a tackle can't be unnecessary if an opposing playing is in possession of the ball and running towards your goal. There were covering players, but it's de Jong's job to make sure the defence aren't troubled as often as they could be. I wouldn't have expected a Newcastle midfielder not to have made that challenge should it have been the other way around.

This sudden character assassination is unjust. There are plenty of players who have made (and who will make) similar challenges to that which injured Ben Arfa, yet, because the freak accident didn't occur, there will be no more words said. Many more players will be injured in fair tackles, seriously or not, in the future.

But that doesn't mean the player responsible for the injury is a vile monster. The world just isn't as black and white as that.

October 2010 Breakdown

Games (all competitions):
Won: 3   **Drawn:** 0   **Lost:** 2

Goals (all competitions):
For: 9   **Against:** 9

Progress:
Premier League: 4th
League Cup: Eliminated in Round Three
FA Cup: -
Europa League: 1st in Group A

Premier League Table

		P	W	D	L	F	A	GD	Pts
2	Arsenal	10	6	2	2	22	10	+12	20
3	Manchester United	10	5	5	0	22	12	+10	20
4	**Manchester City**	**10**	**5**	**2**	**3**	**13**	**10**	**+3**	**17**
5	Tottenham Hotspur	10	4	3	3	11	10	+1	15
6	West Bromwich Albion	9	4	3	2	13	15	-2	15

Europa League Group A Table

		P	W	D	L	F	A	GD	Pts
1	**Manchester City**	3	2	1	0	6	2	+4	7
2	Lech Poznan	3	1	1	1	6	6	0	4
3	Juventus	3	0	3	0	5	5	0	3
4	Red Bull Salzburg	3	0	1	2	1	5	-4	1

November 2010

Lech Poznan 3-1 Manchester City
Europa League Group Stage, Group A
Thursday 4 November, 2010 – 18:00 KO

City: Given, Bridge (Kolarov 69), Boyata, Lescott, Richards, Vieira, Zabaleta (c), Wright-Phillips (Silva 45), Milner (Kompany 77), A Johnson, Adebayor
Unused: Hart, Barry, Jo, Balotelli
Goals: Adebayor (51)
Booked: Richards, Bridge
Man of the Match: Adam Johnson

City started the brighter of the two teams knowing that a victory in Poland would see them qualify from the group. Johnson slipped the ball infield for Milner, whose shot was charged down by the Poznan defender. It broke to Adebayor, but he couldn't get a shot in.

On 23 minutes, Given was beaten all ends up from a free kick driven through his man wall by Peszko, but it was just wide of his post. But, soon after, the home side had found the net, against the run of play. City struggled with a high ball into the box and only partially cleared. Milner got out to close down Injac, but his shot was too quick and it found the bottom corner.

With half time approaching, City seemed to be running out of ideas. Milner, Johnson and Adebayor all couldn't find room for a shot around the edge of the box, before a Johnson free kick missed everybody.

The first action of the second half saw the visitors level. A corner from the right found Adebayor free in the box. He headed it and it was well stopped by the Poznan goalkeeper, but he could do nothing about Adebayor's follow-up.

Silva had a great chance to give City the lead after some fantastic work by Adebayor. The Togolese striker broke down the City left all on his own and worked his way into the box, before chipping to Silva, who improvised the shot and it bounced onto the bar and over.

But, just as it looked like City would leave Poland with a point, Poznan scored to change the game. A free kick from deep was lifted into the box and it looked a comfortable clearance for Boyata. He met it, but his header rebounded back off Arboleda and clipped the post on its way past Given.

As the game entered stoppage time, the ball broke to Mozdzen. From 25 yards out, he smacked a shot straight into the top corner, leaving Given with no chance. From looking like they were on course to earn a point, City returned home with absolutely nothing.

West Bromwich Albion 0-2 Manchester City
FA Premier League
Sunday 7 November, 2010 – 15:00 KO

City: Hart, Boateng, K Toure, Kompany, Zabaleta (Kolarov 88), de Jong, Barry, Y Toure, Balotelli, Silva (A Johnson 68), Tevez (c)
Unused: Given, Richards, Vieira, Milner, Adebayor
Goals: Balotelli (20, 26)
Booked: de Jong, Barry, Balotelli, Zabaleta
Sent Off: Balotelli
Man of the Match: David Silva

The home side started the brighter, but City worked their way into control of possession. Soon enough, City made their dominance pay. Silva was the architect with a delightful reverse-ball to Tevez and the Argentinian fired it low and hard across goal, leaving Balotelli with the simple job of knocking it into the net. He played it back to the opposite corner and over the line.

Two minutes later and it should have been two for City. Yaya Toure found Silva free in the box and the Spaniard tried to open his body up and beat Carson with a curler to the back post, but it was well pushed away by the keeper. Tevez, though, was perhaps the better option square.

Minutes later, City had indeed doubled their lead. Silva was involved once again, with a delightful ball over the top for Balotelli. He brought it down and, with a little bit of luck to beat the defender, he turned and fired in a right-footed shot straight past Carson.

The second half began with some West Brom pressure, and, with 52 minutes on the clock, Cox had an effort from range that beat Hart, but didn't beat the frame of the goal, as it rebounded to safety from the inside of the post.

Balotelli was booked for diving in the area. And, just before he was about to be replaced with Johnson, the Italian was sent off. It was a deserved second yellow card for a kick on Mulumba, who was booked for his reaction to the challenge.

Hart was called into action to tip a Shorey free kick over the bar expertly, before Silva was needed on the line to keep the ball from going into the net by flicking it up onto the bar and away.

Albion continued to press, but City nicked the ball and began to kill the game with some excellent possession football. The home side's frustration told when Mulumba scythed down Tevez to receive his second yellow card and end his side's man advantage.

Manchester City 0-0 Manchester United
FA Premier League
Wednesday 10 November, 2010 – 20:00 KO

City: Hart, Boateng (Kolarov 83), K Toure, Kompany, Zabaleta, de Jong, Barry, Y Toure, Milner (A Johnson 73), Silva, Tevez (c) (Adebayor 90+5)
Unused: Given, Lescott, Richards, Vieira

Goals: -
Booked: -
Man of the Match: Vincent Kompany

It was the home side who started the game brightly, but a driving run from Tevez was swiftly cut out by Vidic, when the former United striker should possibly have taken the shot on from distance. But that was as lively as it got.

With 37 minutes on the clock, Tevez had City's best chance of the game – a free kick in the centre of goal, roughly 25 yards out. He curled it over the wall and it looked to be heading inside the post, until van der Sar got there first.

It took almost until the hour mark for the next chance to arrive. Berbatov was able to volley at goal from inside the box, but his effort was straight at Hart and was nothing he couldn't deal with easily.

With the game heading towards injury time, Zabaleta had the chance to win it for City as he latched onto a Johnson pass that wasn't cut out by Ferdinand. But, after stepping inside Vidic, his left-footed effort was over the bar.

It was the very definition of a bore draw.

Manchester City 0-0 Birmingham City
FA Premier League
Saturday 13 November, 2010 – 15:00 KO

City: Hart, Boateng, K Toure, Kompany, Kolarov (Zabaleta 82), de Jong, Y Toure, Milner (Santa Cruz 67), A Johnson, Silva, Tevez (c) (Barry 84)
Unused: Given, Richards, Vieira, Jo
Goals: -
Booked: Tevez, de Jong
Man of the Match: Vincent Kompany

After a disappointing Manchester derby, the fans at the City of Manchester Stadium wanted a good start to the match with Birmingham. But, to their disappointment, the game started flatly, as if a continuation from midweek.

In fact, aside from exchanging corners neither side could find a shooting chance until midway into the first half. Kolarov found Tevez with a beautiful ball over the top and he laid it on to Johnson. Crowded out, the winger couldn't get a shot away, but it broke to Tevez and he fired low and hard across the box. It was begging for a touch, but it never came.

As half time quickly approached, City had the ball in the net, but it was ruled out for a handball by Tevez as he nipped in front of Foster. The skipper was booked and the game stumbled to the break.

The first minute of the second half almost had City in front. A brilliant ball into the box for Milner to chase put him through and he got a touch to get past Foster, but his shot was cleared off the line by Carr.

De Jong was denied his first City goal by Foster, as he curled one towards the top corner, before Foster made a meal of a shot from outside the box, but Santa Cruz couldn't get there before the Birmingham defence.

It was City's second bore draw in as many games.

Fulham 1-4 Manchester City
FA Premier League
Sunday 21 November, 2010 – 16:00 KO

City: Hart, Zabaleta, K Toure, Kompany, Kolarov, de Jong, Y Toure, Barry (Vieira 82), Silva (Milner 88), Tevez (c) (A Johnson 77), Jo
Unused: Given, Boyata, Wright-Phillips, Adebayor
Goals: Tevez (6, 55), Zabaleta (32), Y Toure (34)
Booked: Zabaleta
Man of the Match: David Silva

City started the brighter and, with recent disappointing draws to United and Birmingham, an early goal would be just what the doctor ordered. And the medicine soon arrived through Tevez: Barry found him inside the area and he turned brilliantly to set up a one-on-one with Schwarzer. There was nothing the Fulham keeper could do and City had the lead.

A Fulham set piece then almost resulted in a brilliant City breakaway goal. A sneaky pull back to Murphy on the edge of the box was blocked by Silva and Tevez found Kolarov steaming into the home side's half. He took a touch around the defender to set himself through on goal, but a brilliant save from Schwarzer denied him his first for the club.

Just after the half hour City doubled their lead. Zabaleta latched onto a poor clearance from Duff and hit it first time from the edge of the box. It brushed Duff on its way through and shot straight past Schwarzer.

And, as Fulham looked for a way back into the game, City added their third. Tevez was allowed to turn and run at the Fulham defence and, when it looked like he might take on the shot, he slid in Yaya Toure. His first touch was brilliant and allowed him to roll it across Schwarzer into the bottom corner of the net.

With an hour gone, Tevez should have made it four for City. Some neat interplay on the halfway line between Yaya Toure, Zabaleta and Tevez left the two Argentinians to combine, sending the striker through on goal. He ran into the box and looked to bend it around Schwarzer with the outside of his foot, but it was saved for a corner.

From that corner, though, he did get his second. It was only half cleared by Etuhu and Zabaleta unleashed another thunderbolt from the edge of the box. It flicked off Tevez, over Schwarzer and into the net.

With 15 minutes to go, Fulham pulled a goal back. A corner was half cleared by the City defence and Gera shot first time from the edge of the box. It flicked off Yaya Toure's ankle and past Joe Hart, who couldn't react to the deflection. That didn't damped the City fans' spirits, though, who made sure the ironic calls of "boring, boring City" rang through Craven Cottage.

Stoke City 1-1 Manchester City
FA Premier League
Saturday 27 November, 2010 – 15:00 KO

City: Hart, Richards, K Toure, Kompany, Kolarov, de Jong, Milner (A Johnson 82), Barry, Silva, Balotelli (Jo 90), Tevez (c)
Unused: Given, Lescott, Boateng, Vieira, Wright-Phillips
Goals: Richards (81)
Booked: Tevez, Richards
Man of the Match: David Silva

It was the home side who began the game the brighter, with Hart in action straight away, punching away a long throw, before City gave the ball away in midfield and he needed to be alert to make a great double-save, first with his legs from Fuller and then his hands from Jones.

De Jong was then dispossessed in midfield by Delap and, fortunately for the visitors, Jones couldn't take advantage. Another Delap long throw in caused trouble in the City box, with Hart missing the punch and Huth volleying over.

With 10 minutes to go before half time, City seemed to have found their feet and were getting themselves back into the game. Kolarov had a shot from range, but it bobbled through to Begovic in the Stoke goal, who saved comfortably.

City finished the half the stronger as a poor backpass almost let Tevez in, but Begovic was off his line sharply to clear. From the resulting throw in, Tevez, Silva and Balotelli caused all kinds of problems in the six-yard box, but nobody could put the ball in the net in the scramble.

City began the second half in control of the game. Some great possession play opened up a shooting chance for Kolarov from the edge of the box, but it was on his right foot and he skied it. Stoke then had a dangerous breakaway blocked for a corner by Kompany.

From that corner, Shawcross got up before Hart and nodded towards goal. But Milner was on the post and was able to clear off the line, before the ball crossed it into the net. The Stoke players claimed the goal and a handball, but it was neither.

Silva had a shot well wide, with Barry trying to get a touch to steer it towards the net, before City took the lead with a piece of brilliance from, of all people, Richards. It was a neat turn from the right back to flummox the defence on the edge of the Stoke box, setting himself up with a shooting chance and he directed the ball past Begovic and into the net.

City tried to play keep-ball for the final 10 minutes and it was all looking good, despite a free kick from the Stoke left being headed over Hart's goal being a warning shot.

Unfortunately for the visitors, it wasn't a warning they heeded and a backheel from Tuncay, as he controlled a long ball on the edge of the box, sent Etherington through and he fired past Hart and into the net, equalising with 90 seconds of stoppage time to play.

PATIENCE IS A VIRTUE

STOP THE PRESSES! ADAM JOHNSON IS UNHAPPY WITH LIFE AT MANCHESTER CITY AND WANTS TO LEAVE THE CLUB UNLESS HE STARTS TO PLAY MORE OFTEN! HE SAID SO HIMSELF, WITH WORDS FROM HIS OWN MOUTH! EVERYONE PANIC! RUN FOR YOUR LIVES! WON'T SOMEBODY THINK OF THE CHILDREN? ETC. ETC.

I might have over exaggerated the situation a little, but isn't that what everyone else has done?

Here's what Adam Johnson actually said, speaking to The Sun after the Manchester derby: "Every footballer has to think about it when the time comes. It is still early but I definitely would consider it. It is disappointing when you are not playing from the start in games like [the Manchester derby]. I was itching to get on. I was dying to play from the start not just come on.

"The manager has to make decisions but I was gutted to be left out. With the players we have it will be a rotation but I am full of confidence and I just want to be playing. I have got to train and get on with it, nothing is going to change. I have to keep the right frame of mind and get in the team because I want to play for the national team as well."

Of course, there's not really much in what he's said that suggests he's making an ultimatum to Roberto Mancini. Yet that doesn't stop The Sun running with 'Adam Johnson's Manchester City Quit Hint'. After checking The Telegraph, The Daily Mail, The Independent and The Guardian, the story was reported in pretty much the same way. And, after checking The Daily Express, I suspect that Princess Diana might have died...

The fact that Johnson understands that he needs to work hard in training and insists that he will do that is glossed over (after all, it's not actually the quotes that people will remember). The quotes where he says that are buried near the bottom of the story, while the report centres around the implication that he might need to leave City in search of first team football sometime at some unspecified point in the future.

That could be in two years' time if he is still playing in dribs and drabs or in 10 years' time when there is younger talent available to whoever is in charge of the club ("Every footballer has to think about it when the time comes"). There's no 'play-me-or-I-will-leave' threat there: He's just confirmed that he's unhappy at starting most games from the bench. In fact, it reads more like he's looking forward to getting on the pitch for City, not looking at which clubs he can move to next transfer window.

Since this article has appeared in The Sun, I've heard City fans talking about Johnson "spitting his dummy out" or "making thinly veiled threats" or "running to the tabloids". Of course, none of which are likely to be true. Saying something is disappointing is not to spit one's dummy out, for one thing, while affirming a desire to play regularly isn't a thinly veiled threat. And it would seem most likely that The Sun approached City (or England) for an interview with Johnson and posed the question 'would you consider leaving if you needed to get first team football?'

It's cracking journalism: It's turned a dull story that, without that question and subsequent quote, would barely be touched, into a story that every City fan has an opinion about. And, of course, The Sun has a few more pound coins in the bank account. And then the other papers got in on the act by using the quotes along with the words 'speaking to The Sun, Adam Johnson said…'

I understand the frustration of the fans. Coming off the back of two disappointing goalless draws and reading that one of the club's prospects for the future isn't happy at not starting matches isn't the ideal opening to the week. That being said, however, there are positives to be taken with City's 'dip in form'.

City have actually conceded 10 league goals all season and eight of them came in October over four matches. It would seem that Roberto Mancini has gone back to basics: The foundation of any good team is a solid defence and, with Birmingham being City's seventh Premier League clean sheet (from a possible 13) this season, City are showing they have just that.

Watching an inherently defensive performance isn't a great way to spend a Saturday afternoon, but, given the choice between attractive, free-flowing football and another season without success and occasionally dull, but mostly effective and efficient performances with success, can we, as City fans, honestly say we'd prefer not to win something?

The reason, I think, that City are currently struggling to open teams up is because they are allowing their opposition too much time to get back into position. Moving the ball quicker doesn't give them that time and allows gaps to be exploited, resulting in more chances and, potentially, more goals. Add that to the current defence and you're no longer talking about a manager who's on the verge of losing his job, but a manager who's on the verge of revolutionising a club that's been a laughing stock for years.

Speaking of which, to the fans who are disillusioned with the current state of affairs: A laughing stock is not what City are. That was a title reserved for being beaten by York City to sink to the lowest point in the club's history. Neither is this a crisis nor a disaster: That is needing to beat Stoke and pray that results elsewhere go our way.

This is just a blip.

So, City aren't currently playing like Real Madrid or Barcelona and they aren't winning every game by three or four goals. But is anyone in the Premier League doing that?

There are sure signs of improvement at City.

We just need to be a little patient.

November 2010 Breakdown

Games (all competitions):
Won: 2   **Drawn:** 3   **Lost:** 1

Goals (all competitions):
For: 8   **Against:** 5

Progress:
Premier League: 4th
League Cup: Eliminated in Round Three
FA Cup: -
Europa League: 2nd in Group A

Premier League Table

		P	W	D	L	F	A	GD	Pts
2	Chelsea	15	9	2	4	29	10	+19	29
3	Arsenal	15	9	2	4	32	17	+15	29
4	**Manchester City**	**15**	**7**	**5**	**3**	**20**	**12**	**+8**	**26**
5	Tottenham Hotspur	15	7	4	4	23	20	+3	25
6	Bolton Wanderers	15	5	8	2	28	22	+6	23

Europa League Group A Table

		P	W	D	L	F	A	GD	Pts
1	Lech Poznan	4	2	1	1	9	7	+2	7
2	**Manchester City**	**4**	**2**	**1**	**1**	**7**	**5**	**+2**	**7**
3	Juventus	4	0	4	0	5	5	0	4
4	Red Bull Salzburg	4	0	2	2	1	5	-4	2

December 2010

Manchester City 3-0 Red Bull Salzburg
Europa League Group Stage, Group A
Wednesday 1 December, 2010 – 20:05 KO

City: Given, Boateng, Lescott, K Toure (c) (Richards 83), Zabaleta, Vieira, Milner, Wright-Phillips, A Johnson, Jo, Balotelli (Adebayor 71)
Unused: Hart, Kolarov, Barry, de Jong, Silva
Goals: Balotelli (18, 66), A Johnson (79)
Booked: -
Man of the Match: James Milner

With seven minutes gone, Wright-Phillips warmed the crowd up with a brilliant run and cross that needed an intervention from Schiemer to put it behind. It set the stall out for City's role in the game: Dominance.

Soon enough, City got the reward their weight of pressure deserved. Zabaleta put a low ball into the box and Balotelli, from the penalty spot, cheekily flicked out a foot and directed it into the bottom corner of the goal.

Balotelli nearly doubled the lead soon after, as he got to the ball ahead of the onrushing Tremmel, but his flick over the goalkeeper's head was off target. He managed to keep it in play, but couldn't force it over the line and had nothing in the way of support to help him.

Soon into the second half, it was 2-0. Johnson won the ball on the edge of the Salzburg box, before slipping Vieira through. The veteran scuffed his shot, but it broke to Balotelli at the back post and he guided it into the net, with the visiting goalkeeper helpless.

With 15 minutes to go, Given was called into a rare moment of action as he had to make a good save from range, before City added to their goals tally for the night. Johnson picked up the ball wide on the left and cut inside. After taking on and beating three men, he came face to face with the goalkeeper and, on his wrong foot, he found the bottom corner. It was a brilliant individual effort.

City saw out the game with Adebayor unlucky not to find the net from just inside the box, but it didn't matter. A draw between Lech Poznan and Juventus in the other Group A game saw City through to the knockout stages of the competition.

Manchester City 1-0 Bolton Wanderers
FA Premier League
Saturday 4 December, 2010 – 15:00 KO

City: Hart, Zabaleta, K Toure (Lescott 32), Kompany, Kolarov, de Jong, Barry, Y Toure, Silva (Richards 85), Balotelli, Tevez (c) (Milner 90)
Unused: Given, Vieira, Jo, A Johnson

Goals: Tevez (4)
Booked: Y Toure, Tevez, Kolarov
Sent Off: Kolarov
Man of the Match: Vincent Kompany

City started the game quickly, pressing Bolton and looking for the early goal. And that's just exactly what they got – Tevez, fresh from having gotten his eye in with an effort straight at Jaaskelainen, was sent through by Yaya Toure and he made no mistake, slipping it past the goalkeeper.

Both the City players and the City fans wanted a penalty on 15 minutes, as Silva weaved his way into the box and fired in a shot. It was blocked en route to the goal, but it looked to have been by the arm of the defender. The referee, though, gave a corner and not a spot kick.

With half an hour gone, Yaya Toure misplaced a defensive header and it needed Kolarov to get the ball away, before City had a goal ruled out for offside – Barry was clearly ahead of play, but there were questions as to how active he was, as he let the ball run for Silva, who found Tevez to slot it home. On another day, that would have been City's second of the match.

Zabaleta then had a golden chance to double the lead, but his one-on-one was blocked, after he ran on to a delightful chipped pass from his fellow countryman, Tevez.

After the break, Bolton should have pulled level with their best chance of the game. City were caught short at the back and Davies had the chance to volley from the edge of the box, but it was just over the bar. Balotelli then hit the post, after Tevez and Silva caused confusion in the visitors' box.

City were soon peppering the Bolton goal with shots, but with 20 minutes to play, it was almost 1-1, save for Kompany. The big Belgian prevented Hart's blushes, after the young keeper came off his line to collect a routine free kick and, unchallenged, let the ball slip through his hands. It carried on through towards the net, but the centre-back was there first to clear.

Two minutes later, Kolarov picked up a yellow card for a late challenge in the City half, before a delightful run by Kompany opened up the Bolton defence. He carried the ball to the edge of the box and produced a wonderful flick to Kolarov, but his shot was driven wide.

But then, as it looked like City would be comfortable going into the final minutes, Kolarov slid in late on Ricketts. The linesman flagged for a foul and the referee concurred, giving the left back his second yellow card and sending him for an early shower.

West Ham United 1-3 Manchester City

FA Premier League
Saturday 11 December, 2010 – 15:00 KO

City: Hart, Boateng, K Toure (c), Kompany, Zabaleta, Y Toure, de Jong, Barry, Silva (Milner 87), Balotelli (A Johnson 61), Jo
Unused: Given, Richards, Lescott, Vieira, Santa Cruz
Goals: Y Toure (29), Green (og 73), A Johnson (81)
Booked: Balotelli, de Jong, Zabaleta
Man of the Match: David Silva

City started the brighter of the two teams, controlling the play in the opening stages in the West Ham half. Zabaleta tried to feed it through to Jo, before Silva did manage to find the Brazilian on the left, but his low cross was held by Green.

A minute later, the same combination should have put City into the lead. Silva found Jo and he played it in to Balotelli on the edge of the six-yard box. But, unmarked, the Italian couldn't find the net and his side-footed effort rolled wide of the far post.

With 26 minutes on the clock, Yaya Toure picked up the ball in the midfield and drove towards goal. He carried it from halfway and into the West Ham box, but, instead of taking the shot with his left foot, he used the outside of his right and it was an easy save for Green, who was able to hold it.

Barrera had a pop from range, but it was watched well wide by Hart, before City went up the other end and took the lead. Yaya Toure found Barry wide on the left and the England international's return pass was hit first time, just inside the area, with his left foot and it found the top corner emphatically.

It was the home side who started the second half the better, with some pressure on Hart's goal. City, though, while struggling to get the ball away at times, weren't troubled and West Ham couldn't force a decent shot on target.

As the game entered the final 15 minutes, City were able to take it by the scruff of the neck and move into complete control. Yaya Toure ran from the edge of the box, past Tomkins and into the area to fire in a low shot. It hit the post, bounced off the back of Green and into the net for the visitors' second goal of the match.

And soon enough, City were showing their dominance. Silva played a beautiful through pass to Johnson and the substitute took the ball around Green and slid it into the net, taking the visitors joint top of the Premier League.

But, there was a blemish on the copybook to come for City.

With the game heading towards stoppage time, Tomkins was unmarked from a West Ham corner and he rose to head the ball past Hart, with the aid of a deflection off Kolo Toure. It was a silly goal for the away side to concede and put a dampener on an otherwise excellent performance.

Juventus 1-1 Manchester City
Europa League Group Stage, Group A
Thursday 16 December, 2010 – 18:00 KO

City: Given, Boateng, Richards, Boyata, Bridge, Wright-Phillips (Chantler 90), Milner, Vieira, A Johnson, Nimely (Zabaleta 61), Jo
Unused: Taylor, Ibrahim, Kay, Mee, Elabdellaoui
Goals: Jo (77)
Booked: Zabaleta
Man of the Match: Adam Johnson

Having already qualified for the next stage of the Europa League, City fielded a weakened side for the trip to Turin. However, a positive result would always be preferred, as the Blues will have wanted to finish on top of the group to try and have the best draw possible in the next round.

And it was the visitors that started the brighter and should have taken the lead almost immediately. Richards charged down the right flank and delivered a low cross towards Jo, but the striker couldn't connect to the ball and slot it home. It was a let off for the hosts.

Boyata had to be alert to stop Del Piero from getting his shot away, putting in a cracking tackle in the area, before Nimley almost got his first City goal with a header from a Johnson free kick, but it was just wide.

A dangerous Juventus free kick was flicked wide by Sissoko, before the home side took the lead, somewhat against the run of play. Del Piero worked up to the by-line and got his low cross in through the six-yard box. Gianetti worked his way in front of Boyata and was able to flick the ball home, on the stroke of half time. It had looked like the scores would be level at the break.

Five minutes into the second half, Jo had the ball in the Juventus net, but it was wrongly ruled out for offside, before Johnson almost squeezed an effort home, but he couldn't quite force it in.

With just over 10 minutes to play, Jo equalised for the visitors. Johnson found the Brazilian on the edge of the box and he took a touch, turned neatly and fired into the bottom corner.

Richards almost put the visitors in front immediately, but he couldn't quite turn Johnson's cross into the net. It finished 0-1 in Salzburg, leaving City to top the group.

Manchester City 1-2 Everton
FA Premier League
Monday 20 December, 2010 – 20:00 KO

City: Hart, Zabaleta, K Toure, Kompany, Kolarov, Y Toure, Barry, Silva, Milner (A Johnson 45), Balotelli (Jo 83), Tevez (c)
Unused: Given, Richards, Boateng, Vieira, Wright-Phillips
Goals: Jagielka (og 73)
Booked: Kompany, Barry, K Toure
Sent Off: K Toure

Man of the Match: Pablo Zabaleta

Knowing they could be top of the league for Christmas with a victory, City started the game with some good possession. But, within just three minutes, it was all undone: A free header from Tim Cahill inside the six-yard box put the visitors in front, with the home side's defending leaving a lot to be desired.

With 19 minutes on the clock, it got worse. With Zabaleta off the pitch for treatment to a head wound, Cahill and Baines exploited the space and, after Kolo Toure couldn't reach to intercept the first cross, the ball fell to Baines inside the box. He curled it around Hart and into the net, with a first time hit on his wrong foot.

And City had a mountain to climb.

There were signs that the home side might get back into the game before the break, but chances were few and far between. Balotelli volleyed over from a corner, before City appealed for a handball in the box, but the referee waved the shouts away.

Fellaini went into the referee's book for a stamping challenge that left Tevez on the deck, before a superb free kick from Kolarov was matched by Howard, springing to his left to touch it around the post. Yaya Toure blasted over the bar, before City appealed for a penalty again. A handball against Phil Neville was the cry, but it was turned down.

After half time, it really was all City… but it was Everton who had the goals and it was they who were content to defend deeply and park the bus. Anichebe saw yellow for a late tackle on Hart, before Kolarov wasted an opportunity to get a good ball into the box from a free kick, wide on the right.

With 30 minutes of the game to play, the visitors were reduced a man. Anichebe brought down Zabaleta with a silly challenge as the City man was heading towards his own goal and the referee deemed it worthy of a second yellow card. The man advantage, though, didn't greatly help the home side, as it made the visitors even more reluctant to open the game up.

With 64 minutes played, City had another penalty shout – this time, handball by Jagielka, but the referee, once again, said no. A minute later, Silva's shot was blocked by Neville's arm in the area again, but, despite the City players being convinced it was a spot kick, the referee played on. The fans were beginning to feel hard done to.

On 73 minutes, though, City were back in the game. Yaya Toure's driven cross towards the back post flicked off the knee of Jagielka and beat Howard, reducing the home side to a one-goal deficit.

Three minutes later, it looked like City had equalised. Balotelli beat the offside trap to run on to a Silva pass, but his deft flick over Howard rebounded back into play off the post, before Howard pulled off a world class stop to deny Tevez, who looked certain to score.

With five minutes to play, the City players were shaking their heads in disbelief as Peter Walton turned down another penalty appeal, as the ball struck

Hibbert on the arm in the box and appeared to be another nailed on spot kick.

City's misery was then compounded, with two stoppage time yellow cards for Kolo Toure. First, he brought down Distin in the Everton half and prevented a breakaway, then, a minute later, did the same to Bilyaletdinov.

The Blues had missed the chance to spend Christmas on top of the league.

Newcastle United 1-3 Manchester City

FA Premier League
Sunday 26 December, 2010 – 15:00 KO

City: Hart, Boateng, Lescott, Kompany, Kolarov, Y Toure (Vieira 83), de Jong, Barry, Silva (A Johnson 70), Milner, Tevez (c) (Balotelli 86)
Unused: Given, Zabaleta, Richards, Jo
Goals: Barry (2), Tevez (5, 81)
Booked: Silva, Lescott, Hart, Johnson, Balotelli
Man of the Match: Gareth Barry

The game was only 90 seconds old when City showed how they intended to approach it. The visitors opened the scoring through Barry, with a helping hand from the Newcastle defence as well. Krul played a short ball out that was stolen by Tevez and he laid it on for Barry to find the net, through the keeper's legs. It was a late Christmas gift of a goal on Boxing Day.

And it got better for the away side just two minutes later. Tevez found Milner wide on the right and his ball straight back into the box found the little Argentinian striker, who was able to slot the ball into the top corner from close range, giving City the perfect start. It all came from a mistake in the home side's midfield.

A minute later and the home side could have been back in the game. Carroll had the chance to head into the net from close range, but Hart was on hand to pluck the effort out of the air and hold it, making it look a much simpler save than it actually was.

A minute from half time, Tevez gave the ball away in midfield and allowed Newcastle to build an attack. It led to a diving header from Carroll, but that flicked off Nolan and spun wide of the post.

City started the second half quickly, just as they had done the first, earning themselves a corner as Newcastle still looked like they were on their half time break. Kolarov's vicious cross was cleared, before his shot from the rebound skewed wide of the post.

Soon, the home side reduced the deficit. Barton swung a corner into the middle and it was met by the unmarked Carroll, who planted it into the net. Hart picked up a yellow card for complaining that he was fouled by Nolan and the City keeper had a point, but referee Chris Foy wasn't moved.

But City showed what they were made of as the clock ticked past 80. Milner found Tevez on the left and he broke through the challenge of Barton. A quick one-two with Johnson gave the Argentine the chance to cut inside and shoot – the shot flicked off two defenders and finished in the net, via Coloccini's bottom.

It secured the three points for City and was the icing on the cake of an excellent performance. It had been a very tough game for the Blues.

Manchester City 4-0 Aston Villa
FA Premier League
Tuesday 28 December, 2010 – 15:00 KO

City: Hart, Richards, Lescott, Kompany, Zabaleta, Vieira, Y Toure (Jo 63), de Jong (c) (Bridge 77), Silva (Milner 59), A Johnson, Balotelli
Unused: Given, Boateng, Barry, Tevez
Goals: Balotelli (pen 8, 27, pen 55), Lescott (14)
Booked: Milner
Man of the Match: David Silva

With large changes from the side that won at St James' Park, an out-of-form Aston Villa side could have had their hopes of a resurgence buoyed. City quickly snuffed out their chances however, as a bright start led to Silva almost finding Balotelli in the box.

But, a minute later, the same two players combined and Lichaj hauled the big Italian down, gifting the home side had a penalty. Balotelli dusted himself down and coolly slotted the ball past Friedel, sending the American the wrong way to put City in a commanding position.

And the second goal was soon in coming, as Lescott rose well to nod the ball towards goal. Bannon thought he had headed it clear, but the assistant flagged that it had crossed the line and the referee gave the goal.

Aston Villa threatened an immediate response, but Downing's free kick was well over the bar, before a City move consisting of 35 passes without a Villa touch effectively ended the game before half time.

After a spell of knocking the ball between midfield and defence, City saw their chance and Yaya Toure found Silva, whose shot was saved by Friedel, leaving Balotelli to slot in the rebound. It was one of the best team goals that had been scored in the City of Manchester Stadium.

With 34 minutes on the clock, Silva almost made it four, but his effort was deflected just the wrong side of the post, as Friedel was beaten, after some good work from Johnson on the right wing.

The first big chance of the second half fell, unsurprisingly, to the home side. A Johnson corner was cleared only as far as Vieira. The veteran took a touch and fired it towards goal, but Friedel was equal to it, pushing it around the post

And it was a sign of things to come: A minute later, Johnson weaved his way into the box and was tripped by Albrighton. The referee had no hesitation and awarded City their second penalty of the game. Balotelli slotted it home for his hat-trick, as coolly as his first.

Delph had an isolated shot for Villa, but it was well pushed around the post by Hart, before Downing sent another free kick well over the bar. Lichaj then fired towards goal from six yards, but Hart, again, was on the top of his form to make the save, as Villa looked in vain for a late consolation goal.

THE WRATH OF THE LAST MINUTE GOAL GOD

Right at the end of the 1998-99 football season, Manchester City were involved in perhaps the most famous Nationwide League Division Two Playoff Final ever. And I'm not exaggerating – it was a dreadful game that sparked to life eight minutes from the end as, first, Carl Asaba and, second, Robert Taylor put Gillingham two goals in front. As the clock struck 90, Kevin Horlock pulled one back for City, before, at the end of stoppage time, Paul Dickov equalised.

And, it would seem that, at that point in that game, City angered whichever God it is that is in charge of handing out last minute goals. Because, since then, I'm struggling to remember many last minute goals that changed the game in City's favour. There was, of course, Adam Johnson's stunner at Sunderland (1-1). And who could forget that time that Micah Richards did it at Aston Villa (1-1) and then swore on the telly? He also did it at Everton (1-1), while Macken did it at Tottenham (4-3) and Robinho at Blackburn (2-2). Then there's Kiki Musampa (1-0, Liverpool), Stephen Ireland (2-1, Reading) and Danny Califf (1-0, own goal, FC Midtjylland).

Contrast that to the events of last weekend: Matthew Etherington added himself to a list that contains (in no particular order) Paul Scholes, Mateusz Mozdzen, Wayne Rooney, Tim Cahill, Ryan Shawcross, Dirk Kuyt, Michael Jakobsen, Michael Owen, Darren Bent, Gary Speed, Jimmy Bullard, Manuel Arboleda, Sanli Tuncay, Martin Vingaard, Glenn Murray, Richard Dunne (own goal) and Roman Bednar, all of whom have scored last minute, game changing goals against City.

And to think people say I don't hold grudges... ha!

It seems odd that I'm moaning about City not scoring enough in the last minute by naming eight times when they have done it. But that's all I can remember from the last 12 years, while City have conceded seven of them since Roberto Mancini took charge. It's also slightly ironic that I praise Mancini so much for his defensive coaching.

It's almost as if City never learn their lesson: It's generally not a good idea to leave a member of the opposing team unmarked in the box with just seconds remaining when leading a game by one goal. Or, worse, when drawing. And it certainly feels like it's always City conceding the last minuters than scoring them.

Having watched the first half of the draw with Stoke through my fingers as the home side went closer than was really necessary to scoring, I was starting to enjoy the second half. Obviously, that was because I was watching with my City hat on and, come the second half, City were starting to take control of the game.

In fact, by the time City scored, not many people will have expected a Stoke equaliser; it looked like, as the City pressure around the Stoke penalty area began to build, the home side had missed their chance and would have to settle for trying to keep City out. That being said, though, very few sides keep Stoke blank at their own ground and perhaps it was that complacency that cost the goal.

While I think the draw was a fair result – Stoke by far dominated the first half, but, in the second, didn't seem to have a look in, while it was roles reversed for City – it's disappointing to have taken the lead at a difficult place to go with 10 minutes (ish) of the game remaining and not to go on and win. To have dealt with the first half pressure, the long throws, the corner kicks, the set pieces, the tall men in the box, the kitchen sink and whatever else Stoke hurled towards City, yet lose a goal to an untracked run made it feel like a worse point than it was.

If you had offered 1-1 at the start of the day, I would have taken it without question. I've seen City fail to deal with Stoke's threat on numerous occasions, so I would have been happy with a point before kick-off. Traditionally, City struggle at that ground (1-0, 3-1(aet), 1-1). But, even so, having been so close to stealing all three, it's hard not to be disappointed, especially on the weekend when United and Arsenal won.

And, while the result mirrors the corresponding league result from last season, I would venture that it was an improved performance. Last season and the season before at the Britannia Stadium, City struggled to equalise against a team with 10 men (they managed it last season, but not the one before). But every long throw that went into the box caused havoc and, right at the death, Ryan Shawcross was unlucky not to have scored the winner (again with seconds to play), having had what looked to be a perfectly fair goal ruled out for a foul.

Yet, last weekend, City coped well. Save for the odd moment of panic, Kompany and Toure were good in the air, Hart was decisive coming off his line and winning the ball when he did, and, for all the pressure, the Stoke goal never came. The City goal never looked like coming at that time, granted, but the defending was much better.

So much better, in fact, that as half time came and went, City were able to use it as a platform to build on. They got themselves on top of the game and scored, albeit through a moment of brilliance that I suspected surprised Micah Richards as much as it did everyone else. Would City last season have done that? Probably not.

Mark Lawrenson on Match of the Day suggested that Balotelli and Mancini didn't fancy the game because it was cold and snowing. That would be Messrs Balotelli and Mancini, formerly of Milan, an Italian city that famously has never even heard of cold or snow.

Joe Lovejoy in The Guardian speculated that City's squad of foreigners (seven of which were English) struggled for being a fair-weather team, which would have been a valid criticism, had 13 of the 18 not forged a successful career here for more than two seasons. Though he did also describe the team as 'Northern Softies', making them both English and foreign.

Anyway, my admittedly sarcastically written and very roundabout point is that City didn't draw the game because of something silly like the weather. It was a moment of bad defending that did them in.

Oh, and the wrath of the Last Minute Goal God.

The pesky bleeder.

THIRD PLACE FOR CHRISTMAS

There are some things in life that we know for certain. The smelly guy with the greasy hair and whiskey bottle inside a brown paper bag will always be the one that chooses to sit next to you on the bus. It's always during that important meeting with your boss that you mother calls your mobile to find out if she can visit for the weekend. And it's always the weekend that you're going to an away game that she invites herself.

Of course, if you're a City fan, you'll have gone into Monday night's game with Everton with that feeling of inevitability in the pit of your stomach. Everton, struggling this season and hovering just above the relegation zone, coming to the City of Manchester Stadium to play City who, with a win, could go top of the league for Christmas day – it's odds on for a home win, surely…? City's defence don't let much through easily and, on their day, they can score some pretty decent goals.

Even if they managed a draw, they'd spend Christmas day in second place.

So now it's Christmas Eve and, with no more fixtures to be played before tomorrow, City sit in third. Can any of us actually say we're surprised at this? It's one of those inevitabilities of life as a City fan; if there's an easy way to do something or a way to reward the fans with something nice every now and then, you can sure as hell bet City will do it the hard way. If they do it at all.

It must be hard-wired into the club's DNA. We have a phrase for it that has been doing the rounds since well before I started going to watch them: Typical City. City beat the top of the league by three goals, then lose to the bottom team the week after – Typical City. City are the subject of a takeover and become the richest club in football, only to subsequently spend that Christmas in the relegation zone – Typical City. City go joint top of the league after a great performance without one of their most important players and, that evening, said important player hands in a written transfer request – Typical City.

And, would you know it, it was Typical City FC and not Manchester City FC that turned up on Monday evening. I'm not saying that the game was an easy one, far from it. What I am saying is that, with most of the league games last weekend falling victim to the weather, City knew before kick-off that a victory would leave them top of the league. So, naturally, they didn't start playing until they'd given Everton a two goal head start.

For the record, I feel 'given' is the correct word since Everton didn't exactly have to work hard to get those two opening goals. My Sunday league team could have scored those two opening goals with the state of City's defending, though, in fairness to Everton, my Sunday league team wouldn't have been able to see out and win the game from that position. They've got me in goal, for starters.

In fact, Everton's defending is something that we should praise the visitors for, too. City piled on the pressure for about 70 minutes and the only way they could score was a deflected cross from Yaya Toure. The story of the game is summed up in City's shooting statistics: 32 shots, four on target. Nearly all of City's shots were from range or blocked (suspiciously with arms on several occasions – Phil Neville played a blinder in goal for Everton), while the visitors scored all of their shots on target.

True, they spent most of the game time wasting or in their own box, but it's not against the rules to park the bus as they did. It wasn't pretty to watch, but I daresay their fans don't care seeing it as they won the game. And it's down to City to score the goals necessary to go on to win the game (which would be helped without such an atrocious start to the match).

It would also be quite hypocritical of me to criticise their style of play, given that it's exactly what City had to do whilst strapped for cash under Stuart Pearce in order to stay in the Premier League. It's always far too holier than thou to say how football should be played and many teams have been successful in many different ways.

I've no doubt that City will win something and soon. In fact, if they don't, then questions need to be asked, starting with what the hell did everyone at City do in a past life to upset the footballing Gods and how bad was it? It must have been something quite bad if they conspire to stop City winning something despite such an investment as the one they have received.

Certainly, though, the concept of 'Typical City' is an interesting one. It's been around the club for decades, yet managers, chairmen, boards, squads of players, shirt sponsors, kit colours, divisions, tactics and even stadiums have changed since it was first introduced into your average Citizen's lexicon. How is it possible for City to have a poor record against one team that stretches back for ten or more years? The only constant in City in that period is the fans.

Can the 'Typical City' attitude be the entire problem? Could it be, no matter how much money is thrown at the team and no matter what improvements are made to the stadium, pitch and training facilities, that City will continue to struggle on the big occasions (Everton, Tottenham, Manchester United in the Carling Cup) because of the 'Typical City' sword that dangles over them? Could it really be that City will win something when we as fans stop thinking that the worst will happen because 'that's what City do'?

We know the atmosphere at Eastlands isn't brilliant, but a collective groan after the first misplaced pass or a wholesome sigh when someone miscontrols the ball doesn't help anyone.

2010 is nearly gone, so let's leave 'Typical City' behind with it. It's Christmas Eve and City aren't top of the league. Bah Humbug, eh? What an awful season it's turning out to be. It's not as if, on this day two years ago, we were sitting in eighteenth place, having just lost to West Brom, playing a quality of football that would disappoint my Sunday league team.

Christmas in third place.

It's not all bad.

December 2010 Breakdown

Games (all competitions):
Won: 5   **Drawn:** 1   **Lost:** 1

Goals (all competitions):
For: 16   **Against:** 5

Progress:
Premier League: 2nd
League Cup: Eliminated in Round Three
FA Cup: -
Europa League: 1st in Group A, qualified for the Round of 32

Premier League Table

		P	W	D	L	F	A	GD	Pts
1	Manchester United	18	10	8	0	39	17	+22	38
2	**Manchester City**	**20**	**11**	**5**	**4**	**32**	**16**	**+16**	**38**
3	Arsenal	19	11	3	5	39	22	+17	36
4	Chelsea	19	10	4	5	33	15	+18	34
5	Tottenham Hotspur	19	9	6	4	29	23	+6	33

Europa League Group A Table

		P	W	D	L	F	A	GD	Pts
1	**Manchester City**	**6**	**3**	**2**	**1**	**11**	**6**	**+5**	**11**
2	Lech Poznan	6	3	2	1	11	8	+3	11
3	Juventus	6	0	6	0	7	7	0	6
4	Red Bull Salzburg	6	0	2	4	1	9	-8	2

January 2011

Manchester City 1-0 Blackpool

FA Premier League

Saturday 1 January, 2011 – 15:00 KO

City: Hart, Boateng, Lescott, Kompany, Kolarov (Zabaleta 60), de Jong, Barry, Y Toure (Vieira 85), Silva (Milner 64), A Johnson, Tevez (c)
Unused: Given, Richards, Wright-Phillips, Jo
Goals: A Johnson (34)
Booked: -
Man of the Match: Nigel de Jong

City began the first game of 2011 with all guns blazing and had two excellent chances to take the lead in the opening 90 seconds. First, Tevez slid a shot wide as he stole the ball on the edge of the box, before Silva sent a low cross towards Toure, but he couldn't stretch to reach it.

Blackpool then had a golden chance to take the lead and probably would have done through Taylor-Fletcher were it not for a brilliant saving tackle from Lescott, yards away from the goal.

With 13 minutes played, it was Hart who was called upon to make the first save of the game, as a poor clearance found its way to Taylor-Fletcher in the box. He turned and shot towards the top corner, but Hart got across well to push it behind.

Just after the half hour, City's hard work came to fruition. A corner was only half-cleared to Johnson on the edge of the box and the winger took a touch to control before firing low and hard through the crowd. It flicked off Crainey's ankles and beat Kingston into the back of the net.

A minute later, Tevez had the chance to double City's lead after Yaya Toure was hauled down in the area by Varney. The little Argentinian, though, pulled his penalty kick wide and Blackpool were off the hook. It was an uncharacteristic error.

With 54 minutes on the clock Hart was called into action again, saving from Phillips, before a break from Yaya Toure could have seen City in a more comfortable position but for the intervention of Kingston's left boot.

20 minutes from time Tevez should have killed all of the Blackpool threat, as he picked up the ball from Johnson and was through on goal. He rounded the goalkeeper and tried to switch it back to his right foot, but he slipped in the process, giving the defence time to get back.

Arsenal 0-0 Manchester City

FA Premier League

Wednesday 5 January, 2011- 19:45 KO

City: Hart, Richards, Zabaleta, Kompany, K Toure, de Jong, Barry, Milner, Y Toure, Jo (A Johnson 65), Tevez (c) (Boateng 90+4)
Unused: Given, Bridge, Lescott, Wright-Phillips, Vieira
Goals: -
Booked: de Jong, Barry
Sent Off: Zabaleta
Man of the Match: Vincent Kompany

It could have all gone wrong for the visitors with just 90 seconds played, as van Persie was almost left with an open goal from a square pass by Wilshere, who could have shot but, thankfully for City, it rolled straight past the Dutchman and he didn't put it in.

Eight minutes in, van Persie struck the foot of the post as Hart was unsighted and Arsenal were piling on the pressure. But City were holding strong: Hart got down well to deny Wilshire, van Persie skied a free kick and Zabaleta was in the thick of the action with several great tackles on Walcott. The England man then slid a great chance wide of the post, after he turned in the box.

Fabianski had to clear to stop Richards getting to the ball first, before a City corner came to nothing as Tevez mis-hit his return pass when free at the back post. The breakaway, though, saw Arsenal hit the post twice – first van Persie crashed one past Hart, and the rebound fell to Walcott, who did the same.

With 33 minutes played, Jo chipped a ball for Tevez to chase, but the bounce took him wide and, with very little support in the centre, the Argentinian opted to volley at goal and it was just over the bar.

Early in the second half, van Persie shot wide, before it took a world class save from Hart to keep the scores level. Van Persie had an attempt from outside the box and it was destined for the top corner, before the England international's fingertip intervention.

In stoppage time, Zabaleta ran the ball out of play and Sagna wasn't happy with the City man's defending. He pushed his head into Zabaleta's twice, before the Argentinian full back pushed him in the chest and both players were shown a red card by the referee.

Leicester City 2-2 Manchester City
FA Cup Third Round
Sunday 9 January, 2011 - 16:00 KO

City: Hart, Boateng, Kolarov, K Toure, Lescott, Vieira, A Johnson, Wright-Phillips (de Jong 45), Milner, Jo (Zabaleta 73), Tevez (c)
Unused: Given, Boyata, Santa Cruz, Ibrahim, Nimely
Goals: Milner (23), Tevez (45)
Booked: -
Man of the Match: James Milner

City's FA Cup campaign for this season got off to the worst possible start – just 45 seconds into their third round tie with Leicester and they were behind. A short corner was whipped into the box and Bamba got up before Boateng to nod the ball past Hart, leaving the visitors on the backfoot from the off.

It didn't take long, though, for the response: From a moment of brilliant play between Milner and Tevez, the English midfielder pulled City level. After a quick one-two, he cut inside the Leicester defence and smashed the ball into the bottom corner with his left foot for his first goal in a City shirt.

Johnson had a glorious chance to put City in front as he slid in to Tevez's low cross, but he could only poke the ball wide, with Jo in a better position at the back post.

Just as it looked like the teams would go in level, City stole the lead. A short corner was poorly defended by the home side and a low Milner cross left Tevez free to back-heel the ball in at the near post.

Leicester began to press the City goal in the second half and, when it seemed that City had ridden the storm, a mistake from Hart let the home side off the hook. A simple catch was fumbled into the path of King, who needed no second invitation to poke the ball into the net.

With 15 minutes to play, Milner was City's saviour, heading the ball off the line as Bamba had, once again, got up before the City defence. At the other end, de Jong should have had his first City goal, as a great turn from Tevez left him with almost no work to do, but Weale got across to make the save.

With minutes to play, City could have stolen the game with an effort from Tevez, but the goalkeeper was there again to block.

Manchester City 4-3 Wolverhampton Wanderers
FA Premier League
Saturday 15 January, 2011 – 15:00 KO

City: Hart, Zabaleta, Kompany, K Toure (Lescott 54), Kolarov, de Jong, Barry, Y Toure, A Johnson (Silva 84), Tevez (c) (Milner 82), Dzeko
Unused: Given, Boateng, Vieira, Jo
Goals: K Toure (41), Tevez (51,66) Y Toure (54)
Booked: -
Man of the Match: Carlos Tevez

It was Wolves who began the game looking like the team who could go top, rather than the home side, and the visitors' pressure paid off on 13 minutes. A bit of pinball in the City box from a poor clearance by Kolo Toure left Milijas to tap the ball into the net.

Fletcher could have doubled the lead with a free header, but it was straight at Hart, as the City fans began to wonder whether the home side were going to turn up. They had another heart-in-the-mouth moment, as Kolarov had to throw himself in front of a shot to prevent what looked to be a certain goal, as Wolves capitalised on a sloppy pass.

With half time quickly approaching, Dzeko had a shot deflected wide and City sent the big men forward for the corner. It found its way to Kolo Toure at the back post and he took a touch, before firing a shot at goal. Hennessey got a touch, but couldn't prevent it from creeping into the back of the net.

It was almost as if a completely different City team came out for the second half. With five minutes played, a great piece of individual skill put City in front. It was the captain, Tevez, who picked up the ball just inside the box and beat two defenders to get himself a one-on-one. He slid it under the goalkeeper and City looked to have put their poor first half showing behind them.

Three minutes later, it got better with a clinical breakaway. Tevez slipped the ball to Dzeko on the left and he cut inside to find some space, before placing a deft pass in to Yaya Toure and putting him through on goal. Toure made no mistake and slotted it into the net, to give City a two goal advantage.

Dzeko had a shot deflected just wide, as it looked like it was going to sneak in at the near post, before City added to their lead. The corner was flicked clear as far as Zabaleta who, as it looked like he might have a go from the edge of the box, chipped it back in to Tevez, unmarked, and he nodded it home off the underside of the crossbar.

But, almost immediately, Wolves had a chance to reduce the deficit. Lescott, with a clear foul in the box, gave Doyle the penalty kick and he fired it home, sending Hart the wrong way and, with over 20 minutes to play, the visitors began to believe they could get back into the game.

With four minutes left, the away side set the game up for a grandstand finish. Zubar found himself space inside the City box and had a free header from a left wing corner – Hart was beaten and de Jong thought he'd hacked it off the line, but the linesman said otherwise and awarded the goal.

With four of five added minutes played, Wolves came within inches of an equaliser as a shot was deflected past Hart, who was left helpless but, fortunately for City, it was just wide of the post.

Manchester City 4-2 Leicester City
FA Cup Third Round Replay
Tuesday 18 January, 2011 - 19:45 KO

City: Hart, Zabaleta, Kolarov, Kompany, Lescott, Vieira, Milner, Y Toure (Jo 79), A Johnson, Silva (Barry 64), Tevez (c)
Unused: Given, Boyata, K Toure, de Jong, Nimely
Goals: Tevez (16), Vieira (37), A Johnson (38), Kolarov (90+1)
Booked: Vieira
Man of the Match: James Milner

The visitors started brightly and forced a corner from a deflected header that almost beat Hart, before Johnson found himself through on goal, but he wasn't able to give the home side the lead.

Yaya Toure couldn't find Tevez or Silva as he played a low cross into the box and Weale was able to see the ball safely behind. But he could do nothing about the next effort, one that put City in front. Tevez received the ball from a throw-in and beat two challenges into the area, before lashing it into the top corner, silencing the visiting fans.

But, just two minutes later, Leicester had a chance to get back into the game. Dyer broke into the box past Kolarov and Vieira, brushing the latter and going down. The referee took his time, but decided the contact was enough to award the penalty, which Gallagher drove into the net.

But, just before the break, another City goal came. Tevez played a nice ball over for Zabaleta and he drove his way to the by-line. His pull back landed to the feet of Silva, who shot at goal on his weaker right foot and forced a good save from Weale, but Vieira was there at the back post to stab home.

Then, as the City fans were taking their seats, they were celebrating again. A defence-splitting pass from Silva slipped Johnson through for his second one-on-one of the night and this time he made no mistake, slotting the ball past the goalkeeper from outside the box.

Tevez skied a shot on 54 minutes after some neat interplay between Yaya Toure and Johnson, before the Argentinian had the chance to put his penalty miss against Blackpool behind him. Through on goal, he was tripped by Hobbs, but his penalty was straight down the middle and saved by Weale.

With 83 minutes played, the visitors set up an exciting finish. After a large slice of luck where the ball bounced kindly off the referee, Dyer raced on to a pass through the centre that neither Kompany nor Lescott could quite reach and he placed the ball past the on-rushing Hart.

But, as the game entered stoppage time, it was Kolarov who wrapped the tie up. After a piece of patient build-up, Johnson cut into the box and poked the ball to the left back on the edge. He took a touch and found the space to fire a low drive across Weale and into the bottom corner.

Aston Villa 1-0 Manchester City
FA Premier League
Saturday 22 January, 2011 – 17:30 KO

City: Hart, Boateng, Kolarov, K Toure, Kompany, de Jong, Y Toure, Barry (A Johnson 56), Silva, Dzeko, Tevez (c)
Unused: Given, Lescott, Zabaleta, Vieira, Milner, Jo
Goals: -
Booked: Kolarov
Man of the Match: Aleksandar Kolarov

Having seen Arsenal and Manchester United win with large margins earlier in the day, City needed a victory to regain second place in the league. But it was the home side that started the brighter, as Hart had to clear from Bent, before former City skipper Dunne got up from a free kick to head over.

It was corners where City were causing the home side problems, with Kolarov's wicked deliveries, but Kolo Toure couldn't capitalise with a volley on his left foot. Tevez couldn't react quickly enough as everybody missed it in the six-yard box, and the ball rolled under his foot. City should have been ahead.

Instead, it was the home side that got themselves in front. Sloppy play from City at the back gifted the ball to Villa. Young took on the shot from the edge of the box and Hart could only parry it into the path of Bent, who scored on his debut for the hosts.

With 22 minutes on the clock, Kompany almost had City level. His header from another fantastic Kolarov corner was powered towards the roof of the net, before the intervention from Friedel. Dzeko was inches from converting another Kolarov delivery. The former Villa man Barry almost levelled for the visitors shortly after, as he nodded a Boateng cross just wide, with the goalkeeper beaten.

City continued their dominance of the game after half time, with Tevez firing the first chance wide just seconds in. Villa could have nicked a second after a difficult backpass was sliced by Hart straight to Agbonlahor, but the hosts couldn't capitalise.

City camped themselves in the Villa box, as Johnson wriggled his way to the by-line and found Tevez, but the little striker's shot was superbly blocked by Collins. De Jong was denied his first City goal by a flick onto the post from the feet of Clark.

With five minutes to play, Dzeko got up above of Collins and headed inches wide of the post and Kolarov's shot took two deflections before finishing just the wrong side of the upright.

Notts County 1-1 Manchester City
FA Cup Fourth Round
Sunday 30 January, 2011 - 14:00 KO

City: Hart, Zabaleta (Kolarov 77), Richards (Kompany 88), Boateng, Lescott, Vieira, Barry (c), Milner, Y Toure, Jo (Silva 63), Dzeko
Unused: Given, K Toure, de Jong, Guidetti
Goals: Dzeko (80)
Booked: Milner
Man of the Match: Micah Richards

With eight minutes played, City could have been in front. Dominating the early possession, they worked it wide to Richards on the overlap and he fired in a low cross to the centre, where Yaya Toure threw himself at it. He connected with the ball, but the keeper flung out a foot to deflect the effort over the bar.

Jo was inches away from connecting to a Milner cross as half time approached, before Milner nearly latched onto a Darby header back to his goalkeeper. County could have put City under pressure in stoppage time, but the free kick from the centre drifted over everybody in the box.

But then, early in the second half, the home side took the lead. Hughes appeared to be fouling Zabaleta in the box, but the referee didn't agree and that led to a deflection behind. Bishop rose to nod the corner into the net ahead of Dzeko and the visitors had it all to do.

With 69 minutes on the clock, Barry was denied a brilliant equaliser by a superb save from Nelson. A City corner was nodded as far as the edge of the box, Barry took a touch and fired in the shot towards the top corner, but the keeper got up well to flick it over the bar.

Then, as it looked like it was going to be another upset, City got their equaliser. Notts County were tiring and a long ball out of their defence was nodded to Boateng by Hart. The German played in Richards who, after a neat touch around the defender, smashed the ball across the six-yard box and there was Dzeko to put the ball in the net for his first City goal.

DON'T BLAME US IF YOU CAN'T SCORE!

Good grief. I mean, seriously, wow. The overreaction to Manchester City's performance at The Emirates is unbelievable. A football team went to another stadium and played for a point and that's it. You'd think they'd started a nuclear war, or been involved in an international drug smuggling scam, or put a cat in a bin, or something. Maybe that's a slight overreaction, too, but heigh ho, what's good for the goose and all that.

I find it very amusing, more than anything, when the accusation of 'anti-football' is branded about. I have slated our own supporters for this when moaning about teams parking the bus. It's a term of snobbery and only cracked out of the cliche cupboard when a side has been dominant and failed to win. City fans did it when Birmingham came to Eastlands.

And now Arsenal fans are doing it when City went to The Emirates. You know, like it's City's fault Arsenal didn't (couldn't) score. It wasn't Birmingham's job to let City score, just as it wasn't City's job to let Arsenal score. If you have 68% of the possession, but only manage five shots on target, you only have yourselves to blame.

Defending is just as much a part of football as attacking is. City did the former very well and the latter took a bit of a back seat. It's almost as if playing for a draw at one of the best clubs in the league is a crime. In fact, I was rather forcefully told by an Arsenal fan after the game that "even fucking Blackpool came here and attacked" and, in fairness to him, he's right, they did. And look what it got them: -6 in the Goal Difference column.

Does Arsenal's FA Cup victory over Manchester United in 2005 mean less because they defended for 120 minutes and then won on penalties? Of course it doesn't. I'd be interested to see what those Arsenal fans booing City think.

It seems though, of the comments (mainly on Twitter) from Arsenal fans I've seen about City's choice of style for Wednesday's fixture, most, if not all, have missed the point entirely. It's all well and good saying things like "if that's what £200m buys you, they you are welcome to non-football" or "Man City are the most boring side in the Premier League!" or "spending £300m+ and only getting a point, if I was a City fan I would be furious" or "I'm disgusted I paid £72.50 to watch Man Shitty park the bus".

One fan went as far to say City played 12-0-0 because of the goalposts. I assume he forgot that the size of the goal doesn't change each week and that putting the ball in-between the posts instead of onto them is a job for the attacking team?

The point is, though, (aside from the fact that the later the evening went on, the total City had spent on the team rose, it seemed, until it peaked at about £1bn – seriously), City don't park the bus in front of their goal every week. In fact, it's happened twice this season: Wednesday evening and in the first half at White Hart Lane. City may have the best defensive record in the league, but they have also scored more than, for example, Tottenham and, somehow, it's Tottenham who are being portrayed as the free-scoring saints and City as the smash-and-grab merchants.

City, like Arsenal, have put on some fine attacking displays this season. And they will put on some more as the season goes by. So they had to defend like beavers in order to secure a point at The Emirates. Off the back of four games in 10 days, 10 out of 12 points is a good haul, especially as the final game was the toughest of the fixtures. Total football was never going to be on the agenda; City have saved that for the teams it will be most successful against.

Paying £72.50 for a ticket to a football match is obscene, but that's not because your team didn't break my team down. It's because £72.50 to watch any game of football is obscene. And if you're disgusted with anyone, it should be your own team for not putting one of their chances in the net. And for setting the price that high.

It's not the away team's job to entertain the home fans.

Hearing Arsenal fans complain about City's style last Wednesday does feel somewhat hypocritical. It would be pertinent to consider their own club's history of grinding out 1-0 victories by shutting the shop, pulling the shutters down and setting the alarm when having taken the lead before criticising.

I have been impressed with City's defensive record this season. I'm not used to it; we're more than halfway through the season and I'm yet to fully appreciate that, if City are under pressure with 10 minutes to go, the chances are they won't concede. For a City team to be playing keep-ball for the last five minutes while leading by one goal is unnerving. I'm far too used to panic stations, hoof it anywhere and defending deeper than a military submarine on manoeuvres.

At no point this season have City claimed to be title contenders, in fact, quite the opposite. When asked, both management and players alike have played down City's title ambitions. It's the fans and the media that have played it up. Sure enough, come mid-April if they are still where they are now, then they are very much in the mix, but right now they still have a long way to go and a lot to learn. Spending hundreds of millions assembling a team isn't like playing Football Manager. Players won't settle, high numbers of players in and out makes it difficult to gel a team, managers don't know their best combinations… but, most importantly, throwing money at a club won't win you the Premier League title. There's much more to it.

Just because x number of millions have been spent on a team doesn't mean that they will suddenly go out and dominate. It's taken a long time for some City fans to learn this lesson. City are a work in progress. A work in progress that won a well-earned and hard fought point away from home on a Wednesday evening.

It's very easy to say that City won't be title contenders because no title contender would park the bus at an away game. However, you would also think that an entirely different title contender would break down a stubborn defence when playing at home.

Don't blame the opposition when you don't score.

EFFICIENT, EFFICIENT CITY

"I can see a very nervy one-nil victory," I said, when taking part in a game of Predict The Manchester City Score for a City podcast that I host, expecting Wolves to come to The City of Manchester Stadium, park the bus and for it to be all City, yet the team being unable to find the second goal (leading to a tense final few moments). As happened with Blackpool. And Bolton. And Birmingham (though City failed to get the first goal).

I, unlike Mick McCarthy, hadn't done my homework on the opposition. Credit where it's due, Wolves didn't get what they deserved from their performance – City were only good for about 15 minutes of the entire match. The rest of the time they were distinctly average, while Wolves pressed and caused trouble every time they went into the home side's box. McCarthy didn't give the home defence time to pass the ball out, which led to long balls and, subsequently, City losing possession.

In many ways, I was actually quite close to reading the game correctly, though for entirely the wrong reasons. City did win by one goal. It was a nervy finish, where Wolves threw the kitchen sink. I couldn't have been more wrong about the middle bit, though.

Having scored four times, it seems silly talking about a nervy finish. I thought the days of cowering behind the person in front of me, watching both teams score freely, were over when Roberto Mancini arrived. It's rare that a team will score three times against City (though Wolves have scored five in total this season, which, I suspect, will be the most any team scores against them – tempting fate, obviously).

Nevertheless, City were 4-1 up with 25 minutes to play. And, having been fortunate to have gone in to the dressing rooms from a first half dominated by the visitors at 1-1, everybody in the stadium thought they had ridden their luck and were now pumping up the goal difference. But, a silly penalty and a goal that might or might not have crossed the line later, and suddenly, the comeback was on, when it really shouldn't have been.

In many ways, I hope that this is a lesson to some (not all) City fans. Far too many of us (myself included, on several occasions, this season) seem to think that all the club needs to do to win a game by three, four, five goals is to walk out onto the pitch. "It's only Wolves, we will win this game at a canter" is a phrase that tripped far too easily off the tongue over the past week. A fortnight earlier, it was "It's only Blackpool, we can beat these easily."

Yet neither turned out to be straightforward in the end.

No game in this league is easy. It's a cliche I know and I feel very dirty for writing it, but it's true: All games are difficult, but some games are more difficult than others. But with the investment comes a raise in expectations and 'four goals good, two goals bad' appears to have become the philosophy for certain people. The more important philosophy, though, should be 'four goals good, two goals good also, as long as we've kept a clean sheet'.

Granted, those who expected City to win big before kick-off on Saturday almost had a point – from being 4-1 up on 66 minutes, it should have finished as a big win. In fact, the three conceded goals worry me a little: A poor clearance from a normally reliable centre-back (made up by his equaliser), a needless foul for a penalty, and a free header from a corner (whether it actually crossed the line or not – in fact, this argument is a nice excuse for losing a goal through poor marking). I expect these defensive frailties are a blip, because, despite Saturday's result, City's defence is still the best in the league: 19 conceded in 23 matches, compared to Manchester United's 19 in 21 and Chelsea's 19 in 22.

Despite the criticism of having been playing defensive football, yet still having scored more than Tottenham, the team dubbed as the season's entertainers by Fleet Street, City have been picking up results. When flowing attacking moves have been seen on the pitch and when the team is leading by a couple of goals, it's become the fashion for the City fans to sing 'boring, boring City' in an ironic manner.

But, if being solid at the back, keeping clean sheets (11 in the league this season) and winning games by one or two goals is considered boring, then I'll take that boring City over the one that both scores and concedes for fun. I know that the latter might be more entertaining for the neutral, but I'm not a neutral. And City have caused more than enough people to develop heart conditions over the years, it's only fair they stop.

In fact, call me selfish, but I'd actually quite like to win something in the next few seasons and, by keeping clean sheets, any team will win more than they draw. Any good team is built on solid foundations and behind the best defence in the Premier League is one of the best goalkeepers in the Premier League.

Roberto Mancini has shown this season that he likes his defence tight and, on the whole, it has been. He doesn't underestimate the opposition as it seems a lot of fans have been doing recently. He doesn't think that a game will be a walkover because the opposition are below seventh in the table. It would be nice to score six or seven in a match, don't get me wrong, but it's not a necessity. It's high time that fans didn't go to games and get frustrated that the team isn't three goals up at half time (slight exaggeration).

Mancini's City aren't a machine that grinds out 1-0 victories with unattractive football. There's good football played along the way. In fact, no, there's been some excellent football played along the way. So perhaps a more appropriate chant would be 'efficient, efficient City'.

Though, I suppose, that doesn't quite scan.

INTERVIEW: SVEN GORAN ERIKSSON

Tuesday 18 January was a day of reunions. Roberto Mancini was paired up with his former mentor for the second time in nine days and that former mentor was paired up with his former club, too. Sven Goran Eriksson's Leicester City had earned a very credible 2-2 draw with Manchester City in the FA Cup Third Round earlier in the month and that meant that the former England manager would be returning to The City of Manchester Stadium for the replay.

This time, though, he was visiting the away dressing room. "It's a little bit smaller than the home dressing room," he laughs. "It was very good to come back. I have lots of good memories, but I didn't want to have gone there for the second game in the FA Cup.

"I would have preferred to beat City here in Leicester, because I felt we had the chance, but didn't take it," he says, thinking back to the game.

The Swede, though, is very philosophical about the eventual outcome of the tie. "In two games they [City] were the better team and we lost. And now they have a real chance of winning the FA Cup. And I hope they will." There are clearly still very warm feelings towards the club, despite the acrimonious way in which he and City parted company.

Sven's time with City got off to a flying start. The team had needed some serious investment from the season before, a campaign which had seen City score just 10 home league goals and not one of them came after New Year's Day 2007. For a while, it had looked like the following season would be another struggle, but soon news broke of a takeover.

Thaksin Shinawatra took control of the club and immediately appointed Sven as his number one, giving him the chequebook to bring in some new players too.

"I knew that they had had a poor season the season before," Sven remembers. "I think the players and everyone in the club understood that it was necessary to bring in some new players or we would have been struggling against relegation. Nobody wants to do that, of course, and the owners at that time were aware of that, too.

"We signed a lot of players in a rather short time," he continues. "I think we were lucky because more or less all of the players made a good contribution to the team and to getting results. We started the season very well and better than I thought we should have done; better than anyone thought we would."

Sven signed eight players that pre-season: Rolando Bianchi, Geovanni, Elano, Gelson Fernandes, Martin Petrov, Javier Garrido, Vedran Corluka and Valeri Bojinov. On the whole, there were positive contributions from them all – though Bojinov was unlucky to have fallen foul of a serious knee ligament injury in just his third game.

One of those eight, though, was struggling in Manchester. Rolando Bianchi got off to a great start, scoring the opening goal on his debut in City's 0-2 win at West Ham. But, he didn't grab himself another league goal for almost four months and, in the January transfer window, he moved to Lazio on loan until the end of the season.

"That's my fault," Sven says, talking about the Italian striker. "He didn't fit in as well as I thought he would have done. But I think all of the other signings did an extremely good job for the club."

City's start to the season was a stark contrast to the form of the year before: Three games, three wins, no goals conceded. The fixture list, though, as it so often does, had a sting in the tail for the Blues. The third of those games being a tie with Manchester United; it wasn't an ideal match for City to be playing having had so little time to assemble their team and get them gelled together.

"I wished at that time that we'd had more time to prepare. It was more or less every day that we had been signing a new player," Sven says, despite City eventually going on to win the game. "But the players were very clever and they were good players.

"It was my first derby in Manchester and you could feel it the whole week before," he continues. "It was something special. I remember when I signed for City, one of the supporters came to me and said: 'Sven, don't talk about Europe or the league. Just beat United twice and that's it. That's the most important thing.'

"The most important thing, though, was the final result for the club. You could feel the derby and, if you compare it to Lisbon or Rome or anywhere I've been before, it's great. It's probably the biggest derby I've been involved in."

The following match, City's unbeaten start came to an end as they visited The Emirates Stadium and Arsenal. Despite Robin van Persie missing a second half penalty, the Blues couldn't quite hold on and eventually went down to a Cesc Fabregas goal with 10 minutes to play. It was the first goal City had conceded in almost six hours of football under Sven.

But did that good start to the season put the team under pressure?

"In one way, I think so," the then manager remembers. "But I think everyone was very happy – the players, the fans, the people in the club. Certainly until Christmas, but with the team we had at that time, we shouldn't have won the league and I don't think we could have won the league.

"Everything's possible in football. We had a very good team, but not one that was that good that we could compete with the best two or three teams in the league over a long period."

But, as good as City's start was, the second half of the season was the opposite. If the form up until Christmas was top four material, the form in the new year was very much relegation fodder. In the first 19 games of the campaign, City won 10 and drew five. While, in the final 19 games, that became five wins and five draws.

Amongst that poor run of form, though, was one standout moment for most fans. Having already won the first Manchester derby of the season, City travelled to Old Trafford on Sunday 10 February, 2008 – the game where the home side marked the 50th anniversary of the Munich air disaster.

Sven remembers it well: "It was a special day because it was a memorial day for the tragic air accident of Manchester United. In that way it was very special and I will always remember for all my life the minutes before kick-off, when it was one minute of silence.

"I remember, throughout all the week before, some of the people from City were nervous that City fans might boo them or something. And I think it was a great minute of civilisation and education. You couldn't hear anything inside the whole stadium and it's one of those moments that I'm very proud of."

If the fans did the club proud during the build up to the game, the players did their bit in the subsequent 90 minutes. Goals from Vassell and new signing Benjani were enough to secure City their first derby double since 1969-70.

"We weren't lucky," Sven says of the second derby. "We were very good and deserved to win that game. If you talk about the first game at home, we played okay and we won, but I think we were brilliant the second game and deserved to beat United at that time.

"It felt good [to win the first derby double for City in over 35 years] and it's written in the history books, so whatever happens they can't take that away from anyone who was involved at that time."

But that derby victory was a shining light in quite a poor run of form. And this had quite a large effect on the manager, especially with murmurings in the press about discontent behind the scenes.

"It became too many rumours about my future in the club," he says, looking back. "Thaksin's relationship with me was totally broken down. He never talked to me. He didn't want to talk to me during the last couple of months.

"Of course, the players knew. The whole ambience, from being great, became…" Sven's thoughts trailed off. It was clear we both knew the extent to which the relationship between chairman and manager was affecting the club. "I think everyone at that time was a bit disappointed with everything that was happening off the pitch.

"You have to try to do the best you can and it wouldn't have become a problem if only I knew about it [Shinawatra's intentions to sack Sven at the end of the season]. I didn't know about it, but I was rather sure it would happen.

"As soon as it comes out to other people in the club, the players or the staff it becomes very difficult. And, at the end, the fans knew it, too. It shouldn't have happened.

"I think he [Shinawatra] could have sacked me at the end of the season, but he should never have let anybody suspect that that was what was going to happen. That was his mistake.

"I take the blame for the last games of the season, but I think he should take equal blame because, as a football director, you can't act like that."

While his time with City ended with a sour taste in the mouth, Sven harbours no bad feelings towards the club. But would he have preferred to have had a crack at City with the current finances available?

"I had an extremely good time at Manchester City. If I could have chosen my time to come to City, I should have come a couple of years later," he laughs. "Then things might have been quite different."

January 2011 Breakdown

Games (all competitions):
Won: 3   **Drawn:** 3   **Lost:** 1

Goals (all competitions):
For: 12   **Against:** 9

Progress:
Premier League: 3rd
League Cup: Eliminated in Round Three
FA Cup: Round Four ongoing (replay scheduled)
Europa League: 1st in Group A, qualified for the Round of 32

Premier League Table

		P	W	D	L	F	A	GD	Pts
1	Manchester United	23	14	9	0	51	21	+30	51
2	Arsenal	23	14	4	5	48	22	+26	46
3	**Manchester City**	**24**	**13**	**6**	**5**	**37**	**20**	**+17**	**45**
4	Chelsea	23	12	5	6	42	19	+23	41
5	Tottenham Hotspur	23	10	8	5	32	26	+6	38

February 2011

Birmingham City 2-2 Manchester City

FA Premier League

Wednesday 2 February, 2011 – 19:45 KO

City: Hart, Kolarov, Kompany, Richards (K Toure 37), Boateng, Barry, de Jong (Vieira 45), Milner, Silva, Tevez (c), Dzeko
Unused: Given, Zabaleta, Lescott, Jo, Guidetti
Goals: Tevez (4), Kolarov (40)
Booked: de Jong, Kolarov
Man of the Match: David Silva

City couldn't have wished for a better start to the game at St Andrews, as Silva picked up the ball on the edge of the Birmingham area and tried to make room for the shot. Crowded out by defenders, he opted instead to slide Tevez through on goal. The Argentinian striker fired the ball back across Foster and into the bottom corner, after just four minutes.

But, after 21 minutes, the home side were back level. A free kick from the left flank was poorly crossed into the City box, but nobody dealt with it and Zigic was left to flick the ball under Hart.

City lost Richards to a serious looking head injury, as the defender was down for almost seven minutes for treatment before being stretchered from the field, as things started to go downhill for the visitors.

But then, when the game restarted, Dzeko won a free kick on the edge of the box after he was dragged to the floor by Gardner and up stepped Kolarov. He rifled it, low, hard and with plenty of bend, into the bottom corner, as Tevez and Silva lurked. The goal was somewhat against the run of play.

The second half was a tight affair, with both sides unable to carve out a good chance. Just as it looked like City had done enough to earn all three points without really getting out of second gear, the Birmingham pressure paid off. Phillips turned into Vieira in the box and the striker went to ground, leaving the referee to point at the spot. It was harsh, but Gardner didn't care as he smashed it past Hart.

The final chance of the game fell to the visitors, as Kolarov stepped up to take a free kick from roughly the same position as he'd scored in the first half. He came very close at the far post, but it was just wide and City came away from St Andrews with only one point when they could, and perhaps should, have had all three.

Manchester City 3-0 West Bromwich Albion

FA Premier League

Saturday 5 February, 2011 – 15:00 KO

City: Hart, Zabaleta, Boateng, Kompany, K Toure, Kolarov, Milner, Barry, Silva (Razak 90), Y Toure (Dzeko 64), Tevez (c) (Wright-Phillips 87)
Unused: Given, Lescott, Vieira, Jo
Goals: Tevez (pen 17, 22, pen 41)
Booked: Zabaleta
Man of the Match: Carlos Tevez

West Brom got their first chance on goal after a foul by Kompany right on the edge of the box. Brunt whipped the kick around the wall and Hart pulled off a good save to push it well away. He was in action again shortly after to touch a volley from the edge of the box wide of the post and then to knock an Olsson header over the bar.

But, just as the visitors were getting into their game, they shot themselves in the foot. A nice ball from Tevez let Kolarov, who had stepped up to left midfield for this match, turn in the box and he was brought down by Reid for a certain penalty. Tevez stepped up and, having missed his previous two, showed no pressure as he sent the keeper the wrong way.

Four minutes later, it got better for the birthday boy. Tevez played a neat one-two with Silva after having beaten two West Brom defenders and found himself through on goal. He slowed it down, composed himself and slipped the ball past Myhill.

Olsson was needed to put in a last ditch challenge on Tevez to prevent his hat-trick, before Kolarov decided against the intricate build-up that City had been playing and fired in a ferocious effort from 30 yards that needed fingertips from Myhill to touch it onto the bar. Tevez got another chance for his third, after a handball into the box and the Argentinian belted the penalty away.

The visitors should have pulled a goal back on 62 minutes, as Fortune found himself clean through on goal after some shocking defending from City. His shot beat Hart, but it was into the side netting and City were off the hook.

With just over 10 minutes to play, Tevez should have had his fourth after the ball broke to Barry at the back post. He dragged Myhill out of position before rolling it sideways to Tevez, but the man on form scooped the ball over the bar when faced with an open goal.

Manchester United 2-1 Manchester City
FA Premier League
Saturday 12 February, 2011 – 12:45 KO

City: Hart, Zabaleta, Lescott, Kompany, Richards, Kolarov (Wright-Phillips 52), Barry, Milner (Dzeko 60), Y Toure, Silva, Tevez (c)
Unused: Given, Boateng, K Toure, Vieira, Jo, Dzeko
Goals: Silva (64)
Booked: Kompany, Milner

Man of the Match: David Silva

It was City who had the best chance of the opening minutes, as Tevez slipped Silva through inside the box, but the little Spaniard poked the ball wide as van der Sar closed him down.

A spell of United pressure was twice dealt with by Richards flying headers, before a dummy from Yaya Toure left Silva with the chance to break. He ran at the United defence, but couldn't slip the return to Toure in, sending him too wide and the momentum of the move was lost.

Giggs found some space on the left and crossed to the back post where Fletcher was free, but his header was straight at Hart and the City keeper held on to the ball. It was the first real bit of danger from the home side.

Just before half time, United took the lead against the run of play. A ball over the top fell to Nani via Rooney and he slotted the one-on-one past Hart. City had been the better side, but they found themselves behind.

And it was the visitors who started the second half the better, but they needed to score while they were on top. Rooney denied Richards a goal by heading off the line from a City corner, before Silva found van der Sar's gloves as he got the chance to shoot from the edge of the box, on 56 minutes.

With 64 minutes played, City got their equaliser. Wright-Phillips drilled a low cross into the box and Dzeko hit it whilst falling backwards. His shot rebounded off Silva's back and looped into the net. City deserved to be on terms, though there was a huge slice of luck with the goal.

But then, with 12 minutes to play, City were stung again. A deflected cross in from the right found Rooney between two defenders and he scored the goal of the season – an overhead kick from the left side of the box. It was United's second goal against the run of play.

The home side were lucky not to concede a penalty as Vidic elbowed Dzeko in the box, but the referee missed it. But that was the last of the action and United ran down the clock by the corner flag. It will be little consolation to them, but City know that the gap between the sides is now minimal.

Aris 0-0 Manchester City
Europa League Round of 32, First Leg
Tuesday 15 February, 2011 – 17:00 KO

City: Hart, Richards, Kolarov, K Toure, Boateng, Wright-Phillips (Balotelli 77), Barry, Y Toure, Silva, Tevez(c), Dzeko (Zabaleta 86)
Unused: Given, Kompany, Jo, Vieira, Lescott
Goals: -
Booked: Dzeko
Man of the Match: David Silva

City had a tough test in Greece, visiting a stadium with a hostile atmosphere and a team that were unbeaten there in over 40 years of European football, having beaten the reigning Europa League champions earlier this season.

Boateng was too casual in trying to clear and it almost presented the home side with a chance, before Kolo Toure got enough in the way of a shot to take the sting out of it. The visitors could have been in more trouble after a mix-up between Hart and Barry, resulting in the keeper handling outside his box, but Neto put the free kick wide.

It was a typical European night, as the game meandered to half time. The first action of the second half saw Aris win themselves a corner and Kolarov clear under pressure, before Wright-Phillips hit a shot straight at the goalkeeper from outside the box.

Toja fired straight at Hart, before it could have been the visitors who had the advantage, as Barry found Dzeko's head, but a fine one-handed save from Sifakis denied him the goal.

With 70 minutes played, Dzeko fired wide. Kolo Toure was then in the right place to get a backwards header away from the City goal, before Balotelli tried an overhead kick, but to no avail.

Manchester City 5-0 Notts County
FA Cup Fourth Round Replay
Sunday 20 February, 2011 - 14:00 KO

City: Hart, Zabaleta, K Toure (c), Lescott, Richards, Vieira, Y Toure (Barry 81), Kolarov, Silva (Jo 87), Balotelli (Tevez 60), Dzeko
Unused: Taylor, Boateng, Kompany, Nimely
Goals: Vieira (37, 58), Tevez (84), Dzeko (89), Richards (90+1)
Booked: Balotelli
Man of the Match: Patrick Vieira

For the opening stages, it was the visitors who were on top of the game: Hart had trouble with a first minute free kick, before Hawley picked up the ball on the corner of the box and curled an effort around the keeper. Many in the ground thought it was in, but it hit the inside of the post and bounced out.

And that was the wake-up call that City needed. Richards put in a perfect cross for Dzeko, who got up to head well, but it was straight at the goalkeeper, and he pushed it over the bar.

City then made their pressure pay. A great cross from Silva was met by the head of Vieira and the veteran nodded it through the goalkeeper's legs, via Pearce's hand, to give City the lead.

As the hour mark approached, Vieira doubled his tally and City's lead, with another header from another corner. The ball was flighted perfectly for the Frenchman's head and he connected with power to leave the keeper standing.

The concern, though, was for Balotelli and Pearce, after a nasty clash of heads.

With just over 10 minutes to play, Hart needed some acrobatics to keep the clean sheet in tact, as Gow hit a volley from the edge of the box. It looked like it would fly past the young England keeper, but he got up well to get both hands on it and force it over the bar.

Tevez got in on the goalscoring action and he grabbed his 50th in a Manchester City shirt. He latched on to a brilliant Dzeko pass, took the ball around Nelson and slid it into the net from an acute angle. And then Dzeko added to City's goal tally. A brilliantly weighted pass from Barry sent Tevez through. He drew the goalkeeper and chipped the ball into the six-yard box for Dzeko to head into the net from a yard out.

In stoppage time, it got even better. A corner from the left wing fell to Micah Richards and he took a touch to control, before volleying it into the top corner with his left foot.

Manchester City 3-0 Aris
Europa League Round of 32, Second Leg
Thursday 24 February, 2011 – 20:05 KO

City: Hart, Boateng, Kolarov, Lescott, Kompany (Zabaleta 36), Barry, Y Toure, Silva (Wright-Phillips 81), Balotelli, Tevez (c) (Vieira 81), Dzeko
Unused: Taylor, K Toure, Wabara, Jo
Goals: Dzeko (9, 12), Y Toure (75)
Booked: Kolarov
Man of the Match: Edin Dzeko

City were the more lively of the two sides from kick-off and it looked like the hosts were going for the jugular. Kolarov whipped a first minute free kick over the bar, before Dzeko got his angles wrong from a corner and side-footed wide.

The home side's left back tried another free kick shortly after from the right wing, but that too was over the bar, as City tried to make their early possession and pressure pay.

Soon enough, it did and they were in front. Lazaridis couldn't deal with a ball over the top, allowing Dzeko to steal in and fire across the goalkeeper and into the bottom corner with a fine finish.

And it got better. A breakaway down the left flank was quickly switched to the right, via Silva and then Tevez. Dzeko moved the ball from his right foot to his left, cutting inside, and he fired it into the same corner as he scored his first to double City's lead.

With a minute of the half to play, Dzeko should have had his first City hat-trick, as he was sent clean through on goal by Tevez. The big Bosnian tried rounding the goalkeeper, but a combination of him and his defenders got enough on the ball.

As the game appeared to be meandering to an end – City were keeping hold of possession and Aris were pressing, but unable to create too many clear cut chances – Balotelli almost put the tie beyond doubt. Breaking down the right, he skipped into the box and fired a low shot across goal. But it hit the post and bounced out, with Dzeko unable to re-adjust to the rebound.

Yaya Toure then added City's third of the night. A corner was cleared to him on the edge of the box and he took a touch to control before firing it back and, with the aid of a deflection, he found the bottom corner.

With just minutes to play, Dzeko could again have had his hat-trick, but the ball skipped off the surface and ran away from him after Balotelli had done well to flick it on. Nevertheless, City were safely through to the last 16 and face a tie with Dynamo Kiev in the next round.

Manchester City 1-1 Fulham
FA Premier League
Sunday 27 February, 2011 – 15:00 KO

City: Hart, Boateng, Kolarov (Milner 77), Lescott, K Toure, Zabaleta, Barry, Y Toure, Balotelli, Tevez (c), Dzeko (Vieira 62)
Unused: Taylor, Wabara, Jo, Wright-Phillips, Guidetti
Goals: Balotelli (26)
Booked: Balotelli
Man of the Match: Pablo Zabaleta

With 16 minutes played, Tevez and Zabaleta linked up well and it could have been better, but the Argentinian full back couldn't get enough on Boateng's cross to worry the visiting defence. Fulham, though, soon showed that they hadn't come to Eastlands to let City play. Beginning to get a foothold on the ball with some possession in midfield, they attacked quickly with Murphy firing over.

But then, as the visitors appeared to have settled into the game, Balotelli put City in front with a shot from absolutely nothing. Tevez had the ball on the left side of the penalty area and knocked it back to the Italian. He took a couple of touches inside and curled it expertly into the bottom corner, when there appeared to be very little danger.

A Fulham free kick could have been more fruitful after it was played to Duff on the left. He fired in a low cross that Johnson couldn't force towards goal and City were able to scramble clear.

Just after the interval the visitors got their equaliser. A quick break down the right let Johnson through and he fired a low ball across goal for Duff to smash in at the back post.

With 20 minutes to play, City had a series of corners that Fulham were struggling to deal with. Both Balotelli and Kolarov were firing the ball into the box, but it wouldn't go in. In all of that action, Kolarov almost scored a cracker

– a volley from mid-way into the Fulham half – but Schwarzer touched it over.

As the game wore on, City's efforts became increasingly desperate and Fulham appeared happy with a point. Perhaps the best chance to win the game fell to Tevez. He was played through by Milner and almost flicked it past Schwarzer, but for the keeper's fingertips.

In the end, City had to settle for a point, but that made it four seasons in a row where City had taken the lead in this fixture and gone on not to win maximum points. A bad day at the office for the Blues, but there's still a long way to go.

MANCHESTER CITY FANS AND THE BIPOLAR DISORDER

I sometimes wonder if Manchester City fans suffer from bipolar disorder. It could be a condition that comes on after a few years of supporting a club that shoots itself in the foot at any given opportunity, or it could be something innate that means subconsciously we all tend to lean towards the Citizens. There isn't really much room for a grey area: Championship challenge or relegation. Brilliant signing or total flop. There doesn't seem to be any middle ground.

After the 2-2 draw at Birmingham, I would hazard a guess that The Samaritans were busier than usual, as City did what they do best and struggled against a hard working side at the wrong end of the league. To be fair to Birmingham, though, they played well and deserved their point. Even if the penalty for the equaliser was dodgier than a pub-bought DVD being played on the latest laptop bought on a second-hand market on the cheap. From a guy known locally as 'Dodgy Terry'.

But, off the back of a game where City were twice leading and should have seen out the final whistle in a winning position yet didn't, you would have thought that the club had been doomed to a season of mid-table mediocrity or, worse, confirmed as relegated. In no particular order, I heard or read comments from a large number of fans along the lines of: "Hart should be dropped!", "That's it, the season's over!", "Dzeko is no better than Jo!", "Adebayor scored, why did we let him go?!", "We need to get Mourinho in to save us!", "Vieira should be taken out the back and shot!"...

Roll that forward to the evening of a routine home victory against West Brom and suddenly the title challenge is back on.

I suppose it's easy to jump to irrational conclusions on the back of a game that was within City's control and they have let slip away. I'll be honest, I was quite frustrated that Wednesday evening and I don't think it would have been right not to be. But we still need to calm down before shouting our mouths off.

Joe Hart's had a blip in form recently, but has shown his ability for most of the season and won City many points. The season isn't over because there's also the FA Cup and Europa League to play for. Dzeko is gradually getting better, Adebayor and Mancini clearly don't see eye to eye, changing the manager now is a ridiculous suggestion and Vieira's knowledge and experience will be invaluable at the end of the season, if not on the pitch.

Though I do think someone might have shot at Vieira and hit the wrong man on Wednesday evening, given what happened to Phillips in the box. Talk about a soft penalty.

Anyway... a penalty was given, a penalty was scored and a draw was the result. It felt like two points dropped because City had twice led. But United and Tottenham only managed a draw at St Andrews and Chelsea lost there, too, so it's clearly not an easy game in Birmingham.

But, despite that negative feeling leading up the West Brom fixture, City did the unlikely – they did what they were supposed to do. They won the game and played well. Instead of giving several fans in the stadium premature coronaries, a skill they've perfected down the years with stunts of sheer lunacy, usually in the last minute. But there was none of that.

The problem is, with an increased level of performance and a big investment comes a higher level of expectancy. Fans, perhaps wrongly, go to matches against the teams towards the bottom of the table and expect an easy game and a big win; a sentiment summed up by Angry Lady, sitting behind me at Eastlands, who shouted towards a West Brom defender "get out of his way!" as Zabaleta tried to get a cross in.

Teams won't roll over and die, defences will try and stop attacks and Angry Lady will always be shouting that Tevez should "earn his wages" (that one came when he spooned a shot over the bar, despite already having a hat-trick).

It doesn't make sense to get agitated when City haven't scored inside the first 20 minutes. I don't like using cliches, but there are no easy games and no team is in this division by accident (I lied, I love using cliches). What counts is that City at least win the game, without a good performance, if necessary.

On the other side of the fence, one win doesn't make the season. True, results went in City's favour last weekend and they were the only side in the top four to have won. And they are only five points off the top. But they have played a game more – and I think we, as fans, ignored that there were games in hand to play when we were sitting top of the league and talking of the title.

In other words, optimism got the better of us.

We should be optimistic, though, don't get me wrong. City are better than last season. But the idea that this would be a bad season for not winning the title or being out of the 'title race' in February is ludicrous and is perhaps symptomatic of the "I-Want-It-Now" McSociety we're living in.

I'm sure the title challenge will come in future, but fourth was a priority at the start of the season. And it's not unreasonable to reassess to third (possibly even second) given the current standings.

Results could go City's way and they could be within reach of the title with five or six games to play. But nobody should be too upset if that isn't what happens. We shouldn't be thinking of dropping 10 players, changing the manager, or shooting Patrick Vieira if we don't win the league. Maybe if we don't finish in the top four.

We're in a marathon, not a sprint (cliche alert). One result doesn't define the season and the collective mood swings of the large proportions of the fans aren't necessary. We're not fighting relegation; we're not sitting mid-table with nothing to play for; we're still in two cup competitions as well... so let's sit back, relax and enjoy the (good) ride, for once.

Lithium on standby.

DERBY DAY IS THE WORST DAY OF MY LIFE

So, it's here again for another year. It's going to happen and there's nothing we can do about it and there's no way we can get away from it. It's like when your mother-in-law arrives just in time for kick-off and talks all the way through the first half, shuts up for half time, before continuing her discussions through the second half, blissfully unaware that you're trying to watch the match. Though, to be honest, if she wanted to distract me for 96 minutes tomorrow, she would be welcome to (bear in mind I'm single and haven't got a mother-in-law, so it's going to have to be a very quick courtship and wedding at this late stage).

I hate derby day. As simple as that. I hate it. It's a truly horrible day. In fact, I'd go as far as to say it's the worst day of the football season. And some fool decided that it should happen at least twice. Clearly someone's off their rocker.

It never fails to leave your stomach feeling the way it does after you've had a bug for three days and haven't eaten. It never fails to put your body under more stress than taking an exam that your life depended on you passing. I'm not aware of such a test existing, but it'd definitely spice up A Level exam halls.

One reason why it makes me (and I assume other Manchester City fans) feel like this is simple. The result is amplified: Wins feel better, defeats feel worse, while draws feel like even damper squibs than they were. But the biggest reason of all, however, is actually that we're Manchester City fans. Doing things the easy way isn't in the club's nature, so getting through derby day isn't a simple achievement.

United fans have it easy. It's win-win in their camp. They win, they get to taunt some City fans. They lose, they get to pretend that Liverpool is their big fixture. Though, of course, we all know they do care thanks to the outrage felt at the Welcome to Manchester billboard, the (now cancelled) party to celebrate City's lack of success and the (club endorsed) banner that shows the years where we have won nothing... thank you for showing such concern in little ol' City.

That's what makes the game so difficult to endure. It's a horrible day, invented so neutrals can watch as people like me suffer nervous breakdowns and a whole manner of heart problems decades before we should. I love winning derbies, I just hate the actual playing of the game.

And then there are the neutrals! The media build-up is incredible: You would think that no football match is ever going to be like it until the end of recorded time ever (which, at Old Trafford, will have about seven or eight added minutes). The strange and ever-so paradoxical thing is that I'm now a part of that crazy build-up to the game.

But, with the stakes higher this season than they have been in any season for a long time, the one thing I feel pretty assured in saying is that this will be a nervy game. And that might well help City, since we've been pretty good on the break this season and pretty strong defensively. But if that's how Mr. Mancini decides to set up, then this could be one of the longest 90 minutes of our lives.

Not including stoppage time, obviously.

February 2011 Breakdown

Games (all competitions):
Won: 3   **Drawn:** 3   **Lost:** 1

Goals (all competitions):
For: 15   **Against:** 5

Progress:
Premier League: 3rd
League Cup: Eliminated in Round Three
FA Cup: Qualified for Round Five
Europa League: Qualified for the Round of 16

Premier League Table

		P	W	D	L	F	A	GD	Pts
1	Manchester United	27	17	9	1	61	25	+36	60
2	Arsenal	27	17	5	5	57	27	+30	56
3	**Manchester City**	**28**	**14**	**8**	**6**	**44**	**25**	**+19**	**50**
4	Tottenham Hotspur	27	13	8	6	38	31	+7	47
5	Chelsea	26	13	6	7	46	22	+24	45

March 2011

Manchester City 3-0 Aston Villa
FA Cup Fifth Round
Wednesday 2 March, 2011 - 19:45 KO

City: Hart, Zabaleta (c), Boateng, Lescott, Richards (Boyata 84), Vieira, Y Toure (Jo 81), Barry, Kolarov, Silva, Balotelli (Tevez 61)
Unused: Taylor, Wabara, M Johnson, Dzeko
Goals: Y Toure (5), Balotelli (25), Silva (70)
Booked: Balotelli
Man of the Match: Patrick Vieira

It was City who came out of the blocks the quicker, and from a fifth minute corner, they made their early pressure pay. Vieira got a flick on Kolarov's wicked delivery and the ball bounced back off Clark, leaving Yaya Toure to swivel and smash the ball past Friedel from inside the six-yard box.

The goal did spur the visitors into a bit of life, with Bannan firing over the bar after a low cross had found him inside the area. But then, just as Villa appeared to be settling into the match, City doubled their advantage. A brilliant pass from Vieira set Balotelli through on goal and it was some finish from the Italian on the half volley, placed in the top corner off the post.

As the half drew to a close, Villa upped the tempo to try and get back into the game. Agbonlahor couldn't get the better of Boateng in the area before Heskey shot from just inside the box, forcing Hart into a good save. The shot spilled to Delfouneso, but Kolarov was there to put it behind.

In the second half, Balotelli was close to finding Yaya Toure with a driven free kick from the corner of the box, before Tevez joined the action and immediately got himself into the thick of it. Soon after, it was his presence in the box that left a Kolarov cross to be nodded down to Silva. He took a touch and fired it straight past Friedel to seal the game.

City tried to finish off the game in style, but a brilliant instinct save from Friedel denied Tevez from a great Barry pass, before Tevez flicked it to Silva who found Jo, but the Brazilian could only fire it straight at the goalkeeper.

Manchester City 1-0 Wigan Athletic
FA Premier League
Saturday 5 March, 2011 – 17:30 KO

City: Hart, Richards, Kompany, Lescott, Zabaleta, Vieira, Barry, Y Toure, Silva (de Jong 84), Balotelli (Kolarov 69), Tevez (c) (Dzeko 86)
Unused: Taylor, Boyata, Boateng, Jo
Goals: Silva (38)
Booked: Richards, Barry, Kompany

Man of the Match: David Silva

After a strong performance in the FA Cup in midweek, the home side will have been looking for a good start in this tie to get them back on track. But it was the visitors who started the brighter, putting City under some early pressure with a corner headed over by Rodellega.

City stepped up their play and should have taken the lead as the first half progressed. Silva the architect, he twice weaved his way to the by-line to get in a low cross, but twice City couldn't find the finish. First, Barry couldn't get a shot in as he had to stretch to control and then Yaya Toure was crowded out. Rodellega had a shot blocked from inside the City box, before Richards was perhaps lucky to have stayed on the pitch for a late tackle on Caldwell.

With just over the half hour gone, it was Wigan's turn to think they should have been ahead. A cut back could only be cleared to McCarthy in the box and the Wigan man smashed his shot wide, with Hart left as an observer.

But then, City got themselves in front with a big helping hand from Al Habsi. Silva weaved his way into the box and fired a shot at goal, straight at the goalkeeper. But the Wigan shot-stopper must have taken his eye off the ball and it went straight through him, between his legs and into the net.

Despite being in front at the break, City struggled to get going in the second half. It took Yaya Toure to head away from a corner, before Alcaraz hit the post from a Watson flag kick. Hart was then called into action as a corner was only partially cleared and fell to the feet of McCarthy at the edge of the box. He volleyed it straight back at goal and the England international threw himself at it to push the ball behind.

With seconds to play, it was Sammon who missed Wigan's most guilt-edged chance. He found himself through on goal, bearing down on Hart and, with just the goalkeeper to beat, he slid the ball wide of the post.

Dynamo Kiev 2-0 Manchester City
Europa League Round of 16, First Leg
Thursday 10 March, 2011 – 20:05 KO

City: Hart, Richards, Lescott, Kompany, Zabaleta, Barry (c), Y Toure, Kolarov (Wright-Phillips 82), Silva, Dzeko, Balotelli (Tevez 57)
Unused: Taylor, Boateng, Boyata, de Jong, Vieira
Goals: -
Booked: Balotelli, Tevez
Man of the Match: David Silva

With Dynamo Kiev having won their last Europa League tie by a large aggregate scoreline, City knew that this first leg would be a tough game. Temperatures were low and the pitch was rock solid, but it was the visitors who had the first chance, as Balotelli volleyed over from a deep corner.

With nearly 20 minutes on the clock, City were given a shooting opportunity in the Kiev half as Silva was fouled, but from the resulting free kick Kolarov could only find the arms of Shovkovskiy.

But, with City having the better chances, it was Kiev who took the lead. The ball was fired back into the box after it was half-cleared and neither Hart nor Kolarov could get there first, leaving Shevchenko to knock it into the net.

The first talking point of the second half concerned Mario Balotelli... City kicked off with 10 men, while Balotelli was late arriving to the pitch. From there, Shevchenko shot over from the edge of the box and Zabaleta was lucky to escape a yellow card for a rash challenge in the Kiev half.

But, just as it looked like City were getting themselves back into the game, they were pegged further behind. A flicked header from Kompany inside the area unluckily fell to Gusev. Richards couldn't react and Gusev smashed it past Hart for Kiev's second goal of the night and City were desperate for an away goal.

Wright-Phillips almost had an instant impact as he tried to slide the ball through to Richards – who was playing as a makeshift centre-forward – but it was just over hit. Gusev then had a deflected effort well held by Hart.

With just over a minute before stoppage time, Hart got in to block a three-on-one breakaway and keep City in the tie, but they have it all to do next week.

Manchester City 1-0 Reading
FA Cup Quarter Final
Sunday 13 March, 2011 - 16:45 KO

City: Hart, Richards, Kompany, Lescott, Kolarov, de Jong (Barry 84), Vieira (Balotelli 70), Y Toure, Wright-Phillips (Boyata 90), Silva, Tevez (c)
Unused: Taylor, Razak, Jo, Dzeko
Goals: Richards (74)
Booked: Kompany, Richards
Man of the Match: Nigel de Jong

With the FA Cup draw having already been made before kick-off, City knew that a victory over Reading would set up a mouth-watering Manchester derby at Wembley. And it didn't look like City wanted that place in the semi final, as the game got off to a slow start, with neither team taking the initiative.

Wright-Phillips was denied by a great save as he broke into the area and, from the rebound, Silva was stopped by an even better block, as he attempted to slot it into the net while the goalkeeper was still on the ground. Yaya Toure should have scored when he found himself one-on-one with Alex, but he drilled his shot straight at the goalkeeper.

The second half arrived and City tried to continue where they left off – but hoping to turn that pressure into goals. Tevez was unlucky not to find the net with a cute flick after some good work by Silva to wriggle free in the box, before Wright-Phillips won the ball on the edge of the area. He crossed for Tevez, but the Argentinian's shot was miskicked and didn't make the goal.

With 66 minutes played, Richards headed down into the ground and it was looping in at the back post until a touch from Alex put it behind for a City corner. It was a sign of things to come, though, and eight minutes later, the right back connected to a Silva set piece and powered the ball into the back of the net.

That prompted a spell of pressure from the visitors. They weren't, however, able to create a clear cut chance – the best coming from Long as he got the better of Lescott, but couldn't beat Hart, who was able to hold on to the forward's shot.

Manchester City 1-0 Dynamo Kiev
Europa League Round of 16, Second Leg
Thursday 17 March, 2011 – 18:00 KO

City: Hart, Richards, Lescott, Kompany, Kolarov (Milner 89), de Jong, Barry (A Johnson 71), Y Toure, Silva (Dzeko 76), Balotelli, Tevez (c)
Unused: Taylor, Boyata, Vieira, Wright-Phillips
Goals: Kolarov (41)
Booked: Tevez, Kompany, Silva, de Jong, Y Toure
Sent Off: Balotelli
Man of the Match: Nigel de Jong

Needing two goals without reply to just force extra time, City were up against it from the off. And they were out of the traps quickly. Tevez had a run at the Kiev defence, but couldn't find a way through before Balotelli, somehow, missed an open goal from two yards, skying a Richards cross. Balotelli then accidentally blocked a Silva shot that would have worried the goalkeeper.

But then, as City were looking for a way back into the game, their task got a lot harder. Balotelli's evening got worse when he was shown a straight red card with 10 minutes of the first half to play, for a karate-kick style challenge onto Popov's chest, as he tried to clear the ball.

Though the hosts gave themselves a helping hand soon after. A free kick on the edge of the box was tapped to Kolarov and, after taking a touch to get the ball out of his feet, the left back thundered a shot through the penalty area and into the net. The keeper should have done better, but City weren't complaining.

Kiev were themselves lucky to keep 11 men on the pitch after a high challenge on Tevez on the edge of the box. From the resulting free kick, Richards launched himself at the cross, but his header cleared the crossbar. Lescott then saved City from needing to score even more by heading a corner off the line, as Hart was beaten.

As the board went up for added time, Dzeko turned and drilled a fierce shot at goal, but the goalkeeper was across well to make the save.

As a final roll of the dice, City had a free kick on the edge of the box: Yaya Toure drilled the ball in and Tevez was millimetres away from getting a touch into the net, but he couldn't and the keeper was able to take the shot with ease. The damage was done in the first leg.

Chelsea 2-0 Manchester City

FA Premier League
Sunday 20 March, 2011 – 16:00 KO

City: Hart, Richards, Kompany (c), Lescott, Kolarov, Barry, de Jong, Y Toure (Balotelli 81), Milner (A Johnson 81), Silva, Dzeko
Unused: Taylor, Boyata, Boateng, Vieira, Wright-Phillips
Goals: -
Booked: Milner, de Jong, Barry
Man of the Match: Nigel de Jong

It was City who started brightly and pressed into the Chelsea half. Dzeko couldn't get a shot away as he broke down the left, before Toure stung Cech's gloves and Silva's cross from the rebound was missed by both Dzeko and Richards.

But then it was the home side who should have opened the scoring. Milner wanted a foul on the right wing, but it wasn't given and Chelsea were able to break with Torres. He found Kalou, who tripped up over his own man Ramires when through on goal, and Hart was able to collect the loose ball.

The ball then broke for Kalou on the edge of the box and he cut inside. Neither Milner nor Richards could get the challenge in and Kompany forced it away. Cole, latching onto the rebound, scooped his shot well over the bar, as Chelsea began to grow into the game.

Lescott and Barry combined to deny Torres a shooting opportunity, after Kompany had found Dzeko, but Toure couldn't quite slot Silva in after the Bosnian's lay-off. Some Chelsea possession resulted in a Lampard effort from the edge of the box, but it was on his left foot and was nowhere near Hart's goal.

Kolarov hit a free kick straight at Cole, before there was a scramble in the City area as Torres fired in a cross and Lescott could only loop it into the air. Hart, though, was off his line quickly to punch.

Kompany was caught out of position after Richards gave the ball away in the middle, but Lescott did his job in holding up Kalou and de Jong put in a fantastic tackle to deny Torres a shot on goal. The resulting corner bounced up in the box, but Milner was able to clear.

Chelsea carved out a great opportunity to take the lead five minutes into the second half, as Kolarov gave the ball away on the halfway line, but Malouda's effort from the penalty spot – via Torres and Kalou – was tame.

Dzeko fired a shot straight at Luiz and then did well to win a free kick on the left wing. Milner delivered it and found Dzeko's head. Cech was beaten, but so was the post, as the ball drifted behind.

From a left wing free kick, Kolarov wasn't tight enough to Luiz and he headed past Joe Hart from the edge of the six-yard box and City's 80 minutes of hard work was undone.

As City piled forward, they were hit on the break. Ramires found himself through on goal and he slotted it past Hart to take the hosts above the visitors with a game in hand.

THE CITY PLAYER ENTITLED TO HAVE A CHIP ON HIS SHOULDER

There are some footballers you know that you can just light the touch paper and then watch them fly off the handle. For example, I would never consider excluding the goalkeepers from a 5-a-side training game when Roy Keane was in my international squad, should I want to avoid several bust ups that result in his acrimonious departure from the World Cup. It's probably not a good idea, for instance, to be a fan of the opposing team standing near the tunnel, if Eric Cantona has just been sent off. You get the idea.

Step forward Mario Balotelli. The City player that opposition fans love to hate, Balotelli is the one player that, when he starts for City, you're never quite sure what you're going to get: An anonymous 90 minutes, a hot-headed substitution, a red card for a silly kick-out, two yellow cards for dissent, a brilliant hat-trick, moments of pure genius with the ball at his feet… any of those things (and more) could happen, little of it a surprise.

His first City appearance yielded his first City goal: Away in Romania to FC Timisoara, he scored the only goal of the game and set City on their way to the group stage of the Europa League, before quite seriously injuring his knee. It hasn't helped him that that injury ruled him out for large spells of this season and, despite a scoring record of 10 goals in 18 games, City still haven't seen the Italian's best form. And, clearly, if 10 goals in 18 appearances isn't his best form, a lot of Blues won't be able to wait to see it.

If there is one player in City's team, though, that would be entitled to have something of a chip on his shoulder, it's Mario Balotelli. As a small child, he had serious intestinal problems that required a series of life-saving operations to fix. His parents, both Ghanaian immigrants living in Italy, asked the country's social services for help because of cramped living space. Balotelli was then fostered and, as he grew up into the life of a professional footballer, his biological parents asked for their son back – a move that Balotelli himself disagreed with, describing them as 'glory hunters' and believing they only wanted him back because of his success.

And Mario's problems didn't end there. Despite a desire to represent Italy, he was denied the chance to join the Under 15s and Under 17s squads because of bureaucratic issues: To the country in which he lived and the country he was from, he wasn't an Italian citizen. Yet, his wish to play for Italy couldn't have been stronger, a point re-iterated when he turned down a call-up from Ghana.

Then throw into the mix a career in Italy shrouded by racism: In only his second senior cap for Italy in November 2010, he was subjected to abuse by a section of his own fans. These fans also held aloft a banner reading "No to a multi-ethnic national team".

And it's not just while he was representing the country; while he was with Inter Milan, sections of the Juventus support targeted him and taunted Balotelli with vile racial abuse. When City travelled to Turin to play Juventus, Balotelli was reportedly relieved that he didn't have to make the trip; a decision made by

Roberto Mancini, very aware of the problems the striker had faced there in the past, and a decision taken on the basis that City had already qualified.

Yet it is this boy who has 10 goals in 18 appearances, this boy who has had injury problems throughout his first season in England, this boy who has suffered racist abuse for most of his life, this boy who was denied the chance to represent his country because of a daft law, this boy who has had a turbulent upbringing... he is the one who is petulant and troubled. It's easy to forget that he is just a kid with the weight of the world on his shoulders.

So he doesn't smile, who gives a damn? His reasoning, on his arrival at City, was simple: Scoring is as normal to him as any other everyday activity is to everyone else and one wouldn't smile cooking dinner or driving to work. And who cares if he looks glum if his scoring record stays as good as it is?

The problem is, Balotelli's reputation precedes him. He's the petulant child that shows dissent when things don't go his way. Several times already this season, he has been shown yellow cards for his reaction to decisions; reactions that are no different than those of the likes of Rooney or Terry or Gerrard. Yet you can count on one hand collectively the number of yellow cards those players receive for that reaction over the course of a season.

And yet, this week, we have seen a brand new Mario Balotelli. This is a Mario Balotelli that acted as the peacemaker in a 'disagreement' between Aston Villa's Richard Dunne and City's Yaya Toure in the FA Cup Fifth Round tie. The man normally associated with causing trouble was the one man who was preventing it from happening.

His goal in that game, too, was something I was surprised hasn't garnered more attention. The ITV commentators were totally underwhelmed, but it was one of the best goals you'll see this season. A first time, side-footed, placed, half-volley, from a ball that was on its upward motion after bouncing from over his shoulder was greeted as if it were a tap-in.

And that off the back of Roberto Mancini's open criticism of the forward after the 1-1 draw with Fulham. Balotelli scored another corker that match, too, but, as Mancini pointed out, he didn't do much else. Normally, I would feel very uneasy with a manager openly criticising his players, but Mancini has got form (Adam Johnson, Joe Hart, Carlos Tevez) and it has worked. And if there's anyone who knows how to get the best out of Mario Balotelli, then it's the man in the Eastlands dugout.

For the moment, Mario's in the middle of what he needs: A quiet few games, with a few goals and without controversy. He doesn't need to grow up, as so many pundits have commented; in fact he's probably the one player in City's squad that has grown up quicker than anybody else, given what he has dealt with in the past.

Perhaps it's time everybody else got off his back and just let him do his job.

HOW CITY'S EUROPEAN WOES ARE LIKE ROBERTO MANCINI'S HAT

Last night wasn't especially great if you're a Manchester City fan, like myself. It began with an uninspired performance, got a bit worse with a striker who had an allergic reaction to the type of grass on the pitch. A two goal deficit to overcome without the aid of an away goal added a bit more to the misery, and that's before we throw in a poor performance to boot. You would think that it couldn't possibly have been worse last night, but, unfortunately, it was.

There has been one constant throughout City's season that we, as blues, could rely on. One thing that we knew, if all else failed, that we could count on to remain solid and dependable in the face of adversity. But, last night, that constant was snatched from us in one moment of madness in the Kiev cold.

I'm talking, as everybody else is, I'm sure, about Roberto Mancini's hat.

The moment that that monstrosity parked itself on Roberto Mancini's scalp was the moment that it became clear to all City fans that his sense of style – so often revered by the media and so often envied by fans of teams with less stylish managers (Tony Pulis, I'm looking in you and your baseball cap's direction) – had deserted him. Never have City fans seen such hideous managerial headwear since Alan Ball, complete with flat cap, was at the helm. Although, there was, famously, Mario Balotelli's impression of Feathers McGraw from earlier this season, but he hasn't ever managed City and it, therefore, cannot count.

In many ways, Mancini's hat was the perfect metaphor for City's performance in Kyiv. It wasn't in keeping with what had gone before it for the previous seven months of the season and, not only was it difficult to look at, but you knew that it could have gone on all night and never once been right.

It actually started off quite well – City were coping competently with Dynamo Kiev's counter attacks and looking slightly threatening at times with some spells of pressure. But, and if there's one thing that we can criticise Roberto Mancini's City for it's this, City failed to turn any of their spells of pressure into clear cut chances. There were half-chances at best – nearly moments where the shot didn't come, or they were speculative volleys from tight angles.

Then, there was a bit of self-foot-shooting from City for the opening goal. Kolarov and Hart could both have done better and Shevchenko could have done us a favour by showing some of his Chelsea form and skying it or something, but, with over an hour of the match to play, it wasn't a disaster. There was still time for City to pick up the tempo and play some of that good football we've been spoiled with this season.

But, in typical City fashion, that didn't happen and, as the game wore on and the visitors went in search of that equaliser and away goal, the inevitable happened and Kiev scored again. A cross that shouldn't have come in came in, and there followed an unlucky flick off one of the centre-backs and the right back being a bit too flat footed for my liking and, before we know what's going on, City have a mountain to climb.

Though, to be fair, the conditions on that mountain can't be much colder than they were in Ukraine.

I was then astounded to read several opinions around the City supporting Twitter feeds and message boards that going out of the Europa League could be a blessing in disguise. It's a bloody good disguise if it is, because it passed me by – the Europa League being a competition that City could, before last night, at least, have realistic expectations of winning. I mean, it's not like City have been winning trophy after trophy, so the chance of one more would be nice...

The age-old problem is the build-up speed. So many times this season, City have been keeping the ball well – though, last night, that was a struggle at times – but the movement has been too slow. It's a bugbear of mine when I hear cries that "backwards passes are bad passes" because they're not. Not every pass needs to be forwards, providing it drags the opposition out of position and messes up their shape. That allows the forward players to exploit the space.

But, last night, again, that build-up was too slow. So, while the passing did drag the Kiev players out of position, the lack of urgency allowed them to get back into position before the space could be exploited. That left the team shooting from range or giving the ball away in the final third trying to pass it through a wall of shirts... and susceptible to a quick breakaway. Unfortunately.

City remain in the competition thanks to the skin of the skin of their teeth (or, in other words, the fact that, right at the end, Joe Hart made sure we didn't need to score four goals without reply to win), but the position is no less than precarious, at best. Kiev have proven how effective they are on the counter attack and that will be their gameplan at Eastlands – they've no need to risk giving City space to find two goals, so they'll look to keep it tight and kill off the home side on the break.

And, with a two goal deficit to recoup, City will have to push forward, leaving them open to being counter attacked. An away goal for Kiev could well be the end of any European success for City this season. In fact, coming away from Ukraine two goals behind and without an away goal is worse than leaving Germany trailing Hamburg 3-1 two years ago.

City need to step it up for the final run in. And Roberto Mancini needs to lose the hat. In fact, no, he needs to destroy the hat. Then there's no chance it'll be seen in his vicinity again.

March 2011 Breakdown

Games (all competitions):
Won: 4   **Drawn:** 0   **Lost:** 2

Goals (all competitions):
For: 6   **Against:** 4

Progress:
Premier League: 4th
League Cup: Eliminated in Round Three
FA Cup: Qualified for the Semi Final
Europa League: Eliminated in the Round of 16

Premier League Table

		P	W	D	L	F	A	GD	Pts
2	Arsenal	29	17	7	5	59	29	+30	58
3	Chelsea	29	16	6	7	53	24	+29	54
4	**Manchester City**	**30**	**15**	**8**	**7**	**45**	**27**	**+18**	**53**
5	Tottenham Hotspur	29	13	10	6	41	34	+7	49
6	Liverpool	30	13	6	11	41	36	+5	45

April 2011

Manchester City 5-0 Sunderland

FA Premier League

Sunday 3 April, 2011 – 16:00 KO

City: Hart, Boyata (McGivern 70), Kompany, Lescott, Kolarov, de Jong, Y Toure, Silva (Wright-Phillips 79), Balotelli, A Johnson (Vieira 67), Tevez (c)
Unused: Taylor, Barry, Milner, Dzeko
Goals: A Johnson (9), Tevez (pen 15), Silva (63), Vieira (67), Y Toure (73)
Booked: Kolarov, Vieira
Man of the Match: Vincent Kompany

Balotelli had the opening shot of the game, but his furious drive was charged down, as the hosts looked for the early goal. And, a minute later, that goal came courtesy of Johnson. He received a return ball from the right from Yaya Toure and smashed it into the net from just inside the box.

And just when Sunderland needed to keep it tight, City hit them with a quick counter attack. Tevez was played in with a neat ball over the top and all Bardsley could do was bring him down in the box. The skipper, though, dusted himself down and slid the penalty into the corner of the net to double City's lead.

The first action of the second half saw Roberto Mancini prove that he's not lost it, as he expertly controlled a high ball, after Kompany had cleared towards the dugout. Johnson could have put City three goals in front after some fantastic interplay between Silva and Tevez, but he was just offside.

City, though, pulled themselves further ahead. Tevez broke quickly down the right flank and played an early, low ball in for Balotelli. The Italian's shot was blocked, but Silva popped up on the edge of the six-yard box to slot into the net and seal game with just over an hour played.

Johnson was replaced to a standing ovation by Vieira. And it turned out to be an inspired substitution, as Vieira's first touch of the ball saw him knock it over the line, despite Mignolet's best efforts to stop it.

With just under 20 minutes to play, City did their goal difference even more good, as Yaya Toure got his name on the scoresheet. Cattermole got himself in trouble on the right wing and tried to look for his goalkeeper with a chipped pass. Some smart centre-forward play by Tevez though, made sure that Toure could nip in and chip the ball over the on-rushing Mignolet.

Liverpool 3-0 Manchester City

FA Premier League

Monday 11 April, 2011 – 20:00 KO

City: Hart, Boyata, Kompany, Lescott, Kolarov, Barry, Y Toure, Milner (Silva 59), A Johnson, Tevez (c) (Balotelli 13 (de Jong 83)), Dzeko

Unused: Taylor, Zabaleta, McGivern, Wright-Phillips
Goals: -
Booked: -
Man of the Match: Gareth Barry

Kuyt had the first shooting chance of the game, after a neat chest down from Carroll to Suarez and a block by Barry could only fall to the Dutchman. His effort, though, was skied well over Hart's crossbar. Hart was in action a minute later, though, as Suarez found himself one-on-one with the England keeper, who touched his low shot onto the post. Boyata then headed a Tevez cross over the bar at the other end.

With 12 minutes on the clock, the Liverpool pressure told. A speculative shot from inside the City half deflected off Kompany as far as Carroll on the edge of the box. The big striker took it first time and smashed it past Hart, who got a hand to the ball, but couldn't keep it out. It went from bad to worse for City, though, who then lost Tevez to injury seconds after the restart.

Soon after, Liverpool doubled the lead. A ball to the back post was blocked by Kompany and it broke to Kuyt on the right side of the box. Kolarov didn't close him down quickly enough and he slotted it past Hart.

From the restart it was three. It was sixes and sevens at the back as Kolarov didn't climb with Carroll and he nodded it home after just 35 minutes.

The second half started as the first ended. Kolarov was caught out of position and Carroll found some space in the middle of the pitch to shoot at goal, but Barry was there to block. Kuyt then found a free header inside the box from a corner and should have made it four.

Carroll nearly grabbed his hat-trick on 88 minutes, as Lescott was denied a foul against Kuyt, before Kolarov was beaten too easily by Suarez and he found the Geordie's head at the back post. It was worrying Hart, but it was just over the bar. City's worst performance of the season left them with the worst possible build-up for the coming FA Cup semi final.

Manchester City 1-0 Manchester United
FA Cup Semi Final
Saturday 16 April, 2011 – 17:30 KO

City: Hart, Zabaleta, Kompany (c), Lescott, Kolarov, Barry, de Jong, Y Toure, Silva (Vieira 89), A Johnson (Wright-Phillips 80), Balotelli
Unused: Taylor, Boyata, Milner, Jo, Dzeko
Goals: Y Toure (53)
Booked: Zabaleta, Balotelli, de Jong, Kompany
Man of the Match: Vincent Kompany

The third Manchester derby of the season took both sides to Wembley for the FA Cup Semi Final. City hadn't really done themselves justice in the previous two derbies this season, so there couldn't have been a better time to set that right. Though it was the red half that started the better, with Hart on hand to produce a brilliant save, racing off his line to deny Berbatov on a one-on-one.

Seconds later, Berbatov should have done much better: Nani smashed a low ball across the face of the City goal and the Bulgarian slid in with Kolarov to try and get the first touch. Hart dived across, but was beaten and Berbatov did get his foot on the end, but somehow he put it over from two yards out.

Soon enough, City got into their stride. Silva found Balotelli in the box, but he wasn't able to get a shot away. Instead, the ball found Barry, who turned his marker and managed to fire an attempt at van der Sar's near post, but it hit the side netting, with some of the City faithful thinking it had dropped in.

Balotelli stung the hands of the goalkeeper with a rasping shot from 35 yards, before Lescott couldn't control a volley at the back post on his wrong foot from the resulting corner. Yaya Toure ran at the United goal, and it took a great block from Vidic to see the ball behind. Kompany was inches wide with a shot from the edge of the box after a corner, too, as City began to dominate.

City had grown into the game and finished the half well on top, but didn't have the goal their weight of pressure deserved. But, after the restart, that didn't take long – a poor clearance from van der Sar was lucky to fall to the feet of Carrick. He, though, presented the ball straight to Yaya Toure and the Ivorian broke into the box and slotted a slide-rule shot under the United keeper, right in front of the City fans.

Johnson then played a short corner to Silva, before receiving the return ball. United didn't close him down and he wriggled along the by-line to fire a low cross towards Balotelli. Van der Sar got there first, but lost the ball and, fortunately for the keeper, it rolled behind for a corner, when it could have rolled into the net. Yaya Toure then tried a back post volley, but Ferdinand was able to block it to safety.

Hart produced a fine save to keep the blue half of Manchester in the lead, as Nani's free kick deflected off Balotelli's head. The City keeper adjusted well and flicked the ball onto the bar, leaving the defence to clear.

Scholes ended United's chances of making the FA Cup Final, as his high challenge on Zabaleta left the full back in a heap and the Reds a man down for the final 20 minutes of the game. Yaya Toure could have finished United off, but he couldn't quite get to the ball ahead of van der Sar, as he powered through to the box.

City were in the final.

Blackburn Rovers 0-1 Manchester City
FA Premier League
Monday 25 April, 2011 – 20:00 KO

City: Hart, Zabaleta, Kompany (c), Lescott, Kolarov, Barry, de Jong, Y Toure, Silva (Boyata 90), A Johnson (Dzeko 72), Balotelli (Vieira 84)
Unused: Taylor, Milner, Wright-Phillips, Jo
Goals: Dzeko (74)
Booked: Barry, Balotelli, de Jong
Man of the Match: Nigel de Jong

City started the game on the front foot, controlling the early possession and trying to work an opening. Barry tried to lift a pass to Balotelli, who couldn't quite get there ahead of the Blackburn defence, before Zabaleta crossed for Silva to volley and, with Robinson helpless, he hit the inside of the post.

Benjani then found some space in behind Kompany and he squared the ball for Emerton to cross. He tried to return it and find the head of Benjani, but the Belgian defender got there first. Roberts wanted a penalty for a challenge by Kompany in the area and it could have been given, the referee perhaps dissuaded by the theatrical fall by the home side's forward.

Benjani flicked a header beyond his own man at the back post in a decent position for Blackburn, before Kompany attempted to connect to a Kolarov corner. Balotelli picked up the loose end and fired a shot straight at Salgado, allowing Robinson to collect. Samba came closest for Blackburn, flicking a header past a rooted Hart, but just wide of the far post.

The visitors got off to a similar start in the second half as they did the first: Johnson got down the right and crossed for Silva, but it was flicked away just before he could connect. Kolarov then found the Spaniard, who chipped it to Yaya Toure at the back post and his header needed pushing over by Robinson.

Silva then slipped the ball to Yaya Toure into the box. He found Silva again, and he shot across goal. It was cleared as far as Dzeko, who grabbed his first league goal, smashing it into the net, after taking a neat touch to control.

With three minutes to play, Jones was kicking himself that he hadn't equalised for the home side. Kompany didn't know Roberts was behind him when he attempted to clear and caught him. The referee pulled the game back, despite a good Rovers advantage, and Jones headed over from the cross.

WHO ARE YOU AND WHAT HAVE YOU DONE WITH THE REAL MANCHESTER CITY?

It's always a good feeling to blow out the cobwebs. When you've spent the last few weeks running on almost empty and you've only just been managing to get through the day, it's nice to sit down, relax and take the load off your feet. And, as Manchester City showed last weekend, footballers are just like the rest of us when it comes to that arena. The demolition of Sunderland resulted in City's biggest winning margin of the season and, coincidentally, the biggest since they had demolished Burnley at Turf Moor exactly a year to the day earlier.

In the last few weeks, it's been very difficult to see just where City were going to get their goals. Tevez was stuck on 50 and whatever he tried just didn't come off. Dzeko has looked isolated when played as a lone striker. Balotelli has weighed in with the odd one, but attention has been distracted by his new hobbies of darts and karate.

In fact, I've said several times that, when Tevez isn't scoring, City have struggled. True, the solidity of the defence has come in handy in those weeks – if you can only score one goal a game, clean sheets are vital and Joe Hart has 23 of the buggers so far this season. So, while City have been out of form, it hasn't affected the league position so badly.

Now, though, one international weekend later, and a rest for some of the City players, and it's almost as if a completely new Manchester City have emerged. One that has pace in the attack, rather than one that would keep possession well but rarely trouble their opponents. One that was happy to move the ball quickly, rather than one that wanted three or four touches per player. One that looked dangerous, rather than one that looked toothless.

Ignoring the obvious performers for once, the game with Sunderland produced some good performances from players that have, for one reason or another been missing recently.

To start with, Yaya Toure was no longer playing football like he was a metaphor for a rhino trying to disco dance. Instead, he was sharp, his passing was on target, his runs weren't laboured and lethargic, and, not only did he use the ball well, but he used it intelligently. Since the end of January, it was almost as if he couldn't work out what he should be doing with it: He was taking it from the defenders and, when he had the opportunity to turn, he would play the quick return pass to try and open the space for someone else. When it needed that quick ball to the other centre-back, he'd try and turn on it and put himself under pressure. His passes would go astray and he looked knackered.

Fast forward to last Sunday and you could see the effect that a weekend off had had on him. He was actually injured for the Ivory Coast's game after picking up a knock at Stamford Bridge and so didn't feature for his country, but it was clear that he had needed it. He was an ever-present in City's packed run of fixtures – eased now due to no cup replays and elimination from the Europa League – and, for the last month, it had looked like he could barely run.

Not anymore, if Sunderland was anything to go by.

Then there was the reintroduction of Adam Johnson. On his first start since his injury, he was instrumental in City's victory. While Silva and Balotelli and Milner and Kolarov can do a job in the wide areas, none of them hugs the touchline in the way that Johnson does.

Without him, City tended to look very narrow because... well, because they ended up playing very narrowly. With him out on either flank – because he is comfortable on either left or right foot – the opposition defence can't sit as tightly and pack the middle as much as they would like. This gives Tevez et al slightly more space to do their work.

And, if anything, Tevez's touch just hasn't been right recently and that's down to, in no small part, the number of opposition players he has around him and the lack of support he sometimes finds himself with.

With Johnson dragging the defence out to one flank and, on Sunday, Balotelli dragging them out to the other, not only was there space for the little forward to exploit, but plenty of room for the midfield to get into the box and support him – Silva scored because of a break from midfield, Yaya Toure scored because of a break from midfield...

Despite such a good attacking performance, though, it seems very unfair not to comment on the strength of the defence. Joe Hart is closing in on the club record for clean sheets in a season, and he has, in no small part, been helped out by those in front of him. Vincent Kompany has been drawing the plaudits, but it's Joleon Lescott who has really stepped up to the plate.

He was shaky when he arrived and shaky for the most part when called upon last season. He has looked a completely different player since the turn of the year. He was a surprise inclusion in the derby squad in February and has barely put a foot wrong since coming into the team, looking strong and solid. In fact, I would go as far as to say he is now half of the best centre-back pairing in the Premier League, despite my obvious bias and limited viewing of other pairings. Both he and Kompany have been nothing short of immense.

There should also be a notable mention here for Dedryck Boyata, too. He isn't a full back, though you'd never have guessed with the way he played there on Sunday and against Chelsea way back at the start of the season. The future's bright for this one.

And all this after a weekend when Tottenham, Chelsea and Arsenal dropped points! This isn't what City are supposed to do: Surely, the correct thing to do would be to miss out on yet another opportunity to grasp onto that Champions League place? Fourth is looking increasingly difficult for Tottenham. Not only do they find themselves six points behind City, but, should they win that game in hand and beat City in their upcoming tie, the goal difference is still a large obstacle and they would still be behind City because of that.

With an FA Cup Semi Final to look forward to and the heels being dug into the top four positions, everything appears to be coming up roses for City.

Which begs the obvious question: Who are they?

And what have they done with the real Manchester City?

THE WRONG SIDE OF THE WORLD

It was just gone quarter past two on the afternoon of 16 April, 2011 and I was sitting in a bar in Montclair, New Jersey. Actually, that's a lie; I wasn't sitting down at all. I couldn't. I'd just had the most nerve wrecking 45 minutes of my entire life. And a combination of relief, elation and stress-induced-fidgetiness had meant that I was, in fact, pacing up and down inside a bar in Montclair, New Jersey, legs wobbling and hands shaking.

Manchester City had just won the FA Cup Semi Final against Manchester United and had done so with consummate ease. Though, I had only seen the second half, so hadn't had to live through the opening stages of the game.

It never was the plan to miss the semi final. The holiday that had me in America was booked for that weekend for three reasons: One – it was a cheaper weekend to go to New York; Two – it was FA Cup Semi Final weekend and we didn't expect City to still be in the competition when we booked it; Three – if City weren't in the FA Cup Semi Final, as expected, it was Tottenham at home, and we never win that one.

Once it was clear City were through, I thought if I was cut off from the game, then I wouldn't be able to worry about it; I wouldn't have to worry about the chances United created, the chances City missed. I'd not have to care about defenders slipping at crucial times or a goalkeeper, who'd barely put a foot wrong all season, making a mistake. All of that would be out of my control. I could relax, enjoy the holiday and find out the score when I got home.

Turns out, that's not the case. I knew it would cost me money, but I tried to log into Twitter to see the teams or the score, despite being in the backseat of a large car on the highway. I had no connection, though. I had to put my phone in my pocket and grit my teeth. Not knowing how well or badly your team is doing in a local derby semi final is worse than knowing they're losing.

Luckily, City weren't losing.

So, we arrived in Montclair just in time for me to dart out of the car, sprint into the bar and use the bathroom. Drinking an entire bottle of soda isn't the best way to deal with not knowing about the semi final, either. But, the important thing was, we were there in time for the second half. There was me, my mum and dad, and our family friends living in Pittsburgh, Lisa and Brian. Brian is a lapsed City fan, originally from Manchester.

The plan had originally been to watch the match in New York City, in a bar that was given the Heart of the City award by the club: The Mad Hatter Saloon. I wanted to be with other blues, blues who would celebrate a win, console a defeat, and bite their nails all the way through. But we overslept and wouldn't have gotten there until after the 90 minutes.

So we stopped halfway.

We ordered fries. I ate none. I sat down. I stood up. I had a sip of my drink. I felt ill. A United fan sat next to me, red shirt on, shouting things at the screen showing the match. I remained numb, City shirt on, and clenched my fists. Then I unclenched them. Then I clenched them again.

Then City scored. I wasn't sure what to do. I wasn't in the City of Manchester Stadium, I wasn't in a bar with other City fans. I couldn't just leap into the air and jump around. I was in a quiet bar with my family and family friends. I'd look out of place. Odd. Weird. Strange.

The United fan chose to swear.

City continued to have United on the ropes. The clock ticked down. Slowly. Too slowly. A deflected free kick was touched onto the bar. Paul Scholes was sent off. The United fan swore again. The final whistle went. City won.

And Balotelli winked.

I spent the rest of the day with a spring in my step, but there was always the prang of regret that I wasn't in London, that I wasn't in Wembley, that I wasn't with my friends. New York is a wonderful city. Montclair, New Jersey, is a beautiful American town, lifted straight from the movies. But I just didn't want to be there that evening.

Looking back, though, it's a good job City won. The game was on day three of a six day holiday; there were still three days to go. In the past, whenever City had lost a league derby, with nothing resting on it, I had moped around for days, feeling sorry for myself. Imagine doing that in one of the most brilliant cities on the planet, after such an important game.

I had never seen anything that good as a football fan. Seeing the comeback at Wembley in 1999 was good, better than good, but it wasn't that. That game saved City as football club.

But the FA Cup Semi Final made City as a football club.

The laughing stock was no more.

It was just a shame I was on the wrong side of the world at the time.

April 2011 Breakdown

Games (all competitions):
Won: 3   **Drawn:** 0   **Lost:** 1

Goals (all competitions):
For: 7   **Against:** 3

Progress:
Premier League: 4th
League Cup: Eliminated in Round Three
FA Cup: Qualified for the Final
Europa League: Eliminated in the Round of 16

Premier League Table

		P	W	D	L	F	A	GD	Pts
2	Chelsea	35	21	7	7	66	28	+38	70
3	Arsenal	34	18	10	6	67	36	+31	64
4	**Manchester City**	**33**	**17**	**8**	**8**	**51**	**30**	**+21**	**59**
5	Tottenham Hotspur	34	14	13	7	50	43	+7	55
6	Liverpool	34	15	7	12	51	39	+12	52

May 2011

Manchester City 2-1 West Ham United

FA Premier League

Sunday 1 May, 2011 – 16:10 KO

City: Hart, Zabaleta, Kompany (c), Lescott, Kolarov, Barry (Dzeko 75), de Jong (Milner 45), Y Toure, Silva, A Johnson, Balotelli (Vieira 87)
Unused: Taylor, Boyata, Wright-Phillips, Jo
Goals: de Jong (11), Zabaleta (15)
Booked: Zabaleta, Barry, A Johnson
Man of the Match: Gareth Barry

It was City that started the brighter, with Yaya Toure having a shot blocked and Balotelli heading wide from a corner. And, soon enough, that early goal came through the most unlikely of sources. A Silva shot was deflected behind for a corner and that cross was cleared to the edge of the box, where de Jong was waiting. He placed it expertly into the bottom corner and got his first ever City goal, in almost 100 games for the club.

Just four minutes later it got better, and from another unlikely source. Silva picked up the ball on the right and spotted the run of Zabaleta in behind the full back. He chipped a delightful ball over the top for the Argentine to run on to and his low shot was helped over the line by the defender, via his own crossbar.

City began to slow down in possession and allowed West Ham to get back into the game. Hart produced another save similar to his against Berbatov at Wembley, this time as Keane broke the line, before the visitors pulled a goal back. Ba reacted first as the ball hit Lescott's hand and he fired it past Hart.

With 10 minutes of the second half played, City were almost further in front. Balotelli was found by Silva on the far side of the box and he cut it back onto his right foot, before aiming for the top corner. Green was rooted, but was relieved to see it crash back off his crossbar.

City had another golden chance to wrap up the points when Silva was onside and played through for a one-on-one with Green. He took too many touches and couldn't find room for the shot, so he squared for Balotelli, whose shot was cleared off the line by Tomkins.

City were able to see out the game with possession of the ball. It didn't matter that the third goal never came, despite a Zabaleta successfully chasing down Green, because City were able to hold on and fourth place in the Premier League is looking good for the Blues.

Everton 2-1 Manchester City

FA Premier League

Saturday 7 May, 2011 – 15:00 KO

City: Hart, Zabaleta (Balotelli 80), Kompany (c), Lescott, Kolarov, Vieira (A Johnson 78), de Jong (Jo 90), Y Toure, Silva, Milner, Dzeko
Unused: Given, Boyata, McGivern, Wright-Phillips
Goals: Y Toure (28)
Booked: Kompany, Kolarov
Man of the Match: Nigel de Jong

City started brightly. On eight minutes as Silva produced a wonderful piece of control inside the area after Kompany had played a high diagonal ball. He turned Hibbert inside out and flashed a shot across goal, but it was wide.

Three minutes later and City should have been in front. A delightful ball to the back post by Milner found Silva and he cushioned it down for the late arriving Vieira, but he put his side-footed volley over the bar.

City began to take control and they carved another golden chance as Silva broke into the box. He tried to square it past Howard, but was only able to pick out Everton shirts. A minute later, he found Yaya Toure on the right, who smashed it past the keeper and into the top corner, putting the visitors ahead.

A brilliant piece of defending from Jagielka denied Kolarov a certain goal in the area, after some neat interplay between Silva and Yaya Toure left him through on goal, but the Everton centre-back got a foot on the ball first.

The first action of the second half saw Kompany pull out the best tackle he's made all season. A Baines shot from a free kick deflected to the edge of the six-yard box and seemed a simple tap in past Hart, until the Belgian centre-back got his toe in first to force the ball behind for a corner.

A defensive header by Dzeko from a corner allowed City the chance to break away and Yaya Toure found himself through on goal, but he couldn't force the ball past Howard on his one-on-one.

And then, with 65 minutes played, Everton punished City for their slack finishing. Kompany lost Distin in the box from a set piece and he nodded past Hart to equalise for the home side against his former club. City should have been more than one goal in front and they paid the price for being wasteful.

Everton pushed for the second goal immediately and City were on the backfoot. Osman rose higher than Kompany in the area and headed towards the back post, giving Hart no chance and moving the home side in front.

Milner had a shot deflected over at the death, but it was the closest City came and they couldn't pull it back.

Manchester City 1-0 Tottenham Hotspur
FA Premier League
Tuesday 10 May, 2011 – 19:45 KO

City: Hart, Richards, Kompany (c), Lescott, Zabaleta (Kolarov 58), de Jong, Milner, Y Toure, Silva (Tevez 84), A Johnson (Vieira 67), Dzeko

Unused: Given, Boyata, Wright-Phillips, Balotelli
Goals: Crouch (og 30)
Booked: Milner
Man of the Match: Vincent Kompany

The penultimate midweek of the season and City had their rearranged fixture with Tottenham to play before thoughts could turn to the FA Cup Final. And it was almost a repeat of last season's rivalry, although this time Tottenham were behind on points and City could qualify for the Champions League with a victory over last year's tormentors.

Though it was the visitors that got off to the better start with some pressure from Modric and Lennon, it was City who fashioned the best chance for an early goal. Dzeko should have given the home side the lead, as Silva found him on the edge of the six-yard box, but Cudicini spread himself well to block.

Modric should have put the visitors in front on 28 minutes, but his placed shot was just inches wide of Hart's post, with the City keeper scrambling.

Against the run of play, the home side got their goal. A break in the Tottenham pressure came with a City corner and it was taken short between Milner and Silva. The visitors weren't switched on and Milner had the chance to drive a low cross into the six-yard box. Lescott and Kompany were nearby, but the vital touch came from Crouch, scoring in the same net as he did last season, but this time for a different team.

The second half came and with it came the expected Tottenham onslaught. In the opening stages, it took a fantastic save from Hart to deny Pienaar an equaliser, as he flicked the ball around the post. The visitors must have been sick of the sight of the City keeper this season.

Tevez then joined the action and almost immediately forged a game winning chance, as he broke into the area and knocked the ball for Vieira to shoot. The big Frenchman waited for Cudicini to go to ground and just lifted it over him. It was goalbound until a brilliant header from Gallas put the ball over the bar.

The visitors' attacks became more desperate as the game entered stoppage time and the centre-back pairing of Lescott and Kompany were eating every one of the balls into the box up, leaving City the chance to break. Kompany tried it, as did Kolarov, but neither could force that second goal.

This season, City would finish, at the very lowest, fourth.

Manchester City 1-0 Stoke City
FA Cup Final
Saturday 14 May, 2011 – 15:00 KO

City: Hart, Richards, Kompany, Lescott, Kolarov, Barry (A Johnson 73), de Jong, Y Toure, Silva (Vieira 90), Balotelli, Tevez (c) (Zabaleta 89)
Unused: Given, Boyata, Milner, Dzeko

Goals: Y Toure (74)
Booked: -
Man of the Match: Nigel de Jong

With the City fans hoping for the chance to tear down the banner at Old Trafford and the Stoke fans hoping for their first ever FA Cup Final victory, the nerves were high at the start of the game. But it was City who settled the quickest. The first corner of the game was flicked away after Richards tried to get a header in towards goal, before Tevez forced a decent save from Sorensen with a low shot to his right.

With 11 minutes played, Yaya Toure had a pop from 30 yards and the ball looked set to burst the net until, at the last moment, it swerved away from the goal and whistled millimetres wide of the post, with Sorensen desperately flinging himself towards the shot.

The first Delap long throw in came to nothing, as the City defence dealt well with the set piece, after Balotelli had had a shot blocked and de Jong had fired an effort over, as City dominated the opening stages. Huth was lucky to stay on the pitch for a loose elbow in a challenge with Balotelli.

Balotelli forced a wonderful save from Sorensen as he flicked the Italian's goalbound effort around the post when it looked destined for the top corner. Kompany then had a go and the Stoke keeper produced another good save, after the City centre-back had picked up the loose pieces from Silva and taken the shot on from the edge of the box.

The City fans were beginning to wonder if it was going to be their day, as their side continued to dominate the game, but couldn't seem to take one of their many chances. Silva missed the most guilt-edged of them all in the first half, as it rebounded from Sorensen to his left foot and, with virtually an open goal in front of him, he volleyed the ball into the floor and it bounced over.

The second half started much in a similar way to how the first half ended. Kolarov wasted a good chance when in behind the Stoke defence. Hart was then needed to deny Jones, after he gave Lescott the slip, and the City keeper was out quickly to smother the shot smartly.

Silva could have given City the lead, but the ball fell to the Spaniard's right foot inside the box and, in checking the ball back onto his left foot, he was crowded out and lost the opportunity to find a finish.

As it looked like the game was going to be frustrating for City, the breakthrough came. The ball was played low into the box and it looked like the chance had gone after Balotelli's shot was blocked. That was until it broke to Yaya Toure eight yards out. The Ivorian put his foot through it and gave City the lead right in front of their own fans.

It was the same player that scored and in the same end as in the previous round, as City found the lead that their play had deserved.

But then came the inevitable Stoke onslaught: A series of corners in added time had City scrambling to get the ball clear. Sorensen joined the attack and

Hart had to come off his line to punch away, before Vieira was in the right place to block.

City were able to see out the remaining time to take their first trophy in 35 years and celebrate with their own imitation banner from the Stretford End. The celebrations were just beginning in the stands, as Tevez lifted the FA Cup for Manchester City.

Manchester City 3-0 Stoke City
FA Premier League
Tuesday 17 May, 2011 – 19:45 KO

City: Hart, Richards, Kompany, Lescott, Zabaleta, de Jong, Milner, Y Toure, Silva (Dzeko 57), A Johnson (Wright-Phillips 68), Tevez (c) (Boyata 88)
Unused: Given, Kolarov, Barry, Vieira
Goals: Tevez (15, 65), Lescott (53)
Booked: -
Man of the Match: Carlos Tevez

Having seen Arsenal drop points, the home side were confident of a repeat performance from Saturday to lift themselves into the driving seat for third place in the league. In truth, it was rarely in doubt, as City continued their good play from the final against a deflated Stoke side.

It took just 15 minutes for the opening goal and there were no surprises who got it. City's all-time leading scorer at Eastlands added another to the tally as, after a quick one-two with Milner, Tevez stepped inside one challenge and around another to lash the ball into the top corner, with Sorensen helpless.

Stoke threatened for the first time in the game with just over 20 minutes played and it was with a deep cross into the box that Hart came to punch, but missed. Carew collected the ball and lashed a shot at goal, but Richards was there to block bravely with his face, leaving him dazed... but he was back on his feet quickly.

The first action of the second half saw City double their lead. Richards powered his way through two tackles and went down under a third from Wilkinson, though the free kick appeared very harsh on the Stoke man. Johnson curled the ball into the box and Sorensen came to collect, but it was Lescott who got there first, nodding past him and into the net.

Soon after replacing Silva, Dzeko almost found himself on the scoresheet, too. A lucky bounce fell to him on the edge of the box and he closed in on goal. He tried to slide it past Sorensen, but the Stoke keeper was down quickly to smother the ball and hold on, keeping his side in the game for the time being.

Soon enough, though, City were well in front and it was Tevez once again, to pull himself level with Berbatov for the Premier League Golden Boot for the season. A free kick was awarded to City about six yards outside the Stoke box and the captain stepped up to fire it right into the top corner, giving Sorensen no chance of stopping it.

And on 67 minutes, Dzeko smashed the ball into the outside of the post after some good work on the right flank.

With that, City leapt up into third place in the Premier League and Hart's 17th clean sheet of the season earned him the Golden Gloves. All that remains is to see if City can stay in third with a victory over Bolton next weekend and if Tevez can take the Golden Boot.

Bolton Wanderers 0-2 Manchester City
FA Premier League
Sunday 22 May, 2011 – 16:00 KO

City: Hart, Zabaleta (Wabara 87), Kompany, Boyata, Lescott, de Jong, Barry, Y Toure, A Johnson (Dzeko 60), Silva (Milner 78), Tevez (c)
Unused: Given, Vieira, Wright-Phillips, Balotelli,
Goals: Lescott (43), Dzeko (63)
Booked: Tevez
Man of the Match: Gareth Barry

City started the final game of the season the brighter, setting the pace in the blustery conditions at the Reebok Stadium, but they couldn't find the early lead they wanted. As Silva cut the ball back towards Tevez, he should have planted it into the net, but it hit a Bolton leg en route. Kompany then missed a free header.

The home side then missed a similar chance, as Davies nodded wide, before he was lucky to stay on the pitch with a late and high challenge on Lescott. Bolton would have felt they should have had the lead soon after, as Sturridge found Elmander, but he was denied by a great save from Hart.

The City keeper produced another fine save to keep the scores level, with half an hour played, as a flicked header towards the back post could have dropped into the net and Hart extended his fingertips to knock it behind.

The visitors should have taken the lead after some neat play between Tevez and Yaya Toure let Boyata cross. Barry connected and hit the crossbar, before the Ivorian nodded the rebound wide.

With two minutes to play before half time, a fluke header got City the lead. A corner aimed towards the penalty spot was attacked by Kompany, but he missed it completely and it took Lescott totally by surprise. It hit him on the head and looped past Jaaskelainen into the top corner.

On the hour, Dzeko joined the action and Tevez played a great ball for Barry, who crossed for the Bosnian. He missed his first chance thanks to a brilliant block, but he was able to swivel and shoot, planting the ball into the net at the second attempt.

Milner chased down Robinson and won the ball back as it was directed towards his goalkeeper, but his square pass didn't find a blue shirt. Tevez won it back and, via Yaya Toure, he had a shooting chance on the edge of the box, but it was swallowed up by Jaaskelainen. Sturridge then saw a red card for a nasty challenge on Dzeko, which left him on the deck.

With attention elsewhere in the league, the game petered to a close and Tevez wasn't able to add his name to the goalsheet. Eyes went to Old Trafford to see if Berbatov would steal the award, but he wasn't able to and the former United team-mates shared the Golden Boot. City, though, finished level on points with Chelsea, to round off their best ever Premier League season.

THE END OF TYPICAL CITY?

Well, that's that, then. Another season done and dusted. Another 10 months of laughter, crying, delight, despair, anticipation, vomiting, nervousness, silly defeats, unexpected victories and invaluable points – doesn't look such a bad point at The Emirates, now, does it, Robin? – has been and gone, and the time as come to reflect on the highs and lows. Except, I'm a Manchester City fan and, as far as lows have come this season, they're pretty few and far between.

The highs, though, have been plentiful. Two of them stand out more than any, naturally: After all, I'm 23 years old and I was crowing on last season about how we shouldn't be disappointed with that year and how it was our best ever season since I had been born. Well, bugger me with a toasting fork, but we've gone done blown that there season out of the water. Automatic Champions League qualification and lifting the FA Cup; ask most City fans at the start of the season and it presented a tough choice. Many would have accepted fourth position in the league and no trophy. So imagine how we're all feeling to see third and have had two days out at Wembley, one of which resulted in the captain climbing the steps to the royal box as the winner of the competition.

The most vital thing for City was getting into the top four, especially having missed out narrowly last season. There was a delicious irony that it was the player who ensured City couldn't finish fourth last season that ensured they would finish fourth or above this. The goal even came in virtually the same place on the same pitch in the same goal. And it had extra value to me, since it came from a low cross and the bloke behind me had been shouting all game that City should be "crossing it high" because "nothing ever comes of fucking low crosses".

Amused me, anyway.

Having secured that fourth place, City then travelled back to Wembley for the FA Cup final. I was actually more nervous about the final than the semi final for one simple reason: I'm a pessimistic sod and so naturally assumed City would lose the semi final, since United had more 'big game' experience and were the favourites (seemingly able to cope without Rooney better than City could cope without Tevez). So, I was pleasantly surprised when I was wrong. But City went into the final as favourites and if there's any team that can cock it up...

But City didn't cock it up. In fact, they should have won by more, though I doubt many City fans were complaining about that at the final whistle. It's been quite a long wait, after all. I used to think that success for the Blues was similar the 53 bus; you'd wait forever and then end up walking home because it never bloody turned up. Turns out, it's exactly like the 53 bus; it didn't turn up yesterday or the day before or the day before that, but just as you start to wonder if it'll ever arrive, two of them arrive together.

So, what is it that has been the difference between City this season and City last season? Aside from the summer transfer kitty, obviously, because that's clearly the easiest factor to congratulate.

You'd be a fool to think that Roberto Mancini has just bought good players and that's why it's worked. True, it's been an important part of the success, but having the tools and using the tools to the best of their ability, getting them to work together and complement each other, are completely different things.

Take the City defence. The best performing back four, this season, has seen a centre-back pairing of Joleon Lescott and Vincent Kompany. Either side of them, Pablo Zabaleta and Micah Richards have been the outstanding full backs. Interestingly enough, three of these players were signed by Mark Hughes. All of them were available to Mark Hughes for a long time during his stewardship of the club, yet City's defence was leakier than a colander in a rainstorm. Credit where it's due, Hughes could certainly spot a player, but it needed Mancini to be able to make them play together: 29 clean sheets in all competitions speaks for itself, as does needing three goals to draw with Burnley and Bolton.

The team defend as a unit. Hart himself won't take the credit for the clean sheet record, simply for that reason. Roberto Mancini has gotten the defence performing as a unit, too, and not as a series of individuals. Kompany was rightly named as the player of the year, after a season where he has constantly raised the bar in what is expected of him. Lescott is looking like the player Everton sold. Richards should be in the full England team after his second half of the season form. And Zabaleta has bled more for the cause than he has sweated, it seems.

Tevez has, of course, been an important part to City's season. Without him, City would have struggled to score as many as they have done, yet for perhaps the most crucial time of the season, they were able to cope without him. Though difficult, they were able to show they weren't totally reliant on the little Argentinian. That being said, should Tevez leave, he will definitely need replacing; very few strikers play the role that he does.

Then throw into the mix the creative force that has been Silva, who has had a near-perfect debut Premier League season. In fact, only a few more goals could have made it better. His vision, through passes, and general play have been a joy to behold and have elevated him almost immediately into the same bracket as Ali Benarbia or Georgi Kinkladze for City fans.

Yaya Toure picked his moment to start weighing in with a few goals and the turning point for him was seemingly the club being knocked out of the Europa League. He was an ever-present in the team for months, despite the number of fixtures that were filling the list. But once he had had that week's rest, he was a man reborn. His powerful runs forward gave City an excellent breakaway option and two of his biggest goals ended up winning City the cup. Not a bad return on his investment, all told.

And, finally, with Arsenal handing out points to all and sundry towards the end of the season, and with City ending the campaign playing some of the best football they have done in the last three decades, it was in the Blues' own hands to finish third. And they ended up doing that with consummate ease. In fact, had the season been six weeks longer, I'd quite fancy City to have overtaken Chelsea. Since the defeat against Liverpool, City have been playing like a team that had fully gelled together and were a force to be reckoned with.

All of that led City to their most successful season in my lifetime. Their highest ever Premier League finish. The first trophy in the cabinet in generations, poignantly in the same year that two club legends passed away. A victory parade. Perhaps one of the best managers and back room teams since Mercer-Allison.

But this isn't normal for City. City should have hit a bad run of form and slipped out of the top four. City should have battered Stoke in the FA Cup final, but lost to an own goal that deflected off three players and the referee. City shouldn't qualify for the Champions League through league position. Whisper it quietly, but this could be the end of Typical City.

Gone but not forgotten.

Though definitely not missed.

May 2011 Breakdown

Games (all competitions):
Won: 5   **Drawn:** 0   **Lost:** 1

Goals (all competitions):
For: 10   **Against:** 3

Progress:
Premier League: 3rd
League Cup: Eliminated in Round Three
FA Cup: Winners
Europa League: Eliminated in the Round of 16

Final Premier League Table

		P	W	D	L	F	A	GD	Pts
1	Manchester United	38	23	11	4	78	37	+41	80
2	Chelsea	38	21	8	9	69	33	+36	71
3	**Manchester City**	**38**	**21**	**8**	**9**	**60**	**33**	**+27**	**71**
4	Arsenal	38	19	11	8	72	43	+29	68
5	Tottenham Hotspur	38	16	14	8	55	46	+9	62
6	Liverpool	38	17	7	14	59	44	+15	58
7	Everton	38	13	15	10	51	45	+6	54
8	Fulham	38	11	16	11	49	43	+6	49
9	Aston Villa	38	12	12	14	48	59	-11	48
10	Sunderland	38	12	11	15	45	56	-11	47
11	West Bromwich Albion	38	12	11	15	56	71	-15	47
12	Newcastle United	38	11	13	14	56	57	-1	46
13	Stoke City	38	13	7	18	46	48	-2	46
14	Bolton Wanderers	38	12	10	16	52	56	-4	46
15	Blackburn Rovers	38	11	10	17	46	59	-13	43
16	Wigan Athletic	38	9	15	14	40	61	-21	42
17	Wolverhampton Wanderers	38	11	7	20	46	66	-20	40
18	Birmingham City	38	8	15	15	37	58	-21	39
19	Blackpool	38	10	9	19	55	78	-23	39
20	West Ham United	38	7	12	19	43	70	-27	33

Summer 2011

THE CARLOS TEVEZ DILEMMA

Good grief. The season's been over for a week and I'm bored. Bored, bored, bored, bored, bored. The end of the football season always brings about this feeling every year and every year I forget that I'm going to end up feeling this way. August arrives and I'm excited about the new season, but can't take too much seriously because there's a long way to go. Mid-way through the season, the table starts to take shape and you know if you're challenging for Europe, struggling against relegation or ploughing into a title challenge. Then April comes and I just want it to be over, so I can have the definitive sense of achievement on where we have finished. Or disappointment, as has been the case for nearly all of my City-supporting life.

Then, the next day, I miss it all and want it to be August again, so we can start the whole cycle one more time.

Naturally, there's going to be a lot to keep us City fans entertained over the next two and a half months. Every man and his dog will be linked with the club (I suspect there are rules against pets playing professionally, though admittedly, I do need to check that). And, although no matter how much it's jazzed up, signing players, selling players, open-training sessions and pre-season friendlies are just not the real deal. They're like the piece of fruit that's waiting for you after your meal: Better than nothing, but you'd rather be having the chocolate gateau.

And, of course, the one thing that is going to plough on like a steam train rumbling towards a train station in a James Bond film, is the whole will-he-won't-he situation on the Carlos Tevez front. Stories speculating about the Argentinian's future will be as predictable as finding Top Gear and Dragons' Den on Dave during the day time. Don't get me wrong, I quite like Top Gear, but there is a bit of overkill sometimes.

I'm no more informed than my cat when it comes down to whether Tevez will be departing for a new club this summer. In fact, my cat could probably give just an accurate answer as I can, and she's not even that interested in football. She much prefers leaving dead rodents on the doormat and scratching you when you least expect it.

For what it's worth, much as I don't want it to be the case, I do believe Tevez will not be playing for City next season. I'd love to be wrong, but I fear that the resolution to last December's transfer request was, in fact, 'give us until the end of the season and we'll see where we go from there.' Perhaps automatic Champions League qualification and lifting the FA Cup for the team might, hopefully, persuade him to stay, though I worry the conclusion was reached a while ago.

If we assume that Tevez is transferred out of City, then there's a little Argentinian-shaped hole that will definitely need filling. While some of his actions this season might have caused some fans to question his commitment to the club – handing in a transfer request or missing the FA Cup semi final at Wembley, for example – his Golden Boot winning contributions on the goals front can't be denied.

Okay, so there was a spell when Tevez was absent through injury and City didn't do too badly: They won four of the five games he was unavailable for. But those victories all came by one goal, despite plenty of chances heading the team's way and the points (and, in one case, cup progress) were earned the hard way. What those games proved, really, was that City were reliant on Tevez for goals, but just not to the extent that the Sky Sports Soccer Saturday team thought.

The problem for City is that few strikers do the job that Tevez does. I like Balotelli and I like Dzeko, but they just don't play the lone striker role in the same way as the little Argentinian. City's formation and system is geared up to the focal point of Tevez as the striker; his ability to defend from the front not only eases the pressure on the midfield, but it also forces opposition defenders into mistakes or sloppy passes, meaning City can be back in possession.

Overall, it's Tevez's ability to craft goals from absolutely nowhere that has helped City so much, this season. That's not to detract from the rest of the team, either, because City didn't finish third by accident: The defence was more solid than my mum's gravy (served in slices) and the midfield was nicely balanced between protecting the defence and supporting the attack. Though, Tevez doesn't need as much support as the other strikers in the squad – which isn't a slight on those other strikers, either, because I'd go as far as saying Tevez is one of the best, if not the best, lone striker on the planet.

Without Tevez next season, should the club decide to sell him and he decides to leave, then his goals will need to be replaced. Whether that's with a change in Roberto Mancini's system or through trying to replace him like-for-like, it doesn't matter. But the goals will have to come from somewhere.

The interesting decision for Roberto Mancini, though, will come if Tevez stays. A large number of City fans have expressed the opinion that City's captain should be more of a leader. Sure, Tevez has led from the front and his effort on the field can't be questioned, but there were quite a few eyebrows raised when he was given the armband.

When it comes to commitment, ability and leadership, one player has shone in this past ten months; one player who would, perhaps, be a better candidate: Vincent Kompany. Personally, should Tevez leave the club, there would be no question who would be the skipper next season, but should he stay, would it be worth risking alienating the striker by taking the captaincy from him? After all, there's no denying how vital his goals are to City.

So there's going to be a fine balancing act for Roberto Mancini this summer.

A REBOOTED CAREER

On a chilly Saturday afternoon in October 2006, Manchester City put in the worst team performance that many fans had ever seen. And that's quite a bold statement, because there have been some truly shocking displays down the years, but this one was a real stinker. Pummelled 4-0 away at Wigan and without even fashioning a chance, let alone a shot on target, it became clear that 2006-07 was going to be a very long season.

There was one little glimmering light in that game, though. One little beacon of hope, amidst a bunker of bleak darkness that sunk down like a bottomless abyss. A City academy product was given his debut by the then manager, Stuart Pearce. He played in the number 33 shirt, most recently associated with Vincent Kompany. And, in the limited touches he was able to get when City did keep the ball that afternoon, he showed himself to actually have been the best player for the visitors.

His name was Michael Johnson. A man now often forgotten about at City. A man forgotten about by the Premier League, who once saw him as a future City and England legend. A man forgotten about by football.

For a while it went well for him. Okay, so he was dropped straight after that Wigan game – probably to save him the embarrassment of more team performances like that one – but he worked his way back into the side later in that season.

A turning point came for the Blues over Easter. After a series of dire performances for the first three months of 2007, it looked like City would be in great danger of finding their way out of the Premier League. But a battling display against Chelsea and a run of form of 11 points from five games (beating Middlesbrough, Newcastle and Fulham, and drawing with Charlton and Liverpool) saw City safe.

That coincided with the return to the team of Michael Johnson. It's a bit brash to suggest that he alone saved City from the drop that season, but he had a big influence on that run of form. Dunne and Distin, with Barton and Mpenza too, were also hugely involved. And by the time City lost to Arsenal at the Emirates near the end of April, they were safe. We can say that for sure because they only went on to pick up one more point that season, drawing with Watford, and they didn't go down.

But when he was back in the team, Michael Johnson looked the part and fitted into the team like he had been playing Premier League football for a decade. Then, though, City sacked their manager. It didn't come as too much of a surprise, since they hadn't scored a Premier League goal at home in five months. The club changed owners, too. The new manager quickly became a fans' favourite and he brought with him a wealth of talent from around the world.

Sven's City began the season well, losing out only to a fine goal at the Emirates after wins against West Ham, Derby and Manchester United. The goal that beat Derby was City's first at home since Samaras' eight months earlier and was scored by one Michael Johnson. A beautiful curler from the edge of the box with the outside of his foot. He scored the winner against Aston Villa that season, too, a graceful run from midfield ending with him slotting the ball beyond Scott Carson.

Sven was saying all good things about him. His team-mates likewise. The media more so. The City fans even more so; some were saying he reminded them of a former City hero, held in the highest esteem: Colin Bell. In truth, the praise was very premature. He had only been in the team for half a season, but he was definitely one to watch. In fact, he was a lynchpin in Sven's successful City team and he was definitely missed when form took a turn for the worse after the New Year.

The injury that caused him to miss many games that season seemed an innocuous abdominal one. But, while he was out, he had a double hernia operation and, when he did return towards the end of the campaign, he never truly seemed fit and like he had recovered. The season ended and a new manager came in and, this time through City's lack of funds more than anything, he survived the upheaval once again.

Mark Hughes liked him and Johnson started well, linking up with Stephen Ireland and Elano in a distinctly average start to the season. City were taken over. Robinho arrived as a marquee signing. City lost to Chelsea and faced Brighton & Hove Albion in the League Cup. And that trip to the Withdean Stadium was more costly than a simple, embarrassing League Cup exit: There was a recurrence of Johnson's abdominal injury and he didn't play another game that season.

The following summer, City had the chance to truly flex their financial muscle – and they did. Once again, Johnson survived the cull, but this time he had spent over seven months injured and this could have been one of the biggest contributing factors. He was ready for pre-season, where he played (and picked up a minor injury) in a friendly with Orlando Pirates. He was ready for the end of September, where he came off the bench for two minutes in City's 3-1 win over West Ham.

City, though, were soon in the middle of their infamous run of draws and patchy form, and therefore weren't in a position to be re-introducing players from long term injuries into the side. But, with the League Cup game at home to Scunthorpe being over at 4-1, Johnson got about 20 minutes at the end of the match. In that time, he showed moments of passing and vision that the City fans remembered him for, and he went on to score the best goal of the night – a long range effort on his weaker foot. It looked like he was back in the business, though he needed some game time and City's form was still poor as they continued to draw games.

But, on 10 December, 2009, it was announced that Johnson had broken down in training and suffered a serious knee injury. He was back to square one, after almost a year of hard work to get back to fitness and coming so close to achieving it. He's not been named in another City squad since.

After such a long time on the sidelines and such improvements made to City's squad since he was last playing regularly, Johnson fights an uphill battle just to make it back into the team. Nevermind the fight he has on his hands to fulfil the potential he showed back in 2007. There are so many examples of players who have never been the same after long term injuries. It would be easy to think, in fact, that Johnson's ship has sailed from the City port – which would be unfortunate given the time he's had, but football is a cut-throat world.

Today, it's been announced that Johnson is being considered an option by one of his former City managers, now working in The Championship. Leicester City would probably be the perfect destination for him to hit the reboot button. He's played the best (almost only) football of his career under Sven; the games will come thick and fast; and it will be competitive, but not as potentially overwhelming as a Premier League comeback would be.

Providing his injuries haven't had too much of an effect on him, he can still provide a cutting edge through a packed defence. And I don't think there's a single City fan that wouldn't like to see him back keeping fit and playing like we all used to see.

INTERVIEW: JASON MANFORD

The broadcasting icon that is Stuart Hall, in reference to Old Trafford being nicknamed 'The Theatre of Dreams', once remarked that, by contrast, Maine Road (as it was back then, rather than The Etihad Stadium) must be 'The Theatre of Base Comedy'. For years, being a City fan has been quite unique in that sense and Hall – a fan of the Blues himself – hit the nail right on the head. While the trophies rolled in on the other side of town, the relegations and promotions stacked up on this.

But there was one way that us blues could survive the dark times: We developed a self-depreciating sense of humour. The ability to laugh at ourselves is the only thing that could possible have kept some people going, as the club sunk to defeat after defeat, against the odds. One man, though, turned that into his day job.

Jason Manford sprung to the forefront of comedy with an appearance on Jack Dee's Live At The Apollo on BBC1. In that routine, he openly talked about his supported football club: Manchester City. From making jokes between other fans, he took it to a national Saturday prime time audience.

"I think like all City fans, you can't not have a sense of humour," he says. "What's interesting is how City have become so massive recently that you can do jokes on mainstream telly and people get it. There's no editor taking it out because nobody gets it anymore. Ten years ago, you'd struggle.

"I had a gag a while back," he continues. "There was a point when they [City] were sending us emails and letters when you didn't come to the match. I think it was during Kevin Keegan and then Stuart Pearce's era. And you'd get a letter from Kevin Keegan – obviously, not really from him, but from the club – saying '*I notice you weren't at the game on Saturday*'. And you think, it's Keegan, he's only going to cry or something.

"But then you get one from Stuart Pearce and think: '*Oooh, bloody hell, I'd better go!*' He probably did write it himself. In his own blood.

"Being a City fan certainly doesn't hinder it [having a sense of humour]. I remember saying to my dad, when I was about eight or nine, and we were coming home from somewhere and it [the football] was on the radio. On Piccadilly Radio, James H Reeves used to do his show and sometimes it wasn't live commentary, they'd just play music as normal. Then they'd interrupt a song with '*It's a goal!*' or, invariably, '*Oh no!*' and it'd be one of the north-west clubs.

"And all the way through growing up, I remember '*It's a goal!*' was always followed by '*and we're going over to Old Trafford now...*' and it was always a United goal. And, every time, '*Oh no!*' was always City.

"I remember saying to my dad: '*You know what, we should just support United, you know, dad. It seems to be a lot easier to support them. There's a lot of heartache here; you're crying every weekend, you're in a mood all Sunday...*' and it was like I'd come up with this great idea; like I'd solved all his problems.

"And he's only just started talking to me again after that," he laughs. "You can really disown a son! He genuinely said to me that he didn't care if I was gay, straight, Tory, anything... just don't dare be a United fan."

Comedians often talk about writing material that's close to home; after all, it's often said that you should write what you know. Clearly, Jason has done that with his blues-based comedy, but does it ever worry him how the jokes will be received by the other forty-odd thousand on the terraces?

"All City fans have got a good sense of humour," he notes. "You can't be too anti-United or anti-any other club because you still need to sell DVDs and tickets. Generally, football fans have a good sense of humour.

"You do have your nutters and your proper *head-the-balls* who are not going to come anyway and genuinely don't like you because you support City. Most people are normal and go: '*well, I don't like United and I don't like United fans, but actually I work with them and some of my relatives are United fans and some are alright – it's not Palestine.*'"

Despite Jason playing down the teasing of opposition fans, it's impossible not to find out what his best United gag is: "Funnily enough," he replies, "it's one that gets quoted back at me all the time. It just goes: '*United fans are like rats, you're never more than three meters away from one of the...*' and, obviously, there's a little swear word on the end.

"And it's one that, even at the match now, people tell it me all the time.

"But my favourite one is a joke I did about Robinho," he continues. "And I was gutted when he left. Not because he was a brilliant player, but just because I wasn't able to do that joke anymore.

"I once told that joke at a City gig. It was a charity thing and all the players were there, and I decided to just go for it. And Robinho was sat there – and this is why I'll always have time for him – and everyone's had a bit of a chuckle and I've looked over, hoping he was laughing. He was.

"This is a man who'd been speaking English for about three weeks. And I thought that he must have a good grasp of the language, because there's a few double meanings in the joke and it's quite complex.

"After the gig, I'd gone over and introduced myself and he didn't speak any English. I spoke to his manager about it and he said that he [Robinho] had just heard his name, saw everyone laugh and thought he'd better join in."

As Jason's career took off, though, it did affect his watching of his beloved Blues. Notoriously, the best slots for stand-ups to perform is on a Friday or Saturday evening and, when you're on stage at the other end of the country, getting back to Manchester for kick-off can be tough.

"People complain about these games on a Monday night or a Sunday afternoon," he says. "But they're the best games for me. I love a Sunday afternoon kick-off. Saturday, 3 o'clocks are the worst: Game finishes at 5 o'clock – I never leave before the final whistle, I can't do it – and if you're due on in Hull at 7 o'clock, it's a bit of a squeeze.

"But, weirdly," he continues, "[City's sudden rise to success] does ruin my material. I'd go to Liverpool and say '*Ladies and gentlemen, I'm from Manchester!*' and they'd boo. And I'd go '*But I support City!*' and they'd cheer. But now they still boo!

"But, I'd be happy to lose ten minutes of my material if City win everything. That'll do me, I'm happy to do that," he laughs. After all, it is easier to write self-depreciating material than anything else. "There'll always be stuff to joke about. Football is a male soap opera: We've got goodies and baddies, last second script changes, and ridiculous story arcs... it's just our EastEnders or our Coronation Street.

"City are just the latest to go from goodie to baddie. We used to be everyone's second favourite club. We were just those laughable idiots; people who got knocked out of competitions by a balloon. We were just a daft club, with inflatable bananas and ridiculous situations, but then we got all this money, became good and people hate us.

"If you look at United – the most hated club in the world – they're also the most successful club. I know it's hard for City fans to look at United as an ambition, but what we have to do is learn from their mistakes. Let's be as successful as them, but let's keep our roots."

But Jason does have one sure-fire way to deal with anybody who disapproves of who you support: "The trick is, if anyone has a go at you for being a City fan and has a go at us for buying the cups, what you have to do is to accuse them of being a racist. And it works, because it shuts people up.

"You say, '*It didn't seem to matter when it was Abramovich, it didn't seem to matter with Russians, it didn't seem to matter with Americans... but all of a sudden, because it's Arabs, is that what you're saying? Oh, I see. I think I am on to you, my friend.*'

"And suddenly, you're back on the high horse," he chuckles.

August 2011

Manchester City 2-3 Manchester United

FA Community Shield

Sunday 7 August, 2011 – 14:30 KO

City: Hart, Richards, Kompany (c), Lescott, Kolarov (Clichy 74), de Jong, Silva, Y Toure, Milner (A Johnson 67), Balotelli (Barry 59), Dzeko
Unused: Taylor, Savic, Wright-Phillips, Aguero
Goals: Lescott (38), Dzeko (45)
Booked: Dzeko, Y Toure, Kolarov
Man of the Match: Joleon Lescott

It was United that started the game the brighter, with City unable to get their foot on the ball. Kompany gave away a free kick on the left wing, but Young's delivery could only find the Belgian's feet and he cleared. City looked asleep.

Despite being unable to properly get going, though, the Blues took the lead. Milner won a foul off Evra and Silva curled the resulting free kick into the box. Lescott met it before any of the United defence and he nodded it home.

And, just before the break, it got better. Dzeko picked the ball up in the middle of the United half. He turned and fired a stunning effort into the net.

United tried to hit back immediately after the break. Smalling lost Dzeko in the box and he latched onto a Young free kick from deep to lift the ball past Hart, getting the Champions back into the game.

Nani then levelled the count with a stunning goal. United moved the ball well around the edge of the box and the Portuguese man was left to break unchallenged into the six-yard box. Hart came out and he flicked it over the City keeper, to equalise with under an hour played.

With a minute of the game to play, Dzeko had the chance to win the game with a free header in the United box, but it was flicked weakly at goal. United cleared the ball and a breakdown of communication between Kompany and Clichy left the Belgian too much work to do against Nani and he broke clear into the City half. He rounded Hart and won the game.

Manchester City 4-0 Swansea City

FA Premier League

Monday 15 August, 2011 – 20:00 KO

City: Hart, Richards, Lescott, Kompany (c), Clichy, de Jong (Aguero 60), Barry, Silva (Milner 82), Y Toure, A Johnson (Savic 75), Dzeko
Unused: Taylor, Zabaleta, Kolarov, Balotelli
Goals: Dzeko (57), Aguero (68, 90+1), Silva (71)
Booked: -
Man of the Match: David Silva

It was a slow start from the home team, who appeared to be struggling to get their possession game going, as Swansea tried to keep City quiet. Silva hit the bar, after he was found by Johnson. His side-footed effort beat the goalkeeper, but it didn't beat the frame of the goal, and the visitors were off the hook.

With almost an hour played, Silva turned well in his own half to keep the ball. He found Johnson who broke into the Swansea box and fired a shot across goal. It was well saved by Vorm, but only to the feet of Dzeko, who knocked the ball back into the empty net to give the hosts the lead.

Aguero joined the action immediately and it didn't take long for the Argentina international to get off the mark at his new club. Eight minutes into his debut, he was on hand at the back post to convert a Richards low ball across the six-yard box, much to the fans' delight.

The new boy then had a hand in creating a goal for the man of the match. Dzeko neatly kept the ball on the right flank, before knocking it on to Aguero steaming into the box. He flicked it over the goalkeeper and managed to then extend his leg to keep the ball in play and cross to the back post. Silva was arriving late into the box and he made no mistake in hitting the net.

And there was nothing Vorm could do about the final goal of the night – which would be the icing on the cake for the debutant Aguero. He picked up the ball mid-way into the Swansea half and knocked it out of his feet. With nobody closing him down, he decided to have a hit from 25 yards and it whistled into the bottom corner, completing a fine opening night display from the Blues.

Bolton Wanderers 2-3 Manchester City
FA Premier League
Sunday 21 August, 2011 – 16:00 KO

City: Hart, Richards, Lescott, Kompany (c), Kolarov, Milner, Barry, Silva (Zabaleta 89), Y Toure, Aguero (Tevez 68), Dzeko (A Johnson 80)
Unused: Pantilimon, Clichy, Savic, Balotelli
Goals: Silva (26), Barry (37), Dzeko (47)
Booked: -
Man of the Match: David Silva

It was a bright start to the game that saw a neat ball from Silva put Kolarov in behind the Bolton defence, who smashed it across the six-yard box. Milner got the touch, but Jaaskelainen managed to block.

Bolton looked to have ridden the storm as City pressed, but, after some good work from Richards breaking into the box, the visitors took the lead. The right back found Silva on the edge of the box and the little Spaniard took a shot. It went straight through Jaaskelainen and into the net.

Soon, City had their second. The ball was played to Barry on the edge of the box from a corner and, from 25 yards, he fired it into the top corner with

Jaaskelainen left flapping at thin air.

But the home side responded immediately. Petrov fired in a low cross towards the penalty spot after he was found by Cahill. Klasnic was first to it and he hit the back of the net on the volley, reducing the deficit.

The first action of the second half saw Dzeko get himself on the scoresheet. A ball was knocked on by Milner and Robinson committed to the challenge, but didn't win it. It broke to the Bosnian and he made no mistake in finishing.

But, as City were dominant in the game, they conceded a second and Bolton, once again, reduced the deficit. Davies climbed higher than Lescott from a free kick and nodded the ball towards goal. Hart threw himself at it, but couldn't reach it, and it flicked off the post and into the net.

Tottenham Hotspur 1-5 Manchester City
FA Premier League
Sunday 28 August, 2011 – 13:30 KO

City: Hart, Zabaleta (Richards 64), Lescott, Kompany (c), Clichy, Nasri, Barry, Silva, Y Toure, Aguero (Savic 75), Dzeko
Unused: Pantilimon, Milner, A Johnson, Tevez, Balotelli
Goals: Dzeko (35, 41, 55, 90+2), Aguero (60)
Booked: Barry, Zabaleta, Y Toure, Savic
Man of the Match: Edin Dzeko

Tottenham could have taken the lead early on: Bale missed a sitter for Tottenham, after Lennon cut the ball back across goal from the right wing. With Hart bearing down on him, he skied his shot high and wide.

Clichy and Nasri linked up well, before Nasri played a lovely one-two with Aguero to set up the crossing opportunity. The Frenchman found Dzeko in the box and he found the back of the net, stealing in to get his toe on the ball.

Clichy blocked a Corluka cross for a corner, which Lescott cleared. From that clearance, Yaya Toure broke away with Silva and Nasri, before the cross found Dzeko in the box and he doubled the visitors' lead with a brilliant header, with his back to goal.

From a City corner early in the second half, Dzeko got his third. The initial cross was cleared by the defence, but it was picked up by Yaya Toure. His low centre was smashed into the net from two yards by the Bosnian.

Aguero then got himself on the scoresheet with an hour played. He picked up the ball on the left flank and nipped in past the defender. Faced with Friedel, he smashed the ball into the top corner.

It was all go: Kaboul pulled a goal back for the home side with a free header from a corner, as the Tottenham man found space in the box. But the last word went to Dzeko, who played a nice one-two with Barry, before side-footing a wonderful left footed effort into the top corner.

KUN AGUERO: THE YOUNG MAN WITH THE BIG FUTURE

In the July of 2003, a young man of 15 years (and 35 days) joined the action for Independiente in their match against Club Atletico San Lorenzo de Almagro, breaking the record for being the youngest ever player to take part in an Argentine First Division match. The previous record had been held for 27 years, by one Diego Maradona, whose daughter Giannina would later become that young man's wife. That young man was one Sergio Leonel Aguero del Castillo. Sergio Aguero.

That 15 year old was slowly bled into the first team at Independiente. His first goal came in November 2004 and that was the catapult for him to become a regular. As he matured in his home country, he began to attract the attention from Europe. It would have been a bizarre change in fortunes for him: Growing up, his father earned the equivalent of £20 a week and that was what his family had to feed him and his six siblings. Their home was tiny, with a dilapidated tin roof and a rag sheet as its front door.

Football was his escape route. His first Christmas present was a ball. Aged nine, he would spend his days playing the game in the streets, honing his skills – shooting, passing, dodging kicks from less skilful players. He had attracted the attention of local scouts. By the time he was 12, he was playing five times every Saturday.

Suddenly, this boy who had spent his early years in a small house in an area surrounded by gang violence and drugs was propelled to the heights of La Liga, when he signed for Atletico Madrid aged just 18. And the Spanish side knew exactly what they were getting; his record in his home country was 23 goals in just 54 matches – almost one goal every two games. This raw talent was worth €23m.

It didn't take long for him to make an impact in Europe, though probably not for the right reason: Taking a leaf out of his future father-in-law's book, Aguero used his hands to score the deciding goal against Recreativo Huelva. It was only his second goal for the Madrid club, but it wasn't long until his record began to take on a familiar slant – in his second season, he was third highest scorer in the division and had netted important goals against the league's giants Barcelona, Real Madrid and Valencia.

But it wasn't all positive for the forward at his new club. Perhaps unsurprisingly for a young man living on the other side of the world, he was homesick. He gained weight as he developed a taste for burgers, fast cars and nights out in the most expensive of the expensive night clubs. Though soon that changed when he met Giannina Maradona. She was the calming influence he needed.

Four and a half years on the continent led to Aguero attracting the interests of the biggest of the big clubs. His goalscoring record wasn't what it was in his homeland, but nevertheless it was still impressive: 74 goals in 175 appearances, better than a goal every three games. During that period, he helped Atletico qualify for the Champions League for the first time in ten years, provided the assists for both goals in their Europa League final victory over Fulham and went on to impress on the international stage with Argentina.

Perhaps it was his slow introduction to international football that helped him become such a prolific striker for his country, too. He was wanted by many to join the 2006 senior team for the World Cup, but missed out on the squad due to his inexperience. In truth, this was probably a huge aid to his development. He didn't have the pressure of a great footballing nation on his shoulders too early.

He was able to join up with the Under 20s squad for their World Cup tournament the following year. He captained the side in the final, where he scored the game's equaliser in their 2-1 victory, and also won the tournament's Golden Boot (highest goalscorer) and Golden Ball (best player). He then added an Olympic gold medal to his trophy cabinet, a year later.

City's interest reportedly dates back to 2008, when the club was first taken over by Sheikh Mansour. But Aguero remained in Spain until last month, when the Blues finally made their move, shelling out £38m (including potential add ons) for his services. If anything, this is probably both the perfect time for him to join City and the perfect time for City to have him join. With his fellow countryman seemingly on his way out of the club, there will be plenty of opportunities for Aguero to shine.

He's no longer the young boy who needs protection from the weight of expectation put upon his shoulders. He's left a club where he was the best player for a brand new challenge: One where he will need to work hard to better himself; one where he can win trophies with a club that is also looking to better itself year on year; one where he's not a big fish in a small pond.

His introduction to City is somewhat similar to most of his career. Despite signing in time to travel with the squad to Dublin for the pre-season tournament, the fans had to wait to see him. He got blisters on his feet and borrowed the manager's boots. Many expected him to be in the squad for the Community Shield, especially if he were to be ready for the Premier League opener the weekend later. Again, he didn't get off the bench.

Roberto Mancini appeared to be easing the new man in. An injury to holding midfielder Nigel de Jong just after City took the lead against Swansea left the man in the dugout needing to make a change. Sensing that Swansea were tiring, it was the perfect time to switch formation and slowly introduce Aguero. Of course, Sergio had other ideas: Tapping in the second, assisting the third from a seemingly impossible position, before stealing the headlines with a blockbuster of a fourth.

Swansea may well be opposition who are expected to be relegation fodder this season, but they are in the top division for a reason – they deserve to be. However, there were pundits who were concerned that Monday night's show was just a one-off, asking how Aguero would cope with a wet winter's night at Stoke. Well, judging by his career so far, the answer appears to be pretty obvious.

He'll do just fine.

A RISK WORTH TAKING

It was an overcast day in Manchester when the surprise first reared its head. The overcast nature of the weather wasn't the surprise, given it was August and this was Manchester. Anyone in Manchester expecting anything other than the threat of rain towards the end of August is a fool. There used to be a phrase 'what happens today in Manchester, happens in the rest of the world tomorrow' – so if the rest of the world is reading, tomorrow's going to be overcast.

But it was on one of these traditionally dull summer days that news hit the wires that Owen Hargreaves, the perennially injured former Manchester United midfielder, was having a medical with Manchester City for a pay-as-you-play deal. Everybody double checked to see if they'd read it correctly. Twitter went haywire. Joe Hart used the word '*Wowzers*'. City fans were confused and United fans decided it was the **ULTIMATE BETRAYAL** from a man who had no emotional connection to their club for any reason other than having played there for a bit.

As I see it, a move for Owen Hargreaves doesn't post any real risk for City. If, as one would assume it would be, the deal he is offered is that he would only collect wages on the weeks he was taking part in first team action, then there's nothing for City to lose here. When he was fit, he was one of the best midfielders in England – a mainstay in the England side and voted the best England player in 2006, ahead of both Gerrard and Lampard. If he isn't fit, then he doesn't get paid.

Ok, so he's been injured. And injured for a while. But we have all seen the videos he posted to YouTube to prove his fitness. Since suffering a recurring knee problem – patellar tendonitis – he has had a torrid time of it. When it finally looked like he would be able to restart his playing career, he was forced to be substituted five minutes into the game after pulling his hamstring. After that point he wasn't considered for the first team, despite getting back training with Manchester United.

With Hargreaves having offered to play for United for free, it seems clear that he is desperate to prove his fitness. It also suggests that he understands his body's limitations; perhaps he feels his body can't complete 38 Premier League matches, plus extras in the cup. And even the most optimistic of footballers couldn't expect to have spent more of the last three years in the physio room than on the pitch and then go on to walk into a place in a midfield that contains the likes of (amongst others) Gareth Barry, James Milner, Yaya Toure, Nigel de Jong, David Silva or Samir Nasri.

However, maybe the role that Mancini would be offering Hargreaves is more than simply being a member of the playing squad. Perhaps it's more about his experience and influence, rather than his actual playing abilities (of which there are no questions, either) and his fitness (where the big question mark lies). It could be that the manager is after City's next Patrick Vieira.

Last season, Vieira's role in City's successful FA Cup campaign cannot be understated. He scored vital goals in the competition early on. He was the calming influence for the manager to bring on during the closing stages of the semi final and the final. And, on top of all that, he's helped the younger players' development over his time with the club; asked who they looked up to, the World Cup winner was usually their first answer.

And Hargreaves' achievements aren't too shabby, either: Four Bundesliga titles, three German Cups and two Champions Leagues. And it could be the Champions League victories that are attracting Roberto Mancini. He's been there, done it, bought the t-shirt and had the operations to prove it. City's squad does have Champions League experience, even if it's the club's first year in the competition. It's still a young squad, though, and that little bit age with experience wouldn't go amiss.

While it would be silly to talk about City as potential winners of the Champions League, if Hargreaves' influence has the same effect that Vieira's did on the FA Cup, then perhaps City could get through two or three more rounds than they would have done without it.

It seems bizarre that the most puzzling aspect of this transfer move turns out to be the offence a large number of United fans have taken to it. One of them went as far as commenting that moving to City would be a big 'two fingered salute' to Manchester United. It's not like the player is a free agent or able to choose wherever he'd like to sign based on the offers he receives, after his previous club decided he was surplus to requirements, is it? Oh.

He offered to play for United for nothing. He was willing to give his services (whatever he was able to, that is) to his former club without a wage. That doesn't seem to be anything like disloyalty. To cry disloyalty, when the club decide not to take that offer up and he chooses to go elsewhere is a bit rich. What should make him decide that he won't sign for one of their rivals? He's desperate to play football and prove that he's still got it. Why would he turn down the chance to do that?

Incidentally, his offer of playing for nothing followed by his agreement to a 'pay-as-you-play' deal completely puts out the fire of the good ol' 'only-move-to-City-for-the-money' chestnut.

For what it's worth, there are also a fair number of United fans wishing him all the best for the future, even if that future is with their rivals. Though, if I see the 'fallen through the transfer window and is injured again' joke once more, I may smash something.

Overall, this appears to be a very shrewd bit of business by City. If he is fit – reports suggest that City's medical team are not only impressed by his fitness, but stunned at his condition – then he can provide cover for the first team when he's needed. He can be the player that can come in and control certain games or come off the bench to make sure that City get the result they want. He's proven at the top level and will (hopefully) be available when Yaya Toure heads for the African Cup of Nations.

While if it doesn't work out for him at City, then the club doesn't lose: they've paid no transfer fee and the player has only been paid when he's been playing. And the player has had a chance to prove that he's still capable at the top level.

Above all else, Roberto Mancini's record in the transfer market has, on the whole, been very good. There is only Jerome Boateng who can be described as a poor signing from the manager, because, as haphazard as he is at times, Aleksandar Kolarov has had his good points.

Is Owen Hargreaves worth the risk?

Most definitely.

August 2011 Breakdown

Games (all competitions):
Won: 3   **Drawn:** 0   **Lost:** 1

Goals (all competitions):
For: 14   **Against:** 6

Progress:
Premier League: 2nd
League Cup: -
FA Cup: -
Champions League: -

Premier League Table

		P	W	D	L	F	A	GD	Pts
1	Manchester United	3	3	0	0	13	3	+10	9
2	**Manchester City**	**3**	**3**	**0**	**0**	**12**	**3**	**+9**	**9**
3	Liverpool	3	2	1	0	6	2	+4	7
4	Chelsea	3	2	1	0	5	2	+3	7
5	Wolverhampton Wanderers	3	2	1	0	4	1	+3	7

September 2011

Manchester City 3-0 Wigan Athletic

FA Premier League
Saturday 10 September, 2011 – 15:00 KO

City: Hart, Richards, Kompany (c), Lescott, Clichy, Y Toure (Razak 80), Milner, Silva, A Johnson, Tevez (Nasri 60), Aguero (Balotelli 70)
Unused: Pantilimon, K Toure, Zabaleta, Dzeko
Goals: Aguero (13, 63, 68)
Booked: -
Man of the Match: David Silva

City took the initiative from the off with the early pressure on the visitors' goal. Johnson fired over with a volley that wouldn't drop in time for him to catch properly before the Wigan defence closed him down.

Tevez came close to marking his first start of the season with a spectacular overhead kick, as the ball dropped to him after Kompany nodded a corner towards the back post. But, with Al Habsi coming towards the ball, Lescott tried to flick it into the net, but he inadvertently nodded it over.

But shortly after, City took the lead. A great move down the left flank between Tevez and Silva presented the ball to Aguero in the box. He carried it around the defender and shot low to Al Habsi's right. The keeper wasn't able to get near it and the ball nestled into the corner.

With 17 minutes on the clock, City had the chance to double their lead. Silva was clearly fouled in the box and the referee had no hesitation in giving the penalty. Tevez stepped up, but it was a poor spot kick and Al Habsi guessed correctly to make the save.

Nasri joined the action on the hour and immediately set about creating City's second goal. Silva threaded the ball through to the former Arsenal midfielder and he, in turn, slotted it on to Aguero, setting him free in the box. The Argentine made no mistake in finding the net, rolling his shot beyond Al Habsi.

Seven minutes later, he got himself the match ball. Silva's brilliant assist put Aguero through on a one-on-one and he waited for Al Habsi to commit, before passing the ball into the bottom corner.

Manchester City 1-1 Napoli

Champions League Group A
Wednesday 14 September, 2011 – 19:45 KO

City: Hart, Zabaleta, Kompany (c), Lescott, Kolarov (Clichy 76), Y Toure, Barry, Silva, Nasri (A Johnson 76), Dzeko (Tevez 81), Aguero
Unused: Pantilimon, K Toure, Savic, Richards
Goals: Kolarov (74)

Booked: Zabaleta
Man of the Match: Yaya Toure

City got their first ever Champions League game off to a fast start, taking the initiative to the visiting side and looking for an early goal. Nasri came close with a low drive that flashed just wide of the post, before Silva had an effort from a free kick deflected over the bar.

But Napoli soon began to show why they shouldn't be underestimated. Kompany dived in on the edge of the box and didn't win the ball, leaving Lavezzi the chance to turn in the area. He did and looked to place his shot in the top corner; Hart was beaten, but it bounced down off the bar and Kolarov was able to clear.

With ten minutes of the half remaining, City struck the bar, too. A brilliant move left Silva with the ball on the by-line inside the box and he got his head up to find Yaya Toure. His first time effort smashed past the goalkeeper and crashed into the crossbar.

The second half saw Napoli hit the post through Hamsik after his effort took a nick off Kompany. Both Aguero and Lescott had chances flash over the bar: The striker volleyed over with a cheeky attempt, before the defender had a free header in the box from a corner, but he couldn't direct it goalwards.

With just over 20 minutes to go, Barry gave the ball away on the edge of the opposition's box and the visitors broke with speed. Kompany was left with a two-on-one and Cavani had space to shoot. He didn't need a second invitation and slotted the ball through Hart's legs to give the Italian side the lead.

City hit the bar again as they looked to respond immediately. Aguero had an effort from inside the six-yard box, reacting instinctively to get his shot in. It beat the goalkeeper, but clipped the post and away to safety.

The equaliser, though, wasn't long in coming. Zabaleta won a free kick on the edge of the box and Kolarov stepped up to take it. He whipped it up and over the wall, sweeping it into the bottom corner: The goalkeeper was rooted to the spot, although he'll probably be disappointed to have been beaten by it.

In the end, City were the dominant team and should probably have done better with the amount of possession and pressure they had. But, having fallen behind, a point in the opening game isn't the end of the world: It could have been better but, equally, it could have been a whole lot worse.

Fulham 2-2 Manchester City
FA Premier League
Sunday 18 September, 2011 – 15:00 KO

City: Hart, Richards, Kompany (c), Lescott, Clichy, Y Toure, Barry, Silva (Zabaleta 69), Nasri (A Johnson 81), Dzeko, Aguero (Tevez 83)
Unused: Pantilimon, K Toure, Balotelli, Kolarov

Goals: Aguero (18, 46)
Booked: Barry
Man of the Match: David Silva

City started the game the brighter: Richards played a neat ball out to Dzeko on the right wing. He fired a cross in that was half-cleared, but Silva picked up the pieces and slid it into Aguero in the box. With the Fulham players appealing for an offside, he turned and placed the ball into the corner, giving the visitors the lead.

It was all City mid-way into the first half, as Silva was onside in the box. He clipped it back for Dzeko, who slammed a left footed shot at goal, but another fine save from Schwarzer kept it at 1-0.

From the second half kick-off, City doubled their lead. Clichy played a high ball to Dzeko, who nodded the ball down for Aguero to shoot and he found the bottom corner. The goal came 12 seconds into the second half and the first Fulham touch after the break was Schwarzer's, picking the ball out of the net.

On 55 minutes, largely against the run of play, Zamora pulled a goal back for the home side. His first touch took the ball away from Richards and he smashed an effort past Hart into the top corner. Hart then pulled off another great save from Dempsey, pushing a header over the bar from a Fulham corner.

With 15 minutes to play, Fulham pulled it level. Zamora controlled the ball in the box and laid it back to Murphy. His shot deflected off Kompany and left Hart helpless. From a leading position, City dropped two points and should have done better from being two goals in front.

Manchester City 2-0 Birmingham City
League Cup Third Round
Wednesday 21 September, 2011 – 19:45 KO

City: Pantilimon, Onuoha, Savic, K Toure (c), Kolarov, Zabaleta, Hargreaves (Milner 57), Bridge (Rekik 78), Razak (Scapuzzi 86), Tevez, Balotelli
Unused: Taylor, Clichy, Suarez, Aguero
Goals: Hargreaves (17), Balotelli (38)
Booked: -
Man of the Match: Owen Hargreaves

The game started slowly, but it was all City. Balotelli had a shout for a penalty turned down as he weaved his way into the box, before Zabaleta took an opportunistic volley on from the edge of the box with his left foot, but the ball sailed over the bar.

Soon, City's domination paid off. Balotelli knocked the ball down for Hargreaves on the edge of the box and the former United midfielder hit an effort towards the top corner of the goal. Doyle threw himself at it, but couldn't get close, and it nestled in the back of the net.

Tevez then prodded an effort over the bar, after Kolo Toure had won a header from a Kolarov corner, before Balotelli was inches away from connecting with a low cross from the left.

As the game was meandering towards half time, City doubled their lead. Kolarov broke down the left flank and looked to drive in one of his trademark smashed crosses. But, instead, he slid the ball back to Balotelli, who was just inside the box, and he was able to deftly redirect the ball into the bottom corner, across the goalkeeper.

Pantilimon had to be alert from a series of Birmingham corners, before the defence were able to get the ball clear. Kolarov then had an effort from range blocked and Tevez whipped a free kick just wide of the far post, before Balotelli smashed a shot straight at the goalkeeper. Tevez should then have made it three, as he was sent clean through, but, having carried the ball from the halfway line, his shot was straight at Doyle and Kolo Toure couldn't put the rebound in.

Manchester City 2-0 Everton
FA Premier League
Saturday 24 September, 2011 – 12:45 KO

City: Hart, Richards, Kompany (c), Lescott, Clichy, Y Toure, Barry, Silva , Nasri (Savic 83), Dzeko (Balotelli 60), Aguero (Milner 79)
Unused: Pantilimon, Kolarov, Zabaleta, Tevez
Goals: Balotelli (68), Milner (89)
Booked: Y Toure
Man of the Match: Joleon Lescott

The game got off to a slow start. Rodwell earned himself a yellow card for a late tackle on Silva – and it seemed to set the stall out for the next few minutes, with mainly Silva on the receiving end of some questionable challenges. Neville was next in the book for clipping the Spaniard's heels, before Osman joined him for an unfair challenge on Richards as he got away from him.

It was more about the tackles than the actual football as the game moved past the half hour, as Yaya Toure went into the book for a late sliding tackle on Coleman. City couldn't get the ball down and Everton were happy to keep breaking up the play.

The second half got off to a lively start, as Richards caused confusion in the Everton box with a low cross that needed Distin's intervention.

Balotelli joined the action on the hour mark, as Roberto Mancini looked for something different to break down the watertight Everton defence. And then, just eight minutes after coming on, the Italian changed the game. Aguero received the ball on the right and carried it across the box, looking for the shooting opportunity. It didn't come, but he laid the ball back to Balotelli, whose first time, side-footed effort clipped Jagielka and found the bottom corner, with Howard scrambling across.

As the game headed for stoppage time and Everton looked to see if they could salvage a point, the home side confirmed their victory. Silva blocked a loose ball in the centre of midfield and was able to get to it first to keep possession. He was on his own with three defenders for company, but was able to hold on to it until Milner was got up to help. He found the City substitute and he prodded it past Howard to get his first goal of the season.

Bayern Munich 2-0 Manchester City
Champions League Group A
Tuesday 27 September, 2011 – 19:45 KO

City: Hart, Richards, Kompany (c), K Toure, Clichy, Y Toure, Barry (Kolarov 73), Nasri (Milner 69), Aguero, Silva, Dzeko (de Jong 55)
Unused: Pantilimon, Zabaleta, Lescott, Tevez
Goals: -
Booked: Aguero, Clichy, Y Toure, K Toure
Man of the Match: Joe Hart

City started the game on the front foot, pressing the Bayern Munich goal and should have had a penalty after just two minutes. Former City defender Boateng appeared to foul Silva as the Spaniard turned in the box, but the referee played on and Bayern eventually got the cross clear.

Richards broke into the box after a one-two and went down under a challenge from Boateng and was unlucky to see the referee wave play on: The former City centre-back got nothing of the ball and was living dangerously.

With seven minutes to play to the break, the home side took the lead. Ribery was able to cut inside on the left flank and fire a shot in from the edge of the box. Hart got down to save it, but the rebound fell to straight to a Bayern shirt. The Englishman got across well to save the second shot, but he could do nothing about the third strike from Gomez from four yards out.

And seconds before the break, the home side doubled their lead. A free kick was flicked to the near post and Hart pulled off another world class save to keep it out. But Gomez was at the rebound first and smashed it into the net. There wasn't even time for City to kick off and they were two behind at the interval.

Bayern started the second half as they ended the first: In control of possession. A ball chipped over the top was close to being met by Muller as Kompany slipped, but Hart was off his line quickly to catch. Kolo Toure was then needed to head a deep cross away, before Ribery's shot was charged down by Richards.

Silva then gave the ball away to Rafinha on the edge of the box, but Kompany was there to block before Hart was called upon. Gomez was unmarked in the six-yard box as Ribery crossed and should have gotten his hat-trick. City were on the ropes and were unable to get a kick of the ball.

In stoppage time, Kolarov broke into the box, as Silva slipped the ball through, and he fired an effort across goal, but it was scuffed and well wide. Two silly goals conceded from City did the damage after a very promising first third of the game, but once behind, the visitors never looked like they would get back into the match.

A BLESSING IN DISGUISE

When you see grown men and women frothing at the mouths and seething with pure, unadulterated anger, it's usually because something terrible has happened: Their son has crashed the car. Their daughter has come home with a boyfriend and she's still far too young. The wife has found the husband's porn collection. But the level of anger amongst City fans on Sunday, on a scale of one to Malcolm Tucker, was high off the top end of the charts.

To be honest, the draw with Fulham has a few similarities with that day you didn't clear the internet history and your wife found your porn collection. It should never have happened, you should have been a hell of a lot more careful about what you did that Sunday afternoon and when it's all over there's an overwhelming sense of shame and disappointment.

And believe me, I cleaned that metaphor up. A lot.

The problem is, after the first four matches of the season, we have all been getting carried away. Though, in my opinion, of course, with good reason: Four goals against Swansea, three at Bolton, a demolition of Tottenham and overturning Wigan (without really getting out of second gear) go some way to build confidence. And, of course, being two goals in front and throwing that away is inexcusable; every team should be able to hold on to a lead, especially when they have been comfortable in the game.

Expectations were (rightly) high. Pre-match predictions on Twitter regularly included threes, fours, fives (and even one seven) in the goals for column for the visitors, while it seemed blues fans believed the best the home side could hope for was one. Again, however, leading 2-0 after twelve seconds of the second half should mean that the away side would take the points.

Obviously, control of the game slipped from City's grasp like a piece of soap in a bath full of washing up liquid and, once it had, they were unable to get it back again. Fulham had the initiative. And then they had two goals, too. While we can analyse the defending until the cows come home – poor marking going someway to explain them – I think it's more interesting to reflect on why this might have happened and what effect this could have on City in the future.

They say change is the enemy of complacency. And, looking back to before City's first venture into the Champions League, I'm beginning to think that complacency was starting to infiltrate the fans' ranks. I'm willing to hold my hands up and say that I completely underestimated Napoli. I knew they had a few quality players within their squad, but I didn't think they would be a match for City: They were a Pot Four team and, as such, not as good as my beloved blues, right?

How wrong was I?

The weekend before taking a point away from the Etihad Stadium, they turned over Cesena on their own ground. The weekend after, AC Milan pitched up in Naples and left with a 3-1 defeat. Suddenly, this group that I was expecting to be a tough test, but one that City would overcome in a manner akin to their league form, is a lot tougher than I thought.

I can't speak for all fans, of course, but judging by the reactions in the stadium on that Wednesday evening, I think a lot of people felt as I did. I was looking forward to a good game, but one that I expected City to win by two or three goals. Perhaps if City had scored in their major dominant spell in the first half that would have been the case, but, again, hindsight is an easy thing to use.

And that, perhaps, is the key to the ill feeling following the draw with Fulham. Expectations are that City will go into most games this season and come away with maximum points; certainly that was the case at Craven Cottage. I mean, after we had steam-rollered Tottenham, I went on record to say that I could honestly see City winning every league game leading up to the first Manchester derby – on Sunday 23 October. That would have been eight league victories on the bounce.

But here's the thing: I'd fallen into the trap of thinking how I'm now warning against. Any team that expects to turn up and that be enough to win a Premier League game is in for a big shock (maybe with the exception of when playing Sunderland, circa 2005, because, let's face it, they were abysmal). City have enough quality to beat every team in this league; so it shouldn't be difficult.

What a big trap that is.

Obviously, I don't think Roberto Mancini will let his players think like that. No matter who the opposition is, he will always understand the threats they pose and the dangers of complacency – that winning routine. When a team is struggling, they say losing is a habit and breaking a losing spell is difficult. Equally, when a team is winning, it's easy to get carried away and think the job is done long before it is.

A game isn't won when the second goal goes in. However, I felt like Sunday's match was, despite there being 44 minutes to play. Judging by the way the players switched off, it would seem a few of them believed that too and they've been taught the harsh lesson of what happens when you switch off.

And that could be what makes dropping our first points of the season at Craven Cottage a blessing in disguise. There are 33 more games to play and we find ourselves sitting two points off the top of the league. There are a potential 99 more points for every team in the league to add to their total and I guarantee that not one of the 20 will do it. Manchester United will drop points. Chelsea will drop points. City will drop points. Everyone will.

If you're going to drop points, it's much better to do it when there's plenty of time to recover the situation. Imagine if this situation had occurred in May and we were toe-to-toe with United for the Premier League title with two games left. And we drew that penultimate match when United won. One fixture is no time at all to make up the two point deficit.

That means it's up to City to take advantage of other teams' failings more often than it happens the other way around. It's not often that United lose, but then, these days, City don't drop points too often, either. Any involvement in the title isn't over until, mathematically, City are unable to catch the team in the lead. Or no other team is able to catch them.

Perhaps this very minor setback will put our feet back on the ground. This season could well be one of the best ever in City's history, but it's not going to be easy. Every game will be tough. If we have scored three, we should go for goal number four. If we're leading by one goal in the final stages, we should be keeping the ball and seeing out the victory. We should be keeping clean sheets. And we, as fans, can't be getting on edge and disgruntled if we haven't scored within the first fifteen minutes.

The players will have had a telling off from the management for letting a two goal, comfortable lead slip. It shouldn't have happened, but it did. And that's that; water under the bridge. It's been and gone. The time to put it right is over the next 33 games.

So let's all just calm down a little, eh?

And, for the record, after being brought back down to earth last Sunday, I think City will still be able to go unbeaten until that first Manchester derby…

Roll on defeat against Everton, then.

INTERVIEW: TONY BOOK

At the beginning of last season, it was perhaps a surprise to some that Roberto Mancini named his club captain as Carlos Tevez. There was always the 'leading by example' case that could be made because of the Argentine's work rate on the pitch, but, looking deeper into it than that, the choice was slightly baffling. Tevez doesn't speak much English and he's not the type of character to 'fire up the troops'.

However, come the end of the season, it was Carlos Tevez that was lifting the FA Cup for Manchester City. He might not have been the classic captain material, but he'd led the team to their first trophy in over three decades and became the first player to climb the steps of Wembley to lift a major cup since Tony Book.

"I had a job to make my way up the steps at Wembley to go and pick up the trophy," Book laughs, thinking back to his time wearing the armband for the Blues. "It was just an amazing feeling to be presented with the trophy and to show it to the fans, it just takes your breath away.

"And then, when you travel back the day after and get off the train at Wilmslow and get on an open deck coach and see the thousands and thousands of blue fans, with their scarves and the kids. It's just an amazing feeling."

Book took the captaincy from Johnny Crossan, when the Irishman moved to Middlesbrough in 1967. He says that he thinks he was picked to take the armband because of his experience, despite only having been a professional player for a short time.

"I came in and I think it was because of the age I was," he says. "Malcolm [Allison] had known me as captain of Bath and then I'd captained down at Plymouth as well. I think it was down to the experience I'd had, but not just as a professional footballer – as a part time professional, too.

"There were a lot of young lads who had come through the system; the likes of Glyn Pardoe, Alan Oakes, Mike Doyle, Harry Dowd. They'd all come through the ranks and age-wise I had the most experience."

And it was quite the rise to the captaincy for Book. It had looked for a long while that his career would never reach the higher levels of the game and that he was going to be a part time footballer for the extent of it. He remembers how it all began: "When I left school, I always wanted to be a footballer. I went from playing schoolboy football into youth football. I was a little inside forward in those days and I was just trying to play at a consistent level in the West Country, where I lived. I played for a little team outside of Bath called Peasedown Miners Welfare.

"But then I joined the army. And, in them days, it was good to be in the army if you were a footballer because they used to have to play six amateurs amongst five professionals in a team. So, as an amateur as I was then, I got a chance.

"And, being in the army, you do as you're told. For some reason, the Sergeant who was in charge said to me he wanted me to go and play at right-back. So that's how I started there. While I was in the army, I then went to Chelsea for trials through one or two of the other players who were professionals where I was camped out."

On leaving the army, though, Book had a letter from Chelsea explaining that they didn't believe he would be good enough to make it as a full time professional footballer. Instead, he returned to the West Country and signed for his home town team of Bath. There, he spent seven and a half years, becoming club captain and winning the Southern League title.

And then a new arrival at Bath changed Book's life completely.

"Somebody came into my life," he says, with a wry smile. It was Malcolm Allison. He'd gained some experience of coaching at West Ham and then at Cambridge University, but Bath was his very first management position. And that started a close connection between the two men.

Soon, Allison was given the chance to manage Toronto City. He took up the offer and his captain followed him to Canada. But it was a matter of weeks until he was coaching in England again, this time at Plymouth – though Book stayed in North America for three months longer, where he was voted the best full back in Canada. But later in the year, aged thirty, Book completed a £1,500 move to Plymouth, though not everything was as straightforward as it seemed.

"They [Plymouth] thought they were signing a 28 year old," he remembers. "Malcolm, in his wisdom, said to me: '*Tony, I've told the directors that you're 28. Is there anything we can do to sort that out?*'

"Luckily, very luckily, my mum had my birth certificate folded," he continues. "And right on the fold line was the 1934, so it was quite easy to say that it was '36 instead of '34."

Allison moved on after a year at Plymouth, becoming assistant manager to Joe Mercer and it wasn't long before Manchester City were knocking on Book's door. In a matter of months, he'd moved from a career in part time football to a Division One captain. And Book's experiences show how much the life of a professional footballer has changed.

"It was amazing that we came together," he says. "They [Mercer and Allison] looked at the team and decided what they needed and they went out and got the likes of Mike Summerbee, Colin Bell, Francis Lee. And with the nucleus of the young lads, it all came together and we had some great times together.

"We used to be away every two or three weeks," he continues. "They'd take us to Southport or to Blackpool after games we'd played at Maine Road. We'd go there for the weekend. We'd get together on a Saturday night and have a few drinks. Then, the next morning, we were out on the beach doing some work. We'd play hard, but we'd also work hard."

In the first year that Book was named captain, he played every game for the Blues and led them to the First Division title. But, the following season, City had started the struggle and the run of form wasn't helped by Book's achilles injury. Because of his age, the doctors decided against operating and the captain missed four months of the season, only returning in the January.

He remembers what happened: "Tommy [Booth] was a young lad who'd just got into the team at the time and he'd started doing well. He was speaking to Malcolm [Allison] one day and had said, *'I'm a little bit concerned about the way things are going.'*

"'*Don't worry,*' Malcolm had said, '*we've got Skip coming back after a long injury. We'll go out and win the FA Cup this season, when he gets back.*' And that's the type of confidence he had in people. I came back in the January and we played away at Newcastle in my first game back. We got a draw and brought them back to Maine Road, and we won that one. And we went on to win the FA Cup."

Book's achievements didn't end on the pitch, however. After Johnny Hart stepped down as City manager due to ill health, Book took charge of first team affairs until Ron Saunders was appointed. He then became number two to the new manager, before taking over as the number one just six months later.

Taking the reigns, though, wasn't easy: "I'd been playing with them and, as I said, we were a tight group of players who got on great with each other. And I had the most difficult job to do because I had to break up that side. They were getting a little bit older and I had to try and change it around and get success as well. But things had to be done and I tried to do them to the best of my ability and we didn't do too badly.

"We finished up runners up to Liverpool, losing the championship by a point. We won the League Cup. We got into Europe four times out of the five years I was manager," he says. "It was difficult, but I enjoyed it. It was a great period in my career."

Book holds one accolade, though, that can never be taken away from him. In 1976, in managing the club to the League Cup, he became the first person to win the competition as first a player and then as a manager. It's an achievement he's quite modest about.

"When I look back," he says, "I've never given it a lot of thought. This club had done so much for me in giving me a chance and it's just good that I've been able to do something to pay them back."

September 2011 Breakdown

Games (all competitions):
Won: 3   **Drawn:** 2   **Lost:** 1

Goals (all competitions):
For: 10   **Against:** 5

Progress:
Premier League: 2nd
League Cup: Qualified for Round Four
FA Cup: -
Champions League: 3rd in Group A

Premier League Table

		P	W	D	L	F	A	GD	Pts
1	Manchester United	6	5	1	0	22	5	+17	16
2	**Manchester City**	6	5	1	0	19	5	+14	16
3	Chelsea	6	4	1	1	12	7	+5	13
4	Newcastle United	6	3	3	0	7	3	+4	12
5	Liverpool	6	3	1	2	8	8	0	10

Champions League Group A Table

		P	W	D	L	F	A	GD	Pts
1	Bayern Munich	2	2	0	0	4	0	+4	6
2	Napoli	2	1	1	0	3	1	+2	4
3	**Manchester City**	2	0	1	1	1	3	-2	1
4	Villarreal	2	0	0	2	0	4	-4	0

October 2011

Blackburn Rovers 0-4 Manchester City
FA Premier League
Saturday 1 October, 2011 – 15:00 KO

City: Hart, Zabaleta, Kompany (c), Lescott, Kolarov, Y Toure, Milner, A Johnson (Savic 79), Silva, Balotelli (Dzeko 88), Aguero (Nasri 28)
Unused: Pantilimon, Clichy, Barry, de Jong
Goals: Johnson (56), Balotelli (59), Nasri (73), Savic (87)
Booked: Zabaleta
Man of the Match: James Milner

The game got off to a lively start, and Balotelli should have put the visitors into the lead with just under ten minutes played. Silva weaved his way into the box and forced a good save from Robinson. The rebound fell to the Italian on the edge, but his effort was skied over the bar, with the goal at his mercy.

Some more neat City build up on 36 minutes gave Balotelli the chance to strike, but his effort was a yard wide of the post, as Robinson flung himself at it. At the other end, Hart was down smartly to hold on to a shot from Yakubu.

City started the second half on top, as Balotelli was inches away from giving City the lead in spectacular fashion, as he tried a curling effort from inside the box, but it bounced off the post with Robinson beaten.

But then, Kolarov swung the ball into the box from a corner and it was cleared as far as Johnson. From 20 yards, he curled it towards the top corner and found the back of the net, with Robinson nowhere near it.

And, minutes later, it got better for the visitors. Yaya Toure spread the play to Kolarov on the left and some neat play between Silva and Nasri let the Frenchman get in a cross. It was Balotelli at the front post who got across his man and toe poked the ball at waist height to beat Robinson from close range.

With just under 20 minutes to play, Nasri finished the game for the visitors. From a Blackburn corner, the away side broke away with a five-on-four. Nasri found Silva inside the box and he pulled it back to the Frenchman. His shot was deflected off Lowe and into the bottom corner.

From a City corner, Stefan Savic got himself his first City goal. He rose unmarked to nod it into the net, with Robinson left flapping at thin air.

Manchester City 4-1 Aston Villa
FA Premier League
Saturday 15 October, 2011 – 15:00 KO

City: Hart, Richards (K Toure 66), Kompany (c), Lescott, Clichy, Y Toure (Silva 66), de Jong, Barry, Milner, A Johnson (Hargreaves 79), Balotelli
Unused: Pantilimon, Kolarov, Nasri, Dzeko

Goals: Balotelli (28), A Johnson (47), Kompany (53), Milner (71)
Booked: Barry
Man of the Match: James Milner

Soon City got into their stride: Balotelli had an effort that Milner backheeled onto the post, before a Barry cross was inches away from a decisive touch and Yaya Toure forced a comfortable save out of the former City keeper Given.

And, on 28 minutes, the pressure paid off. A corner wasn't well cleared by the visiting defence, leaving it to be prodded back into the danger zone by Richards. Balotelli was there and he executed a neat over-head kick to smash the ball past Given from six yards out.

As soon as the game restarted from half time, City found themselves further in front. An over the top ball from the left was missed completely by Warnock as he tried to volley clear and Johnson made the most of the opportunity to coolly roll it past the on-rushing Given and into the bottom corner.

Almost immediately, City added their third. Johnson found an unmarked Kompany with a corner kick and the Belgian made no mistake in heading home.

Richards and Given then collided from another corner and City lost the right-back to injury. While they were down to ten men, as Mancini waited to hear on the defender's fitness, a cross into the City box wasn't dealt with and broke to Warnock at the back post. He rattled the crossbar as he smashed the ball into the net, giving the away side hope of a comeback.

City, though, were in no mood to let their visitors off the hook. Milner played a beautiful cross-field pass to Johnson, who brought in Barry. The ex-Villain gave it back to Milner on the edge of the box and he swept the ball into the top corner, restoring City's three goal lead.

Manchester City 2-1 Villarreal
Champions League Group A
Tuesday 18 October, 2011 – 19:45 KO

City: Hart, Zabaleta, Kompany (c), Lescott, Kolarov, de Jong (Aguero 63), Y Toure, Nasri (Milner 81), Silva, A Johnson (Barry 39), Dzeko
Unused: Pantilimon, Savic, Richards, Clichy
Goals: Marchena (41 og), Aguero (90+3)
Booked: -
Man of the Match: Pablo Zabaleta

In a match that City really needed to win in order to give themselves a fighting chance of keeping up with Napoli and Bayern Munich in the group, the home side got off to a very bad start. De Jong gave the ball away on the edge of his own box and Rossi took it on to shoot. Hart could only parry and Cani slotted the rebound into the back of the net after just four minutes.

But just as it looked like City were going to stumble to the break a goal down, the breakthrough came for the home side. Kolarov picked up the ball on the left flank and he drove a low ball into the box for Dzeko to attack. Just before he could get a touch, Marchena tried to clear and could only find the back of his own net.

Dzeko could have made the half time oranges taste better as he went through on a one-on-one with seconds of the first period remaining, but his shot was straight at the goalkeeper and Lopez was able to push the ball to safety.

As it looked like City were going to be frustrated for another evening in the Champions League, the breakthrough came – with just ten seconds left on the clock. Milner played a great reverse ball to Zabaleta and he fired a low cross into the box. Arriving at the back post to tap it into the net was Aguero.

Manchester United 1-6 Manchester City
FA Premier League
Sunday 23 October, 2011 – 13:30 KO

City: Hart, Richards, Kompany (c), Lescott, Clichy, Barry, Y Toure, Milner (Kolarov 89), Silva, Aguero (Nasri 75), Balotelli (Dzeko 70)
Unused: Pantilimon, K Toure, Zabaleta, de Jong
Goals: Balotelli (22, 60), Aguero (69), Dzeko (89, 90+3), Silva (90+1)
Booked: Balotelli, Kompany, Dzeko, Richards
Man of the Match: James Milner

The opening pressure of the game came from the home side, as Richards gave away a free kick on the right flank, but Young's ball was cleared by the City defence. Anderson headed well wide at the back post, as Rooney chipped the ball in from the right. Richards was then on hand to produce a diving header to clear from Anderson.

But then, somewhat against the run of play, the visitors took the lead. Clichy slipped when trying to cross, but was able to win a throw in on the left. Silva found some space to receive the ball in the middle and found Milner. His return ball into the box was behind the Spanish international, but Balotelli was there to coolly slot it into the far corner.

City suddenly had wind in their sails: Clichy picked up the ball on the left and carried it right to the edge of the United box. His ball square found Aguero and he dinked it to the middle, but it was slightly too high for Balotelli's head and United got it away.

A mis-kick by Evans in the six-yard box let City off the hook from a United corner, when the home side's centre-back should have pulled the hosts level. Aguero then had the chance to shoot inside the United box, but it was well blocked by a combination of defenders.

The second half saw City win a free kick on the edge of the box and Jonny

Evans dismissed. Balotelli slipped past the centre-back and was through on goal when he was pulled down right on the line.

Lescott did well to dispossess Welbeck in the box, as United looked for their equaliser on the break. Young should have done better in the City area, as he found space to shoot. It hit Milner and then Young again and Hart was rooted to the spot, but the deflection was wide of the post.

And, as United were starting to create some chances, City hit them with a second goal. Some brilliant build up from Milner and Silva left the England international through on goal inside the six-yard box. He found Balotelli at the back post and the Italian netted his second of the game.

City soon added their third. A neat flick from Balotelli found Milner on the right wing and he nudged the ball on to Richards. The full back drove to the by-line and fired a ball into the box, for Aguero to beat de Gea with 20 minutes left.

With ten minutes to play, United pulled a goal back. A one-two between Hernandez and Fletcher resulted in the Scotsman side-footing the ball from the edge of the box into the top corner, with Hart helpless.

But City made it four with a minute of normal time to play. A Silva corner was flicked to the back post where Lescott knocked it back into the middle. Dzeko was in the right place at the right time to knee into the unguarded goal.

And it got even better for the visitors: Silva found himself clean through on goal and slotted the ball through de Gea's legs to make it five for City, virtually straight from the kick-off.

United looked to see the rest of the game out, but Silva won the ball in midfield and produced the pass of the season to find Dzeko, as he steamed past the home side's defence. Clean through on goal, he finished with his left foot to complete the humiliation and condemn United to their heaviest ever Premier League defeat at Old Trafford.

Wolverhampton Wanderers 2-5 Manchester City
League Cup Fourth Round
Wednesday 26 October, 2011 – 19:45 KO

City: Pantilimon, Zabaleta, K Toure (c), Savic, Kolarov, de Jong, Razak (Milner 85), Scapuzzi (Rekik 74), Nasri (Suarez 67), Johnson, Dzeko
Unused: Taylor, Onuoha, Bridge, Balotelli
Goals: Johnson (38), Nasri (40), Dzeko (41, 65), Scapuzzi (51)
Booked: Savic
Man of the Match: Edin Dzeko

It was a much changed City side that made the journey to Molineux and they struggled to get settled against a tough Wolves team. Kolo Toure managed to just about clear the danger, before Pantilimon had to be alert to pluck a good cross out of the air. Savic saw yellow for an edge-of-the-box block, before

Kolarov was lucky not to concede a penalty for handball.

With 18 minutes on the clock, Wolves made their pressure pay. Milijas took advantage of more poor defending from the visitors and smashed the ball past Pantilimon to give the home side the lead. It had been coming.

City looked to respond on 24 minutes, but Razak didn't have the pace to escape from Elokobi, before Scapuzzi should have hit the target with a neat turn and shot from 10 yards out. But, the travelling fans didn't have to wait long until the visitors were level. The goal came through a stunning effort from Johnson, after Dzeko had laid him off on the edge of the box.

And it immediately got better for the away side: Johnson slid a great through ball for Nasri to run onto and the Frenchman slotted it into the back of the net with a neat, low drive.

Just as the visiting supporters took their seats, they were up once more, as City made it three goals in four minutes. Scapuzzi did well to keep the ball alive inside the Wolves box before unleashing a rather tame shot at de Vries. But the home side's keeper didn't deal with it and Dzeko was on hand to smash the rebound into the net.

In the second half, Kolarov broke down the left flank and found Scapuzzi in the box. His first effort was saved by de Vries, but he couldn't hold onto it and only parried it straight back into the danger zone. The young Italian was able to get enough on it at the second attempt and force the ball over the line.

Just after the hour mark, City added their fifth of the evening. It was a very tidy passing move that started on the right flank and, after a neat one-two between Nasri and Dzeko, the Frenchman found Scapuzzi breaking into the box. There, he delivered a low cross to Dzeko; the Bosnian couldn't and didn't miss.

Almost immediately, though, Wolves responded. The ball was cut back to O'Hara inside the City box and he found the target across Pantilimon, who wasn't able to keep it out and wasn't helped by the defenders in front of him.

Manchester City 3-1 Wolverhampton Wanderers
FA Premier League
Saturday 29 October, 2011 – 15:00 KO

City: Hart, Richards, Kompany (c), Lescott, Kolarov, Y Toure, Barry, Nasri (Balotelli 71), Aguero (Savic 76), Silva, Dzeko (A Johnson 65)
Unused: Pantilimon, Zabaleta, Milner, de Jong
Goals: Dzeko (52), Kolarov (67), Johnson (90+1)
Booked: Barry, Dzeko
Sent Off: Kompany
Man of the Match: Aleksandar Kolarov

It was a difficult first half for the hosts, who began brightly as Hennessey was called into action to tip a dipping shot over the bar for a corner. Aguero blasted an effort wide of the post when Richards drove down the right flank and forced a low ball across, and he should have done better.

Dzeko wanted a penalty with 36 minutes on the clock after it seemed Stearman had wrestled him to the ground and a brilliant save from Hennessey kept the scores level soon after, as he got a Dzeko shot over the bar as the City forward broke into box.

Soon after the break, it was the hosts who got their noses in front. Hennessey, who had played well for the visitors, dwelled on the ball for too long on the edge of his box and his rushed clearance was blocked by Aguero. The ball landed kindly for Dzeko just outside the area and, faced with an open goal, he was never going to miss.

The introduction of Johnson proved to be the difference shortly after: He ran at the Wolves defence and slid the ball to Silva. His shot was pushed out by Hennessey and Kolarov was in the right place to slot home.

With 15 minutes to play, though, City found themselves a man down and facing a penalty. A shot from the edge of the box was parried by Hart and it looked like Doyle was going to be first to the rebound until he was pulled back by Kompany. The referee gave the penalty and had no choice but to show a red card to the home side's skipper. Hunt stepped up and sent Hart the wrong way.

For a while, the ten men were on the backfoot as the visitors took advantage of their extra body with some possession in the City half. Hunt fired a shot well over the bar, before Lescott was needed to put in a strong tackle on the edge of the box.

But, as the away side looked to pull themselves level, the hosts went on to win it. The ball was cleared to halfway, where Balotelli nicked it and was able to run through at goal. He checked back as the defence got into position and tried to send Toure through. He found Johnson and, from 30 yards, the substitute curled the ball into the bottom corner of the net and sealed the points for blues.

THE MAN PEOPLE LOVE TO HATE; OR THE MAN PEOPLE SIMPLY HATE?

Over the past few weeks I've been actively avoiding the Carlos Tevez affair like a man pretending to be asleep with his iPod headphones in when the ticket collector comes down the train's aisle, but I've been violently woken by the man in the hat and am now dragged kicking and screaming into the subject. After all, the incident in Munich happened almost a month ago. But, as bizarre as this sounds given how I'd written in the summer that City's success this season would depend on keeping Tevez, I just don't care.

And that's the truth: Whatever happens to Carlos Tevez now just doesn't interest me one bit.

At the time of writing, City have played nine Premier League games this season and have scored a total of 33 goals – a Premier League record and equalling the record for the English top flight (Everton managed 33 goals in nine games in 1894-95). In seven of the nine games, City have scored three or more goals. In the league, Sergio Aguero has scored nine, Edin Dzeko six and Mario Balotelli five.

In contrast, during his brief appearances for City this season, the extent of Carlos Tevez's contributions to the team have been a missed penalty. And nothing more.

I don't mean that to sound as harsh as it perhaps does, but there's much more value in talking about the strikers who are doing the business on the pitch than the one who has been found to be in breach of five contractual regulations by a disciplinary panel. And don't get me wrong, I'm happy that we have had two brilliant goalscoring seasons out of Tevez; without his goals City wouldn't have won as many matches as they have done in the last two years. But the power in the City-Tevez tug of war has shifted completely.

Last season, Tevez was the main man. So much so that, after his injury in the heavy defeat at Anfield, City fans everywhere were wondering just where on earth the goals would come from in the following games, most notably the FA Cup semi final against Manchester United. As it happened, in the time that Tevez was missing, City won four of their five games, though all of them were by one goal – United (n, 1-0), Blackburn (a, 1-0), West Ham (h, 2-1) and Tottenham (h, 1-0). While City did play well in all of those games, the chances weren't being converted; Carlos Tevez's job wasn't being fulfilled.

Now cast your mind to the morning of Sunday 23 October. The pre-derby nerves had kicked in. The starting line-up hadn't been announced, but you knew that it would involve a combination of Aguero, Dzeko and Balotelli and that there would definitely be no sign of Carlos Tevez. While we were all thinking 'I hope we win today,' not one City fan I spoke to that morning or in the days before had thought 'if only we had Tevez for this match.'

And there's the power-shift. Previously, the threat of losing Carlos Tevez's goals was huge for City. But, this season, City have lost those goals and have gone on to break a Premier League record, equalling one that's stood for 117 years. City's dependence on Tevez's goals has gone and, as such, the need for Tevez to be in the team is no longer there. Of course, it isn't the ideal situation to have lost a quality striker – despite City's lack of dependence on him, he is still a quality striker – but having been found guilty of five breaches of contract, it's hard to see how he has a future at the club.

Whatever happened on the bench that Tuesday evening in Germany has served to do only one thing: It's strengthened Roberto Mancini's position in charge at City and totally undermined Tevez's. The fans' reaction was immediately obvious at the 4-0 drubbing of Blackburn. The old adage about no player being bigger than the club had never been truer and the team have been proving all season that Carlos' decision to burn his bridges won't change what happens on the pitch. And there's no way Mancini is going to be moved: He's won the club's first trophy in over three decades, he's secured the team in their highest ever Premier League finish (ensuring Champions League group stage qualification in the process), he's got the club playing the best football seen in generations and, on top of all of that, he's just managed City in the game where they put six goals past United at Old Trafford.

In fact, I'd wager there hasn't been a City manager as secure in his job as Mancini since the Mercer-Allison era.

Something tells me, though, that this saga is far from over and that it will end in a hideous manner: Much the same way as that afternoon when you'd had too much to drink and told the mother-in-law just exactly what you thought of her. Except, unlike the mother-in-law, this situation probably isn't going to be resolved with numerous apologies and a bunch of flowers.

More likely a cut-price transfer in January and a firm good riddance from the fans of a club who formerly adored him. And, to be honest, I think the City fans have put up with a lot from Tevez: Transfer requests, constant reports of unhappiness, a general desire to leave, the whole bloody two restaurants thing... and a large proportion of fans were willing to forgive and forget, given the Argentine's attitude on the pitch which, up until the evening of Tuesday 27 September, was unquestionable.

However, couple the findings of the internal inquiry with the fact that the club's other strikers and midfielders have been banging in the goals, that goodwill and forgiveness has been spent. While Tevez was by far and away the club's leading goal threat, the baggage he carried was something we were all willing to put up with. But now Dzeko has settled, now Balotelli is writing headlines on the pitch (and off them, but, let's be honest, we all love that he's a bit of a fruitloop), and now Aguero is lighting up the Premier League, Manchester City are doing just fine without Carlos Tevez.

But, until he moves on at least, Carlos Tevez is not doing just fine without Manchester City.

October 2011 Breakdown

<u>Games (all competitions):</u>
Won: 6   **Drawn:** 0   **Lost:** 0

<u>Goals (all competitions):</u>
For: 24   **Against:** 6

<u>Progress:</u>
Premier League: 1st
League Cup: Qualified for the Quarter Final
FA Cup: -
Champions League: 3rd in Group A

<u>Premier League Table</u>

		P	W	D	L	F	A	GD	Pts
1	**Manchester City**	10	9	1	0	36	8	+28	28
2	Manchester United	10	7	2	1	27	12	+15	23
3	Newcastle United	10	6	4	0	15	7	+8	22
4	Chelsea	10	6	1	3	23	15	+8	19
5	Tottenham Hotspur	9	6	1	2	18	14	+4	19

<u>Champions League Group A Table</u>

		P	W	D	L	F	A	GD	Pts
1	Bayern Munich	3	2	1	0	5	1	+4	7
2	Napoli	3	1	2	0	4	2	+2	5
3	**Manchester City**	3	1	1	1	3	4	-1	4
4	Villarreal	3	0	0	3	1	6	-5	0

November 2011

Villarreal 0-3 Manchester City

Champions League Group A
Wednesday 2 November, 2011 – 19:45 KO

City: Hart, Zabaleta, Kompany (c), Savic, Clichy, de Jong, Y Toure (Aguero 74), Milner, Nasri, Silva (A Johnson 65), Balotelli (Kolarov 82)
Unused: Pantilimon, Lescott, Barry, Dzeko
Goals: Y Toure (30, 71), Balotelli (pen 45+2)
Booked: Balotelli
Man of the Match: David Silva

City's second away Champions League game got off to a very flat start, as both teams tried to feel the other out. Hart was alert to deal comfortably with a long range shot from Perez, before the visitors got their boots on the ball and managed to wrestle control of the game away from the hosts.

Soon, it fell to Yaya Toure to neatly gave the away side the lead. Silva won the ball back and knocked it to the Ivorian on the edge of the box. He turned and used the space well to get a shot in, finding the bottom corner of the goal.

With seconds of the half remaining, a nutmeg from Balotelli gave him the chance to break into the box and, with nothing on in the centre, he went down under a challenge from Marchena and the referee pointed to the spot. The Italian picked himself up to coolly send the keeper the wrong way.

In the second period, Balotelli tried a shot on goal from halfway into the Villarreal half, but it was over the bar. Nasri had an effort soon after, from some neat play by Silva and a powerful run from Zabaleta, but his shot was sliced the wrong side of the post. It was still all City and Hart had been a spectator.

With 20 minutes to play, City got their third goal on the break. Nasri and Clichy worked well on the left flank to keep the ball and find Balotelli breaking into the Villarreal half. He, in turn, knocked it square to Toure, who took a touch to step away from the defence and set up a one-on-one. He made no mistake and slotted into the bottom corner of the goal.

Queens Park Rangers 2-3 Manchester City

FA Premier League
Saturday 5 November, 2011 – 17:30 KO

City: Hart, Richards (c), Savic, Lescott, Kolarov, Y Toure, Milner, Barry (Balotelli 75), Silva, Aguero (A Johnson 68), Dzeko (K Toure 88)
Unused: Pantilimon, Zabaleta, Clichy, Nasri
Goals: Dzeko (43), Silva (52), Y Toure (74)
Booked: Balotelli
Man of the Match: James Milner

The game started at a furious tempo and it was the hosts who began the brighter. City's passes weren't accurate and several times in the opening stages the visitors either gifted the ball to their opponents or passed out of play.

With just over 20 minutes played, Ferdinand should have given QPR the lead. A deep free kick was nodded behind for a corner and Barton found Helguson at the back post. He headed it across goal and the centre-back was inches away from connecting, but, fortunately for the visitors, it bounced behind.

A dubious free kick was given to QPR on the right flank; it was delivered into the box by Barton and it was met by the head of Bothroyd. Hart had no chance as the header dropped into the bottom corner. It had been coming and it was the first time the Blues had gone behind in the league this season.

City were furious with the referee as QPR were allowed to break away when Aguero appeared to have been fouled on the edge of the box and it took a great double save from Hart to keep the score at 1-0. Wright-Phillips sprinted down the left and Bothroyd's shot was expertly saved, before Helguson's diving header was pushed away, with the goal gaping.

But, as the home side looked to get to the break in front, the visitors got an equaliser. Dzeko cut in from the left wing and carried the ball past Ferdinand, who went to ground. His shot found the bottom corner at Kenny's near post and City were level, largely against the run of play. With the interval approaching, City were suddenly on top and Aguero hit the post from range.

Early in the second half, the visitors got themselves in front: Milner broke away from defence and fed Dzeko on the left. He fired a low ball into the box for Silva to control, dummy and spin expertly. The hosts' back line bought the dummy and the Spaniard had time to fire past Kenny at his near post.

But QPR weren't lying down and soon got themselves an equaliser. Traore managed to get a ball into the box and it deflected for Bothroyd to head at goal at the back post. That header was on target, but it hit the back of Helguson, who was just onside in front of Hart, and the deflection beat the England keeper.

Minutes later, though, and City were back in front in a topsy turvy tie. Barry switched the play to Kolarov on the left and he delivered a great ball into the box. Yaya Toure met it and headed it straight past Kenny.

Helguson hit the bar from a header at the other end, after a deep ball in from Barton's free kick as the hosts stepped it up again. Faurlin skied an effort from the edge of the box after a spell of head tennis in City's area. Kenny came forward for a last minute corner, but Helguson headed Barton's cross wide.

Manchester City 3-1 Newcastle United
FA Premier League
Saturday 19 November, 2011 – 15:00 KO

City: Hart, Richards, Kompany (c), Lescott, Clichy, de Jong, Y Toure (Barry 85), Milner, Nasri, Aguero (A Johnson 77), Balotelli (Silva 69)

Unused: Pantilimon, Kolarov, K Toure, Dzeko
Goals: Balotelli (pen 41), Richards (43), Aguero (pen 72)
Booked: -
Man of the Match: James Milner

Newcastle started the game brightly by pressing the home side in possession of the ball. Aguero chanced his arm from outside the box with a neat turn and shot, but it was just over the bar with Krul flapping at thin air. Balotelli forced a good save from the visiting keeper, as he headed towards goal – either side of the Newcastle shot-stopper and it would have been the opener.

Hart was called into action mid-way through the first half as the visitors had their first meaningful spell of possession. A one-two on the edge of the box bypassed Kompany and Lescott, leaving Ba with the chance to shoot. He couldn't find the corner of the net and the keeper forced it behind.

And just as the game appeared to be trundling to half time goalless, a moment of City pressure earned the home side a penalty, after Yaya Toure's shot at goal was blocked by the arm of Taylor. Balotelli stepped up and he wasn't put off by Krul, sliding the ball into the bottom right corner.

Two minutes later, City had doubled their lead. A ball into the box looked to have bounced to the Newcastle defence, but Richards pressed Taylor, who didn't have as much time as he thought. The City full back blocked his clearance and volleyed the ball into the net with his left foot.

With the hour mark approaching, a good exchange between Nasri and Aguero almost put Balotelli in, but the chance was cleared from a yard in front of the line as Taylor got back to recover well. Silva then sent Richards through on goal and he was tripped, resulting in the hosts' second spot kick of the day – with Balotelli substituted, Aguero found the back of the net.

As stoppage time approached, the visitors pulled a goal back. Hart was out quickly to block an effort from Ameobi, but the rebound deflected to Gosling and, faced with an open goal from four yards out, he was never going to miss.

Napoli 2-1 Manchester City
Champions League Group A
Tuesday 22 November, 2011 – 19:45 KO

City: Hart, Zabaleta (A Johnson 86), Lescott, Kompany (c), Kolarov, de Jong (Nasri 71), Y Toure, Milner, Silva, Balotelli, Dzeko (Aguero 82)
Unused: Pantilimon, Clichy, Savic, Barry
Goals: Balotelli (33)
Booked: Balotelli, Silva, Kompany, Kolarov
Man of the Match: James Milner

The game started with the visitors doing their best to quieten the home fans by keeping the ball and frustrating the Napoli players, but it was Hamsik who had the best chance of the opening exchanges, as Yaya Toure gave the ball away in midfield. A cross to the penalty spot picked out the Napoli midfielder and, with a free header, he could only find Hart's gloves.

Hart was in action again to push an Inler effort over the bar, as the hosts looked to take advantage of their early pressure – and from the resulting corner, they did. A low ball into the near post was played in towards Cavani and flicked off Hart's knee and into the back of the net.

Silva looked for an immediate reply from the edge of the box, but the goalkeeper was right behind it as City looked very shaken. However, as City started to press, they got their equaliser. Kolarov fired a low ball into the area and it looked an easy clearance, but it was passed straight to Silva on the edge of the six-yard box. His shot was saved, but Balotelli picked up the rebound and, with an open goal, he was never going to miss the tap in.

But, just as City had been on top at the end of the first half, they found themselves behind virtually straight away at the start of the second. Cavani wasn't picked up as he broke into the box and a low ball from the left flank picked him out. With a first time, side-footed volley, he smashed the ball past Hart, restoring the hosts' lead.

A quick free kick was knocked to Silva on the right flank and he crossed early towards Dzeko. The Bosnian got up, but couldn't climb high enough to connect and Balotelli couldn't stretch to win it at the back post. At the other end, Hart pulled out a cracking save to keep City in the game after Kompany slipped and Lavezzi fired in a low drive at goal.

City were living dangerously and as they continued to press the Napoli back line, the home side broke away again quickly – resulting in Hamsik skipping past Kolarov and smashing a shot against the post. Kolarov was caught ball watching and Hart bailed him out with another fantastic save one-on-one with Hamsik.

City piled on the pressure in the closing stages, but couldn't force a leveller and they'll need something approaching a miracle to make the knock-out stages, with their fate now out of their own hands.

Liverpool 1-1 Manchester City
FA Premier League
Sunday 27 November, 2011 – 16:00 KO

City: Hart, Richards, Kompany (c), Lescott, Clichy, Y Toure, Barry, Milner, Silva (K Toure 90), Nasri (Balotelli 65), Aguero (Dzeko 82)
Unused: Pantilimon, Zabaleta, de Jong, A Johnson
Goals: Kompany (31)
Booked: Kompany, Barry, Balotelli, Milner
Sent Off: Balotelli
Man of the Match: Joe Hart

Liverpool started quickly, trying to get the visitors under pressure, but it was the away side that soon took control of the opening exchanges. A short backpass to Reina almost put Aguero clean through on goal, but the Liverpool goalkeeper was off his line sharply to slide the ball away from the City striker. There were appeals of handball from the visiting players, but the referee waved them away.

Just after the half hour mark, the visitors took the lead. A corner was well won by Silva when he had few other options available to him. The Spaniard took it and found Kompany unmarked on the edge of the six-yard box. He threw his head at it and flicked it into the top corner, via his left shoulder.

But, immediately, Liverpool were level. A huge deflection off Lescott sent an Adam shot straight past Hart and down the centre of the goal, as the England keeper was moving the other way to cover the first effort. The original shot was off target and City were on the receiving end of a big slice of bad luck.

Hart was then alert to block an Adam effort from the edge of the box, after Kuyt had gone one-on-one with Clichy and been forced wide. The breakaway was quick, but the England keeper left a foot in the right place to deflect the ball over the bar.

A brilliant ball across the box by Clichy almost found Aguero on the hour mark, but Enrique was there to concede the corner before the Argentine could connect.

City were slack at picking up the home players from a Liverpool corner and Downing was able to get an effort on goal away from the edge of the box. It bounced off the ground and might have looped in, but for a good save from Hart, pushing the ball over the bar.

Balotelli picked up a yellow card for a cynical foul on Johnson as he broke away and, not long after, he was shown a second for a clumsy challenge on Skrtel as the two jumped for the ball. There was very little in it and it was a very harsh decision against the Italian. His manager, though, wasn't impressed.

With a minute of stoppage time to play, Hart pulled off one of the saves of the season, as he first pushed away Carroll's header, before getting up quickly to block from Suarez, preserving a point for City.

Arsenal 0-1 Manchester City
League Cup Quarter Final
Tuesday 29 November, 2011 – 20:00 KO

City: Pantilimon, Zabaleta, K Toure (c), Savic, Onuoha, de Jong, Kolarov (Aguero 32), Hargreaves (Razak 80), A Johnson, Nasri, Dzeko
Unused: Taylor, Richards, Bridge, Rekik, Suarez
Goals: Aguero (83)
Booked: Hargreaves
Man of the Match: Edin Dzeko

The game got off to quite a slow start with both sides much changed and feeling each other out. Johnson had City's opening gambit with an effort cutting in from the right wing – it had Fabianski scrambling across his goal, but it was just over. Pantilimon was soon in the thick of the action, pulling off a fine save to deny Park at the back post.

It took until midway through the first half until either side was able to fashion another shooting chance and it went to the hosts. Chamberlain took on the ball outside the City box and fired in a fierce attempt towards the top corner, but Pantilimon was equal to it, producing a fine one-handed save to tip it over.

The second half quickly arrived and it was the Blues who got into their stride. Dzeko turned smartly on the edge of the box to get a shot away, but it whizzed just wide of the post. But from there, the home side took control: Pantilimon first punched away a cross, before palming a shot away and Zabaleta was needed to steal the ball away from Chamberlain as he closed in on goal.

With just under ten minutes to play – and with Arsenal appearing the more likely to score – the visitors took the lead. Dzeko won the race to the loose ball in the City half and played a delightful pass through the middle to almost set Johnson through. His touch back to Aguero was perfect and the Argentine stroked the ball into the net clinically. It was one of the best breakaway goals City have produced this campaign.

With the hosts desperate for an equaliser, Fabianski joined the attack. But it was almost detrimental to their cause as Pantilimon picked out Johnson breaking from defence and it took a good header from the Arsenal keeper to stop him finishing the game off.

JUST HAVE A LITTLE PATIENCE

"Fucking Man City?" The Glaswegian roared into my right ear. "Why the fuck are they showing fucking Man City? I came in here to watch fucking Liverpool." He was shorter than I was, but I didn't fancy myself to back me up in this situation – he'd had a few drinks, looked like he could kill me with a stare and my punch is as weak as this very metaphor. I was never going to step down from my bar stool and say "Actually, me and m'friend here wouldn't mind watching them."

I actually just shrugged sheepishly and turned away.

I was sitting in an Irish bar in the centre of Brussels, namely O'Reilly's, and had, not thirty seconds earlier, asked if the barman would switch the big screen from Chelsea vs. Liverpool to Arsenal vs. Man City. He wasn't sure, then he saw that my friend was a regular customer (one who drinks a shot of tequila every time City score, no less – you should feel for him (and his wallet) so far this season). And he switched the game.

"Tequila shot after every City goal?" He asked me.

I just stared back. I don't drink.

Given how City had been scoring this season, I could have died that night.

Mike, the barman, looked at the Glaswegian and said to him: "We've got the second half of Liverpool." I'm not quite sure how that worked, but I was willing to go with it. "You can watch it in the back room. All of the screens in the front room are linked and we're showing Man City."

I prayed he wasn't going to add "for these fellas" and point at us. I might not have been here to type this if he had. This Glaswegian had, apparently, told a Belgian man the night before to pick the window he'd like to be thrown through, after he'd made a comment about his girlfriend. I'm neither a lover, nor a fighter. I'm more of a… coward. I wasn't going to upset him.

Fortunately, though, he took his round of drinks back to his table and we got on with watching City. Then not a lot happened, really. The Carling Cup Quarter Final at The Emirates has to be City's dullest game of the season so far – though, to be honest, that probably says more about the other games this year. It's the first time City have really had to grind out a result in a game with no real threat from either side: Pantilimon was forced into a couple of good saves, while City continued to miss the target from range at the other end and it was the one moment of quality that took the tie.

And over this season so far, there have been a few calls of concern – even that feels a bit strong, granted – about the form of Joe Hart. Errors in parrying shots and his distribution with his feet being two of the biggest areas of recent criticism; the biggest examples being goals against Villarreal and Wolves (though he was bloody good at Anfield, even if his save from Carroll wasn't as good as mine at five-a-side a few weeks ago).

There were questions raised that perhaps his form had slipped because there was little in the way of competition now that Shay Given had departed for Aston Villa. Possible and I would argue that was still the case – I can't foresee a situation where Pantilimon or Taylor is selected for a league game ahead of Hart, where the Englishman is available.

What Tuesday evening did show, though, was that if Hart was unavailable for one or two matches, the Romanian would be able to deputise and not do a bad job. Ok, so there'd probably be a few hairy moments with crosses, but with a full strength back four in front of him, there would certainly be a lot of help.

It's funny that this game came after Liverpool, the first time City have really been hanging on this season. And in the space of three days, we discovered that the Blues are capable of both hanging on in there when need be and producing the one passage of play out of nothing that can win a game – if I'm being honest, I was expecting a bit more grief from the Glaswegian when the game went to extra time and he came back for his next round. But a neat move from Dzeko, Johnson and Aguero proved to be enough: From tackle to net in about fifteen seconds. Not bad, eh?

What Tuesday evening proved, though, more than ever is that we need to be patient. Okay, so our team might have been assembled from World Cup winners and Champions League finalists, while the opponents might have been playing in the Championship last season, but that doesn't mean that the goals will just start flowing in. If City haven't scored within the first eight minutes, every misplaced pass at the Etihad is greeted with a collective groan.

One guy behind me says things like "I can see us not scoring today now," and it makes me wonder – there are over 80 minutes left and there's been a couple of sloppy mistakes. These things happen. City are unbeaten at home in over 11 months (or 25 matches in all competitions, to put it another way).

Just have patience. The good stuff is coming, but that doesn't mean we don't have to work for it. As a wise man once said: "Patience. For the Jedi it is time to eat as well."

We'd do well to remember that.

Not sure where I'm going there.

November 2011 Breakdown

Games (all competitions):
Won: 4   **Drawn:** 1   **Lost:** 1

Goals (all competitions):
For: 12   **Against:** 6

Progress:
Premier League: 1st
League Cup: Qualified for the Semi Final
FA Cup: -
Champions League: 3rd in Group A

Premier League Table

		P	W	D	L	F	A	GD	Pts
1	**Manchester City**	13	11	2	0	43	12	+31	35
2	Manchester United	13	9	3	1	30	13	+17	30
3	Tottenham Hotspur	12	9	1	2	26	16	+10	28
4	Newcastle United	13	7	5	1	19	12	+7	26
5	Chelsea	13	8	1	4	28	17	+11	25

Champions League Group A Table

		P	W	D	L	F	A	GD	Pts
1	Bayern Munich	5	4	1	0	11	4	+7	13
2	Napoli	5	2	2	1	8	6	+2	8
3	**Manchester City**	5	2	1	2	7	6	-1	7
4	Villarreal	5	0	0	5	2	12	-10	0

December 2011

Manchester City 5-1 Norwich City

FA Premier League

Saturday 3 December, 2011 – 15:00 KO

City: Hart, Richards, Kompany (c), K Toure, Clichy, Y Toure, Barry, Silva, Aguero (Balotelli 82), Nasri (A Johnson 70), Dzeko (de Jong 82)
Unused: Pantilimon, Lescott, Savic, Milner
Goals: Aguero (32), Nasri (52), Y Toure (68), Balotelli (88), A Johnson (90+1)
Booked: -
Man of the Match: Yaya Toure

City started the game the brighter of the two teams and, if truth be told, there was only ever one way it was going to finish once the hosts had the initiative. Soon enough, Aguero found himself on the scoresheet. Richards broke into the area down the right flank and cut the ball back to the Argentine on the edge of the six-yard box. He looked to be crowded out as he tried to turn, but, from nowhere, he found the gap between three defenders and goalkeeper and prodded the ball into the bottom corner.

Within seconds, he should have had his second goal of the day, as a cut back fell to him at the back post. With the goalkeeper scrambling to get back, it seemed a simple finish, but he – somehow – blazed the ball over the bar. As much as City had dominated the half, they went in just one goal ahead.

But the second half saw the hosts quickly double their lead, with a stroke of good fortune. Nasri curled a free kick into the box, looking for the head of either Dzeko or Yaya Toure. None of the City attackers touched the ball and the defence missed it too, leaving Ruddy to fumble it into the back of the net.

Aguero and Barry both went close shortly after, before Yaya Toure grabbed himself his fourth goal in his last six games. He picked the ball up from Silva on the edge of the box and, after getting it onto his right foot, he curled a shot into the bottom corner, leaving Ruddy with no chance.

With ten minutes to play, though, the visitors gave themselves a glimmer of hope: The City defence switched off at a short corner and it was swung in to Morison at the back post. There, he got up to head the ball into the bottom corner of the goal.

But City restored their three goal advantage with two minutes to play: Yaya Toure and Johnson combined well, to slot the ball in for Balotelli. Ruddy saved his initial shot, but there was nothing the keeper could do to stop the Italian audaciously shouldering the ball into the empty net from half a yard out.

And, in stoppage time, City made it five. A corner was half-cleared by the Norwich defence and good pressure from de Jong and Kompany left the Belgian with the ball on the edge of the box. He looked up and found Johnson free on the right flank. The substitute jinked to his left and just passed the ball into the bottom corner, making it look easy.

Manchester City 2-0 Bayern Munich

Champions League Group A
Wednesday 7 December, 2011 – 19:45 KO

City: Hart, Savic, Lescott, Kompany (c), Clichy, Barry, Y Toure (Balotelli 81), Nasri, Silva (A Johnson 85), Aguero, Dzeko (de Jong 78)
Unused: Pantilimon, K Toure, Zabaleta, Milner
Goals: Silva (36), Y Toure (52)
Booked: -
Man of the Match: Gareth Barry

City knew that only a win would do if they were to stand any chance of making the knock-out stages of the Champions League and, seeing the visitors rest a few players, the hosts set out to attack from the off. Aguero should have opened the scoring with just eight minutes on the clock as Nasri found him unmarked in the box, but his header was over the bar and into the fans.

Lescott had the ball in the Bayern net on 16 minutes, but it was eventually ruled out by the referee for a foul on the goalkeeper. The assistant on the line didn't see it, the assistant behind the goal didn't see it, but the referee thought long and hard before disallowing the defender's header from Nasri's free kick.

Alaba skied the ball over the bar when faced with Hart, before the home side took the lead. A ball from deep from Barry was cutely flicked to Silva by Dzeko. The Spaniard took the ball on his chest and volleyed it from the edge of the box, finding the bottom corner with force.

It was all City: Barry lifted an effort over the bar when there were shouts of handball, Aguero took on and beat the whole Bayern defence to shoot past Butt – though ex-City defender Boateng got back to clear from behind his goalkeeper – and Aguero curled an effort just wide of the post from inside the box.

The first action of the second half saw the hosts double their advantage. Yaya Toure nipped in ahead of the Bayern defence to a Dzeko through ball and he poked the shot under Butt. It was neat, flowing football, but it was dulled by the news the Napoli had taken the lead in Spain, putting City out as it stood.

Nevertheless, the home side continued to press and look for more goals. Nasri smashed a shot just wide of the post and Barry volleyed an effort from the edge of the box at Butt, who got two strong hands on it to push it away.

News from the other game, though, wasn't good. The opening draw with the Italians and the defeat in Naples were the killers, but the City fans got a performance to be proud of in going out of the competition.

Chelsea 2-1 Manchester City

FA Premier League
Monday 12 December, 2011 – 20:00 KO

City: Hart, Zabaleta, Kompany (c), Lescott (Dzeko 85), Clichy, Milner, Y Toure, Barry, Silva (de Jong 75), Aguero (K Toure 64), Balotelli
Unused: Pantilimon, Savic, Nasri, A Johnson
Goals: Balotelli (2)
Booked: Kompany, Clichy
Sent Off: Clichy
Man of the Match: Gareth Barry

City got off to a great start at Stamford Bridge, as Aguero held the ball well on the halfway line under three Chelsea challenges and slid it through to Balotelli. With just 90 seconds on the clock, he skipped away from the sliding tackle from Ivanovic and rounded Cech, leaving him the simple task of rolling the ball into the empty net.

The first spell of Chelsea pressure resulted in a deflected effort from the edge of the box from Meireles but, from the resulting corner, City broke away and should have doubled their lead. Aguero had the chance to shoot in the box on his left foot and, uncharacteristically, put the ball wide, as Cech was closing him down. City were denied a clear penalty as Silva was felled in the box by Bosingwa after a great flowing move put the Spaniard in.

With just over ten minutes to go until the half, the home side found an equaliser. Sturridge burst down the right side of the box and pulled the ball back to the penalty spot where Meireles was ghosting in. He finished first time, giving Hart no chance and dragging Chelsea level when it hadn't looked likely.

With the hour mark approaching, Clichy dived in on Ramires as he tried to break towards the City box and he got none of the ball. Mark Clattenburg had no option but to show him a yellow card and it was his second of the evening, putting the visitors down to ten men and on the backfoot.

Despite City's stout defending, with nine minutes to play, a Sturridge shot struck Lescott's arm and the referee pointed to the spot. It was very harsh, though Lampard didn't care, as he stepped up and scored.

It was City's first defeat in the league since May.

Manchester City 1-0 Arsenal
FA Premier League
Sunday 18 December, 2011- 16:10 KO

City: Hart, Zabaleta, K Toure, Kompany (c), Richards, Y Toure (de Jong 86), Barry, Nasri (Dzeko 86), Silva, Balotelli (Milner 73), Aguero
Unused: Pantilimon, Savic, Lescott, A Johnson
Goals: Silva (53)
Booked: Barry, Aguero
Man of the Match: Gareth Barry

It was a slow start from both sides, who began by feeling each other out. Aguero could have had the hosts in front, before Gervinho had a similar chance for the visitors, but neither opportunity was taken.

Midway through the first half, City could have taken the lead through Balotelli – who'd scored on his last eight starts. The ball broke to him in the box and he took a neat touch to keep it away from the Arsenal defence, before he turned and smashed a shot at goal. But, unfortunately for the home fans, Szczesny was off his line quickly to block and Silva couldn't reach the rebound.

Though the home fans didn't have to wait for long for their side to take the lead in the second half. With just eight minutes played after the restart, Balotelli found space for a shot inside the Arsenal box and Szczesny could only parry. Aguero got there first and prodded the ball on with his head, where Silva was free to slam it into the net from all of two yards out.

Arsenal had the ball in the net almost straight away, but the linesman's flag put a quick end to the visitors' celebrations. Suddenly, the game was very open, as Aguero hit the post, Nasri almost put the ball on a plate for Balotelli with an open goal, while Hart was putting in one of his best performances for City at the other end, preserving the lead.

With 67 minutes on the clock, Zabaleta could have opened his tally for the season with a rasping effort. Szczesny bowled the ball out and the City full back nipped in to steal possession. He carried it to the edge of the box and unleashed a fierce drive on his left foot; the keeper was a spectator as the ball crashed off the post and back out into open play.

In stoppage time, City were thankful to their goalkeeper once again for preserving the lead, as the ball fell to Vermaelen on the edge of the box. He took a touch and set a piledriver towards the home side's net – and it was going in, until Hart got both hands in the way, diverting it over the bar.

Manchester City 3-0 Stoke City
FA Premier League
Wednesday 21 December, 2011 – 19:45 KO

City: Hart, Richards (Savic 59), Lescott, Kompany (c), Clichy, Y Toure, Barry (Milner 84), Nasri, Silva (Balotelli 69), A Johnson, Aguero
Unused: Pantilimon, K Toure, Zabaleta, de Jong
Goals: Aguero (30, 54), A Johnson (36)
Booked: Richards, A Johnson
Man of the Match: Sergio Aguero

City started their final home match of 2011 in full control of the ball and, with the quarter of the hour mark approaching, a moment of inspiration almost gave the Blues the lead. Johnson received the ball on the right flank and cut inside on the edge of the box to unleash a shot. It deflected off the defender as he was closed down and it left Sorensen stranded, but he watched with relief as the ball bounced back off the crossbar.

Nasri smashed a half-volley wide of the far post, as City continued to look for the breakthrough, before the goal finally came through this season's leading scorer. Yaya Toure pulled the ball across the face of the goal and Kompany touched it towards the back post in an attempt to slot it home. It wasn't going in, but it didn't matter, as Aguero re-adjusted to get the final touch over the line, with the visitors appealing for offside.

And, soon after, City doubled their lead. Silva wanted a penalty for a foul by Whitehead in the area, as the Stoke defender put a lot of pressure on the Spaniard to win the ball. The referee waved away the appeals, but Johnson picked up the clearance, knocked it out of his feet, before finding the net from well outside the box.

The first action of the second half saw City add their third goal to their evening's tally. Nasri received the ball in the area and got his head up to smash a low cross towards Aguero and he made no mistake in slotting the ball into the back of the net.

City's three goal cushion meant the remainder of the game was like a training session. The home side took all three points, meaning that only Fulham and Napoli avoided defeat at Eastlands in the whole of the calendar year and that City will sit on top of the Premier League on Christmas Day.

West Bromwich Albion 0-0 Manchester City
FA Premier League
Monday 26 December, 2011 – 15:00 KO

City: Hart, Zabaleta, K Toure, Kompany (c), Clichy, Y Toure, Milner (Dzeko 83), Silva, Nasri (Barry 59), Balotelli, Aguero (A Johnson 75)
Unused: Pantilimon, Savic, Lescott, de Jong
Goals: -
Booked: Yaya Toure
Man of the Match: Mario Balotelli

Early possession in this season's Boxing Day fixture was dominated by the visitors, but it was the home side who had the first chance: Odemwingie found Brunt on the edge of the box and he turned neatly to shoot first time. Hart had it covered, but it flashed just wide of the post and gave City an early scare.

A deflected Balotelli free kick almost found the net, with Foster rooted to his line, but the ball trickled wide of the post. A succession of corners for the visitors then finished with Yaya Toure being taken by surprise by the ball reaching him at the near post and he couldn't convert. Instead, it struck him and bounced behind.

The Italian did have the ball in the net on 34 minutes, but the linesman's flag was up for offside. Silva had a shot from the edge of the box and it looped up off the defender, landing to Balotelli, who volleyed home neatly. But it wouldn't count, Aguero flagged off as he challenged the initial ball in.

The early second half possession was West Brom's, but it was Balotelli who had a go out of the blue from the edge of the box. It beat Foster, but didn't beat the bar, clipping the frame of the goal and ending up in the fans.

On 72 minutes, West Brom could have taken the lead. A ball into the box was cleared as far as Thomas who hit the shot first time and it smashed into the foot of the post and bounced clear. Hart threw himself at it, but he wouldn't have had it covered had it been on target. It was a let off for the visitors, who were struggling to create any clear cut chances of their own.

The home side by no means parked the bus, but City just couldn't break them down – City will be top of the league still, but United's big victory over Wigan leaves them level and will have dented the advantage of City's goal difference.

'TIS THE SEASON TO BE JOLLY

Cast your minds back 369 days to Monday 20 December, 2010. It was cold, bitterly cold, and a covering of snow had ground the country to a halt. MPs were heading home from Whitehall, claiming their Christmas presents on expenses and leaving behind them a scattering of laptops, memory sticks and private documents, containing the personal details of millions of people. And, most crucially, Premier League games had fallen foul of the weather left, right and centre – in fact, if my memory serves me correctly, it was only Manchester City vs. Everton of that round of fixtures that was played.

And there was one vital reason why that was: City could be top of the Premier League on Christmas Day, providing they took all three points from their Merseyside opponents.

Of course, plenty will tell you that the game went ahead because everybody agreed that the conditions for the players were fine and that travelling fans and those around the stadium would be safe. While true, it never seemed in any doubt – City had longer than every other team that weekend, being the Monday evening kick-off, to make sure the conditions were good and they'd done their best to raid the gritting depots of the north west to ensure that the club had the chance of going top on Christmas Day. It was like walking over a gravel driveway to get to your seat that night.

Having pulled out all the stops, City did as they do best and just didn't turn up. Everton strolled to a two goal lead in the first twenty minutes. The most exciting thing City had done in the game until that point was win a corner. It didn't look good and, even when the hosts pulled a goal back, some good saves from both Everton goalkeepers Tim Howard and Phil Neville stopped the Blues getting an unlikely victory.

In temperatures that there should be laws against, the Blues fans trudged home, facing Christmas off the top of the Premier League. Having gotten their hopes up, they should have known better – because that's what City do: They build you up and then let you down. Hypothermia Monday, as it's become known, though, was the last time City have done that to the fans and, in the turn of the new year, the Citizens changed their ways.

They won the FA Cup. They finished in third position, enough to qualify for the Champions League group stages. They won at Old Trafford by a five goal margin. Tottenham were humiliated at the Lane. The year finished with only two teams in all competitions leaving Eastlands with something other than nothing: Fulham and Napoli escaped with draws. Every other team that visited has lost: Blackpool, Wolves, Leicester, West Brom, Notts County, Aris, Aston Villa, Wigan, Reading, Dynamo Kiev, Sunderland, West Ham, Tottenham, Stoke, Swansea, Wigan again, Birmingham, Everton, Aston Villa again, Villarreal, Wolves again, Newcastle, Norwich, Bayern Munich, Arsenal and Stoke again. Out of 28 matches at Eastlands in 2011, City won 26 and drew two, scoring 73 and conceding a mere 13.

Oh, and the club is top of the Premier League at Christmas.

This mightn't sound very significant; City were one win away from the same achievement last season. And, while it might be 82 years since City last sat top of the pile the night that Father Christmas does his rounds and the leaders on 25 December tend not to go on to win the league, there is something worth considering. Last season, City had played two games more and just missed out. This season, City are on equal games.

It's also worth pointing out that it's only three years ago that City spent Christmas in the relegation zone, after a defeat at West Brom. How the times have changed, indeed.

There were rumblings last season of a title challenge, whether it be from fans or sections of the media, especially around the turn of the new year. It was all because City flirted with top spot about that time, but it turned out to be the same relationship you have with the pretty girl in the office: Your eyes meet occasionally and your imagination takes over about how it could all happen, but it doesn't because she's seeing someone else – and it turns out to be the guy that you absolutely hate.

That challenge was always played down by Roberto Mancini and his players, rightly so. City were up there by virtue of the fact they had played two more games than anybody else and I think a lot of people, myself included, kidded ourselves about how close we actually were. In the end, we were nine points off the title; sadly, a more realistic finale to the season when everybody caught up.

This campaign, however, City fans don't have anything to put to the back of their minds this festive season. On level games and in pole position, it's City's to lose, unlike the year before. And, if the 17 games so far are anything to go by, if anybody does finish above the Blues they'll probably win the league. And they'll probably deserve to, as well, given City have demolished most of what's been put in front of them.

It goes without saying that City have performed better this season than they have previously, mainly because they've performed better than nearly every team in the top division ever – you'll have to excuse my vagueness in the opening to this paragraph, my 1890s history isn't too clever – and club and league records have been falling all over the place. And, to give you an idea of the improvement, at this stage last season, City had 32 points. United, the eventual champions, had 37. This year, City have 44.

And every team that's had 40 or more points after 16 games has gone on to win the Premier League. How's about that for an omen?

This season, so far, City have 53 Premier League goals, 15 more than United had at this stage last season. It took until the 2-1 victory over West Ham in May last time out for City to reach this milestone; that was the 34th game of the campaign. City have scored three or more in 12 league games so far; in the whole of the last season, City did that 10 times.

As City fans, we've never had it so good.

'Tis the season to be jolly, alright. Fingers crossed that carries on until May.

December 2011 Breakdown

Games (all competitions):
Won: 4   **Drawn:** 1   **Lost:** 1

Goals (all competitions):
For: 12   **Against:** 3

Progress:
Premier League: 1st
League Cup: Qualified for the Semi Final
FA Cup: -
Champions League: 3rd in Group A, in Europa League Round of 32

Premier League Table

		P	W	D	L	F	A	GD	Pts
1	**Manchester City**	**18**	**14**	**3**	**1**	**53**	**15**	**+38**	**45**
2	Manchester United	19	14	3	2	49	17	+32	45
3	Tottenham Hotspur	18	12	3	3	35	20	+15	39
4	Arsenal	19	11	3	5	35	26	+9	36
5	Chelsea	19	10	4	5	37	24	+13	34

Champions League Group A Table

		P	W	D	L	F	A	GD	Pts
1	Bayern Munich	6	4	1	1	11	6	+5	13
2	Napoli	6	3	2	1	10	6	+4	11
3	**Manchester City**	**6**	**3**	**1**	**2**	**9**	**6**	**+3**	**10**
4	Villarreal	6	0	0	6	2	14	-12	0

January 2012

Sunderland 1-0 Manchester City
FA Premier League
Sunday 1 January, 2012 – 15:00 KO

City: Hart, Zabaleta, Kompany (c), Lescott, Kolarov (Richards 67), de Jong (Aguero 45), Barry, Y Toure, A Johnson, Nasri (Silva 55), Dzeko
Unused: Pantilimon, Clichy, Savic, Milner
Goals: -
Booked: de Jong
Man of the Match: Adam Johnson

A bursting run from Yaya Toure in the opening minute bought City their first corner, but that set Sunderland on the attack early on. Sessegnon sent Bendtner through on goal from mid-way into the City half. He tried to go around Hart, who was out quickly to narrow the angle, and the England keeper blocked well, with Kolarov able to complete the clearance.

A City corner was only half-cleared by the Sunderland defence and Zabaleta was able to find Johnson on the right flank. He worked his way into the box and fizzed a low cross towards Dzeko. His effort was blocked by Mignolet, before Johnson found Nasri free in the area again. The Frenchman's low drive beat the goalkeeper, but it was cleared off the line.

From a corner, the ball fell to Dzeko in the middle and he lashed his volley at goal, but it skimmed the top of the bar. A cross from Johnson caused Mignolet problems, but there was nobody to capitalise on his spill.

With 63 minutes played, Sunderland should have been in front. A flick on from a throw in fell to Sessegnon and Kompany couldn't steal the ball away. He ran through on Hart, who spread himself, and the Sunderland man tried a shot with the outside of his foot. It beat the City keeper, but also beat the post.

As the game headed towards stoppage time, City could have won it: Silva picked up the ball on the edge of the box and shot, but it was pushed away by Mignolet. It fell straight to Richards, whose diving header hit the bar and Dzeko couldn't readjust to get a touch on the rebound.

But as the clock ticked to final second of the game, Sunderland stole the points. Ji broke through the back line and should have been flagged offside as he went through on a one-on-one with Hart. He wasn't and he took it around the goalkeeper and slotted the ball into the back of the net. It was a bad call from the linesman, but City should have put one of their earlier chances away.

Manchester City 3-0 Liverpool
FA Premier League
Tuesday 3 January, 2012 – 20:00 KO

City: Hart, Richards, K Toure, Kompany (c), Clichy, Barry, Y Toure, Milner, Silva (Lescott 76), Aguero (A Johnson 73), Dzeko
Unused: Pantilimon, Zabaleta, Kolarov, Savic, de Jong
Goals: Aguero (11), Y Toure (33), Milner (pen 75)
Booked: Barry
Sent Off: Barry
Man of the Match: Vincent Kompany

The game began tentatively, with both sides feeling each other out in the rain at the Etihad Stadium. It was the visitors who had the first chance to take the lead, as Downing found himself through on goal with just Hart to beat. The England keeper was off his line quickly and made a brilliant block, to keep the scores level – and it turned out to be a very crucial save. Minutes later, at the other end, Aguero took a pot-shot from the edge of the box and Reina made a hash of it, letting it straight though him and into the back of the net.

A minute and a half later, Dzeko, with no support, took a shot on from the edge of the box; it took a huge deflection and spiralled just wide of the post, with the visiting goalkeeper having dived the other way, reacting to the first effort.

Adam was felled on the edge of the City box by Kolo Toure, as he looked to beat the City defender, but the resulting free kick was smashed into the wall. Reina then made up for his earlier mistake by denying Kompany City's second, pushing the centre-back's header over the bar from a corner. But he couldn't keep out Yaya Toure's effort from the next flag kick, as the midfielder nodded the ball past him and into the back of the net.

The second half began with the visitors pressing the home side's goal. But then, just as City were on the backfoot, Barry gave Agger a nudge as the defender stepped around him. They were side to side and the Liverpool defender went down, and Barry earned a second yellow card with just under 20 minutes to play.

If that dampened the City spirits, though, the fans were lifted almost immediately. Yaya Toure broke from his own half and worked his way into the box. There, he went down as Skrtel tackled and the referee pointed to the spot. Milner stepped up, finding the top corner.

Manchester City 2-3 Manchester United
FA Cup Third Round
Sunday 8 January, 2012 – 13:00 KO

City: Pantilimon, Richards, Kompany (c), Lescott, Kolarov, de Jong, Milner, Nasri (Hargreaves 82), Silva (Savic 45), A Johnson (Zabaleta 45), Aguero
Unused: Hart, Clichy, Razak, Suarez
Goals: Kolarov (48), Aguero (64)
Booked: -

Sent Off: Kompany
Man of the Match: James Milner

It was a repeat of last year's FA Cup Semi Final as the third Manchester derby of the season got underway in the rain at the Etihad Stadium. And it was the hosts who looked in full control from the kick-off, as United struggled to get out of their own half. City, though, couldn't fashion a good shooting chance and it was the visitors who took the lead, completely against the run of play: Rooney nodded the ball into the net after a poor kick from Pantilimon.

It got worse for City almost immediately. Kompany slid in to dispossess Nani midway into his own half; he did go in with two feet, but it was more of a scissor motion and a side-footed tackle and, after what appeared to be no small encouragement from Rooney, the referee decided it was worthy of a red card. Nani – the man challenged – seemed happy to play on and Chris Foy appeared to be playing on, but suddenly changed his mind.

Aguero almost equalised with a curling effort straight away, but Lindegaard got across well to push the ball behind for a corner. But that's as good as it got for the Blues fans, as Wellbeck swivelled and shot in the box, finding the bottom corner, after City couldn't get the ball clear.

A rash tackle from Kolarov inside his own area then seemed to end the game: Rooney stepped up to take the resulting penalty and tried for the bottom right corner. Typical of City's luck so far, Pantilimon got across to block, but he was very unlucky that his save bounced straight back to the England centre-forward, who headed into the empty net. It looked all over at half time.

Step forward Roberto Mancini. Two half time changes and a switch in tactics helped City fight their way back into the game, aided by the hosts pulling a goal back virtually from kick-off. Evra brought down Richards on the edge of the box on the right side and Kolarov stepped up to power the free kick into the corner of the net. It was just what City needed.

That changed the atmosphere. With 63 minutes played, Milner nicked a short pass from Scholes to Evra and crossed low for Aguero. The Argentine's first shot was saved, but he reacted first to tap into the open goal. Game on.

With seconds to play, the home side won a corner and piled everybody – including the goalkeeper Pantilimon – into the box. Kolarov's kick found the keeper's head, but he couldn't direct it towards the net and the final whistle blew. City came out of the game with their heads held high and with a lot of pride, but, ultimately, it was United in the fourth round draw.

Manchester City 0-1 Liverpool
League Cup Semi Final, First Leg
Wednesday 11 January, 2012, 19.45 KO

City: Hart, Richards (c), Savic, Lescott, Clichy, de Jong (Kolarov 72), Barry,

Milner, A Johnson (Dzeko 66), Balotelli (Nasri 39), Aguero
Unused: Pantilimon, Zabaleta, Onuoha, Hargreaves
Goals: -
Booked: Nasri
Man of the Match: Micah Richards

It was the visitors who were the quicker out of the blocks. Hart was required to pull off a good save from a one-on-one with Carroll, as the striker turned Savic and closed in on goal. The City keeper then pushed Gerrard's effort from the edge of the box away for a corner, before he got down brilliantly, reacting to a deflection from a shot just inside the box.

With just over ten minutes played, though, a corner for the visitors earned them a penalty. The header was missed in front of Agger and he took a touch on his chest, before being brought down by Savic. There were no questions and the referee pointed to the spot; Gerrard dispatched the kick into the bottom corner.

On the stroke of half time, City should have been level: Richards did well to power past Johnson and get into the box. He pulled the ball back for Milner, arriving on the penalty spot, but the midfielder got his shot all wrong and skied it well wide and well over the bar.

The second half got into a pattern pretty quickly: City struggling to keep the ball and break down the Liverpool defence and the visitors happy to hold on to their advantage under no real threat from the hosts. Aguero intercepted Kelly's short backpass, but Reina did enough to close the striker down.

To round of the home side's frustrations, a two-footed tackle from Johnson on Lescott – worse than Kompany's on Nani at the weekend – went totally unpunished. It didn't merit a red card, but having seen the City skipper sent off for a lesser offence and then having seen the appeal dismissed, it left a bitter taste in the mouths of the Blues in the stands.

City have it all to do at Anfield.

Wigan Athletic 0-1 Manchester City
FA Premier League
Monday 16 January, 2012 – 20:00 KO

City: Hart, Zabaleta (c), Savic, Lescott, Clichy, Milner, Barry, Nasri (de Jong 74), Silva (Onuoha 81), Dzeko, Aguero (A Johnson 90)
Unused: Pantilimon, Kolarov, Rekik, Hargreaves
Goals: Dzeko (22)
Booked: Zabaleta, de Jong, Milner
Man of the Match: Sergio Aguero

The early pressure of the game was on the Wigan goal, as Dzeko looked to get free inside the box in the opening ten seconds, but the defence were able to clear. The hosts, though, hit back immediately, as Lescott missed the ball at the near post and Clichy flicked it away.

On 21 minutes, Dzeko earned City a free kick on the left flank as Alcaraz brought him down. Silva took it and found the big centre-forward unmarked in the box. He planted his header into the corner of the net. It was his first City goal since the start of November.

A City breakaway saw Silva and Aguero have a two-on-two in the Wigan half and the Spaniard did enough to find the Argentine on the edge of the box. He found room for the shot and forced Al Habsi into a good save, before Savic was needed to stop the hosts getting clean through on Hart's goal down the right.

With 20 minutes to play, Hart pulled off a great save to spare Milner's blushes after he'd given the ball away in midfield. It was knocked through for a one-on-one and the City stopper got his foot to the shot from McCarthy and Clichy was able to hook the rebound away to safety.

A blatant handball from Figueroa to deny Aguero a free run on goal from the halfway line had the City fans calling for a late red card, but the referee decided it was only worth a yellow, before Hart needed to collect it to stop the confusion in the City box as a high ball in was only half cleared.

Manchester City 3-2 Tottenham Hotspur
FA Premier League
Sunday 22 January, 2012 – 13:30 KO

City: Hart, Richards (c), Savic, Lescott, Clichy, Milner, Barry, Silva, Nasri, Aguero, Dzeko (Balotelli 67)
Unused: Pantilimon, Zabaleta, Kolarov, Onuoha, de Jong, A Johnson
Goals: Nasri (56), Lescott (59), Balotelli (pen 90+5)
Booked: Clichy, Balotelli
Man of the Match: David Silva

It was a nervy opening from both sides, who spent the first few minutes probing each other, looking for the first chance of the game. With 25 minutes on the clock, City had livened up. Aguero fashioned a shooting chance for Silva, but the Spaniard's shot was a yard wide of the post. Richards broke down the line and got the ball across to Aguero shortly after, but the Argentine's shot was well saved by Friedel, after he'd skipped inside the challenge.

City stepped up their game in the second half. Richards' cross was blocked by Assou-Ekotto's elbow in the area, but it would have been a very harsh penalty. Milner then pulled out a cracking tackle to deny Bale a free run on goal; it was timed perfectly to nick the ball away from the Welshman inside the box.

With the hour mark approaching, Silva found Nasri with a brilliant through ball. The Frenchman was through on goal and, with the veteran Spurs keeper bearing down on him, the former Arsenal man smashed the ball past Friedel and into the back of the net. City's pressure had earned them the lead.

And it got better: From a right wing corner, the ball fell to Lescott at the back post and, from no more than half a yard out, the centre-back scrambled it into the back of the net. It wasn't the prettiest of goals, but it put the hosts two up in three minutes.

Within a minute, though, the visitors pulled one back. A ball over the top wasn't cut out by Savic and he could only flick the ball on. Defoe broke away from the line of defence and skipped around the onrushing Hart, leaving himself with an easy finish into the open goal. It handed the initiative to the away side.

It didn't take long for Tottenham to seize that initiative, either. Bale picked up the ball from 20 yards out after City had struggled to clear their lines. His stunning effort found the top corner and Hart's best efforts couldn't keep it out. In the space of ten minutes, City had gone two goals in front and Tottenham had pulled it back.

With 20 minutes of the match to play, the game became very stretched. Spurs survived a string of City corners, before they broke away at pace, looking to get themselves in front. Balotelli was very lucky to escape a red card for a kick out at Parker after the Italian's shot was charged down.

As the game entered stoppage time, Tottenham should have stolen the points. A mistake by Savic in the middle of the pitch gifted the ball to Bale, who broke on Lescott with a two-on-one. The Welshman sprinted down the line and crossed for Defoe at the back post, who was unmarked and, from a yard out, he couldn't stretch enough and somehow put the ball wide with the goal gaping.

And it turned out to be costly. With under a minute of added time to play, a Clichy clearance bounced nicely for Balotelli to run on to into the box. There, a challenge from King brought his run to an abrupt half and the referee pointed to the spot. Balotelli stepped up and won the game for City.

Liverpool 2-2 Manchester City
League Cup Semi Final, Second Leg
Wednesday 25 January, 2012 – 19:45 KO

City: Hart, Richards (c), Lescott, Savic (Aguero 45), Kolarov, Zabaleta, de Jong (A Johnson 78), Barry, Nasri, Silva, Dzeko
Unused: Pantilimon, Clichy, Hargreaves, Milner, Rekik
Goals: de Jong (31), Dzeko (67)
Booked: Kolarov
Man of the Match: Joe Hart

It wasn't a great start from the visitors, who gifted the hosts a chance to get themselves further into the lead with just six minutes played. Enrique, though, could only find Hart, who saved well with his feet to keep the scores level on the night. It was all Liverpool in the opening stages, and every time City got the ball clear it came straight back at them.

However, it got better for the visitors and, against the run of play, they pulled the aggregate score level and took the lead on the night. De Jong picked the ball up from 25 yards out and, despite slipping, he managed to curl it around Reina and find the corner of the net. Liverpool's away goal had been cancelled out from the most unlikely of sources.

But the lead didn't last long. Richards was adjudged to have handled a fierce drive inside the penalty area and the referee pointed to the spot. It was a very harsh decision – Richards blocked with his foot before the ball ricocheted up onto his arm and it was struck from three yards in front of him – but the referee waved away the protests and Gerrard slotted the spot kick home.

Kolarov picked up a yellow card after he was on the receiving end of a late challenge from Henderson, before Bellamy once again got in behind Lescott, but Richards recovered to block the City old boy's cross. Though, after Silva had wasted a free kick on the right flank, City re-took the lead, again against the run of play – Kolarov smashed a cross low and Dzeko got in at the back post to knock the ball home from inside the six-yard box.

But, just seven minutes later, Liverpool were back level once more. A poor clearance from Lescott put the hosts back on the attack and a quick one-two between Bellamy and Johnson allowed the former City man to slide the ball past Hart, giving the England keeper no chance.

City were once again behind on aggregate.

A last gasp chance from City wasn't enough to retake the lead, as Aguero's overhead kick from a long kick from Hart was straight at Reina. City could feel hard done to with a fair few refereeing decisions, but they could have no complaints as to who was going to progress to the final.

Everton 1-0 Manchester City
FA Premier League
Tuesday 31 January, 2012 – 20:00 KO

City: Hart, Richards, Kompany (c), Lescott (Kolarov 68), Clichy, Barry (de Jong 86), Milner (A Johnson 61), Silva, Nasri, Dzeko, Aguero
Unused: Pantilimon, Zabaleta, Savic, Razak
Goals: -
Booked: Kompany, Lescott
Man of the Match: James Milner

It was City with the opening possession of the game, but it was an Everton corner that almost brought the opening goal after five minutes. Hart couldn't get near to the cross and it was headed beyond him by Stracqualursi, but the former Everton defender Lescott was on the line to head it clear.

With 36 minutes on the clock, City almost had themselves in front. Dzeko won the ball back in the Everton half and held the ball up well. He slipped it to the middle for Nasri and the Frenchman had no thought in his head other than to shoot. He did, he beat Howard, but it crashed down off the crossbar and away to safety. The game was then stopped in bizarre circumstances, after a fan ran onto the pitch and handcuffed himself to Hart's left hand post.

City looked to start the second half where they left off the first. It was Dzeko with the first chance after the break, as he headed towards goal from a Clichy cross, but it was an easy take for Howard. A clearance from Clichy then bounced nicely for Aguero to roll his man and break through on goal. His square ball, though, was behind Dzeko and Nasri picked up the pieces to shoot, but the effort was deflected over. Lescott could have earned City a penalty, but the referee decided he'd fouled Howard and not the other way around.

Aguero tricked himself into the Everton box and was dispossessed by Fellaini. The referee looked twice, before waving play on, and it was a fair challenge. Dzeko couldn't keep the ball as it was then cleared from the City defence and, from the change of possession, a poor touch from Donovan found Gibson, whose shot from the edge of the box deflected off Barry and beat Hart. City were behind on Merseyside again, largely against the run of play.

City were knocking on the Everton door, but the home side were getting men behind the ball and holding firm. The bus was firmly parked and City couldn't find a way through. It was perhaps an undeserved victory for Everton, but it was the bogey team who took the points from the visitors once again.

IN BAD KOMPANY

This week, we've learned that Vincent Kompany will serve a four match ban after his rejected appeal of his red card during Sunday's FA Cup Third Round Manchester derby tie at Eastlands. If I'm being honest, it isn't really too much of a surprise that the FA's panel turned the appeal away. And don't get me wrong here, I think Kompany was very wrongly sent off and the decision should have been overturned. But what I think should happen and what I expect to happen are two entirely different things and, unfortunately, I was correct on the latter.

Though it seems to be, on the whole, only United fans who disagree with me on the former, too.

If Nenad Milijas' red card against Arsenal was turned away by the panel, then the City captain had no chance. As video replays showed, Milijas won the ball. It isn't dangerous. He doesn't use excessive force. In fact, he barely uses any force: The only reason his studs are showing is that it's impossible not to show studs when stretching in that manner.

And that brings us on to Kompany. Who was right to have been sent off because he used both feet, right? Well, this being football, of course it isn't quite as simple as that. For a start, the tackle is made with a scissoring motion (not that type of scissoring, you dirty minded individual) where Kompany's right foot played the ball (with the side of his boot, I'll add) and his left foot doesn't. His left foot is there simply because it's attached to his hips; it's part of his body position. It doesn't catch Nani, it doesn't play the ball. It's not involved in the tackle in any way other than it being attached to the defender.

But the point stands: He used two feet. Two feet equals red card.

Kompany was sent off for 'serious foul play', according to the referee's report. The problem I have here is that the laws of the game deem serious foul play to be the severity of a tackle and not the number of feet used in making it. In fact, here is the ruling (under *Law 12: Fouls And Misconduct*) in full:

> A player is guilty of serious foul play if he uses excessive force or brutality against an opponent when challenging for the ball when it is in play.
>
> A tackle that endangers the safety of an opponent must be sanctioned as serious foul play. Any player who lunges at an opponent in challenging for the ball from the front, from the side or from behind using one or both legs, with excessive force and endangering the safety of an opponent is guilty of serious foul play.
>
> Advantage should not be applied in situations involving serious foul play unless there is a clear subsequent opportunity to score a goal. The referee must send off the player guilty of serious foul play when the ball is next out of play.
>
> A player who is guilty of serious foul play should be sent off and play is restarted with a direct free kick from the position where the offence occurred (see Law 13 – Position of free kick) or a penalty kick (if the offence occurred inside the offender's penalty area).

The closest we get there to the good ol' two-footed challenge argument is the phrase "using one or both legs". From reading that law, we can determine a couple of things: One challenge can be one-footed and dangerous, while another can be two-footed and safe. The key to whether a player should be penalised for serious foul play comes in the opening line: "A player is guilty of serious foul play if he uses excessive force or brutality against an opponent when challenging for the ball when it is in play."

I've not found anything else in the laws of the game that says a player must be dismissed if they use two feet when making a tackle. It's all about the force of the challenge. So, having cleared that up and looking back at the tackle Kompany made on Nani, there is surely no chance that the Belgian defender has used "excessive force", is there? Nani barely even flinches; that's how much force Kompany *didn't* use.

What sticks in a lot of fans' throats, however, is the role that Wayne Rooney appears to have played in this whole drama. The referee, not to be confused with an Olympic cyclist, did appear perfectly happy to play on after the challenge. He didn't look like he was going to blow the whistle and do anything. That is until Rooney waved his arms in his direction, pointing out that two feet were used.

The whistle was blown, the red card was shown, Kompany took the walk.

It's perhaps alarming to think that a referee would be influenced by a player on the pitch in such a manner and, as such, I'd prefer to believe that Chris Foy made his mind up independently. Of course, Rooney's gesticulations may have pointed out that the defender used two feet, but it's up to the referee to decide on the sanction. That's what I believe has happened.

What alarms me more about that scenario, though, is that would mean neither the players nor even the referee fully understand the laws, especially in relation to serious foul play. The assumption is two feet equals red card, which isn't true. Brutality and dangerous play equals red cards. While it's possible Chris Foy has decided that it was dangerous during the game, I just can't believe he's seen it afterwards and stuck to his belief.

Somehow, the panel has come to the same conclusion, despite video replays from various angles. That's less surprising, however, given the number of incorrect red cards that are upheld, correct red cards that are overturned, severe challenges not dealt with because the referee showed a yellow card at the time, incidents ignored because they weren't in the referee's report, arses mixed up with elbows, etc…

It didn't take long for Rio Ferdinand and Wayne Rooney to take to Twitter:

> By the way how can there be any debate about the red card yesterday?? You leave the ground with a #2footTackle = Red card #fact

@rioferdy5, Rio Ferdinand

Funny how people think i got kompany sent off. Im not ref. i didnt give red card. But it was a clear red card. 2 footed tackle

@WayneRooney, Wayne Rooney

Ignoring the bit about the laws of the game and two-footed tackles, which I've covered repeatedly so far, I'd like to flag up something about the latter of the two tweeters up there. Who the fuck is Wayne Rooney to comment on 'getting someone sent off', given his history with Ronaldo during the 2006 World Cup? Who the fuck is Wayne Rooney to take the moral high ground over a red card, given the reason why he will miss the first two games of Euro 2012?

And, also, who the fuck are the FA to appeal an act of brutality from Rooney in an international match – and kicking another player is an act of brutality – and successfully have that suspension reduced to two games from three, while upholding a tackle – which wasn't excessive or brutal – and leaving that suspension intact? The can of worms has been well and truly opened.

Don't get me wrong, however, I'm in no way accusing Rooney or the FA of being corrupt. Nor am I accusing them of cheating. Nor even favouritism. However, I am accusing them of hypocrisy and double-standards.

And this brings us to Rooney's orchestra conducting towards the referee. During the week earlier, Roberto Mancini was roundly criticised for his imaginary card waving towards the fourth official when he felt Martin Skrtel should have seen red (for what it's worth, I disagree with the City manager on this point, but that's not for now). Rooney has received very little by way of criticism for looking like his arms were attached to a windmill.

But what's the difference between shouting something like "ref, he should be sent off" and waving your hands, and shouting something like "ref, he should be sent off" and waving an imaginary card? Both are somewhat 'ungentlemanly' in their actions, but only the latter appears to rile the watching public.

And what's more, there are two key differences: Mancini didn't get what he wanted, while Rooney did. And Mancini apologised for his heat of the moment outburst after the game. If you're waiting for an apology from Rooney, I suspect you'll be waiting for a very long time; I wonder if Rooney would feel hard done to if he were in another Ronaldo circa World Cup 2006 incident or if he'd still feel justified in his actions?

In the end, though, there's not a lot we can do to change the situation. Kompany will serve a four match ban, Chris Foy (like any other referee) will make incorrect decisions, the FA's review panel will continue to make baffling rulings and we all just have to get on with it. However, it isn't nice when your team is up against it for 80 minutes because of a poor decision and then is given a subsequent kick in the knackers when they are further disadvantaged because of a poor decision when dealing with the original poor decision.

INTERVIEW: COSTEL PANTILIMON

When he signed on loan for City in the summer of 2011, there wasn't too much known about Costel Pantilimon. In fact, most City fans – myself included, here – only knew two things: He'd played against the Blues for FC Timisoara in the Europa League in 2010 and that he was quite tall. He's so tall, in fact, that when he did put pen to paper on that loan deal, he became the loftiest man in the Premier League.

As I waited inside a pub in Bredbury, Stockport, I was sitting in one of the back rooms. In the front room, a supporters' club meeting was readying itself for the arrival of two senior players: David Silva and Costel Pantilimon, himself. I was booked in to interview the goalkeeper afterwards and was sticking some last minute adjustments into my notes for things to ask him.

It turns out he'd driven himself to the meeting and hadn't come with the officials from the club, as I discovered when I met one of the press officers who had made the arrangements. I couldn't help hoping that, standing at six foot eight inches, Pantilimon drove a Mini. Such thoughts were quickly booted out of my mind, though, as he walked into the pub, ducking under the doorframe as he did. He said his hellos to everybody and then was introduced to me.

Being your typical, polite, British man in a semi-formal situation, I did what anybody would do: I stood up. Now, I'm no short-arse, but it was at this time that I realised just how huge Pantilimon is. When I shook his hand, it was like I was a three year old child shaking a parent's little finger.

During the meeting, I learned that he had, only that month, made his transfer from Timisoara to City permanent, so there was really only one place we could start. How was he settling into Manchester?

"I like Manchester," he says, as a wry smile appears on his face. Somehow, I knew what was coming next: "The only problem I have is that I don't like the weather. It's incredible. It rains all the time. Everything else is okay – the people, the players, the club, my colleagues. The football's great and it's a good life for a footballer.

"It was very easy for me [to adapt to living away from home for the first time] because I find the people here are very friendly. The fans and the people around town are great and all of these things make my work easy.

"I came here with one thing on my mind: To sign a contract to be here [permanently]. I find my footballing life here and I want to stay here."

This January, Pantilimon got what he wanted and he made his loan move permanent, for a fee reported to be in the region of £3m. But for most City fans, the first time they saw the big goalkeeper play was in last season's Europa League. While City didn't test him too much in either leg – winning 1-0 in Romania and 2-0 back at Eastlands – he showed glimpses of what he was able to do, especially under pressure in the first leg.

"It was two very important games for us," he remembers. "The year before, we'd beaten Shakhtar Donetsk and they were a great team who had won the Europa League final. We'd hoped to do the same thing with City, but we found them to be a very good and very strong team. We lost, but it was two good games."

One year on and he'd obviously done enough to grab Roberto Mancini's interest. With Shay Given departing for regular first team football at Aston Villa, the spot was open at City for an understudy to Joe Hart. And, on hearing of the manager's interest, Pantilimon says there was no question of what decision he was going to make.

"It was a great chance for me," he says. "City now is a top level team. To have this chance is great for my career. It was an opportunity for me to learn. When you play with the best players, you grow up.

"I knew that [he would be understudy to Joe Hart] from the beginning. He's a great goalkeeper and he's England's first choice. But we all work hard and this can only help the team."

Playing in England, though, is a big difference to playing in his home country. After all, the Premier League is often cited as the best in the world. Has making the step up added any pressure to the young man's shoulders?

"No," he insists. "When you're out on the pitch, you enjoy the game. I play football with a smile. I like playing and this is very important. If you can find a good thing in playing football, then you don't feel any pressure. I don't play football for fun, but I enjoy it.

"Here, the Premier League is quicker. There's more contact. It's very different. Romania has a good Premier League, but it's not like here. It's more technical and more physical here.

"But I made this choice because I want to win trophies," he continues. "And I think, with City now, I have this opportunity. I hope that we can start this year, with the Premier League. That's the important one for us. Then, I hope, in the coming years, we can win more and more."

While he might not have featured for City in the Premier League so far this season, he has been the first choice goalkeeper in the Carling Cup run. A clean sheet against Birmingham, followed by a solid display in a victory at Molineux, left the big goalkeeper with a chance to impress as the Blues travelled to the Emirates.

And he was in the thick of the action straight away. Already moving to his left, he changed direction quickly to push away a shot to his right from Arsenal's Park. This preceded a fine one-handed save from a Chamberlain effort from outside the box. His saves were vital in getting City into the coming semi finals with Liverpool.

"I tell people this [the save from Park] is my favourite because it's the last one I've done," he says. "But it was a great game and it was important because we're one step closer to the final. And now we just want to qualify for the final.

"We'd like to win the Premier League, but we're so close to the Carling Cup we'd like to win that, too," he continues. "I've also got my eye on the Europa League because the final is in Bucharest. To play in a final in my country would be great, so I hope we can get there."

Despite his good performances in the League Cup this season, there were perhaps a few eyebrows raised when Roberto Mancini named his team to face Manchester United in the FA Cup Third Round. It was a strong team, however City's first choice goalkeeper was on the bench and Pantilimon had been given the nod.

In the end, he did concede three goals, however to place any blame at the big goalkeeper's feet would be very unfair. The first, a well placed header, would be one that few shot-stoppers on the planet would have reached. The second, a snapshot and turn from inside the box, could have been blocked en route to the net, while he actually saved the penalty that led to the third, conceding only due to bad luck on the rebound.

He says there were mitigating circumstances for the defeat: "I found it a great game, a game where all the town likes it. They live for this game and it's a good game. I know we have a good team and what happened in the FA Cup wasn't true. The result wasn't true.

"These things happen. I don't think it was a red card for Kompany."

A second half fightback from the Blues left Pantilimon in an odd position, too. Goals from Kolarov and then Aguero left the score at 2-3, as the game entered stoppage time. City then won a corner and the tallest man in the Premier League was waved forward by the bench. He connected to Kolarov's flag kick, but unfortunately couldn't direct his header towards goal.

"I was unlucky with [the header against] United," he laughs. "But I don't get that opportunity that often. You don't get many chances [to score] as a goalkeeper, it's happened for me in one of twenty or thirty games!"

January 2012 Breakdown

Games (all competitions):
Won: 3   **Drawn:** 1   **Lost:** 4

Goals (all competitions):
For: 11   **Against:** 10

Progress:
Premier League: 1st
League Cup: Eliminated in the Semi Final
FA Cup: Eliminated in Round Three
Champions League: 3rd in Group A
Europa League: Qualified for the Round of 32 via Champions League

Premier League Table

		P	W	D	L	F	A	GD	Pts
1	**Manchester City**	23	17	3	3	60	19	+41	54
2	Manchester United	23	17	3	3	56	21	+35	54
3	Tottenham Hotspur	23	15	4	4	44	25	+19	49
4	Chelsea	23	12	6	5	41	26	+15	42
5	Liverpool	23	10	8	5	28	21	+7	38

February 2012

Manchester City 3-0 Fulham

FA Premier League
Saturday 4 February, 2012 – 17:30 KO

City: Hart, Richards (c), Savic, Lescott, Kolarov, Barry, Nasri (Milner 55), A Johnson (Pizarro 90), Silva, Aguero (de Jong 80), Dzeko
Unused: Pantilimon, Zabaleta, Clichy, Rekik
Goals: Aguero (pen 11), Baird (og 31), Dzeko (72)
Booked: Kolarov
Man of the Match: Adam Johnson

It was the home side who got off to the better start, controlling the ball and looking for the early opening. It almost came as Aguero found a neat ball through for Dzeko, but the big centre-forward couldn't find the net from just inside the area. As City dominated, they earned their breakthrough: Johnson was tripped in the box by Baird and Aguero slotted the penalty home.

Just after the half hour, Baird's evening got worse. A Kolarov cross missed everybody in the box, but it was rescued by Johnson on the right flank. He crossed the ball back with pace and it hit the Fulham defender on the knee, leaving Schwarzer stranded and City two goals in front.

A sweeping City move on the break from a Fulham corner almost made it three: Aguero got his shot in, but Schwarzer parried and Johnson was offside from the rebound. It took Hangeland's toe to prevent a Dzeko effort troubling the goalkeeper.

In the second half, to get more of the ball for his side, Roberto Mancini introduced Milner and, as the snow began to fall heavily, the hosts wrestled control back, just after the first of the two stoppages while the groundsmen cleared the markings on the pitch.

The visitors' resistance was soon broken: Aguero carried the ball into the box and looked like he was going to fire a shot at goal. Before he pulled the trigger, though, he slid it to his right for the waiting Dzeko, who made no mistake in finding the back of the net.

A deflection inside the City box could have given the visitors a consolation goal, but the ricochet bounced off the post and Richards was able to smash the ball clear.

Aston Villa 0-1 Manchester City

FA Premier League
Sunday 12 February, 2012 – 16:00 KO

City: Hart, Zabaleta, Kompany (c), Lescott, Kolarov, Barry, de Jong, Milner, A Johnson (Nasri 84), Silva (Richards 90), Aguero (Dzeko 89)

Unused: Pantilimon, Savic, Clichy, Pizarro
Goals: Lescott (63)
Booked: -
Man of the Match: Gareth Barry

It was a stuttered start to the game, but Milner had the chance to shoot inside the area early on. He sliced the ball into Dunne and, at the second attempt, it was just about cleared from the box, where Johnson picked it up. He took the shot on, beat his former team-mate Given, but couldn't beat the post, as the ball crashed back off the upright.

With just over ten minutes of the first half remaining, Johnson broke into the box and pulled the ball back. Aguero's deflected shot was blocked en route to the Villa goal, with Barry unable to get onto the rebound. A Kolarov free kick was then curled well over the bar, as City looked for the breakthrough.

With 53 minutes on the clock, Lescott headed a great chance over from a Silva free kick, as he connected inside the six-yard box. Zabaleta had a shot from the edge of the box, but it was easily held by Given.

Just before the hour, Kolarov smashed the ball through a crowded penalty area, but both Silva and Aguero weren't able to get a vital touch and it bounced behind for a goal kick.

A Silva free kick whipped into the box was well headed over by Collins. From the resulting corner, the visitors finally grabbed the lead: Barry headed a deep corner back into the box and Lescott turned and poked the ball past Given.

With just under three minutes of normal time to play, Cuellar got in between markers at a corner and headed the ball over the bar when he should have done better. A brilliant save from Hart then denied Bent, as the board went up for stoppage time. It was a warning shot across City's bows.

After some more great goalkeeping to punch the ball away from Dunne, Hart almost gifted the home side an equaliser in the last seconds as a Barry back header almost slipped from his grasp into the Keane's path. But, fortunately for the visitors, the England keeper was able to recover and grab it.

FC Porto 1-2 Manchester City
Europa League Round of 32, First Leg
Thursday 16 February, 2012 – 20:05 KO

City: Hart, Richards, Kompany (c), Lescott, Clichy, Barry, de Jong, Silva (Kolarov 83), Y Toure, Nasri (Zabaleta 88), Balotelli (Aguero 78)
Unused: Pantilimon, Savic, Pizarro, Dzeko
Goals: Pereira (og 55), Aguero (85)
Booked: Y Toure, Kompany, de Jong, Barry, Nasri, Richards
Man of the Match: Joleon Lescott

It was a typically slow start to the first leg of a European tie, with Porto seeing more of the ball in the attacking third than City, but neither side able to test the opposition's goalkeeper.

Toure was brought down in the middle of the Porto half as he broke, winning City a free kick. Nasri chipped it into the box towards Balotelli, who missed it. But the goalkeeper spilled it and the Italian was almost able to connect with the rebound, but couldn't quite readjust. Richards smashed the clearance at goal and forced a good save from Helton, before Nasri should have opened the scoring with a one-on-one shot from the edge of the box.

With 27 minutes played, the hosts got themselves in front, just as it had looked like City had ridden the storm. Hulk smashed the ball across the box and Clichy couldn't get there ahead of Varela and the striker stabbed it into the net.

Immediately, Balotelli should have levelled the game. He was clean through on goal after a delightful ball from Nasri, but his turn and volley was well pushed away by Helton. With the amount of time and space the Italian had, it should have been City's equaliser.

A neat flowing move from City as the first action of the second period saw Barry find Silva, who, in turn, found Richards on the overlap. The full back powered into the box and smashed the ball at goal. It beat Helton, but it didn't beat the post, as it ricocheted away to safety.

Ten minutes into the second half, City pulled level. Pereira flicked the ball past his own goalkeeper under a challenge from Balotelli, after Nasri had played a ball over the top towards the Italian's run. Helton had come for it, but got nowhere near and the ball trickled into the empty net off the full back's shoulder.

With five minutes of the game to play, City took the lead with their second away goal. Yaya Toure was played through into the area and drew the goalkeeper. He squared the ball for Aguero, who was faced with an open goal and couldn't miss. He didn't, rolling the ball over the line to give City the advantage.

Manchester City 4-0 FC Porto
Europa League Round of 32, Second Leg
Wednesday 22 February, 2012 – 17:00 KO

City: Hart, Richards, Kompany (c), Lescott, Clichy, de Jong, Barry (Milner 58), Nasri (Dzeko 69), Y Toure, Silva, Aguero (Pizarro 82)
Unused: Pantilimon, Zabaleta, Savic, Balotelli
Goals: Aguero (1), Dzeko (76), Silva (84), Pizarro (87)
Booked: Y Toure
Man of the Match: Sergio Aguero

City couldn't have wished for a better start to the second leg of their Europa League tie, as, within the first 23 seconds, the home side had the lead. An interception from de Jong found Yaya Toure, who, in turn, slotted the ball for

Aguero to run on to. He made no mistake with his one-on-one, sliding the ball across the goalkeeper and into the bottom corner of the net.

But, if the home fans were hoping that that goal would open the floodgates early on, they would have been disappointed. Porto tried to get themselves back into the game, but were struggling to create a shooting chance, against a City side that – with an aggregate 3-1 lead – were happy to concede possession on the halfway line.

Moutinho whipped a free kick over Hart's crossbar, before Aguero rounded Helton on the edge of the box and tried to chip the covering defender. He looked to have perfected it, with both the Porto players beaten, but the ball crashed back off the crossbar and away to safety.

While it felt like backs against the walls time for City, in truth the visitors seemed a little toothless – summed up in City adding their second of the night and fourth of the tie. Aguero broke with the ball down the left and squared for Dzeko, who nutmegged Helton and sealed the victory. In the aftermatch, Rolando saw his second yellow card and was dismissed to round off a miserable night in the rain for the visitors.

As the game entered its last ten minutes, the visitors capitulated. Pizarro fought well down the right wing to win the ball back and keep City on the front foot. He took it back from Dzeko, squared for Silva and, faced with an open goal, the Spaniard hit the net.

And it got better for the home fans: Dzeko laid the ball off the Pizarro on the edge of the box, but there wasn't room for the loan signing to shoot. Instead, he chipped the ball over the challenge and bundled his way through into the box, before coolly sliding his one-on-one past Helton to make it four.

Manchester City 3-0 Blackburn Rovers
FA Premier League
Saturday 25 February, 2012 – 17:30 KO

City: Hart, Zabaleta, Kompany (c), Lescott, Kolarov, de Jong, Y Toure (Milner 86), A Johnson (Pizarro 72), Silva, Balotelli (Dzeko 79), Aguero
Unused: Pantilimon, Richards, Clichy, Nasri
Goals: Balotelli (30), Aguero (52), Dzeko (81)
Booked: -
Man of the Match: David Silva

It was one-way traffic from the first whistle, as the hosts looked to get themselves on the scoresheet early on. Balotelli stung Robinson's fingers in the opening minute as he swept a shot at the near post, before a Silva ball into the box was inches away from finding the net via the Italian's head but, somehow, he couldn't connect and the visitors' goal remained intact.

It was Robinson who came out the better again on 27 minutes, after

Balotelli's free kick flicked off the wall and forced the former England international into another good save. It had been all City and the only reason the scores were level was the man in goal for Rovers.

The resistance, though, was breached on the half hour. Kolarov drove the ball into the box and found Balotelli in the centre of the goal. It was a first time flick from the Italian and the accuracy, combined with the pace of the cross, was enough to beat Robinson and give the home side the advantage.

Blackburn could have had a penalty when Pedersen was felled in the box in one of their rare attacks, but the referee decided the contact wasn't enough to have caused his fall – City were lucky.

Kompany nearly had City's second in an almost identical manner to Balotelli's opener: He flicked Silva's corner goalwards with the outside of his foot, but, once again, Robinson kept it out with another wonderful save. Yaya Toure couldn't volley the rebound into the net, slotting it just inches wide of the far post, as the home side pressed for more reward.

City's second goal, though, wasn't slow in coming after the break. Silva's corner dropped right on top of Robinson, who made a hash of his clearance – neither catching nor punching it. Instead, he flapped and it dropped nicely for Aguero to volley straight back into the empty net, despite the attempts of the defenders on the line to stop it.

The game appeared to be petering to a close, as City were happy to keep possession and avoid letting the visitors back into the match. Blackburn, on the other hand, seemed content to have only conceded two, such was the pattern of play. But, with nine minutes to play, Dzeko got City's third to round the evening off in style: Kolarov crossed into the box and it was a powerful header bounced into the net from the Bosnian.

THE STRANGE CASE OF DZEKO AND HYDE

In the mid 1880s, a Scottish poet and author – who shares my birthday, incidentally – wrote a novella about a man with split personalities. It was the tale of a man who was very good when he was good, but very bad when he was bad. This man went from one extreme to the other and it was a mystery to those around him what was going on. Though despite being written a mere 126 years ago, it told a prophecy of something that was coming to Manchester in the year 2011. And, in this story, all that Robert Louis Stevenson got wrong was the name: It should have been called *The Strange Case of Dzeko and Hyde*.

And I don't mean that to sound harsh, because it really isn't. I like Edin Dzeko and I think he's one of the best strikers in the Premier League, however from his year-and-a-bit at City, the one thing that has become clear is that he's either totally unplayable or completely playable. He doesn't really have any distinctly average games: He's either great and could bag a few goals or off the pace and can't trap the ball.

His debut, against Wolves in January 2011, showed he had a bit about him. Despite looking a bit rusty, he displayed one or two moments of good ball control and an eye for a pass, epitomised by his role in Yaya Toure's fantastic breakaway goal and a piece of skill to keep possession mid-way into the opposition half, when under pressure from three defenders and with no support.

But soon, he struggled for form. Domestically, he was struggling with the pace of the Premier League. Naturally, a large part of that has to go down to him being a January signing; traditionally, those players signed in the winter window from overseas do find it more difficult to settle into a squad and find their feet. But there was always that nagging doubt in the back of my mind, at least: What if he wasn't worth the money that had been paid for him?

February arrived and he forced the equaliser in the Manchester derby at Old Trafford, firing a shot so far wide that it bounced neatly off David Silva's pert left buttock and dropped snugly inside van der Sar's post. It went down as a goal for the Spaniard and it was certainly heading nearer to the corner flag than the net when it left Mr. Hyde's boot.

It was only really when the pressure was off towards the end of last season – fourth spot was in the bag and the FA Cup was in the trophy cabinet – when Dr. Dzeko turned up. Perhaps it was a slow build up from his first Premier League goal, when he netted at Ewood Park in the last game in April, that he started to find his confidence. And that, personally speaking, I think is crucial: If there's one thing that Edin Dzeko screams it's that he scores when he's in a confident mood; when things are going his way and when he's been netting regularly.

Clearly, his confidence came back over the summer. Combined with a pre-season training schedule with his new team-mates, he started off the 2011-12 campaign on fire. In fact, the final goal of last season came from the Bosnian's boot and he was the source of the first goal of this. Throw the Community Shield in there and Dzeko had eight goals in five games.

And what happened next is key to why Mr. Hyde returned in September:

Despite scoring four goals at White Hart Lane, Dzeko was an unused substitute for the next match, at home to Wigan. Now, many will say that it won't have too much of an effect (he's a professional and must have been feeling good), but he was in form and everything he was doing was coming off, usually resulting in a goal. After that demotion to the bench – for no reason other than squad rotation – Mr. Hyde didn't score again for a month and a half.

But, while I've just inferred there that Roberto Mancini's management style hasn't helped the striker, the Italian did pull off a masterstroke in getting Dzeko back on a patch of good form. With exactly just a bit more than 20 minutes of the Manchester derby to go, United were still chasing the game, despite the (then) 0-3 scoreline and the manager knew there were more goals to be had. Looking at his bench, he knew that Dzeko needed to get on the scoresheet; he made the swap for Balotelli, even though he was on a hat-trick.

And, as the game entered stoppage time and the Bosnian had missed a couple of good shooting opportunities, the ball bounced in off Dzeko's knee. He was a changed man, once again: A second goal quickly followed, before he netted against Wolves twice in two games and then again at Loftus Road.

But, after that good performance at QPR, he was, once again, an unused substitute against Newcastle. And his goal in City's 2-3 victory in London was the last that he scored until the trip to the DW stadium in January, over two months later. Through November and December, the ball bounced further off his foot when he tried to control it than it did when he tried to pass it, he couldn't win a header and even his work ethic seemed to go missing.

His header at Wigan, though, was exactly what he needed. Hard work won him a free kick on the left flank and a brilliant ball in from Silva gave him little work to do to find the net. And, just like after Ewood Park and Old Trafford, his confidence was back. He converted at Anfield, slotted one in against Fulham and came off the bench to seal a Europa League last 16 place.

From his year-and-a-bit at City, I'm no longer worried that Edin Dzeko hasn't been worth his money. He has. He's scored some great goals, some decent goals, some average goals and some tap-ins. Performance wise, he's had some real stinkers and he's had some real stormers. He's bagged himself 16 goals in all competitions so far this season, so it's obvious he's no flop; but it appears he struggles with the rotation policy at the club.

It's very easy to get on a player's back when he's not playing well – and, Christ, City fans both know and can do that – but Dzeko definitely doesn't need that when he's not in form. He just needs that little bit of luck.

While it's *The Strange Case of Dzeko and Hyde*, we need to make sure that the Mr. Hyde side of him is rarely seen – because, as Stevenson's story goes, the bad side can be repressed. And let's face it, his 16 goals have been crucial in firing the team to the top of the league, smashing records along the way. We know what he can do, he knows what he can do; we just need to back him when he's struggling to do it.

FORGIVE AND FORGET
(AKA – WHY I AM MORALLY A HYPOCRITE WHO JUST WANTS HIS TEAM TO END THE SEASON AS TITLE WINNERS AT WHATEVER COST)

As I was considering how to best handle the Carlos Tevez return, the thought suddenly struck me: I am, morally, a hypocrite. Back when the Argentine didn't come on in Munich and during the ensuing aftermath, I commented that I didn't care what happens to him. I didn't give two smelly farts what he decided to do; I just had the best interests of Manchester City Football Club at heart and, if he was or wasn't a part of that, then I wasn't fussed.

And for months, while the number 32 was AWOL, that was true. I was focused on watching City smash records and top the table and be brilliant without him. While we might have been light on striking options, we have, on the whole, been lucky with injuries and suspensions up top and very rarely has there been a game where the team didn't look like scoring at some point. The fact that the first time the Blues did fail to find the net was on Boxing Day – a mere 18 league games into the season – tells its own story.

Without him, City had been batting records away left, right and centre. And that, combined with his absence, made it very easy not to care about him: His actions meant that he wasn't available to play a part in City's season, so I could have a lack of interest. He wasn't here.

But now he is and I have to be perfectly honest. Morally speaking, I wouldn't like Carlos Tevez to feature for the first team again. City have stood their ground and refused to cut their asking price for the player, and, in turn, the player hasn't got the desired move away from the club: City won that battle of wills. There was only one place my support was going to go and it wasn't to the man whose actions didn't have Manchester City at heart.

For the last few months, barely a day has gone by where the talking point about Manchester City hasn't included (to some degree, at least) Carlos Tevez. City's achievements this season have been at the forefront, don't get me wrong, but most – if not all – of Roberto Mancini's press conferences since the start of October have finished with the question: "What's the situation with Carlos Tevez?" And that was followed by a roll of the eyes from every City fan watching. It feels there's been so much additional baggage for the last four months that RyanAir would have a field day with extra charges.

Other budget airlines are available.

Yet, one apology and a strict training regime later, and the man who has recently been nothing but trouble could be a part of the first team set up. And I really don't want that. I don't want to see a man whose actions have been no help to the team whatsoever waltz his way back into the plans, by way of a carefully crafted statement with club officials and a bit of fitness work. Morally, I'd hate it: Sergio Aguero, Mario Balotelli and Edin Dzeko have been the three strikers who have gotten the club to the top of the league and deserve to be the ones that win City the league; how would they all feel if they're dropped due to rotation or poor form for a man who was AWOL for four months? You couldn't blame them for getting the impression their hard work meant nothing.

And it wouldn't set any sort of example: It would say to the other players and to any potential future players that they can walk all over the club and, if they're good enough – because, for all that's happened, we can't deny that Tevez is a fantastic player – then they'll always have a shot at working their way back into the team. And that makes me feel very uneasy.

They say that, while Tevez's attitude away from the pitch has been questionable, his actions on the pitch have shown that he will always give everything he can. Except that argument took one huge dent when, on the evening of 27 September, he disobeyed managerial instructions and stubbornly remained in his seat on a bench in Germany. The trouble for Tevez was that he held no power cards: City's strike force had been banging goals in without him and the club didn't need to offload him. They could afford to keep him and wait for the right offer when the transfer window opened – something that they did, but the right offer never came.

So far, City have played this perfectly. Mancini has left the door open for a return and re-registered him in the Premier League squad (with spare places, it was the sensible thing to do, even if he was AWOL at the time). And Tevez has continually turned his nose up at the chance of reconciliation, preferring golf in Argentina and commenting that he felt he'd been treated like a dog.

Difficult to agree with, given how City had bent over backwards to accommodate the striker the season before. There had been rumblings that Tevez had wanted to leave since May 2010, but Roberto Mancini handed him the captaincy, virtually guaranteed his starting place and built his team around the Argentine for the following season. There was even forgiveness for the transfer request debacle in December 2010. And then there's everything that's happened since. In reality, it could be fairer to say that it was Tevez himself who had, instead, treated the club like a dog.

However, eventually, be it through advice from a third party or through his own realisation that he needed to show some willing if he was going to earn a transfer away from the club, he apologised. With City not going to sell him in his absence and a contract that isn't running out soon, he was backed into a corner and the only way out was to do as the club wanted him to. And, to be perfectly honest, this sorry doesn't feel like the most sincere there's ever been – AWOL for months, comments to the media and his actions in Munich don't suggest any sort of regret.

That being said, the apology was issued and the club have clearly accepted it: It wouldn't have been released as a statement on the official website unless they were completely happy with it, after all. Though is it possible to forgive and forget, kiss and make up, and thrust him back into the squad, ready for the final push?

Well, here's where it gets tricky and the boundaries get a little blurred. What would you give to see City win the Premier League? How much would you give to see Vincent Kompany et al lift that trophy sometime this May? And this is why I'm morally a hypocrite, because, if it was going to be the difference between City finishing top of the league and City finishing in second place, I would have no problem with Carlos Tevez pulling on that blue shirt and scoring goals – if that is, as he says, what he wants to do from now until the end of the season. And that's despite what I've just written.

I have no problem at all, despite having spent months saying otherwise. Of course, there are fans who would take issue and I can fully understand why. In fact, I admire their principles. But, the truth is, if a fit Carlos Tevez's inclusion in City's matchday squad – be it in the starting line-up or coming off the bench – was enough to bring the title to The Etihad, then my principles that want him to play no part in the success can get stuffed. In a few years' time, I won't care he played a part in lifting that trophy, but I will care that the trophy was in the cabinet.

The interesting aspect to consider, however, is that his inclusion could have completely the opposite effect. While we're talking about the man having the ability to score important goals, we're talking like the rest of the squad will simply accept that he's back and going to join in. Outwardly, I've no doubt that the players will be 'delighted' to have someone of the Argentine's ability around the club again, but that's not a guarantee that it won't cause unrest or disharmony.

His return could mean his goals fire City to the title. However, it's not outside the realms of possibility that it could also be the catalyst that derails the steam train that has, until now, been relentlessly chugging towards top spot in May. It's a very delicate balance.

The biggest bonus here, though, for us fans is that the manager is Roberto Mancini. As evidenced from his time in charge of the club, he suffers no fools. He may appear to be the nice and friendly to the watching world, but behind the scenes I would argue he is ruthless. Anybody who isn't right for the team and for the football club is moved on and replaced with somebody who is. He's a man in total control and if there's anybody that knows the relationships between the players and what decision to make regarding Carlos Tevez, it's him.

The ideal outcome, in my own personal opinion, would be for City to go on and win the league and for Carlos Tevez never to feature in another of the club's matches. But when I take a moment to think about that more deeply, I find that my ideal outcome is simply that City go on and win the league. As long as that happens, I don't really care. Roberto Mancini is the man paid to make the decisions that will win or lose this title and he's got form for getting nearly every one of his calls correct. There's no reason to believe he won't do the same again.

Perhaps I can never forgive Carlos Tevez what he's done this season, but I can certainly put it to the back of my mind and make it the elephant in the room: The club takes precedent over one man and if it's in the best interests of the club to ignore what's happened since Munich, then I can do that, too.

If, morally, that makes me a hypocrite, then so be it.

February 2012 Breakdown

Games (all competitions):
Won: 5   **Drawn:** 0   **Lost:** 0

Goals (all competitions):
For: 13   **Against:** 1

Progress:
Premier League: 1st
League Cup: Eliminated in the Semi Final
FA Cup: Eliminated in Round Three
Champions League: 3rd in Group A
Europa League: Qualified for the Round of 16

Premier League Table

		P	W	D	L	F	A	GD	Pts
1	**Manchester City**	26	20	3	3	67	19	+48	63
2	Manchester United	26	19	4	3	63	26	+37	61
3	Tottenham Hotspur	26	16	5	5	51	30	+21	53
4	Arsenal	26	14	4	8	53	37	+16	46
5	Chelsea	26	13	7	6	47	31	+16	46

March 2012

Manchester City 2-0 Bolton Wanderers
FA Premier League
Saturday 3 March, 2012 – 15:00 KO

City: Hart, Zabaleta (K Toure 19), Kompany (c), Lescott, Clichy, Barry, Y Toure (Milner 82), Pizarro (Dzeko 62), A Johnson, Nasri, Balotelli
Unused: Pantilimon, Kolarov, Silva, Aguero
Goals: Clichy (23), Balotelli (72)
Booked: -
Man of the Match: Yaya Toure

It was a frantic start at the Etihad Stadium, where City could have taken the lead several times in the opening few minutes. Zabaleta pulled the ball back to Nasri, but his effort was blocked en route to goal by a Bolton leg. Balotelli then struck the foot of the post, before Nasri's follow-up was blocked on the line. Balotelli had a golden chance to side-foot home, but he somehow put his effort wide after some good work by Johnson on the right... and the clock had barely hit five minutes.

Balotelli beat the offside trap and slipped at the vital moment, scooping his shot well over the bar. It didn't take long, though, for the hosts to take the lead, but it wasn't without a stroke of luck. Clichy shot from the edge of the box and it was destined for Bogdan's hands, until a deflection beat the visiting keeper and the effort found the bottom corner.

The home side had their goalkeeper to thank that the scores weren't level at the break. Miyaichi stole the ball from Kolo Toure, before curling an effort towards the far post from inside the area. But the England international got a fingertip on the ball and diverted it behind.

With 25 minutes to play, it was almost two as Dzeko wound up to shoot on the edge of the box. But Pratley got there first and tried to stab the ball away from the Bosnian forward; he did, but he beat his own goalkeeper with a lob and the ball crashed back into play off the crossbar. It didn't matter, though, as two minutes later, Balotelli tapped home City's second: Johnson did brilliantly to drive through two challenges in the area, before beating Bogdan with a backheel, leaving the Italian with a tap in.

Sporting CP 1-0 Manchester City
Europa League Round of 16, First Leg
Thursday 8 March, 2012 – 18:00 KO

City: Hart, Clichy, Kompany (c) (Lescott 11), K Toure, Kolarov, Milner, de Jong, Barry (Nasri 59), Silva, Dzeko (Balotelli 71), Aguero
Unused: Pantilimon, Savic, Pizarro, A Johnson

Goals: -
Booked: de Jong, Kolarov
Man of the Match: Aleksandar Kolarov

The early control of the ball came from the visitors to Portugal, but there was a blow for City inside the first ten minutes, losing Kompany to injury. Pereira found space on the edge of the City box and had time to shoot, but his effort was well beaten away by Hart.

City's first corner almost produced the opening goal, as Milner's short ball to Silva was returned to the Englishman. He crossed and Kolo Toure connected, but the Sporting keeper blocked with his foot and nobody in a blue shirt could get to the rebound. A short corner was then well worked to Barry, but his curling effort was just wide of the post.

A low Kolarov cross into the Libson box in the second half caused the home side problems, but both Dzeko and Milner missed the ball and, via a touch from Aguero, it fell to Silva outside the area. His effort, though, was side-footed high and wide, as he tried to curl it into the top corner.

A silly free-kick conceded by de Jong, though, cost the Blues a goal. A shot from Fernandez was blocked by Hart, who was troubled by the bounce right in front of him, and Xandao pounced on the rebound. Hart saved his first effort, but the Brazilian back-heeled past the stranded City goalkeeper at the second attempt, giving the hosts the lead.

Aguero won City a free kick on the left flank just before the hour mark and, with decoys in the box, Milner looked for Kolarov on the edge. He belted it at the top corner; the goalkeeper was beaten, but so was the post. Just.

With four minutes to play, Balotelli connected with a Silva corner at the back post. It looped over the goalkeeper and was close to dropping into the net, but it crashed back off the crossbar and into open play. City have it all to do.

Swansea City 1-0 Manchester City
FA Premier League
Sunday 11 March, 2012 – 14:00 KO

City: Hart, Richards, Savic, K Toure (c), Clichy, Barry (Aguero 37), de Jong, Y Toure, Nasri (A Johnson 86), Silva (Dzeko 87), Balotelli
Unused: Pantilimon, Kolarov, Pizarro, Milner, Dzeko
Goals: -
Booked: de Jong, Balotelli
Man of the Match: Yaya Toure

The home side began the game the stronger, controlling the ball and the early possession. And with five minutes played, Routledge took the ball around Hart and went down, with the referee pointing to the spot – up stepped Sinclair and missed; the England keeper blocking the low penalty to his right.

Kolo Toure blocked a cross from Sigurdsson, but couldn't get the ball clear and it found its way to Graham on the penalty spot, with his back to goal. He turned the Ivorian and got his shot in at goal, but it was wide of Hart's post.

A neat ball into the box from Nasri, after some good possession between Silva, Yaya Toure and Clichy allowed Balotelli to slip in behind the home side's defence. But the defender recovered to concede the corner. From that flag kick, Yaya Toure belted the ball at goal, but it was deflected over.

Balotelli went down under a challenge from behind by Allen inside the area and the referee was unmoved, but there was little difference between the decision at the other end in the first half. A slide-rule Silva pass into the box was just about cut out by Allen, before it got to Balotelli.

Despite the visitors growing into the game, it all counted for nought late in the match. Savic gave the ball away on the halfway line, playing a short pass towards Yaya Toure and it handed possession to the opposition. Swansea broke and worked the ball to the right flank, where Routledge crossed. Moore was unmarked at the back post and he nodded past Hart, with just seven minutes to play.

City had the ball in the net with two minutes left, as Vorm came for Clichy's cross and missed. Richards nodded it into the net, but the flag was up for offside. It was close, but it was the correct call.

Manchester City 3-2 Sporting CP
Europa League Round of 16, Second Leg
Thursday 15 March, 2012 – 20:05 KO

City: Hart, Richards, Savic, K Toure (c), Kolarov, Y Toure, Pizarro (Dzeko 55), A Johnson (de Jong 45), Silva (Nasri 66), Aguero, Balotelli
Unused: Pantilimon, Clichy, Milner, Roman
Goals: Aguero (60, 83), Balotelli (pen 75)
Booked: Y Toure, Kolarov, Savic, Balotelli
Man of the Match: Sergio Aguero

Despite the home side needing two goals to get into the next round from the start, it was the visitors who started the brighter. Fernandez looked for a penalty just before the half hour, going down in the area under a challenge from Savic, but the Serbian won the ball. But then, minutes after, he made his impact on the game: He buried a free kick from the left side of the box into the far corner; Hart got a hand on it, but couldn't do anything to keep it out.

With just over five minutes of the half to play, City's uphill task became a mountain. Izmailov found acres of space on the left flank and crossed the ball low for van Wolfswinkel at the back post. He couldn't miss, smashing the ball into the roof of the net and giving the visitors their second away goal and a 2-0 lead. City needed to score four or they were out of the competition, but they hadn't looked like scoring once in the first half.

But the second half was a different story. Sporting seemed happy with their two-goal haul and sat back, while City went for broke. Mancini introduced Dzeko and, five minutes later, his presence in the box allowed Aguero to find space. Yaya Toure picked him out and the Argentine slotted the ball home, giving the hosts some faint hope.

With 15 minutes to play, Aguero was felled in the box and the referee pointed to the spot: Balotelli stepped up and coolly rolled the ball into the net. The game on the night was level, but City still needed two more goals to qualify for the next round.

With seven minutes to play, a corner into the Sporting box took a touch and found its way to Aguero. The goalkeeper was wrong-footed and City's leading scorer volleyed the ball into the back of the net. The comeback was well and truly on, despite looking so unlikely at half time and the tie was level, though the visitors were going through thanks to their two away goals.

As the game ticked to the final 30 seconds, City won a corner and piled everybody into the box – including Joe Hart. The first ball in was cleared as far as de Jong and the second cross found the City keeper at the back post. He shrugged off the challenge and headed at goal. It was going in at the back post until the fingertips of Patricio pushed the effort wide. There was no time to take the resulting corner and City, for all the second half endeavour, were out, having left it too late in the tie.

Manchester City 2-1 Chelsea
FA Premier League
Wednesday 21 March, 2012 – 19:45 KO

City: Hart, Zabaleta, Richards (c), K Toure, Clichy, de Jong (Tevez 66), Y Toure, Silva (Dzeko 77), Nasri, Aguero, Balotelli (Barry 45)
Unused: Pantilimon, Kolarov, Savic, Milner
Goals: Aguero (pen 78), Nasri (85)
Booked: Nasri
Man of the Match: Samir Nasri

With just nine minutes on the clock, Nasri was inches away from opening the scoring for City. His chest trap from a beautiful ball by Yaya Toure set himself up perfectly to chip Cech. He got the ball over the goalkeeper and it looked to be dropping in. It didn't: Cech reacted well as the effort bounced back off the crossbar and he scooped the ball away from the home side's attackers.

Aguero couldn't finish after a steaming run from Yaya Toure worked the ball into the box, before Toure himself went down under a challenge from Lampard inside the area, but the referee waved away his claims for a penalty. Balotelli then intercepted a bad pass across the visitors' back four and was clean through on goal, but his effort towards the bottom corner was touched around the post by the goalkeeper.

Nasri skied an effort from the edge of the box on a quick breakaway, before the Frenchman almost got lucky – his cross almost dropped in at the back post, until Cech touched it onto the crossbar.

But, just as it looked like City would be the only team to score, the visitors found themselves ahead with something of a smash and grab. A corner into the Blues' box caused them problems and they couldn't get the ball clear. Cahill took advantage, smashing in a shot that deflected off Yaya Toure and beat Hart, who was wrong-footed.

Essien, though, gave the home side a way back. His handball in the area allowed Aguero the chance to shoot from the spot. He sent Cech the wrong way from the penalty, scoring City's 100th goal of the season and the Blues had just over ten minutes to find a winner.

Five minutes before the end, City did get in front. Nasri slipped the ball into Tevez on the edge of the box and he did well to hold off Cahill, before returning it to the Frenchman, who was through on goal. He dinked it over the oncoming Cech and the ball hit the back of the net.

Stoke City 1-1 Manchester City
FA Premier League
Saturday 24 March, 2012 – 17:30 KO

City: Hart, Zabaleta (Milner 84), Richards (c), K Toure, Clichy, Barry (Tevez 74), Y Toure, Silva (A Johnson 62), Nasri, Balotelli, Dzeko
Unused: Pantilimon, Kolarov, Savic, de Jong
Goals: Y Toure (76)
Booked: Barry, Y Toure
Man of the Match: Pablo Zabaleta

It was a tentative opening from both sides, and the early play offered little to write home about. Zabaleta had a left-footed shot deflected behind as he joined in an attack down the right flank, before some good build-up between Nasri, Dzeko and Zabaleta gave Yaya Toure the chance to shoot from the edge of the box. His effort, however, curled over the bar and didn't trouble the goalkeeper.

Nasri and Silva tried a one-two on the edge of the box, but couldn't force their way through a tight defence, before Zabaleta should have done a lot better as he came on to a ball into the area and side-footed his effort straight at the covering defenders.

With five minutes to play before half time, it was Zabaleta to the rescue as he cleared off the line from a Stoke corner. Shawcross had flicked the delivery past Hart at the near post, but the Argentine full back was in the right place to keep the ball out.

Just before the hour mark, Peter Crouch put the hosts in front – largely against the run of play. He received a knock-down from twenty-five yards out and volleyed it into the top corner, giving Hart no chance. It was one of the goals of the year, with the ball not touching the ground from Begovic's goal kick to finding City's net.

City soon responded: Yaya Toure picked the ball up mid-way into the Stoke half and decided to have a pot-shot. It flicked off the head of Shawcross and beat Begovic, who could only push the ball into the top corner and the visitors were level.

But that was as good as it got for City, who couldn't force a second goal.

Manchester City 3-3 Sunderland
FA Premier League
Saturday 31 March, 2012 – 15:00 KO

City: Hart, Richards (A Johnson 45), Kompany (c), K Toure, Kolarov, de Jong, Y Toure, Silva (Tevez 58), Milner (Pizarro 80), Balotelli, Dzeko
Unused: Pantilimon, Zabaleta, Clichy, Barry
Goals: Balotelli (pen 44, 85), Kolarov (86)
Booked: de Jong
Man of the Match: Aleksandar Kolarov

It was a slow start from the home side, who were more than matched by the visitors. Mignolet was called into action to make a block from a Kolarov free kick, before Gardner found the side netting from inside the City box. Chances were at a premium early on.

Dzeko then found Mignolet after a neat move up the pitch from the hosts, before Balotelli nodded over from a corner. But, with City beginning to look like they were getting a foothold into the game, Sunderland found the net: Larsson swept the ball into the corner of Hart's goal, after good work by Sessegnon.

In truth, the home side were looking disjointed and couldn't get going like their previous home record had suggested – but they were offered a get out of jail free card, when Dzeko went down in the area and the referee pointed to the spot. Balotelli stepped up and sent the keeper the wrong way.

But, despite that goal, City went into half time behind. A ball from the right flank was met by Bendtner. His header left Hart with no chance, and the England international was picking the ball out of his net once again. City were causing themselves problems and needed stern words at the break.

Clearly, though, the goal before the break wasn't the wake-up call that the hosts heeded. Ten minutes into the second half, the home side had a mountain to climb as Bendtner crossed to the back post, where Larsson slid the ball over the line. City's unbeaten run at home was hanging by a thread.

Kolarov whipped a free kick just wide of the post, before Tevez had an effort from the edge of the box that was awkward for Mignolet, but the Belgian keeper held onto the shot. Kolarov thumped another free kick wide of the post from the right flank, before Bendtner fired over from the edge of the box: City were getting shots in, but they were shots-to-nothing, at best.

Johnson won a free kick for City on the right flank and it was touched short to Yaya Toure. His cross was cleared, but Balotelli picked up the rebound on the left wing. Cutting inside, he fired a shot at goal and it beat Mignolet to give the home side hope, with five minutes to play.

Immediately, City pulled the game level. Tevez squared the ball to Kolarov on the edge of the box, as the Argentine was crowded out by the penalty spot and had to retreat. The full back powered his boot through the ball and drove it through the area; it smashed past Mignolet and City were on terms.

With two minutes of stoppage time to play, Yaya Toure wasted a good chance from the edge of the box, after Johnson had cut inside. He skied the effort, with better options square. It summed up City's afternoon in front of goal. It was a rescue job by City to earn the draw, but they now needed favours from elsewhere if they were to come out on top in the title race.

NO LONGER TITLE FAVOURITES: A WAKE UP CALL ·

So, it's the morning after the evening after the morning after the night before. And we're not top of the table for the first time in five months. Defeat in Wales, combined with a United victory at Old Trafford ensured that City slipped a point behind their title rivals and their near neighbours, with just ten games to play. And the world looked on in horror, as thousands of children in blue shirts were jeered by their classmates and many of their parents phoned in sick. And Bono and Bob Geldof launched CityAid, because, with the title out of their grasp, the Blues were condemned to yet another season of mediocrity.

Now, I say that not to be offensive and not to be flippant, but just to put into perspective the events of the last couple of days. Worse things have happened, are happening and are going to happen. Even in football, worse things will happen. Ok, so, now we're the chasers. And we, on paper, have the more difficult fixtures. But it's not like we're going to slip out of the league or like we're not going to be playing Champions League football next season or like we're on the verge of bankruptcy.

Don't get me wrong here – I'm not over the moon to be in second place with ten games to go, having been first for so long. In fact, I'm quite fucked off with it, just like you are. However, the title is still very much in our own hands: The equation is quite simple; win every game and we will win the league by, at least, two points. Because both City and United can't win all their games, given we play each other in one of them.

Perhaps I'm over-simplifying the situation. Winning every game seems a very simple solution to a rather complex problem, but it's not too far from what United have been doing. To their credit (words I won't type very often, mind), through their difficult fixtures, United have clung on to City's shirt-tails like a bit of your morning poo that affixed itself to your best top when you didn't realise you'd trapped the back of your clothing under the toilet seat when sitting down on the throne first thing. And City didn't change their shirt, but instead they rather proudly walked into that important meeting, blissfully unaware of the horrible ending that was heading their way that day.

But there'll be more meetings to repair the damage, though the job's going to be a tough one. It's now City's turn to play their run of difficult games during United's easier matches and it's our turn to make sure that we're still within those two points when it comes to derby day. Providing that's the case, the chance to go back to the top of the league (with two games to play afterwards) will be ours and if we don't take it, then we only have ourselves to blame.

Going behind at this stage of the season isn't ideal, but it's not a disaster and it's certainly rectifiable. It's just not very nice to slip up in the manner that we did: Conceding that goal to Swansea, knowing United were winning and we were dropping behind them in the league, was very much like giving a blowjob to a rent boy. There was a sense of foreboding before it happened, an overwhelming feeling of disappointment while it was happening and, when it's over, all that's left is a nasty taste in the mouth.

All we can do now is take care of our own business and we've got ten games to do it in. We might have to face Chelsea at home and Arsenal away, but that's the way it goes; and, who knows, we might well take maximum points from those fixtures. Who would have thought Blackburn would go to Old Trafford and win? Who would have backed Newcastle to spank United at St James' Park... err... The Sports Direct Arena? Who would have thought Sunderland would have nicked our game at The Stadium of Light or West Brom would have taken a point at The Hawthorns?

Exactly. These next ten games are not as easy or hard as anybody thinks. Strange results happen, no more so than at the end of a season, as teams pick up unexpected points all over the place. Those challenging for titles throw them away and those fighting to stay up steal them. And those with no danger of doing anything meander towards the middle of May, liberally sprinkling points towards whoever is kind enough to take them (and there's another eye-opener because that used to be us, just a couple of years ago).

See, the defeat at Swansea prompted two very large reactions from City fans. The first was to throw the toys out of the pram and scream/shout/hysterically cry/hack own head off because the title race was over and there was no chance City were going to fight back (eurgh). And the second was to point out where City used to be ten to fifteen years ago in a bid to point out that we've come a long way and should be happy with our lot (eurgh, also).

Now, I admit, I have a reputation for sitting on the fence (yes, my posterior does contain a few splinters, thank you very much), but this is exactly the time to be perching ourselves neatly between the two arguments. From the first camp, the loss is a reality check: The Premier League is not won until it's mathematically impossible for any team to pass those sitting in first place. Yes, we'd been top for months, but that means the thin end of knob all when the final table is drawn up. Equally, being top of the league (or thereabouts, now), we can't just turn up and expect to win games and that we're now in second place should be a wake-up call to anybody who had developed an air of complacency.

However, from that second argument, it's also prevalent to note where City have come from in recent years. It's taken substantial investment to be able to compete for the Premier League title and, since Roberto Mancini has been in charge of the club, we've improved every year. And we have improved this year, whether we win the league or not. And we will improve again next year. And the year after that.

We do need to be thankful that our final local (league) derby this season should be against United and should play such a major part in who is going to finish as the best team in England, rather than being against Stockport or Macclesfield and deciding whether or not we will be going up/getting into the playoffs/staying in the division. It's important to realise the steps we have taken, but, equally, it's important not to lose that ambition to be the best. There's nothing wrong with being disappointed with what will be City's best ever Premier League finish if we're not champions, but we do need to realise that we are, year after year, getting better.

And so, we have ten games to decide what is going to happen. It's down to the players, the management team and, crucially, the fans. We need to back the team, home and away. We need not to be grumbling or groaning when a pass is misplaced inside the first ninety seconds. We need not to sigh or moan when we haven't scored a first half goal. We need not to be anxious when we're under pressure and tense when the other team are putting up a good fight.

We need to support the team and help them see this through. Perhaps we've been complacent and we've had our bottoms stung for it; it's almost as if we've expected to win, being the league leaders. If United fans act and their team plays like they have already won the league, then they will lose it. But if City fans act and our team plays like United have already won the league, then we have already lost. This isn't over yet.

Come on City.

Let's fucking do this.

TIME TO GET REALISTIC

That's that, then. March is done and dusted and it's a not-so-polite fuck off from me towards the month that has been as good for our title hopes as that last packet of biscuits has been for my training schedule before the Manchester 10k. From a possible 15 Premier League points this month, City have taken eight. Two wins, two draws and a defeat and finishing the month two points off the top of the league, having played a game more than the leaders.

City started the month five points ahead of second place, also having played a game more. Throw in an exit from Europe and only one of City's seven games in all competitions producing a good 90 minute performance from the Blues and it's been the worst month of the season.

Despite it still being mathematically possible, it's at this point where I nail the Mooney colours to the mast and confirm, if the mildly sombre tone of this column so far hasn't already done so, that my towel is in the ring and I have come to the conclusion that City will probably not win the league this season. For me, the time has come to be realistic, rather than optimistic.

The warning signs have been there for a while and a draw with Sunderland isn't where it's gone wrong. In fact, at home isn't where it's gone wrong, given that point against the Black Cats meant that was the first time since February 2011 that City didn't take all three points in a home game. The costly errors have been on the road. Fulham and Liverpool early on were minor setbacks, but nothing we couldn't handle. Same with Chelsea and, to a degree, Everton. But soon, Swansea happened and then Peter Crouch proved why he's a Jedi, being a true-to-life example of Yoda's words: "Try not. Do. Or do not. There is no try."

Nevertheless, hand on heart, I can honestly say I've not been convinced by an away performance of City's after the derby victory in October.

Since then, City have played ten times in the league away from The Etihad Stadium and picked up 12 of a possible 30 points. Of those ten games, City have won three (QPR, Wigan, Aston Villa), drawn three (Liverpool, West Brom, Stoke) and lost four (Chelsea, Sunderland, Everton, Swansea). And they've not been particularly convincing in any of them, unlike the away games before them (Bolton, Tottenham, Fulham (albeit a draw), Blackburn, Manchester United).

Last season, this stuttering away form and near perfect home form (remind you of anyone?) would have been good enough, but, unfortunately (perhaps unluckily) for us, this season, it's not.

In fact, any other season, City would probably still be in front and favourites. But, this season they're not and, the truth is, I wonder where our next away points will come from. Wolves at Molineux is the only game I can see City taking maximum points from; Arsenal, Norwich and Newcastle are away days I really don't fancy.

And now we've hit the situation where United can lose the derby, but still win the league. City need a favour off somebody else. Of course, though, if that favour does come, City really do need to help themselves; something they haven't been doing for the last month, at the very least.

Yet, whatever the outcome, this will be City's best ever Premier League season, given the club has exactly the same points total now as they did at the end of their previous best ever Premier League season – ie. Last season. Year on year for the last three campaigns, we have had our best ever in the Premier League; there's been progress and there have been lessons well and truly learnt. Roberto Mancini's City have always been better with each passing season.

This season, his side re-wrote the record books early on. They stole the consecutive home wins record. They've given United their biggest ever home Premier League defeat. They've played football the likes of which most City fans have only dreamt of. And this is why anybody considering that the manager should lose his job if the club doesn't finish top of the pile is so, so wrong.

Okay, so the progress hasn't quite been as drastic as expected. Last year, we ended the trophy drought and made the step up to the Champions League. This year, barring any disasters, we have stepped up at least one league position, with more points and more goals. And we've genuinely challenged for a title – that still could be ours, however unlikely you or I think it now – instead of flirting with the top spot having played more games than anyone else over Christmas. Mancini has been building on what he's achieved each season and to scrap that and start again with a new man is ludicrous.

Look at where that's gotten Chelsea.

That's not to say we shouldn't be disappointed if we don't win the league. We most definitely should; we've been on top of the thing for months, so not to finish the job is upsetting. However, the future is surely brighter for City than you would immediately think: Chelsea and Arsenal have fallen away and need strengthening to be able to fight for the title again, especially the latter of the two. United are weaker than most seasons (though not as weak as some would have you believe) and they haven't played the quality of football that's set them apart from most of the division – surely, without investment and improvement, they can't keep on scraping through for another 12 months?

Meanwhile, I'd suggest City will come back stronger next season, whether we win the league or not. Think for a moment of next season's title challenge if we don't win it this season; Roberto Mancini isn't going to let the squad go out all guns blazing and fade away again. Now imagine City do win the league this season; Roberto Mancini won't let the squad go out all guns blazing and fade away again.

Think of how you felt last season when Wayne Rooney's overhead kick hit the back of Joe Hart's net. Then think back to October and how you felt the next time those two teams played out that particular fixture, specifically when Dzeko's second wriggled through de Gea. The overhead kick doesn't matter so much anymore, eh?

So be disappointed that we dropped two points to Sunderland. Be disappointed that we handed the initiative to United. Be disappointed if we don't come back and win it. But look at the bigger picture.

That title is certainly coming and it's coming soon.

March 2012 Breakdown

Games (all competitions):
Won: 3   **Drawn:** 2   **Lost:** 2

Goals (all competitions):
For: 11   **Against:** 9

Progress:
Premier League: 2nd
League Cup: Eliminated in the Semi Final
FA Cup: Eliminated in Round Three
Champions League: 3rd in Group A
Europa League: Eliminated in the Round of 16

Premier League Table

		P	W	D	L	F	A	GD	Pts
1	Manchester United	30	23	4	3	74	27	+47	73
2	**Manchester City**	**31**	**22**	**5**	**4**	**75**	**25**	**+50**	**71**
3	Arsenal	31	18	4	9	62	41	+21	58
4	Tottenham Hotspur	30	16	7	7	53	35	+18	55
5	Chelsea	31	15	8	8	53	36	+17	53

April 2012

Arsenal 1-0 Manchester City

FA Premier League

Sunday 8 April, 2012 – 16:00 KO

City: Hart, Zabaleta, Clichy, Kompany (c), Lescott, Y Toure (Pizarro 17), Barry, Milner, Nasri (Kolarov 79), Aguero (Tevez 84), Balotelli
Unused: Pantilimon, Richards, de Jong, Dzeko
Goals: -
Booked: Y Toure, Balotelli, Milner, Zabaleta
Sent Off: Balotelli
Man of the Match: Vincent Kompany

With 15 minutes played, City were lucky to still be level. A corner was played into the visitors' area and van Persie met the ball and looked to have scored. But Vermaelen on the line blocked his own man's effort, before Rosicky put the rebound over the bar.

Balotelli, lucky to still be on the pitch after the referee had missed a late, high challenge from him on Song, then almost got the visitors in front. A corner from the right wing was swung low into the six-yard box and he flicked it at goal, but it was blocked on the line and away to safety.

The second half got off to a much slower start than the first. The two City Argentines got in each other's way and Aguero's header looped towards goal. It needed Szczesny to tip it over, but it was a much easier save than it should have been, with the striker hindered by Zabaleta's presence.

Just after the hour mark, there was another let off for City. Song played a great ball into the box from deep and it was met by the forehead of van Persie. Hart was beaten, left standing, as was Kompany, but the ball rebounded off the post and the visitors were able to get the ball clear.

Hart produced a fine save, tipping the ball onto the post and Vermaelen, faced with an open goal, couldn't force it over the line. The City keeper got across again, before Lescott blocked from Benayoun and it hit the other post before dribbling clear of the goal.

With four minutes of the game to play, City's title challenge was all but over. Pizarro couldn't keep the ball in midfield and Arteta picked it up. unleashed a great strike past Hart and into the bottom corner. It had been coming.

To rub salt into the City wounds, Mario Balotelli was shown his second yellow card of the game for a late challenge on Song in the corner, as the defender cleared the ball.

Manchester City 4-0 West Bromwich Albion

FA Premier League

Wednesday 11 April, 2012 – 19:45 KO

City: Hart, Richards, Clichy, Kompany (c), Lescott, de Jong, Barry, Silva (Zabaleta 81), Nasri, Aguero (Dzeko 73), Tevez (A Johnson 63)
Unused: Pantilimon, Kolarov, Milner, Pizarro
Goals: Aguero (5, 54), Tevez (61), Silva (64)
Booked: -
Man of the Match: Sergio Aguero

City needed a good start to wash away the disappointment of Sunday's result and that's exactly what they got. With just five minutes played, the home side had the lead; Aguero picked up the ball in midfield and carried it straight at the West Brom defence. They backed off and the Argentine had room to shoot from the edge of the box. His effort curled around the covering defenders and beat Foster into the bottom corner.

The second half was where City came alive. It started as Nasri volleyed a Silva cross into the side netting, before Silva blasted a shot from the edge of the box that caught Dawson square in the face and knocked him clean to the ground. The pressure on the visitors was building.

And it soon told: Nasri slipped the ball to Aguero on the left side of the box and, breaking at the goalkeeper, he slid a shot into the bottom corner of the net. He doubled City's lead and the home side were cruising.

That second goal triggered the opening of the floodgates: Next up it was Tevez. Nasri found Aguero running into the left side of the box and, after stretching to keep the ball in, he pulled it back towards the Frenchman. He didn't connect, but behind him was Tevez and, with just the goalkeeper to beat, he made no mistake to smash the ball home.

Minutes later, some brilliant closing down from Clichy forced a mistake and Aguero stole the ball inside the visitors' half. Running at the last remaining defender, he slipped the ball wide to Silva who was in support and the Spaniard drew Foster and delightfully chipped his effort over the goalkeeper.

As the final whistle blew, City's fans waited to hear confirmation of the final score at the DW Stadium. Wigan had won and City had closed the gap at the top of the league back to five points.

Norwich City 1-6 Manchester City

FA Premier League
Saturday 14 April, 2012 – 12:45 KO

City: Hart, Zabaleta, Kompany (c), Lescott, Clichy, de Jong, Barry, Nasri (Y Toure 63), Silva (A Johnson 77), Aguero, Tevez (Richards 81)
Unused: Pantilimon, Kolarov, Milner, Dzeko
Goals: Tevez (18, 73, 80), Aguero (27, 75), A Johnson (90+3)
Booked: Tevez, Nasri
Man of the Match: Carlos Tevez

It was all go from the off at Carrow Road, as Lescott needed Kompany's help to clear the ball, after the Englishman missed his attempt, before the visitors almost opened the scoring as Barry's header was cleared off the line. From the breakaway, Pilkington skipped past both Zabaleta and Nasri, but his shot curled wide of Hart's post.

With 18 minutes played, City took the lead. Tevez picked the ball up outside the area and carried it towards the box. From 20 yards, he smashed a shot at goal and it swerved past Ruddy and into the back of the net.

It was looking like an away performance from the start of the season for City and, just before the half hour mark, Aguero scored his first goal in a blue shirt outside of Manchester or London. A neat Tevez backheel set up his compatriot to half-volley at goal; he gave Ruddy no chance.

Early in the second half, the Norwich recovery looked like it could be on: Hart didn't get the ball away with a weak punch and it fell to Surman inside the box. Keeping his cool, the midfielder dropped the ball into the net.

However, with 73 minutes on the clock, the Blues extended their lead. Tevez reacted quickest to Ruddy's save and got to the rebound ahead of the defender, nodding it into the empty net and restoring the two goal advantage. That advantage quickly became three – Aguero curled an excellent effort past Ruddy from just inside the box and the Blues had scored twice in two minutes.

Five minutes later, City added another. Tevez latched onto a short backpass and took it around the goalkeeper, to slide it into the empty net. It was a hat-trick and he celebrated with a spot of pantomimed golf – all in good humour.

Substitute Johnson clipped the bar with an effort with the outside of his foot, before Aguero smashed a shot into the post; City weren't hanging back and were looking to add to their goal difference.

And, in stoppage time, the Blues had the ball in the net once more: A brilliant ball from Aguero found Clichy, who slipped it back inside to Johnson in the box, leaving him the simple task of slotting it home.

Wolverhampton Wanderers 0-2 Manchester City
FA Premier League
Sunday 22 April, 2012 – 16:00 KO

City: Hart, Zabaleta, Kompany (c), Lescott, Clichy, Y Toure, Barry, Nasri (K Toure 86), Silva (de Jong 59), Aguero, Tevez (A Johnson 75)
Unused: Pantilimon, Kolarov, Milner, Dzeko
Goals: Aguero (27), Nasri (74)
Booked: Y Toure
Man of the Match: Gael Clichy

City made their intentions clear from the start, with Tevez having the first shot of the game from range; it was well over the bar in the opening half a minute.

Just before the half hour, City got themselves in front – and it had been coming. A brilliant ball into the middle from Clichy dropped perfectly for Aguero inside the area and, one-on-one with the goalkeeper, he was never going to miss, sliding it past de Vries. It was exactly what the visitors had deserved.

The half time break came at the wrong time for City and, despite their first half dominance, they couldn't get going in the second period. Wolves found themselves with more possession and it took Zabaleta and Kompany to combine to keep out Ward, before Fletcher tested Hart with a great header from a free kick, but the City keeper pulled off a good stop to keep it out.

Just as the home side looked to be getting back on top, a quick bit of thinking from Tevez set the Blues away. He played a quick one-two with Clichy from a free kick and slid the ball through to the back post, where Nasri and Aguero were queuing up. It was Nasri who beat the goalkeeper for 0-2.

With eight minutes to play, Johnson pulled out a peach of a ball to find Aguero onside and through on goal. But, with so much time, he took a bad touch inside the box and the defenders were able to get back to cover.

Having seen United draw earlier in the day, the Blues now had the title back in their own hands: It all rests on the Manchester derby – a win for City will take them back to the top of the league.

Manchester City 1-0 Manchester United
FA Premier League
Monday 30 April, 2012 – 20:00 KO

City: Hart, Zabaleta, Kompany (c), Lescott, Clichy, Y Toure, Barry, Nasri (Milner 90), Silva (Richards 82), Tevez (de Jong 68), Aguero
Unused: Pantilimon, Kolarov, Balotelli, Dzeko
Goals: Kompany (45)
Booked: Kompany, Y Toure, de Jong
Man of the Match: Gareth Barry

With three points separating the two sides at kick-off, City knew that anything other than a win would see them trailing the visitors with only two games to play. Worse, a United win would leave the Reds needing a single point from their remaining matches to take the league. A City win, however, and the Blues would go back to the summit of the Premier League table on goal difference.

It was the visitors with the early pressure. From their first corner, City struggled to get the ball clear, with a last-gasp block from Kompany and the Blues just about scrambled it away. United wanted a handball from the Belgian, but the referee waved the shouts away.

The Reds didn't test Hart in the opening stages, but they were in control of the game. City were struggling to hold on to possession and hadn't threatened de Gea's goal. Soon, though, that changed: Nasri weaved his way through the visiting defence and slotted it through to Tevez. He smashed the ball back across the box in search of Aguero, but Jones got in the way to clear.

From a corner, Rooney botched his clearance and fired it more up than away. Zabaleta won it and played it back into the box, where Lescott knocked it down for Aguero to volley. He smashed it at goal, but he skewed his effort high and wide of the post.

However, United were defending as well as City attacked; whatever the Blues tried, they just couldn't break through a packed back-line. Aguero almost found room for a shot, but Ferdinand was in his way and the Argentine couldn't force the effort on target.

As the board went up for stoppage time, it looked like the teams would be level. However, Silva delivered a corner into the six-yard box, where Kompany had lost his marker. He connected with it perfectly and his bullet header almost broke the back of the net.

A de Jong tackle on Welbeck had the managers going head-to-head on the touchline, as a disagreement between Roberto Mancini and Sir Alex Ferguson escalated. It showed the importance of the game and the tension in the air.

With ten minutes to play, it was Yaya Toure who could have added to City's tally. He broke away with the ball on one of his trademark runs, but his curling effort from the edge of the box didn't quite swing back in and finished just wide.

Zabaleta and Barry did brilliantly to keep the ball alive in the United half, as Giggs almost got it clear, before some hard work from Toure found Nasri free inside the area. He couldn't dig the ball out from under his feet to find the shot, before he had it nicked away from him by Smalling. City were inches away from sealing it, as the board for stoppage time went up.

With less than a minute remaining, United won a corner and packed the box. The first ball in was cleared, before the second found Rooney unmarked on the edge of the area. He tried to shoot, but Lescott got in the way and, as the rebound was crossed by into the middle, Smalling fouled Hart and the visitors' pressure was over. To the relief of the City fans, the final whistle blew as the ball was cleared down the pitch.

From being eight points behind only a few weeks previous, City had clawed their way back to the top of the table. City and United were level on points, but the Blues' superior goal difference was key. It's advantage City – though the games against Newcastle and QPR won't be easy.

This title will go down to the last day of the season.

INTERVIEW: JOE CORRIGAN

When it comes to the number ones, Manchester City have something of a history. The man between the posts is one of the most crucial positions on the field; a confident goalkeeper breeds a confident defence breeds a confident team. And City have had some good shot-stoppers down the years. The names that spring immediately to mind are the likes of Frank Swift, Bert Trautmann, Alex Williams, or Tony Coton. The man currently with the gloves is also well on course to join that list.

In 1966, however, Manchester City signed a goalie on a youth contract who would go on to be the club's first choice. Three and a half years after signing, he was a double-winner, as City took the League Cup and the European Cup Winners Cup in 1969-70. His name was Joe Corrigan. And, looking at his build, it's hardly surprising that he didn't start out as a footballer.

"I went to Sale Grammar School and I played rugby union," he says, looking back. "It was a great grounding for me to become a goalkeeper; I always wanted to be a keeper. I left school and went into AEI in Trafford Park and then I got a trial with Manchester City. They signed me on that night and it was just an amazing journey from then on.

"It's completely different [how players come through the ranks in the modern day]. You look at the academy here [Manchester City] and the facility the kids have got. I don't think I'd have had a chance in the game today because it's so selective. And anybody who's not the right shape tends to get pushed to one side.

"I was ten years at Liverpool with their School of Excellence and I was working as a first team goalkeeping coach at West Brom and their academy was the same. It's so difficult now, because it's not just a local team anymore. It's a worldwide game."

Corrigan's league debut for City came in a defeat at Ipswich in 1969. He had previously played for the club in a League Cup tie with Blackpool, with Harry Dowd injured and Ken Mulhearn cup-tied. When he nailed down the position as his own, though, he never looked back and became one of the best keepers in the club's history.

"It was one of the real true success eras of Manchester City," he says. "I was fortunate enough to play in a team with the likes of Tommy Booth, Mike Summerbee, Glyn Pardoe, Alan Oakes, Francis Lee – legends of the game. [It's mind-blowing] to be able to be a part of that setup with Malcolm Allison and Joe Mercer as the manager and the club coming from the shadows of Manchester United. In those days, City were the predominant team in the city.

"And then they went through another iffy patch in 1973 and 1974, but Tony Book took over and we had another great era, with Asa Hartford, Joe Royle, Dennis Tueart and people of that calibre. It was just amazing. And it was just an honour to be part of Manchester City for a long, long time."

The conversation turns to Big Joe's appearances for the Blues. He's the goalkeeper who has played the most number of games for City and second-most number of games of any player, behind only Alan Oakes. But he thinks he might have a challenger for that record.

"I think that's going to be beaten by Joe Hart," he says. "If he keeps his head screwed on and his love and passion for the game, I can't see anyone getting anywhere near him. To think the lad's only 23 years of age... he could break every record conceivable at Manchester City and for England.

"I think he's a very, very good goalkeeper," he continues. "I went to watch him when I was at West Brom. Bryan Robson said to me that there was a goalkeeper at Shrewsbury Town, which, ironically, was one of the teams where I went on loan when I was a kid. I went to watch him, came back and said he was a great prospect. He was about 16 or 17 at the time, so I said [the transfer fee would be] £250,000 with add ons.

"We found out not long after that Man City had put £650,000 down and we just couldn't afford that. I was then doing some scouting for the FA and I followed him when he went to Birmingham, the season he was picked to go into the World Cup squad. There, he was fantastic in the games I saw him play and it was, I said at the time, a difficult decision for City when he returned.

"I've known players who have gone on loan and most of them have come back itching to play again. For me, it was fortunate for Joe that they had an international game before the actual season started last year. Shay had come back fit, Joe had just come back from a World Cup and a very successful season with Birmingham and England picked him to play in that game.

"You'd have to ask Mr. Mancini [to be sure], but I think that fact that he played in the game a few days before the season started made it possible for the manager to pick him for the first game. And he's never looked back.

"He's been an absolute star, this season."

And if there's anybody who knows what makes a good goalkeeper, it's Big Joe. What does he put it down to? "Playing behind a good defence!" He laughs. "It's all about confidence. The more experience you get, the better you become as a goalkeeper – as with any position. It's more with goalkeepers, because you learn and get your positioning. The biggest thing, though, is what you have in your chest: If you don't have a big heart, you can't become a great goalkeeper."

He also thinks that goalkeeping has changed like no other position on the field since he was last between the sticks: "I feel sorry for the keepers that are playing today. The ball they use today is unbelievable. It's different from the ball we played with. It moves so quickly.

"People ask why goalkeepers don't catch the balls anymore; it's frightening the amount of movement that's in it. You need good hands and feet and you need to be more of an outfield player because you can't pick up backpasses like we used to. That's changed goalkeeping, for me, for the better.

"The pitches... you don't ever see a dirty goalkeeper anymore. They go off the same colour as they went on, apart from if it's wet. We used to play on pitches that you couldn't believe: Leeds United, Derby County, Maine Road... it was just the done thing, you just got on with it.

"The kit's different, too. The boots and gloves – we didn't play with gloves when I first started. We used to buy our own string gloves when it was wet, icy or snowy."

Perhaps the most unfortunate aspect of Corrigan's career was that he was held in such high regard at the same time as Ray Clemence and Peter Shilton. Despite his performances for City, he never truly got the chance to impress on the national stage. But he doesn't have any bad feelings about his luck.

"I feel proud to be mentioned in the same breath as them. We were very fortunate in those days. I had nine caps for England and I think I still hold the record for the most number of England B caps. If I'd have just got one cap... to play for your country, you can't get any higher, whether you play one game or a hundred and twenty games, you've still reached that pinnacle.

"It's a matter of opinion. I always thought I was the best in the world. They always thought they were the best in the world. And if you didn't think you were the best in the world, then you shouldn't have been playing a game to start with.

"I had a fantastic career. I was club captain at Manchester City, won trophies and I played for my country."

WHY ALWAYS THEM?

While it was in the September of 2008 that Sheikh Mansour took control of Manchester City Football Club, the 2008-09 campaign for the Blues wasn't the best on the pitch. In fact, it ended with the team outside all of the European places and had a Christmas Day in the relegation zone wedged into the middle of it. That was the last time that City met United just twice over the course of a season; every year since then, there has been more than the minimum two Manchester derbies.

Those two derbies of 2008-09 were bleak for City: Two defeats, no goals and barely a shot in either. There was so much between the two sides, you'd never have believed the gap had looked smaller the year earlier – when Sven's side had twice beaten their local rivals. Fast forward to a new manager and throw in a few new players and progress had stalled somewhat.

But that's when City got serious. In a manner, the club declared war on the team from across town. With a summer of additions – including the high profile signing of Carlos Tevez – the Blues had suddenly gone from a team with no European football to one that was pushing to finish fourth in the Premier League. That transfer saga was the start of where the bad blood began to get worse between the two Manchester clubs. Previously, City's mid-table woes and relegation battles had mattered little to United's title challenges and European nights, and vice-versa.

The sides met twice a year and battled it out, with the bragging rights at stake. There were a few days of lying low in work for the losing side's fans, but other than that, that was it.

But that Tevez switch signalled the start of City's rise; the now infamous poster being a cheap dig that got United's back up and had those in charge of the Reds foaming at the mouths. They were rattled. It added extra feeling to that first meeting between the two sides and it felt, for the first time in a long time, that City were somewhere near to pushing United all the way. It was the first step in the Blues' re-emergence from the wilderness; they went in off the back of four wins. Of course, we all know how it ended: Michael Owen stole the points with a goal in added time to added time.

We might not have realised it then, but that game marked the beginning of a new era of Manchester derbies. This was no longer the haves against the have nots; this was the beginning of a fight for power. City were trying to wrestle it from United and it was no longer simply bragging rights at stake. This was league position and future success for City. For United, it was a battle to stay in pole position and to avoid being eclipsed by their nearest rivals.

Before that match in 2009-10, Sir Alex Ferguson uttered his famous "not in my lifetime" quote – in answer to the question of whether City would go into a derby match as favourites. Not only has he since been proven wrong on that front, as the Blues have now gone into a derby with shorter odds than United, but he has himself passed comment on it, claiming the Blues were where the money should be placed for this season's FA Cup tie.

As much as us City fans don't want it to be true, the fact of the matter is United aren't going to just go away. They've had dominance over England for nigh on twenty years and, as is the case with any sort of evil empire, the idea of giving up power isn't one that is ever jumped at. The inconvenience of the matter is that, to become top dogs in this country, City are going to have to dismantle what United have built brick by brick. Mario Balotelli almost hit the nail on the head; he said 'Why always me?', when he should have asked 'Why always them?'

Since the takeover and since City have been climbing the table in their quest for success, they have had to overcome United at every significant point. The coincidental and slightly queer fact that the Reds have been constantly standing in the Blues' way for every little achievement is quite symbolic of the fight as a whole. They have what we want and we have to forcefully take it from them. To be a success, we have to stop them from stopping us.

Back in 2009-10, City had their best chance yet of picking up silverware, having just smashed three past Arsenal's kids and made it to the semi finals of the League Cup. Leaving the ground, fans were desperately trying to find out who the club had drawn. And then the news broke: Manchester United. To make matters worse, it was the most difficult draw, being the home leg first and the away leg second.

The Reds, having played a weakened side all the way up to that point, signalled their intent to the competition and towards City. One could be forgiven for thinking United were more concerned from stopping the Blues winning the cup, rather than winning it themselves; the policy of playing fringe players stopped immediately when it became obvious City were serious about lifting the trophy that so many teams shun. United won that battle, but only just.

The progress for City took another dent later that season. The push for a Champions League place over Tottenham, Aston Villa and Liverpool appeared to be swinging into the Blues' favour, until one Manchester United rocked up at the City of Manchester Stadium. A last minute goal – the third that campaign – again won the game for the visitors, and that sparked a run of form that saw City lose out to Spurs in a penultimate match 'playoff'. While City had clearly improved, they were still some way behind United.

Then came last season. City managed to earn one more point in the Manchester derbies than the campaign previous, but that was a somewhat soul-destroying and wholly forgettable 0-0 draw at Eastlands, the undoubted highlight of which being the final whistle, when fans could finally go home and wonder how better they could have spent that ninety minutes. In fact, it's the fixture in February that is more telling – City turned up at Old Trafford and were marginally the better side, a marked improvement on the year before. They only lost that game due to a freak, out-of-this-world, unbelievably good goal, that, on another day, would have landed somewhere on the M60.

But that wasn't the half of it. With City looking to end a trophy drought of over three decades, the FA Cup was going well and had been suspiciously kind to the Blues. The big sides were dropping out and City had been given favourable draws against lower league opposition and, on the one occasion they drew a Premier League side, it was at home. But then, just before the quarter final with Reading, the balls were pulled out of that strange bowl thing on ITV and, if they got through, City would be paired up with United. At Wembley.

Once again, the Reds were blocking the path of City's progress.

This time, City came out on top – and deservedly so. Rooney was missing, as was Tevez, and both sides went toe-to-toe for the honour of being an FA Cup finalist. The banner at Old Trafford proudly displayed the years since the Blues had won a major trophy (not that they care, obviously); it wasn't officially sanctioned by the club, but clearly endorsed, as, had they wanted it gone, it could quite easily have been removed. Roberto Mancini had previously failed on his first attempt to fulfil his promise of tearing it down.

There wasn't going to be an easy way for him to do it. It looked like if he was going to do it, he was going to have to get the better of United. First it was the League Cup. And then the FA Cup. As we know now, he kept that promise. He went on to complete the cup run by seeing off Stoke in the final and lifting the trophy last May.

The next time the two sides would meet was the Community Shield: The opening game of the season; the curtain raiser. And, back in August, nobody would have predicted just how significant the two teams that contested that match would be. It's telling now that the showpiece for the FA Premier League would be contested by the two teams vying to win it nine months on. City threw away a two-goal lead to lose that game and, from that point on, proceeded to smash records in the opening months of the season, as team after team were dispatched en route to October and a trip to Old Trafford.

A United win would see them leapfrog the Blues into top spot. A City win would see them open up a five point gap at the table's summit. It would turn out to be the Blues' biggest step yet in taking a wrecking ball to Sir Alex Palpatine's empire. Six huge hits were sustained that day and City inflicted United's largest ever Premier League defeat at Old Trafford. Fans that had been arguing that the gap between the two clubs was getting shorter began to argue that it was actually getting wider: That blue had become more dominant than red.

Of course, that was too premature.

The FA Cup was next: The third round draw threw these teams together once again. But for an unjust red card, it could have been a different story; but a club mustn't lament its bad luck. United made it into the pot for the fourth round, though City gave them a scare, with one man fewer for eighty of the ninety minutes and from three goals behind. That first cup might have gone in the trophy cabinet, but the second one after it was still not going to be an easy task, as this season proved.

And now it comes down to this. This evening, City host United for the final time in the Premier League this season. A home win will see the Blues back on top of the league on goal difference. A draw will play right into the Reds' hands, giving them a three point lead with two games to play. An away win will all but confirm the title is heading to Old Trafford. While many of us hoped that the title race would be over well before this match, when the fixtures were announced it was always going to be inevitable that this would play a key role.

United have stood in City's way in everything they have tried to do since the takeover. If City are to knock United into second place in this country, then they will have to do it both literally and metaphorically. In the wartime metaphor, the battles have been tight and close, and, for three years, City have been gradually gaining ground, while United have stagnated. But in the literal world, the Reds have stopped the Blues on several occasions in the past.

A win this evening will go some way to swinging the balance of power and will take the war to its next level. United stood in City's way for Champions League qualification and that was eventually overcome. They stood in the way of a trophy to break the duck and that was eventually overcome. They now stand in the way of league progress. It's do or die. All or nothing. Win or lose.

To exorcise the ghosts of the past, the torment of United's success compared to the Blues' exploration of England's lower leagues, City simply need some success of their own. To get it, however, it seems like they are always going to have to get the better of their rivals.

The next battle in the war begins tonight.

April 2012 Breakdown

<u>Games (all competitions):</u>
Won: 4   **Drawn:** 0   **Lost:** 1

<u>Goals (all competitions):</u>
For: 13   **Against:** 2

<u>Progress:</u>
Premier League: 1st
League Cup: Eliminated in the Semi Final
FA Cup: Eliminated in Round Three
Champions League: 3rd in Group A
Europa League: Eliminated in the Round of 16

<u>Premier League Table</u>

		P	W	D	L	F	A	GD	Pts
1	**Manchester City**	36	26	5	5	88	27	+61	83
2	Manchester United	36	26	5	5	86	33	+53	83
3	Arsenal	36	20	6	10	68	44	+24	66
4	Tottenham Hotspur	35	18	8	9	59	39	+20	62
5	Newcastle United	35	18	8	9	53	46	+7	62

May 2012

Newcastle United 0-2 Manchester City
FA Premier League
Sunday 6 May, 2012 – 13:30 KO

City: Hart, Zabaleta, Kompany (c), Lescott, Clichy, Y Toure, Barry, Nasri (de Jong 62), Silva (Richards 86), Tevez (Dzeko 70), Aguero
Unused: Pantilimon, Kolarov, Milner, A Johnson
Goals: Y Toure (70, 89)
Booked: Barry, Y Toure, Zabaleta
Man of the Match: Yaya Toure

It was Newcastle that started the game with more possession, but it was the visitors with the first spell of pressure. Nasri and Yaya Toure had shots blocked, before a short corner routine allowed Silva to shoot first time in the box. That effort, though, was deflected behind, before Krul pulled off a neat save from a low shot from Silva across goal.

It should have been City that took the lead with five minutes of the half to play. The ball broke to Barry on the edge of the box with room to shoot, but a brilliant save by Krul kept it out. The rebound bounced straight back to him and this time he beat the goalkeeper, but couldn't get it past Santon on the line.

Seconds after the introduction of Dzeko, City put the ball in the net with their next attack. De Jong played a neat one-two with Dzeko, before finding Aguero. He squared for Yaya Toure. The Ivorian placed his shot into the bottom corner of the goal and the Blues squeezed themselves in front.

Soon, Newcastle were still in the game thanks only to Krul. On a one-on-one with Yaya Toure, the keeper stood up and the midfielder slipped. He found Aguero, who appeared to have an open goal. He seemingly lifted it into the net, until Krul's hand came out of nowhere to tip it over the bar.

It was all Newcastle going into the final stages. Richards made a brilliant block from an Ameobi effort on the edge of the box and, on the break from that corner, Clichy slipped Yaya Toure in and he took a touch, before slotting it past Krul to double City's tally with a minute plus stoppage time to play.

Manchester City 3-2 Queens Park Rangers
FA Premier League
Sunday 13 May, 2012 – 15:00 KO

City: Hart, Zabaleta, Kompany (c), Lescott, Clichy, Y Toure (de Jong 44), Barry (Dzeko 69), Nasri, Silva, Tevez (Balotelli 76), Aguero
Unused: Pantilimon, Kolarov, Richards, Milner
Goals: Zabaleta (39), Dzeko (90+2), Aguero (90+4)
Booked: Aguero

Man of the Match: Pablo Zabaleta

City began the game knowing that a win would more than likely seal their first ever Premier League title. For the visitors, a draw would be enough to keep them in the division. While, at the Stadium Of Light, Manchester United could steal City's thunder if they could better the Blues' result.

It was City on top from the off and QPR were happy to see the hosts control possession, but remain firm. Soon, there was bad news from Sunderland: United were a goal ahead and, as it stood, were top of the league.

But, soon enough, City were in front, too: Yaya Toure slipped onto the end of a pass into the box and fed it through to Zabaleta on the overlap; he smashed a shot at goal that Kenny could only parry onto the post and into the back of the net. City were back on the top of the table.

After the break, the game changed. Cisse broke away from the City back line after Lescott misjudged his header and it fell perfectly for the striker to volley. He did and it beat Hart, pulling the visitors level.

QPR were defending stoutly and City were looking sluggish. Barton swung an elbow at Carlos Tevez on the edge of the box and it was spotted by the linesman. The referee produced a red card and, to compound matters, the former City midfielder kicked out at Aguero, before aiming a headbutt in Kompany's direction.

The red card, though, didn't adversely affect the visitors. On 65 minutes, QPR broke away down the left flank and a cross into the box found Mackie unmarked, breaking into the box. He met it with his head and powered the effort past Hart and Lescott on the line and City, needing to win, were suddenly behind and not looking like scoring.

Roberto Mancini went for broke. He threw on Dzeko and Balotelli and City piled men forward into the box, but despite corner after corner and cross after cross, the Blues couldn't force a shot. Dzeko forced Kenny into a good save with his feet. It didn't look like it was going in.

A goalmouth scramble ended with a good double save by Kenny from Aguero, the second preventing the ball from crossing the line from inches out. Balotelli headed at goal, but Kenny was on form again to push it away, also.

The board went up for stoppage time. City had five minutes to score twice – where have we heard that before? The first came from Dzeko. The ball was played into the six-yard box and the Bosnian rose to meet the cross ahead of anybody else. The bullet header was straight past Kenny and City were on level terms, as the final whistle blew in Sunderland. United had won and City needed another.

With a minute to play, the ball was fed into Balotelli on the edge of the box. With his back to goal, he couldn't keep his feet and slipped backwards, but had the presence of mind to nick the ball to Aguero. He beat the challenge and smashed the ball into the back of the net. City were back from the dead.

Manchester City: Premier League Champions.

May 2012 Breakdown

<u>Games (all competitions):</u>
Won: 2   **Drawn:** 0   **Lost:** 0

<u>Goals (all competitions):</u>
For: 5   **Against:** 2

<u>Progress:</u>
Premier League: Winners
League Cup: Eliminated in the Semi Final
FA Cup: Eliminated in Round Three
Champions League: 3rd in Group A
Europa League: Eliminated in the Round of 16

<u>Final Premier League Table</u>

		P	W	D	L	F	A	GD	Pts
1	**Manchester City**	38	28	5	5	93	29	+64	89
2	Manchester United	38	28	5	5	89	33	+56	89
3	Arsenal	38	21	7	10	74	49	+25	70
4	Tottenham Hotspur	38	20	9	9	66	41	+25	69
5	Newcastle United	38	19	8	11	56	51	+5	65
6	Chelsea	38	18	10	10	65	46	+19	64
7	Everton	38	15	11	12	50	40	+10	56
8	Liverpool	38	14	10	14	47	40	+7	52
9	Fulham	38	14	10	14	48	51	-3	52
10	West Bromwich Albion	38	13	8	17	45	52	-7	47
11	Swansea City	38	12	11	15	44	51	-7	47
12	Norwich City	38	12	11	15	52	66	-14	47
13	Sunderland	38	11	12	15	45	46	-1	45
14	Stoke City	38	11	12	15	36	53	-17	45
15	Wigan Athletic	38	11	10	17	42	62	-20	43
16	Aston Villa	38	7	17	14	37	53	-16	38
17	Queens Park Rangers	38	10	7	21	43	66	-23	37
18	Bolton Wanderers	38	10	6	22	46	77	-31	36
19	Blackburn Rovers	38	8	7	23	48	78	-30	31
20	Wolverhampton Wanderers	38	5	10	23	40	82	-42	25

The Rise of the Champions

It's something of a sad affair when you're a 24 year-old male and you can be considered an expert on something that isn't picking your nose or scratching. But I, and I daresay most other City fans of a similar age and demographic, am widely knowledgeable about a subject that could be described, at best, as irritating and, at worst, downright infuriating.

The 2011 FA Cup was City's first trophy in 35 years. The 2012 Premier League title was the first time the Blues have been the best team in England since 1968. If I'm honest, it does make me laugh the horror and shock experienced by Arsenal fans that they – get this – haven't won anything since 2005. How can any team anywhere have no success for seven years? It must be so difficult for them.

I have friends who support Bradford and Wolves. Imagine how they feel.

My earliest memory of a City match is being drenched to the bone wearing a black bin bag in the Platt Lane Stand of Maine Road as Mark Robbins scored a late winner for Leicester in the early 1990s. To be honest, since then, despite often seeing signs to the contrary, it wasn't quite the success story that that five year old had hoped for.

Don't get me wrong, there have been good times. I'll never forget the promotion season under Kevin Keegan, the five added minutes at Wembley in 1999, the derby day victories – especially the Munich anniversary game at Old Trafford, the end of season pushes for Europe… but despite the success signs being present at regular intervals, City have fallen at several hurdles more often than a horse with three legs running the Grand National. The seeds have always been in place, but the flowers have never quite blossomed.

In fact, they normally withered and died.

Though City's problems started long before I can remember, I think the first relegation from the Premier League in 1996 sums up the club better than any long winded metaphor I can conceive. The image of Steve Lomas holding the ball next to the corner flag to preserve a 2-2 draw that would be marginally enough to see City safely down into Division One was trumped only by that of the substituted Niall Quinn bursting from the dugout to inform his team-mate that a point wasn't enough to save the club. It was then generally agreed that City should be searching for a winning goal.

That goal, obviously, didn't come and it was the start of a rollercoaster seven years where City blew every other yo-yo club out of the water and chose to yo-yo between three divisions, instead of the more conventional two. In fact, I got my first season ticket in the 1997-98 season and – just to give you some perspective, here – I didn't watch City play in the same division in consecutive seasons until 2003-04, after they had stayed in the Premier League the campaign before.

Skip forward to April 1997. City had two games left of the season and were battling against relegation to the Second Division. Their games couldn't have been better – they were playing two teams also fighting to avoid the drop – QPR at home and Stoke City away. Two victories would keep the team in the division.

And it was going well when Georgi Kinkladze gave City the lead against QPR. But, as always, it went disastrously wrong when first Mike Sheron levelled.

It was a goal that only City could have conceived. After Martyn Margetson had illegally picked up a backpass and been penalised for it, rather than carry the ball back to his goal and get back into position, he simply handed the ball over to the nearest QPR player, who took a quick kick, squaring to give Sheron an open goal.

It didn't end there. Jamie Pollock then wrote himself in QPR folklore, scoring the own goal that put City's opposition ahead. Credit where credit's due, though, it was a bloody good own goal. So good, in fact, that QPR fans hijacked a poll and voted Pollock one of most influential men of the last 2000 years. He ended up rating higher than Jesus.

City rescued a draw, but that meant that, on the final day of the season, they would have to beat Stoke and hope that one of Portsmouth or Port Vale lost. And, in a turn of events that could only conspire against City, both of those teams won, while City thumped Stoke 2-5. Nothing changed in the league and City were down.

Then, at the end of December 1998, I was sitting in the back of a blue Peugeot 405, at the tender age of 11, listening to Andrew Dawson slot the ball past Nicky Weaver and condemn City to a 2-1 defeat at York. At the time, I probably didn't realise how much of an important moment in City's history it would be, but that defeat left the club in their lowest ever league position – I suppose it's times like this that remind me just how lucky I am that it didn't all spiral on downwards from there, really.

City changed as a club at that point. Before that game, City were prone to losing matches they shouldn't, to dominating home games but coming away with a 0-0 and to handing out points like they were handing out sweets at a child's birthday party. But come the new year, City put a run of results together, got their backsides in gear and dragged themselves up to third position, just missing out on an automatic promotion spot.

When Joe Royle applied the brakes to City's downward slide that December, he was able to shuffle things about to get the club out of reverse and put them into first gear. By the time the playoffs came along, City had gotten up into second gear and climbed out of the league at the first attempt, albeit with a cough and a splutter.

With a squad that was largely unchanged from the season before, City finished the next season in fifth gear and flew into second place, guaranteeing automatic promotion to the Premier League. Though, needing just a point to ensure second place at Ewood Park on the final day of the season, the club didn't half do it the hard way: They were a goal down at half time thanks to Matt Jansen and Blackburn had hit the woodwork four times, while a David Johnson goal at Portman Road meant Ipswich were leading, putting them into second place and City in third.

But goals from Shaun Goater, Mark Kennedy and Paul Dickov, as well as an own goal from Christian Dailly, saw City promoted and the City fans were confident once again. The confidence was boosted by the summer signings of

Paulo Wanchope, Alf Inge Haaland, Steve Howey and, notably, the former World Player of the Year, George Weah. Even the manager himself was talking about the possibility of getting into Europe.

Of course, City were relegated.

In came a new manager, namely Kevin Keegan, and with him some new and exciting players – the gem of the 2001-02 season being a free transfer by the name of Ali Benarbia. But it wasn't a one man team by any stretch of the imagination; Eyal Berkovic played with him in the middle – leading to many satirical and perhaps ill-judged headlines about how Arabs and Israelis can work together. Stuart Pearce joined to shore up the defence, while, despite later admitting he didn't get on with the manager, Shaun Goater hit the form of his life, becoming the first City player since Francis Lee to score over 30 goals in one season.

With the Division One title under their belt and some excellent football played, City moved on to the next level and finished ninth in the Premier League the following season, qualifying for the UEFA Cup thanks to the Fair Play League. The run of form saw City beat United in Maine Road's final derby game. Added to that, the signings of Nicolas Anelka and Robbie Fowler gave the club a bright outlook.

And that meant it was no surprise to any football fan anywhere that the club was nearly relegated again the following season. Aside from another impressive derby day victory and one of the best comebacks in football history at Tottenham in the FA Cup, there wasn't much for City fans to cheer about. The club was knocked out of the UEFA Cup earlier than expected to the Polish side Groclin. In fact, had it not been for David James' penalty saves to preserve draws against Wolves and Leicester, and Leeds' catastrophic goal difference, City could have been in a lot more trouble than they actually were.

Despite starting well, Keegan's tenure at City ended with a whimper. He resigned just after a home defeat to Bolton, allowing Stuart Pearce to take charge for the end of the 2004-05 season, where City fans would be presented with yet another false dawn.

It all started well for 'Psycho'. Apart from defeat at Tottenham in his first game, City finished the season with an unlikely leap towards the last UEFA Cup spot. Going into the final day of the season, City sat in ninth and Middlesbrough sat in eighth spot (which would have been enough to qualify for Europe). Typically, it was City against Middlesbrough at Eastlands that would decide both clubs' fates. City needed to win. For Middlesbrough, a draw would have been enough.

So, at 1-1 with five minutes of the game left, Pearce made his first managerial "last-roll-of-the-dice" decision. With an extra forward on the bench, he opted against putting Jon Macken on in place of Claudio Reyna, choosing instead to play Nicky Weaver and stick David James up front for his height. Then City won a penalty… a goal would leave Middlesbrough less than a minute to find an equaliser and City seconds away from another European campaign.

Robbie Fowler stepped up and missed.

City were gunning well under Pearce, until a series of injuries and suspensions saw the club win only one of their last 10 games of 2005-06 and an utterly awful season of struggle, not helped by a total lack of funds, followed in 2006-07, encompassed by the club's inability to score at home after New Year's Day. In fact, that season, City scored 10 home league goals – three of them in one game. If you missed that match with Fulham, you missed 30 percent of them.

'Psycho' moved on and he was replaced by the former England manager Sven Goran Eriksson. The club was taken over by Thaksin Shinawatra and anticipation spread when news broke that millions of pounds worth of new and exciting players had joined the club. City got their first derby win at Old Trafford in 34 years and enjoyed a first derby double in even longer.

And, at Christmas, it was all looking good and City were in fourth – confidence of a top four finish was at an all time high amongst City fans. But a disastrous second half of the season, culminating in an 8-1 defeat at Middlesbrough, saw the team finish ninth. A European place was gained through the Fair Play League… again.

City's fans, despite having seen it all before, were then treated to another false dawn. This time, after Mark Hughes had been appointed as manager, City suddenly announced a takeover from Abu Dhabi and were – from nowhere – the richest football club in the world. Robinho joined. And, despite a scare in Denmark, they were through to the group stages of the UEFA Cup.

So it was only natural they would win two away games all season, finish lower than they had the season before, lose to both Brighton and Nottingham Forest in the two domestic cups and spend Christmas in the bottom three. How else could it have gone?

Hughes started the next season well. Excellent performances were joined by clean sheets and early victories, but as Christmas approached on the horizon, form began to dip. A 4-3 defeat at Old Trafford in time added on to time added on was a bitter pill to swallow. And it was those four goals where it all started to go wrong for Hughes.

The following game, West Ham at Eastlands on Monday 28 September, was his last league victory until Saturday 5 December. For 68 days, City didn't manage a win in the league. Nor did they slump to a defeat, but rather they drew seven matches, throwing away leads and gifting away silly goals.

After the victory over Chelsea that December, City managed just one more win before Hughes lost his job – in true City style, everybody knew that he had been sacked during the game, including the man himself. In his final three games, against Bolton, Tottenham and Sunderland, City picked up four points, but conceded nine goals. And, ultimately, it was the defence that many people thought led to Hughes' downfall.

Then Roberto Mancini arrived.

City just missed out on the League Cup semi final, losing to another last minute United goal. They just missed out on Champions League football, losing to a late Peter Crouch winner in the penultimate game of the season. The end of the season came and it felt like another false dawn.

But that was buoyed by summer signings of quality players.

Of course, it was a mixed bag to start with – win, lose and draw in the league – but, slowly City turned on the style. One or two blips in form didn't blot the copybook too much and, once the club had gotten into the top four on Sunday 19 September, 2010, they never dropped out of it. For a time in the middle of winter, City flirted with going top.

Roberto Mancini brought success to City with a well oiled machine. For the first time in a long time, City did everything right, both on and off the pitch. And it resulted in automatic qualification for the top European competition and a successful FA Cup campaign, including a satisfying semi final revenge against the team from across town.

That banner came down. There was a parade. City fans cried.

I cried.

But it doesn't end there. The following season, City began with their third trip to Wembley: The Community Shield match with Manchester United. City's performance was a disaster, but, somehow, they ended up two goals in front, on the stroke of half time – thanks to Joleon Lescott and Edin Dzeko. United's pressure told, however, and two quick goals after the break pulled them level.

It was at this point so early in the season that Vincent Kompany's role in the success of the club began to be spelled out. He made a rather uncharacteristic mistake in the final minute, gifting the ball to Nani and the Portuguese winger ran half the length of the field, took it past Joe Hart and slotted it into the net. At that stage, it felt awful to witness, but looking back at the end of the season, Kompany would come out on top.

The response to that defeat was immediate. A record breaking start to the season saw City smash their way to top spot, scoring goals for fun. Notably, Tottenham were dispatched at White Hart Lane 1-5 and United fared even worse, losing out to City at Old Trafford 1-6. It was their biggest ever Premier League home defeat and it was at City's hands. Worse for them, it put the Blues five points clear of them in top spot.

To their credit, however, United battled back. Soon, on level games, the two Manchester clubs were on level points, City only on the top of the league thanks to their superior goal difference. But, just as it looked like it was going to go to the wire, March 2012 happened. A wretched month for City, the club started it two points clear of United on level games. Defeat in the first game of April left the Blues eight points behind, again having played the same number of matches. The points lead had gone. Even the goal difference lead City had boasted was no more – United on +51 to City's +49.

Seemingly, the false dawns were back and big time. It was painful.

Roberto Mancini publicly conceded the title. In every interview, he denied that City could win it and confirmed the club would simply carry on doing their best, but it wouldn't be enough to take top spot. Call it a mind game with United or a mind game with his own players to ease the pressure, either way it worked.

United lost to Wigan, while City thumped West Brom. The gap was five points again. The Reds then threw away a two-goal lead against Everton at home to draw 4-4, while City beat Wolves. The gap was down to three points – with the Manchester derby to play.

For United, a win would see them virtually crowned champions, with them needing one point from their final two games. A draw would keep City at arm's length and likely allow them to retain the league. City *needed* to win, or else it was curtains.

Step forward Vincent Kompany. The captain. Leader. The man who had made the error in the Community Shield to lose the game. The man who had been sent off – wrongly – in the FA Cup third round tie at home for a challenge, again with Nani. On the stroke of half time, his bullet header gave City the lead and it would turn out to be the goal that would decide the game. The Blues were back on top of the league, again on goal difference.

A hard-fought win at Newcastle, matched by United's result against Swansea, left the league going down to the final day of the season: For City, it was QPR at home. Level points and an eight goal advantage meant that, should the Blues win, it would take a goal frenzy from United at Sunderland to steal it from them.

In many ways, it's fitting that Roberto Mancini's successes have come in games over Stoke (FA Cup) and QPR (Premier League). Thinking back to 1998, it was the games against these two clubs that saw City drop into their lowest ever league position and it signalled the worst time to be a City fan. Okay, so the Blues went undefeated against them back then, but that wasn't enough. The 2-2 draw and the 2-5 win left the Blues relegated to Division Two.

Now, 1-0 and 3-2 wins have ended City's trophy drought and left the club sitting as the best team in England for the first time in over four decades. It's remarkable the coincidences that football can throw up sometimes.

That final game of the season, though, was a perfect metaphor for the campaign as a whole. City dominate and take the lead, before getting pegged back to an almost unassailable deficit. They look down and out. Dead and buried. Then, suddenly, and out of absolutely nowhere, City spring to life and steal it in the final seconds.

And, after so many false dawns, this all feels too good to be true. It feels like we're all going to wake up and it's going to have been a horrible trick played on us by our minds: No Champions League, no FA Cup, no Premier League winners medals and City still hanging around Division Two and being the laughing stock of football throughout the world. Yet somehow still playing QPR and Stoke.

But here's the good news: This is no dream.

City are back.

The Turning Points

Signing Vincent Kompany
Friday 22 August, 2008

The signing of Vincent Kompany has been one of the best pieces of business by Manchester City FC in the club's history. From the moment he made his debut in the 3-0 victory over West Ham, he has slotted into the team perfectly. In fact, as each of City's goals that day hit the back of the net, the Belgian was the first player on the scene for the celebrations, despite having only met his colleagues the day before.

Instantly, he was liked by the fans and his value to the team was clear. His performances were regularly top notch, despite being plagued throughout the 2008-09 season with injury. In fact, few realised he was injured, such was the quality of his form.

Under Roberto Mancini, Kompany moved to centre-back in the City team. At first it was to cover injuries, but pretty quickly it became clear that he was the best central defender at the club, as he didn't give many a Premier League striker a sniff of an opportunity, preferring instead to slot them into his back pocket. His leadership qualities are such that he's been promoted to club captain.

A snip at £6m.

Transfer Deadline Day
Monday 1 September, 2008

A day that started with the disappointment in selling a much-liked full back in Vedran Corluka ended in truly bizarre circumstances. City fans around the world were pinching themselves as, on transfer deadline day in 2008, news broke of a takeover of the club from the Abu Dhabi United Group and the club were suddenly able to bid big money for quality players.

By the end of the day, Robinho had joined from Real Madrid when it had appeared that he would be moving to Chelsea and confidence was at an all-time high for a generation of blues. The Brazilian's signature was a statement of intent from the owners and the world began to listen.

The takeover of the club was officially completed later in September.

Defeat At The Hawthorns
Sunday 21 December, 2008

A poor run of results had seen City sliding down the table. The home form wasn't good and the away form was non-existent. With the final game before Christmas, City fans were hoping for a victory over the relegation candidates, if only to brighten the outlook for the run of games coming up.

And it didn't arrive.

The last minute defeat to West Brom left the Blues in the relegation zone for Christmas. There were strong calls for the manager's job, especially after a shocking display that saw City rarely threaten the home side's goal.

A piece of sublime skill from the untried and untested Felipe Caicedo got the visitors back into the game and, at that time, most City fans would have taken a draw. But Roman Bednar popped up with an injury time header to leave the club that had been given huge resources in the bottom three on Christmas Day.

Something had to change. City couldn't go on playing this badly.

Pride In Battle
Thursday 16 April, 2009

After a disastrous first leg in Germany, City got off to a horrible start at home against Hamburg. There were just 12 minutes on the clock when the visitors wiped out City's away goal and left the home side needing three goals just to force extra time.

A disappointing season had left many fans disgruntled with the management and there was speculation that it was only City's European run that had been keeping Hughes in his job. With ticket prices lowered, the stadium full and the crowd buzzing, the comeback was on.

First, Elano won and converted a penalty, leaving City with 73 minutes to find two goals. He then thundered a free kick into the crossbar at one end and curled one onto the post at the other. He had a shot direct from a corner cleared off the line. He had been reborn that evening.

Felipe Caicedo put City in front, five minutes into the second half. He then thought he had made it 3-1, equalising on aggregate, only to look up in despair that the linesman was flagging for an offside.

And it turned out to be the correct call.

City gave everything and nearly rescued an impossible position. But it wasn't to be, though, if the speculation is to be believed, it was a job-saving effort for the manager from the team.

The Billboard
Saturday 18 July 2009

Three little words: 'Welcome to Manchester.'

If there was a point after City's takeover where Manchester United became riled by the Blues, then this was it. A billboard, on the boundary between Manchester and Salford, signalled the arrival of Carlos Tevez, after his defection from the Reds. And not only were United losing one of their best assets to City, but they were having their noses rubbed in it, too.

The signing of Tevez showed City's intent to step it up to the next level. The noisy neighbours wanted to take control and be the top dogs in the city. And stealing players was a signal that City's pulling power had increased. They weren't going to settle for second best anymore and United didn't like it.

Over the course of two seasons, Tevez's goalscoring record was impossible to argue with. He came with a reputation of hard work, but United fans were adamant that he wouldn't score many goals.

How wrong could they have been?

Extra Extra Time
Sunday 20 September, 2009

Mark Hughes was left fuming after Michael Owen won the derby in stoppage time. Understandably so, after time was added for Bellamy's last minute goal celebration: Four minutes were shown by the fourth official and it was closer to six minutes overtime when Given was beaten for the final time that afternoon.

Whether or not that goal should have stood, there were wider issues with this game. It was City's first defeat of the 2009-10 season and every one of United's goals came about through a defensive lapse; whether that was by poor challenges, players out of position or poor marking.

And that began to set the tone for the season. City's defence had been solid before that game, having conceded twice to Arsenal and none others so far that campaign. But following that game, City won just three of their next 12 matches, drawing eight.

Goals began to leak in and calamitous defending from the Blues became something of a trademark. And it was that trademark, which started during the 4-3 defeat to United, that ultimately cost Mark Hughes his job.

Embarrassed At White Hart Lane
Wednesday 16 December, 2009

After the defeat at Tottenham, City had dropped to eighth in the table and found themselves sliding down the league. The performance in the capital on that Wednesday evening was a shambles and, despite the quality running through City's side, there was no passion, drive or hunger. Tottenham won the game at a canter, with their goal unthreatened for the majority of the game.

The defensive frailties had started to become a problem and one-off victories against Chelsea or Arsenal were doing nothing to help the manager, who couldn't seem to get the team playing as a unit. And it was after this defeat that many fans lost their patience.

If reports are to be believed, it is also after this match that the decision was taken to replace Hughes as the man in charge. And Hughes himself looked a beaten man in the dugout.

It was only City's second defeat of the season, however the Blues had won just one of their last 10 league games. If City had any aspirations of finishing inside the top four, something needed to change. The board decided that a new manager was needed.

A Missed Handshake

Saturday 27 February, 2010

A forgettable first half for City at Stamford Bridge looked like it was going to leave the visitors with too much work to do. City hadn't beaten Chelsea away for a long time and hadn't even scored on that ground in ten years. But a misjudgement by Terry and an error from Hilario saw Tevez end that run, scoring from nothing to get the teams level before the interval.

All the talk before the game would be whether Wayne Bridge would accept John Terry's handshake, after the latter's affair with the former's ex-girlfriend. He didn't and that seemed to play on Terry's mind for the entire match, as he struggled to come to terms with Tevez and Bellamy.

A breakaway goal by Bellamy and then a penalty from Tevez virtually sealed the points, before the Welshman added his second as the game neared its conclusion. In the wider picture, this victory put an end to a poor run of form for the Blues and it showed that, on their day, City could beat the best the country have to offer.

The Turf Moor Massacre

Saturday 3 April, 2010

Having seen the teams around them slip-up already that day, City knew that a victory at Turf Moor would set them in good stead for the final push for the top four. Burnley had begun to struggle, but they were still doing enough to worry teams on their own patch. Until City arrived.

Three goals in the opening seven minutes put the visitors in a commanding position and set the alarm bells ringing around the rest of the division. Adebayor, Bellamy and Tevez had given City the record of the quickest ever three goal lead in the Premier League.

Another three goals – from Vieira, Adebayor again, and Kompany – gave City their biggest win of the season and Burnley their worst performance at home. This performance was the springboard for the club to hammer Birmingham the following week and there wasn't a better way to head into the final six matches of the campaign.

City were rejuvenated and firing on all cylinders, looking to be in the right form to give fourth place their best shot. The confidence was back and the goals were flying in from all areas; had the weather not conspired to produce a downpour of biblical proportions, City could have run riot.

Hart Starts
Saturday 14 August, 2010

Having had a season long loan at Birmingham the year before, Joe Hart had been catching the eye. In a newly promoted team, he was beginning to excel and attract the attention of two Italians: one of them in charge of Manchester City and the other in charge of England.

When it came to the opening day of the 2010-11 season, Roberto Mancini had a choice to make. Did he stick with the goalkeeper that had been City's number one the year before, or did he choose the younger and much in form returning loan player? He went for Hart, dropping Given to the bench, and, within the first half hour, his decision was justified.

On the opening day of the season, Hart pulled off saves that didn't seem possible. And then, later in the game, he would go on to better them, much to the frustration of Crouch, Defoe, Huddlestone and Assou-Ekotto.

For the rest of the season, Hart was phenomenal between the sticks, regularly making blinding saves and going on to beat the club's record for the most number of clean sheets in a season.

Dzeko Off The Mark
Sunday 30 January, 2011

Having found it difficult to settle in City's side, Edin Dzeko needed a goal. He had showed flashes of what he could do, but had struggled to get into the games he had been involved in and the ball didn't seem to be bouncing for him.

In the fourth round of the FA Cup, City had been drawn away to Notts County and, on a very muddy and sticky pitch, the home side had battled hard and gotten themselves into the lead. City looked like they were going to crash out of the tournament with a whimper, until a storming run from Richards finished with a peach of a cross.

It landed on Dzeko's foot and, with the goalkeeper beaten, the Bosnian striker couldn't miss. His first goal in a City shirt was vital in keeping the Blues in the cup and, without it, the banner at Old Trafford would have stayed in place. The replay was comfortable and City would go on to lift the trophy.

A Diet Pill
Friday 4 March, 2011

Before the suspension to Kolo Toure, City's summer shopping list most likely contained a centre-back. Behind the former City captain had been the young Dedryck Boyata and the inconsistent Joleon Lescott. And, with almost three months of the season to play, one of the first choice defenders was made unavailable through testing positive for a specified substance.

In stepped Joleon Lescott and immediately he made himself at home. The left foot and right foot partnership between him and Vincent Kompany worked well and the former Everton central defender started to show some form with a run of games under his belt. In fact, he was beginning to look like the player that the Merseyside team had sold, rather than the player that City had had the season before.

Europa League Exit
Thursday 17 March, 2011

While the defeat to Dynamo Kiev meant it was another piece of silverware that City couldn't win, it did bring an end to the dreaded two football matches a week. With City through to the FA Cup semi finals, there was no possibility of a cup replay, either. And it was this combination that reduced the pressure on City's fixture list.

The rest was just what the doctor ordered. The first game back after the international break saw the Blues smash their way past Sunderland. In fact, City hit a patch of form that would eventually see them rise into third place in the table and lift the FA Cup at Wembley.

It's impossible to say that this wouldn't have happened had City beaten Dynamo Kyiv, but certainly the added rest the squad was able to get without those midweek games played a part in such a successful season. Suddenly, City looked sharper, fitter and better able to cope with what was being thrown at them, putting them in the perfect frame of mind just at the right time for the end of the season run-in.

Tevez Limps Off
Monday 11 April, 2011

Losing Carlos Tevez to injury was, perhaps, the biggest blow City could have received before the FA Cup semi final with the enemy. City had been reliant on the little Argentinian for goals for most of the season and, when he hadn't played, the team had struggled to score.

United would be without the banned Wayne Rooney, but, for a large part of the season before Christmas, they had managed to cope without him. City, on the other hand, weren't really sure where the goals were going to come from.

And it was losing Tevez that forced the manager's hand. City had to cope without their star man, otherwise they could be out of the FA Cup and they could slump down the league table. Without the leading goalscorer, the rest of the team had to step up to the plate.

That's exactly what they did. The injury to Tevez came at the wrong time for City, but the team and the manager showed that they had the mental toughness and the ability to overcome big setbacks.

Berbatov's Double

Saturday 16 April, 2011

City were the new kids in town when it came to FA Cup semi finals. United had been there, done it and bought the t-shirt so many times since City had last made that stage of the competition that it took the Blues a short while to warm up. And in that time, somehow, United didn't take the lead.

Joe Hart pulled off one of the most crucial saves he has ever made, denying Dimitar Berbatov from a one-on-one in the opening stages of the third Manchester derby of the season. He raced off his line quickly to slam the door shut in the Bulgarian's face, after some slick football from United carved City wide open.

Berbatov then conspired to miss a guilt-edged chance from two yards, as Nani found him in front of goal and all Hart and Kolarov could do was dive in to try and put him off. And it worked; the United centre-forward skied the effort and City stayed on level terms.

From that point in the match, City got their foot on the ball and began to carve out chance after chance, while United struggled to get a foothold on the game. In the end, Yaya Toure robbed the ball on the edge of the box and scored what turned out to be the game's winner.

Had Berbatov scored one of those early chances, it would have been a very different game and, after the match, the United manager will have been ruing those missed efforts.

00 Years

Saturday 14 May 2011

Having done the hard work of getting to the FA Cup final, City had the difficult job of overcoming a tough Stoke side. Naturally, having just beaten United in the semi finals, the Blues' fans were confident, though the opposition were stubborn and resisted well.

Nerves were high, too. The club hadn't won a major trophy in over three decades and, as such, the supporters were on edge. City always muck it up, right? It's a very City thing to do – get to the final, beat United at Wembley en route and then lose it to the underdogs.

But not this time.

With 74 minutes on the clock, a loose ball inside the Stoke area sat up perfectly and Yaya Toure smashed his foot through it, giving the Stoke goalkeeper no chance. From the previous semi final, it was the same scorer and in the same end. The City fans erupted in celebration and I punched my own father in the face (completely accidentally, your honour).

City hung on and, on the dot of some time around five o'clock, Carlos Tevez led the team up the Wembley steps to lift the trophy. City's cup drought was over and part one of Roberto Mancini's empire was complete. The banner at Old Trafford came down and, rather cheekily, the players paraded the Wembley turf with one of their own – *00 YEARS*.

The platform on which City could build had been established and the foundations were in place.

Wembley Defeat
Sunday 7 August, 2011

The third of City's trips to Wembley in 2011 ended badly, despite the good start that the Blues had gotten off to. United had dominated the opening stages of the Community Shield, but it had been their rivals who had gone into the break with a lead, thanks to two late first half goals from Lescott and Dzeko.

Both strikes had come against the run of play, with United looking like their pre-season had served them better than City's had them. City couldn't keep possession and struggled to push United back and, on the two occasions the ball had been in the United half, it had found the back of the net.

Naturally, the Reds were going to come out strong and fight. Chris Smalling pulled a goal back seven minutes into the second half. Six minutes later, Nani equalised. And, in the blink of an eye, the game was back to where we had been just before City had scored: All United and the scores level.

With seconds to go, however, City had the chance to attack from a deep free kick. They went for it and, as United cleared the ball, an uncharacteristic mistake from Kompany allowed Nani to carry the ball at goal, unchallenged from the halfway line. He skipped around Hart and, in stoppage time, won the game.

The high hopes of the fans had been dashed with another last minute winner from United and a poor performance from the Blues. If the club was serious about mounting a title challenge, things would have to change and quickly, with just a week to go until the start of the season.

Free-Scoring Start

Sunday 28 August, 2011

After the disappointment of the Community Shield defeat, City began the season like an express train. Swansea rocked up at The Etihad Stadium and were sent packing with -4 in the goal difference column after the first match of the season, before the Blues saw off Bolton in a thriller at the Reebok and then smashed five in at White Hart Lane.

In fact, it was fitting that it would be at Tottenham where City's opening to the season would be remembered; the ghosts of the past well and truly exorcised in one performance. Two years previous, Spurs had humiliated the Blues in North London, before denying them Champions League football in Manchester. The season before, City took four points, but only scored once – an own goal. So netting five times on the road was just what the doctor ordered.

With the run of fixtures, City looked unstoppable and were scoring at will. In the whole of 2010-11, the Blues scored three or more in a Premier League game on nine occasions. In 2011-12, the Blues reached that landmark just 11 matches into the season – failing to hit three against just Fulham and Everton.

Any fears that might have arisen after the Wembley loss on the first game of the season were well and truly wiped away. Roberto Mancini had unleashed a very attack-minded City side upon the Premier League.

Mutiny In Munich

Tuesday 22 September, 2011

There are many conflicting reports that came from that night in Munich. In fact, City's 2-0 defeat at the Allianz Arena is often forgotten about when discussing the game, such is the magnitude of what had happened on the bench.

At first, it was reported that Carlos Tevez had refused to come onto the pitch as a second half substitute, however that was soon quashed. The accepted version of events is now that he had been asked by Roberto Mancini to resume warming up in preparation to join the action, but he had refused as he believed he was already warm enough.

That began a five month period where Tevez was unavailable for selection. For a time, he wasn't even in the country, absent without leave in Argentina. It was exactly what City *didn't* need after their first Champions League defeat.

Why Always Me?

Sunday 23 October, 2011

The first Manchester derby of the Premier League in 2011-12 saw City going to Old Trafford on the back of a record breaking start to the season. United were two points behind the Blues at the top of the table and a win would see them move ahead of their city rivals. A win for the visitors, though, would see them open up a five-point lead on their hosts.

United began on top, but could only test Joe Hart with a couple of long range drives; efforts that were meat and drink for the England keeper. And, just after the 20 minute mark, Mario Balotelli coolly slotted a ball into the corner of David de Gea's net, before lifting his shirt to reveal a bodywarmer, emblazoned with the phrase '*Why Always Me?*'. That, after a friend had let a firework off inside his house the night before.

City held onto that lead until half time and it was early in the second period where the hosts lost control of the tie completely. Balotelli, though on goal, was hauled down by Evans, who, in turn, was given his marching orders by the referee. City took advantage; on the hour, Balotelli doubled the lead, before, nine minutes later, Aguero added a third.

United gave their fans some brief hope of a comeback with a goal with ten minutes to play, but a ravenous City ran riot with the hosts' back line in the closing stages. Dzeko added another as Lescott did well to keep the ball in play, before Silva nutmegged de Gea for number five. The Spaniard pulled out one of the passes of the season, volleying for Dzeko to run through and make it six.

The Premier League champions weren't just beaten, but humbled.

Humiliated.

The Bleak Mid-Winter
Wednesday 25 January, 2012

After spending Christmas Day on top of the Premier League, City were in high spirits for their coming fixtures. But, for one reason or another, the Blues just couldn't get their act together for the following month. A Boxing Day draw at The Hawthorns was soon followed by a last minute, offside goal defeat at The Stadium of Light and, despite City's dominance in the games, they twice couldn't find a way through – they were there first two league matches in which the Blues failed to find the net.

It got worse. After a pick-me-up in the shape of a 3-0 home win over Liverpool, City lost their captain for four crucial games, thanks to an incident in the third Manchester derby of the season. Twelve minutes into the game, Vincent Kompany was, as has been conceded by the majority of the football world (save for the FA and the FA's video panel), very harshly sent off for a challenge on Nani. The Portuguese man didn't argue, while Wayne Rooney's protestations angered many fans.

The absent Kompany, combined with poor City play and an equally poor penalty decision at Anfield, conspired to remove City from both of the domestic cups. United clung on to a 2-3 win in the FA Cup Third Round against City's ten man fight-back, while Liverpool were very generously given a penalty to equalise in the League Cup second leg. In truth, though, City were always on the backfoot of the latter tie.

The month was rounded off by a defeat at Goodison Park and it left City on top of the league, but solely on goal difference. United had closed the gap completely and the Blues were left scratching their heads.

The season had gotten difficult.

Forgive And Forget
Wednesday 21 March, 2012

Having returned to Manchester and issued an apology for his behaviour, while removing the legal action he was planning to take against the club and Roberto Mancini, Carlos Tevez was back in a sky blue shirt. With City's season on the rocks, having slipped into second place and a point behind United on level games, the little Argentine came back into the squad for the home match with Chelsea.

City dominated, but it was the visitors who found themselves in front, thanks to a deflected Gary Cahill effort squirming past Joe Hart's desperate dive. Chelsea hadn't deserved to be ahead, but that rarely matters in football; the Blues were struggling to beat Petr Cech and it looked as though the title race was going to be slipping from City's grasp.

But a handball and penalty equaliser later, the stage was set for the returning striker to make his impact. Receiving the ball with his back to goal, he took the pressure well before returning a reverse pass straight back into the path of Nasri, breaking into the area. He controlled and dinked it over the Chelsea goalkeeper, to give City the lead, with just four minutes to play.

Tevez's role in the goal was instrumental.

City were still in with a fighting chance.

No Win In Three
Sunday 8 April, 2012

A point behind United, City faced a difficult trip to Stoke. A tough place to go at the best of times, but when feeling down on luck, it's not a place any side would want to visit. And City hit trouble; Peter Crouch scored one of the goals of the season, a swift turn and volley from well outside the box, to give the hosts the lead, before Yaya Toure rescued a point with one of his own long range drives.

But, by this stage in the season, a point wasn't good enough. It left the Blues three behind United on level games and now City needed to match their rivals point-for-point *and* beat them in the coming Manchester derby to go back to the top on goal difference.

City, however, appeared to have lost it altogether. Sunderland turned up at The Etihad Stadium and scored thrice, with very late goals from Balotelli and Kolarov dragging the Blues from 1-3 down back to level pegging. The draw left City needing favours from elsewhere if they stood any chance of finishing top of the pile in May.

Things transpired to get worse. Under Roberto Mancini, up to this point, City had never failed to win in three consecutive Premier League games. A trip to Arsenal and The Emirates Stadium, though, changed that and the Blues left with nothing, thanks to a late Arteta goal. Balotelli was sent off. City were eight points off the top of the table with six games to play.

The wheels had fallen off the season.

Surely?

The Derby Double
Sunday 8 April, 2012

Roberto Mancini conceded the title.

There was only one team that could possibly win it after that Arsenal defeat and it wasn't Manchester City. That, bizarrely, allowed City to play without any pressure. Three wins followed that defeat, as the Blues stuck four past West Brom, six past Norwich and two past Wolves, relegating the latter in the process.

Meanwhile, on the other side of town, United relaxed. They left the DW Stadium with nothing, as Wigan's fight for survival did City a huge favour, reducing the gap to five points. Then Everton fought back from 4-2 down at Old Trafford to earn themselves a draw, thanks to some sloppy United defending and clinical Toffee finishing. The gap was three points.

The next fixture? City vs. United.

A win for City would see them back on level points with United and, with a better goal difference, it would send them back to the top of the league. It would also clinch their first league double over United since Sven Goran Eriksson was in charge of the club.

The gung-ho approach, though, wasn't without its dangers: A win for the visitors and they would need just one point from their remaining two games to secure the title. City had to be wary, but there was also no sense in holding back; a draw did the home side no good, either.

On the stroke of half time, up stepped Mr. Reliable. Vincent Kompany found the back of David de Gea's net with a bullet header from a stoppage time corner and the Blues took the lead. The visitors couldn't even muster a shot on target during the whole evening – the first time in three years that that had happened.

It was advantage City, again. But only by eight goals.

Forty-Four Years

A lot of things have changed in the world in the time since Manchester City were last Champions of England. In fact, in the 44 years since City last topped the table, there have been some very iconic world events. Below is a timeline of some of the more key incidents between City's titles – we can only hope that the list between this title and the next is nowhere near as long.

1968
11 May: Manchester City are crowned First Division champions.
7 Sept: *Hot Wheels* cars are introduced.
15 Oct: *Led Zeppelin* perform live for the first time at Surrey University.
14 Nov: Yale University allows female students to enrol.
22 Nov: *The Beatles* release the *White Album*.

1969
9 Feb: The Boeing 747 aircraft makes its first flight.
15 May: A teenager, known as Robert R, becomes the first to die of HIV/AIDS.
20 July: Neil Armstrong becomes the first man to walk on the Moon.
15 Aug: The *Woodstock* festival is held for the first time.

1970
10 Apr: Paul McCartney announces *The Beatles* have broken up.

1971
15 Feb: Decimal currency is launched in the UK.
1 Oct: *Walt Disney World* opens in Orlando, Florida.

1972
30 Jan: Bloody Sunday sees 14 unarmed nationalists killed in Derry, N. Ireland.
24 Mar: *The Godfather* film is released in cinemas in the US.
29 Nov: *Atari* release their first commercially successful game, entitled *Pong*.

1973
4 Jan: *Last of the Summer Wine* begins on British TV.
4 Apr: The World Trade Centre opens in New York.
31 Dec: Because of coal shortages, the three day week begins.

1974
8 Aug: US President Richard Nixon resigns after the Watergate Scandal.

1976
21 Jan: The first commercial Concorde flight takes off.

1977
3 Jan: *Apple Computer Inc* is founded.

25 May: *Star Wars* opens in cinemas.

1979
4 May: Margaret Thatcher becomes the first female Prime Minister of the UK.
1 July: The *Sony Walkman* goes on sale for the first time in Japan.

1980
22 May: The best selling arcade game of all time, *Pac-Man*, is released.
8 Dec: John Lennon is murdered in New York.

1981
4 Apr: *Bucks Fizz* win the Eurovision Song Contest with *Making Your Mind Up*.
22 May: Peter Sutcliffe is found guilty of being the Yorkshire Ripper.

1982
2 Apr: The Falklands War begins.
30 Nov: Michael Jackson releases the album *Thriller*.

1983
31 Jan: Seatbelt use for drivers and front seat passengers is made mandatory.
16 Aug: *The Bill* is broadcast for the first time, under the name *Woodentop*.

1985
13 July: The first ever Live Aid concerts raise over £50m for famine relief.

1986
26 Apr: The Chernobyl Disaster kills over 4000 people.
22 June: Maradona scores his *Hand of God* goal against England.
22 Nov: Mike Tyson wins his first boxing title in Las Vegas.

1987
19 Apr: *The Simpsons* airs for the first time as a short in *The Tracey Ullman Show*.
19 Oct: Stock markets around the world crash on *Black Monday*.

1988
21 Dec: Pan Am Flight 103 is blown up over Lockerbie in Scotland.

1989
15 Apr: The Hillsbrough Disaster claims the lives of 96 Liverpool fans.
31 July: *Nintendo* release their *Game Boy* in North America.
9 Nov: The fall of the Berlin Wall begins.

1990
11 Feb: Nelson Mandela is released from prison.

25 Dec: Tim Berners-Lee creates the first webpage on the first web server.

1992
12 Apr: *Disneyland Paris* opens to the public, then called *Euro Disney Resort*.

1993
26 Feb: A bomb explodes outside the north tower of the World Trade Centre.

1994
6 May: The Channel Tunnel opens between England and France.
3 Dec: The *PlayStation* console is released in Japan.

1996
10 Feb: *Deep Blue*, a computer, beats a chess champion for the first time.

1997
29 June: The first in the *Harry Potter* series of books is published.
31 Aug: Diana, Princess of Wales is killed in car accident in Paris.

1998
4 Sept: *Google* is founded by two university students in the US.

1999
1 Jan: The Euro is established.

2001
11 Sept: Nearly 3000 people are killed in terror attacks in the US.
23 Oct: The *iPod* is introduced by *Apple*.

2003
24 Oct: Concorde completes its final flight.

2006
5 Nov: Saddam Hussein is sentenced to death by hanging.

2008
22 Feb: The Northern Rock bank is nationalised.

2009
25 June: Michael Jackson dies in his rented mansion.

2011
7 July: The first artificial organ transplant is completed.
31 Oct: The world's population is estimated at over 7bn for the first time.

Statistical Breakdown

From the start of 2008-09 to the end of 2011-12, City played 218 competitive matches, winning 121 (55.5%), losing 55 (25.2%) and drawing 42 (19.3%). In those 218 matches, City scored 401 goals and conceded 225.

Throughout the 2008-09 season, City played 56 matches. They won 25 (44.6%), lost 23 (41.1%) and drew eight (14.3%), scoring 85 goals and conceding 71.

Throughout the 2009-10 season, City played 48 matches. They won 25 (52.1%), lost nine (18.8%) and drew 14 (29.2%), scoring 96 goals and conceding 56.

Throughout the 2010-11 season, City played 59 matches. They won 34 (57.6%), lost 12 (20.3%) and drew 13 (22%), scoring 97 goals and conceding 48.

Throughout the 2011-12 season, City played 55 matches. They won 37 (67.3%), lost 11 (20%) and drew 7 (12.7%), scoring 125 goals and conceding 50.

Mark Hughes managed City in 77 matches. He won 36 (46.8%), lost 25 (32.5%) and drew 16 (20.8%), scoring 133 goals and conceding 97.

Under Hughes, City came from behind to win four times and lost from being ahead five times. City saved nine points from losing positions and lost 27 points from winning positions. City won 33 games after scoring first.

Roberto Mancini managed City in 141 matches. He won 85 (60.3%), lost 30 (21.3%) and drew 26 (18.4%), scoring 270 goals and conceding 128.

Under Mancini, City came from behind to win 11 times and lost from being ahead five times. City saved 28 points from losing positions and lost 20 points from winning positions. City won 74 games after scoring first.

Mark Hughes' 50th game in charge of City was the 2-1 UEFA Cup quarter-final second leg victory over Hamburg on Thursday 16 April, 2009. Two years to the day later, City beat Manchester United 1-0 in the FA Cup semi final.

City's 50th goal under Mark Hughes was scored by Felipe Caicedo after 27 minutes against Hull at Eastlands on Friday 26 December, 2009. The 100th was scored by Martin Petrov after 31 minutes against West Ham at Eastlands on Monday 28 September, 2009.

Roberto Mancini's 50th game in charge of City was the 3-0 Europa League Group A home victory over Salzburg on Wednesday 1 December, 2010. The 100th was the 1-6 Premier League victory at Old Trafford on Sunday 23 October, 2011.

City's 50th goal under Roberto Mancini was scored by Shaun Wright-Phillips after 21 minutes against West Ham at Upton Park on Sunday 9 May 2010. The 100th was scored by Carlos Tevez after 45 minutes against Leicester at the Walkers Stadium on Sunday 9 January, 2011.

City's 150th goal under Roberto Mancini was scored by Edin Dzeko after 57 minutes against Swansea at The Etihad Stadium on Monday 15 August, 2011. The 200th was scored by David Silva after 52 minutes against QPR at Loftus Road on Saturday 5 November, 2011.

City's 250th goal under Roberto Mancini was scored by Samir Nasri after 86 minutes against Chelsea at The Etihad Stadium on Wednesday 21 March, 2012.

Nigel de Jong played in 94 games for City before he managed to find the net after 11 minutes against West Ham on Sunday 1 May 2011. It took him 7376 minutes to score. That's 122 hours and 56 minutes. Or five days, two hours and 56 minutes. In that time, de Jong was booked 22 times.

After scoring his first City goal, it took Nigel de Jong another 1546 minutes to get on the scoresheet for a second time (in the second leg of the League Cup semi final with Liverpool on Wednesday 25 January, 2012). That's one day, one hour and 46 minutes more football he played. He's getting quicker.

City have three times won 1-6 away from home in the Premier League. The first time was at Burnley on Saturday 3 April, 2010, the second was at Manchester United on Sunday 23 October, 2011, and the third was at Norwich on Saturday 14 April, 2012. All three have come under Roberto Mancini's management.

Over the period of 2008-09 to 2010-12, City had 12 captains: Vincent Kompany (53), Richard Dunne (49), Kolo Toure (42), Carlos Tevez (40), Shay Given (10), Micah Richards (10), Nigel de Jong (5), Pablo Zabaleta (3), Gareth Barry (2), Dietmar Hamann (1), Robinho (1), Patrick Vieira (1).

Excluding penalty shoot-outs, City have scored 30 penalties: Carlos Tevez (11), Mario Balotelli (7), Elano (5), Sergio Aguero (3), Emmanuel Adebayor (1), James Milner (1), Robinho (1), Daniel Sturridge (1).

Manchester United have been City's most frequent opponents since 2008-09, with the two sides meeting 13 times in all competitions. City have won four, drawn one and lost eight, scoring 19 and conceding 20.

City failed to take points off just one team in 2010-11: Everton.

In 2011-12, City took points off every single Premier League side. In the process, they did the double over ten teams: Aston Villa, Blackburn, Bolton, Manchester United, Newcastle, Norwich, QPR, Tottenham, Wigan and Wolves.

Only one side avoided defeat to City in the Premier League in the 2011-12 season: Sunderland.

City have used seven goalkeepers since the start of 2008-09: Joe Hart (139), Shay Given (69), Costel Pantilimon (4), Marton Fulop (3), Kasper Schmeichel (2), Stuart Taylor (1). Gunnar Nielsen played 14 minutes at The Emirates on Saturday 24 April, 2010.

Joe Hart has kept 60 clean sheets for City in 139 appearances (43.2 %) since the start of 2008-09. Hart's longest spell without conceding for City is 499 minutes, between James Beattie's header for Stoke on Saturday 31 January, 2009 and Darren Bent's 94th minute penalty for Sunderland on Sunday 29 August, 2010.

Joe Hart has faced 16 penalties, including penalty shoot-outs, and has saved four (25%) of them. Costel Pantilimon has faced one and saved it, although the rebound was scored.

Since 2008-09, City have been involved in three penalty shoot-outs in all competitions, winning two (Midtjylland, Aalborg) and losing one (Brighton). They have all been away from home.

Between the start of the 2008-09 season and the end of the 2011-12 season, City used 73 players for first team competitive matches. In that time, City gave 17 academy graduates their debuts, 14 of them coming under Roberto Mancini.

On two occasions have substitutes been substituted: Robinho replaced Santa Cruz before being replaced by Wright-Phillips at Everton on Saturday 16 January, 2010. Balotelli replaced Tevez before being replaced by de Jong at Liverpool on Monday 11 April, 2011.

Between the start of the 2008-09 season and the end of the 2011-12 season, City had 48 different goalscorers. Eight own goals were scored by the opposition.

Between 9 January, 2011 and 5 February, 2011, all of City's seven matches were against opposition from the Midlands: Leicester (2), Wolves, Aston Villa, Notts County, Birmingham, West Brom.

City were shown 20 red cards from the start of 2008-09 to the end of 2011-12: Four to Balotelli, three each to Dunne and Zabaleta, two for Kompany and one each for Adebayor, Barry, Bellamy, Boyata, Clichy, Gelson, Kolarov and Kolo Toure.

On one occasion, City had two players dismissed in the same match. Gelson Fernandes received two yellow cards and Richard Dunne saw a straight red in the 2-1 defeat to Tottenham at Eastlands on Sunday 9 November, 2008.

In the whole of the 2010-11 season, City scored four headers in the league. Three of them were from Joleon Lescott (Aston Villa, Stoke, Bolton) and one was from Carlos Tevez (Wolves).

Edin Dzeko's hat-trick at Tottenham (Sunday 28 August, 2010) followed by Sergio Aguero's hat-trick at home against Wigan (Saturday 10 September, 2010) is the first time back-to-back hat-tricks have been scored for City since 1987. Then, Tony Adcock scored three against Huddersfield and, in the next match, three against Plymouth.

Micah Richards' first half goal against Newcastle on Saturday 19 November, 2011 was the 9000th goal by an Englishman in the Premier League.

After City's defeat to Everton on Tuesday 31 January, 2012 (2011-12 season), City had both scored and conceded the same number of goals as they had done in the whole of the season before (2010-11 season).

In 2011-12, City reached their 2010-11 final points total (71 points) by drawing with Sunderland on Saturday 31 March, 2012, with seven more games to play.

During the 2011-12 season, City's lead when on level games with United was, at most, five points. At one point, when on level games, United had an eight point lead over City. Both overcame those deficits to re-take the top spot on various occasions.

Mario Balotelli is the first Italian player to win the Premier League.

Glauber Berti's City career lasted seven minutes.